SOUL EATER

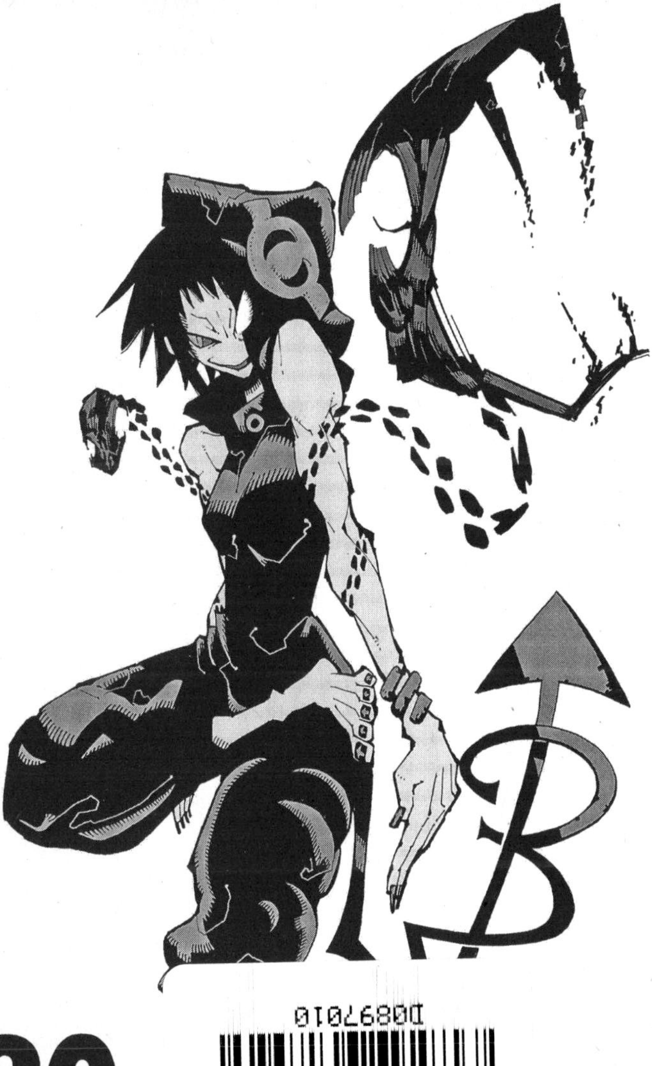

20

OHKUBO

SOUL EATER

vol. 20
by ATSUSHI OHKUBO

Before long the madness breaks out

SOUL EATER 20

CONTENTS

Chapter 82: The Whereabouts 005

Chapter 83: Mad Blood 038

Chapter 84: Recovery 071

Chapter 85: Pursuit 101

Chapter 86: Hellfire 121

Chapter 87: Just a Simple Story about Killing a Person . 139

CHAPTER 82: THE WHEREABOUTS

SOUL EATER

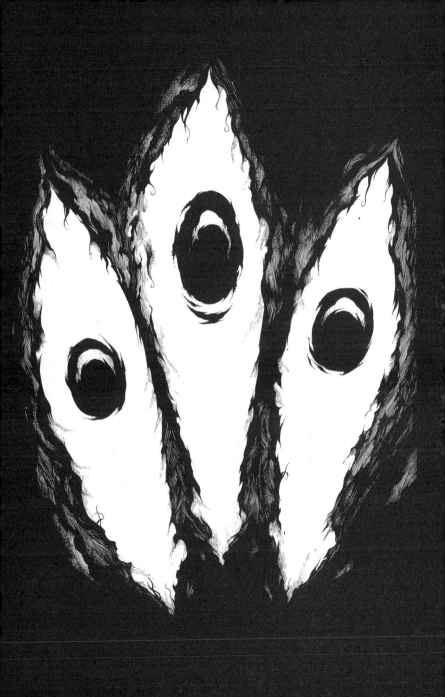

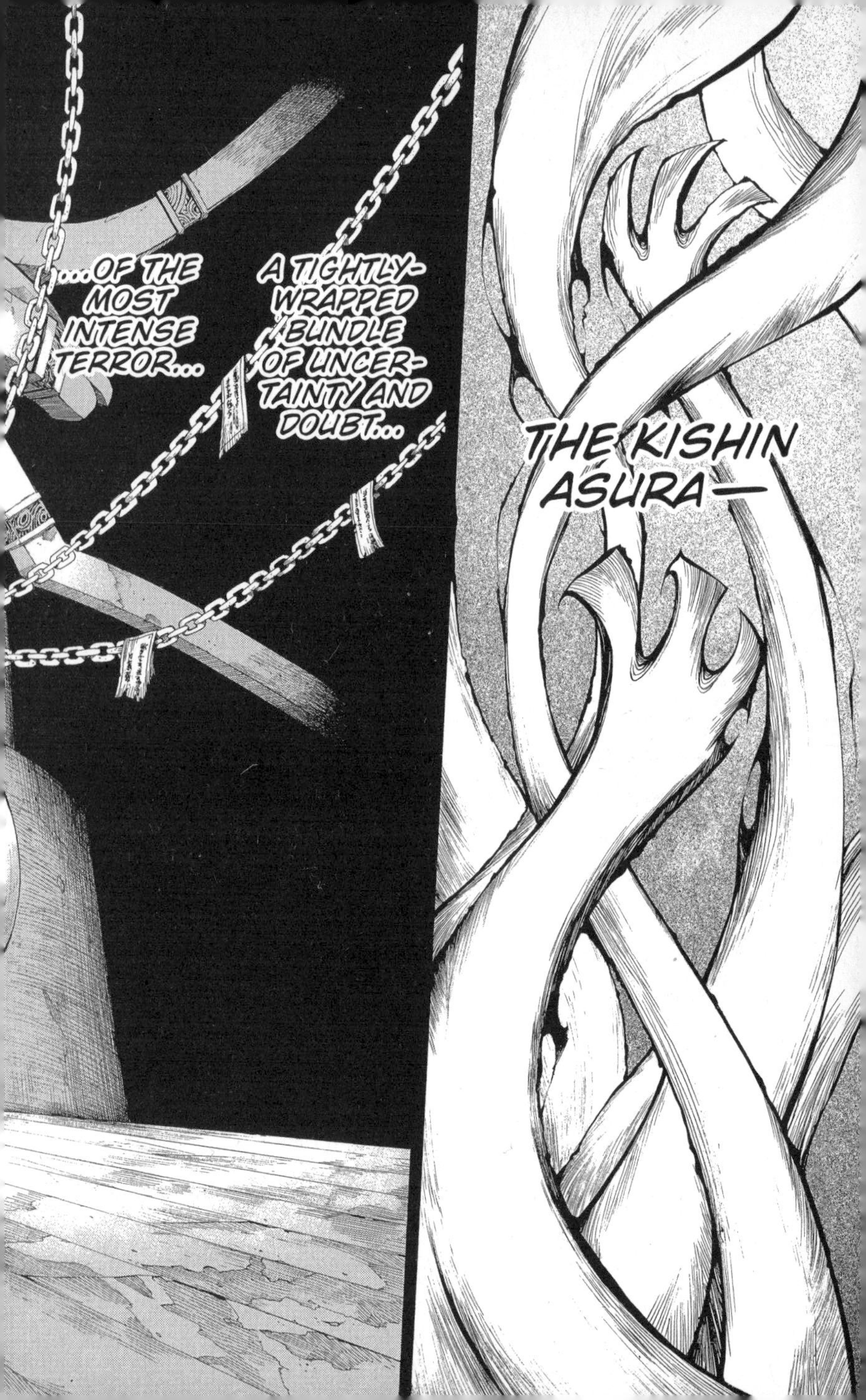
THE KISHIN ASURA—
A TIGHTLY-WRAPPED BUNDLE OF UNCERTAINTY AND DOUBT...
...OF THE MOST INTENSE TERROR...

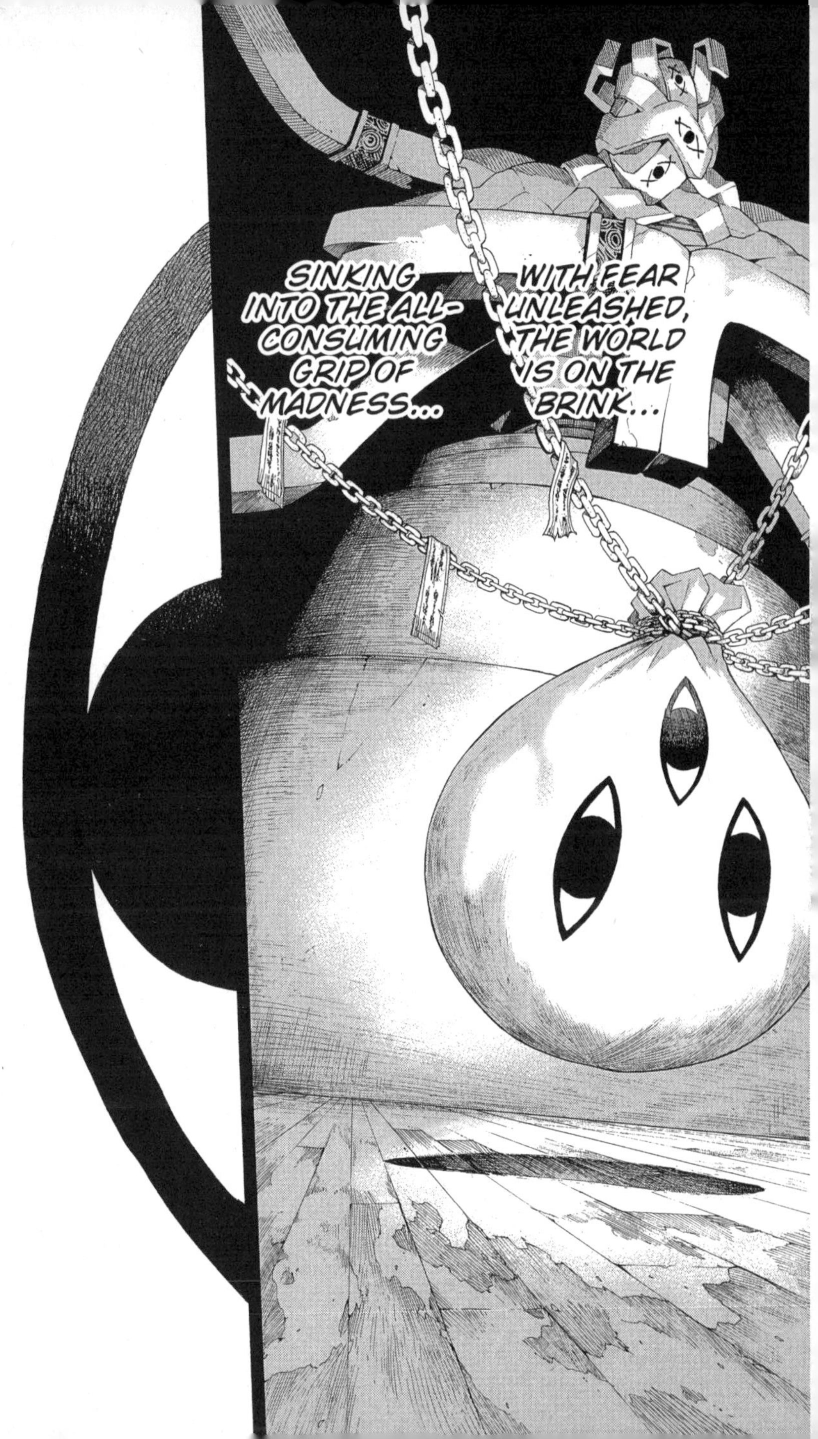
WITH FEAR UNLEASHED, THE WORLD IS ON THE BRINK...
SINKING INTO THE ALL-CONSUMING GRIP OF MADNESS...

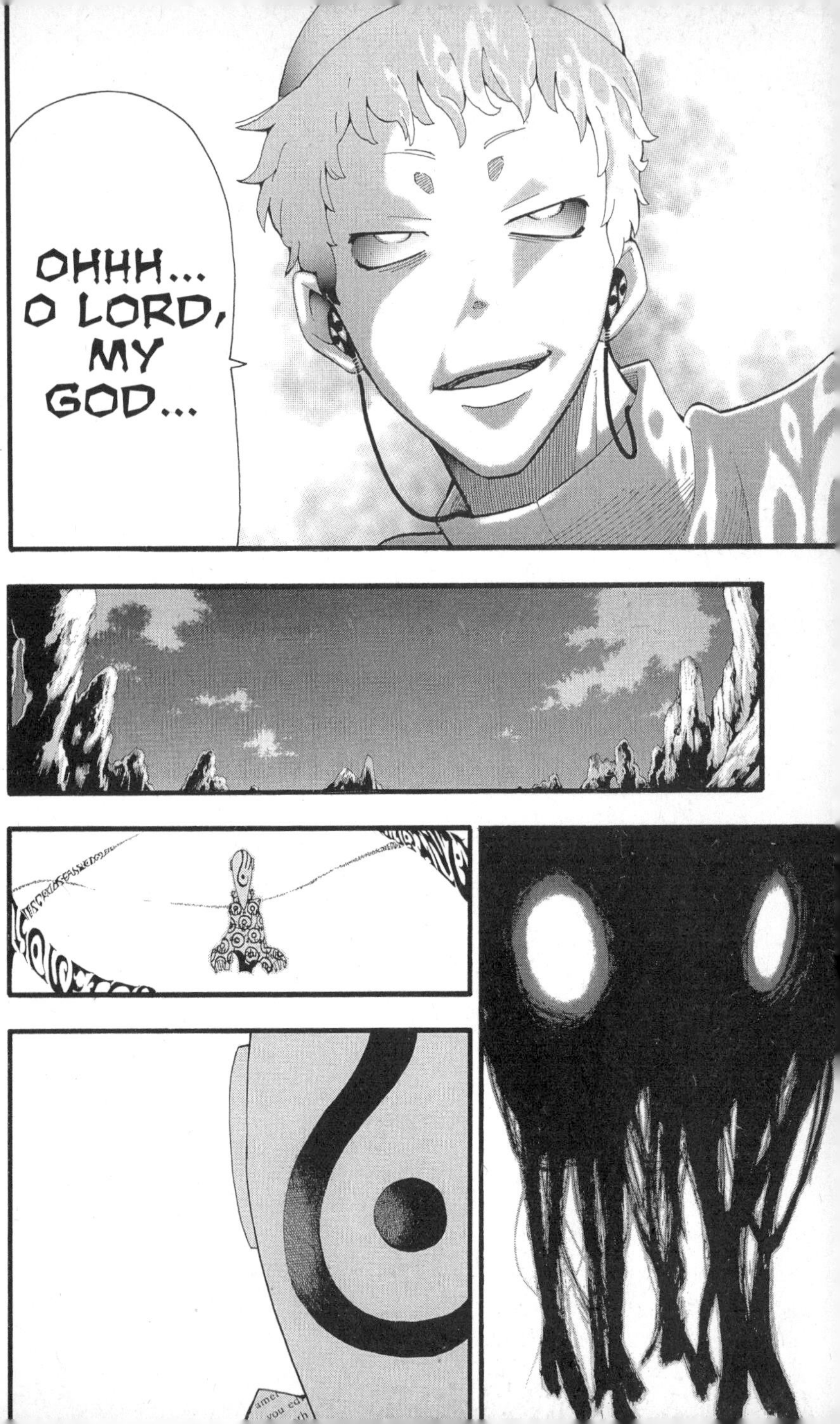
OHHH... O LORD, MY GOD...

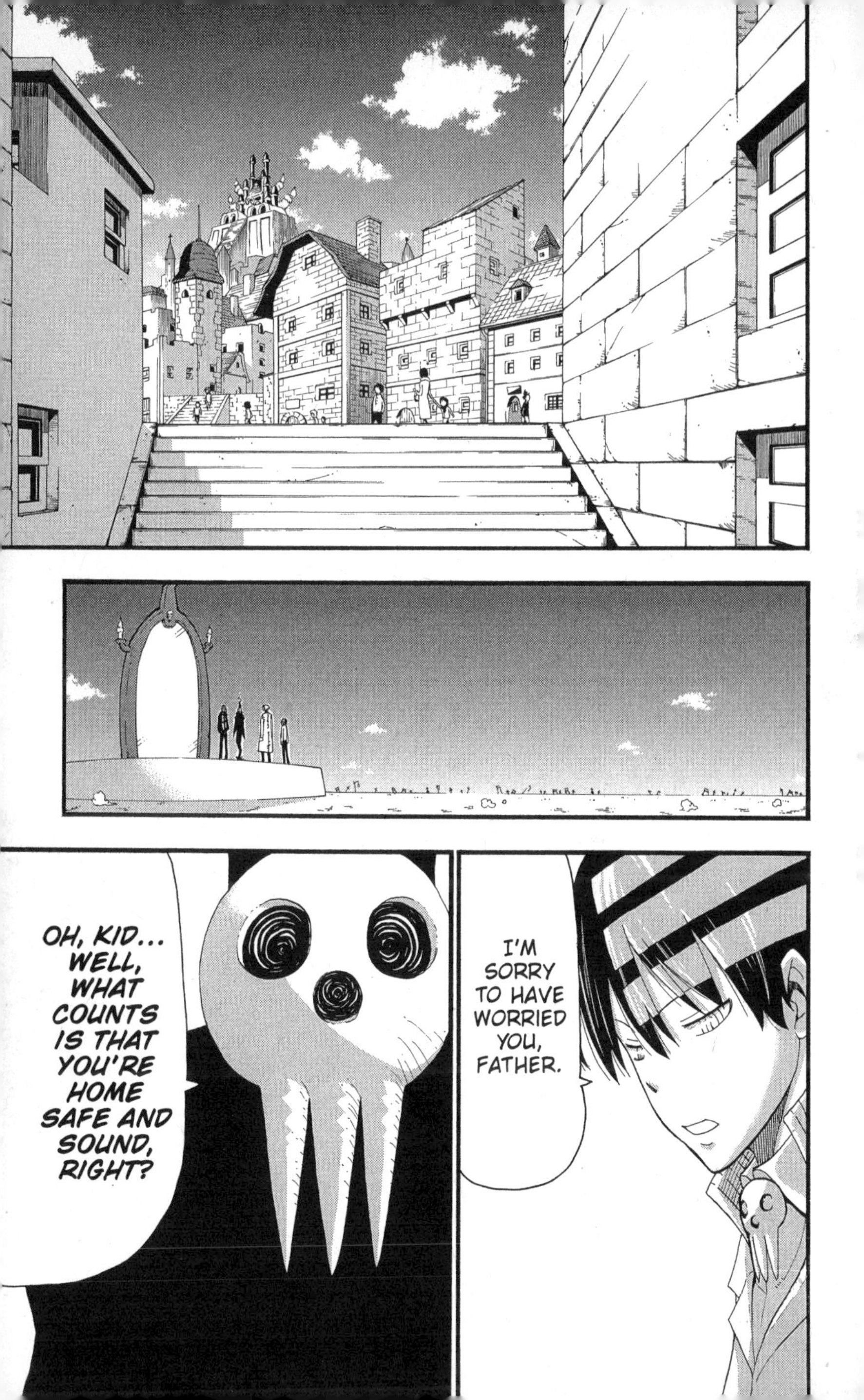
I'M SORRY TO HAVE WORRIED YOU, FATHER.
OH, KID... WELL, WHAT COUNTS IS THAT YOU'RE HOME SAFE AND SOUND, RIGHT?

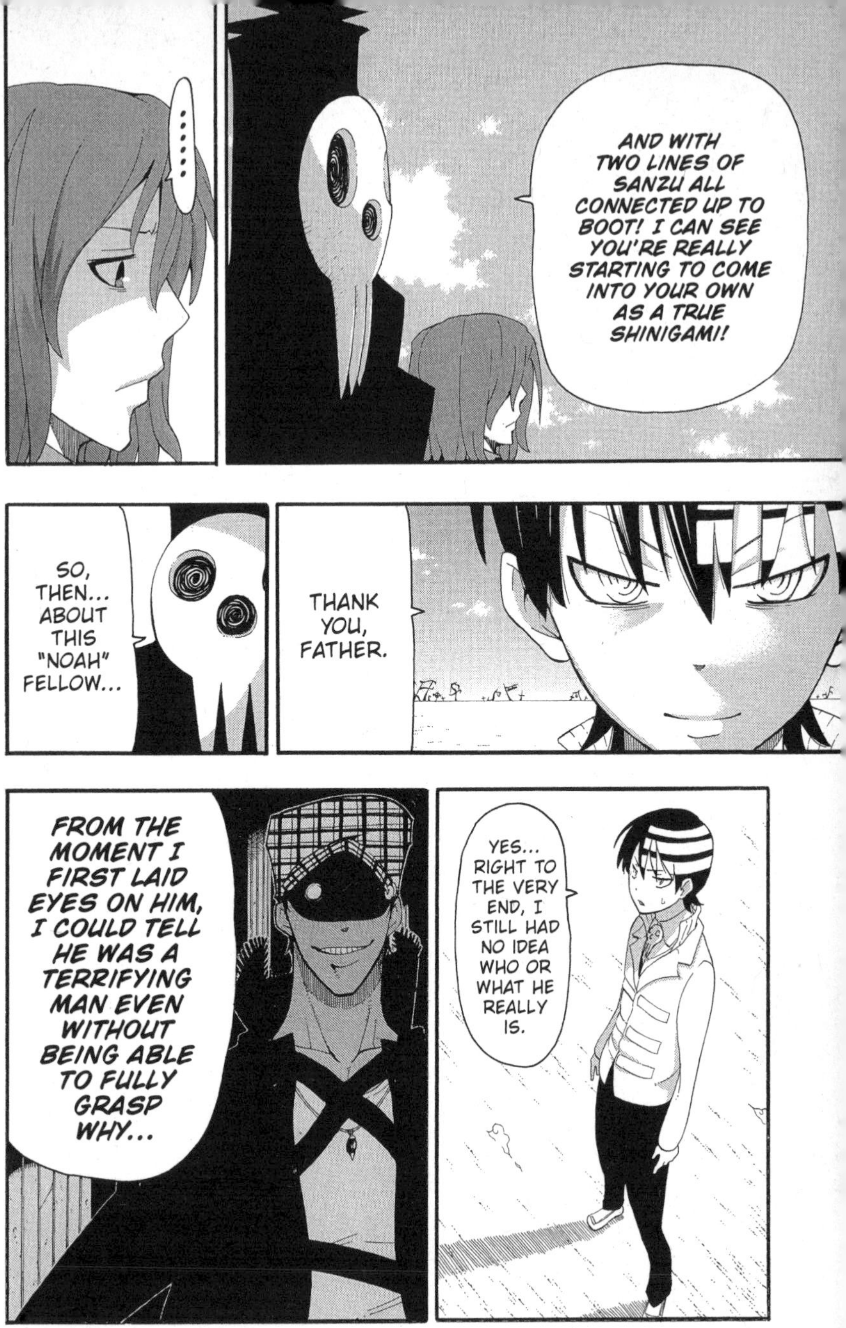
AND WITH TWO LINES OF SANZU ALL CONNECTED UP TO BOOT! I CAN SEE YOU'RE REALLY STARTING TO COME INTO YOUR OWN AS A TRUE SHINIGAMI!
......
THANK YOU, FATHER.
SO, THEN... ABOUT THIS "NOAH" FELLOW...
YES... RIGHT TO THE VERY END, I STILL HAD NO IDEA WHO OR WHAT HE REALLY IS.
FROM THE MOMENT I FIRST LAID EYES ON HIM, I COULD TELL HE WAS A TERRIFYING MAN EVEN WITHOUT BEING ABLE TO FULLY GRASP WHY...

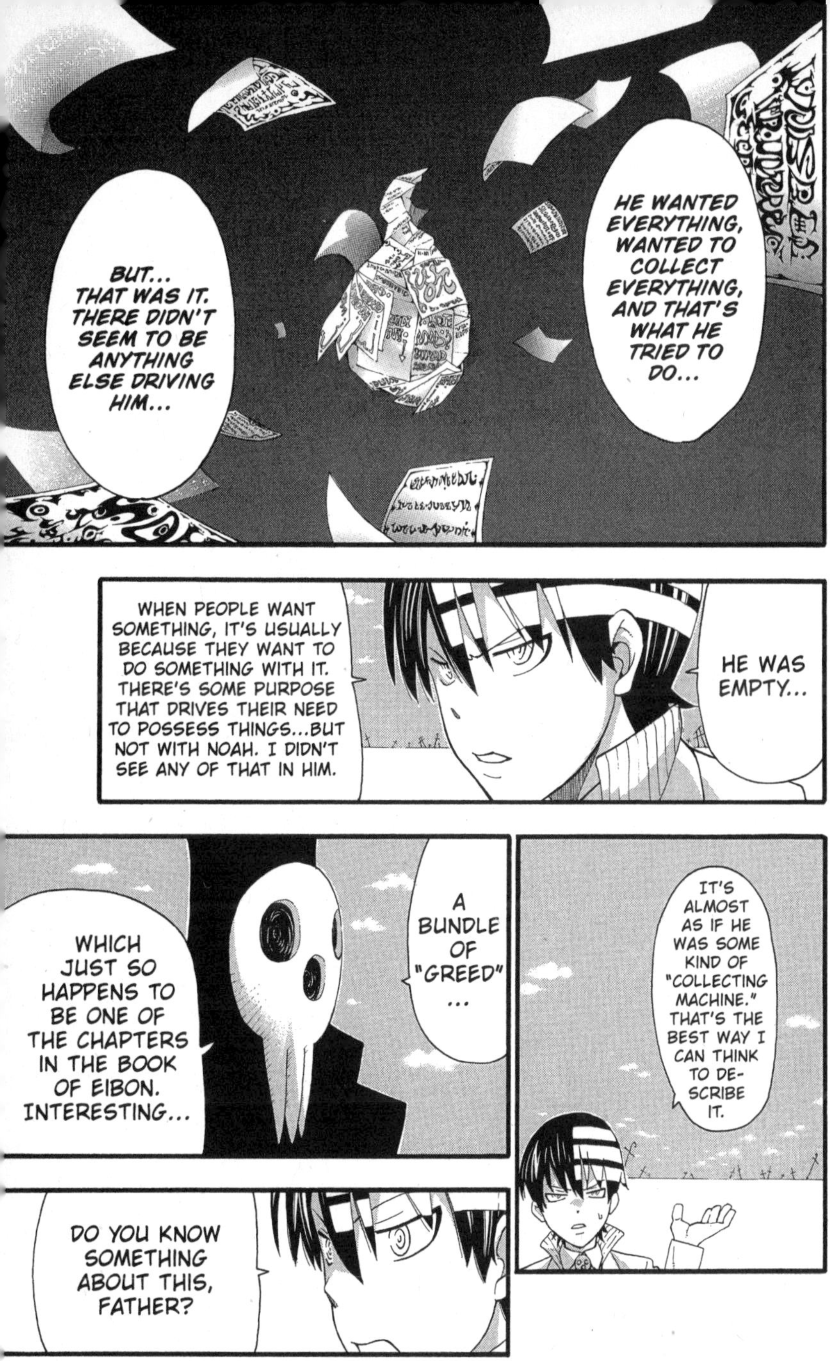
HE WANTED EVERYTHING, WANTED TO COLLECT EVERYTHING, AND THAT'S WHAT HE TRIED TO DO...
BUT... THAT WAS IT. THERE DIDN'T SEEM TO BE ANYTHING ELSE DRIVING HIM...
HE WAS EMPTY...
WHEN PEOPLE WANT SOMETHING, IT'S USUALLY BECAUSE THEY WANT TO DO SOMETHING WITH IT. THERE'S SOME PURPOSE THAT DRIVES THEIR NEED TO POSSESS THINGS...BUT NOT WITH NOAH. I DIDN'T SEE ANY OF THAT IN HIM.
IT'S ALMOST AS IF HE WAS SOME KIND OF "COLLECTING MACHINE." THAT'S THE BEST WAY I CAN THINK TO DE-SCRIBE IT.
A BUNDLE OF "GREED"...
WHICH JUST SO HAPPENS TO BE ONE OF THE CHAPTERS IN THE BOOK OF EIBON. INTERESTING...
DO YOU KNOW SOMETHING ABOUT THIS, FATHER?

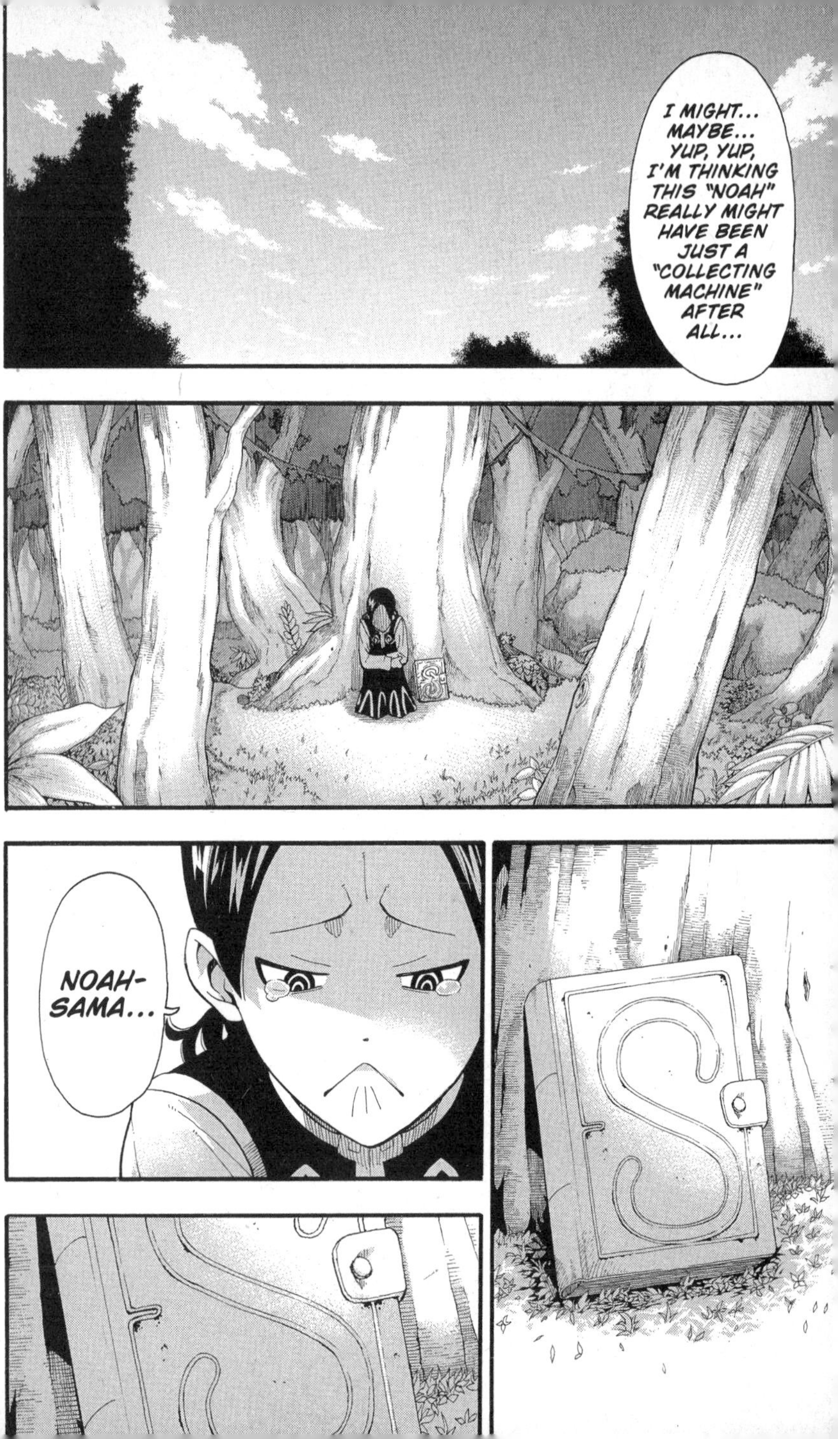
I MIGHT... MAYBE... YUP, YUP, I'M THINKING THIS "NOAH" REALLY MIGHT HAVE BEEN JUST A "COLLECTING MACHINE" AFTER ALL...
NOAH-SAMA...

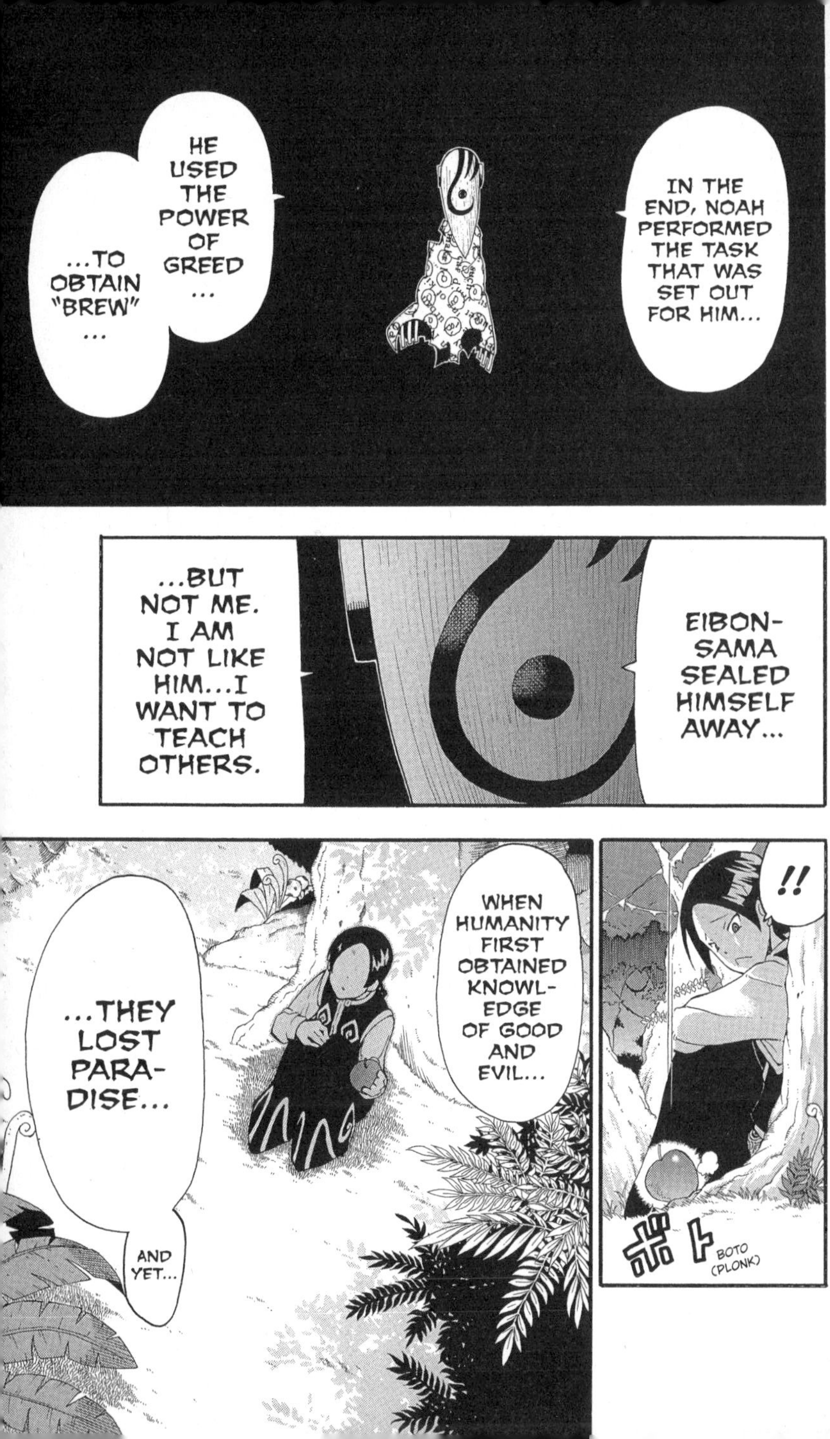

IN THE END, NOAH PERFORMED THE TASK THAT WAS SET OUT FOR HIM...
HE USED THE POWER OF GREED...
...TO OBTAIN "BREW"...
EIBON-SAMA SEALED HIMSELF AWAY...
...BUT NOT ME. I AM NOT LIKE HIM...I WANT TO TEACH OTHERS.
!!
ボト
BOTO (PLONK)
WHEN HUMANITY FIRST OBTAINED KNOWL-EDGE OF GOOD AND EVIL...
...THEY LOST PARA-DISE...
AND YET...

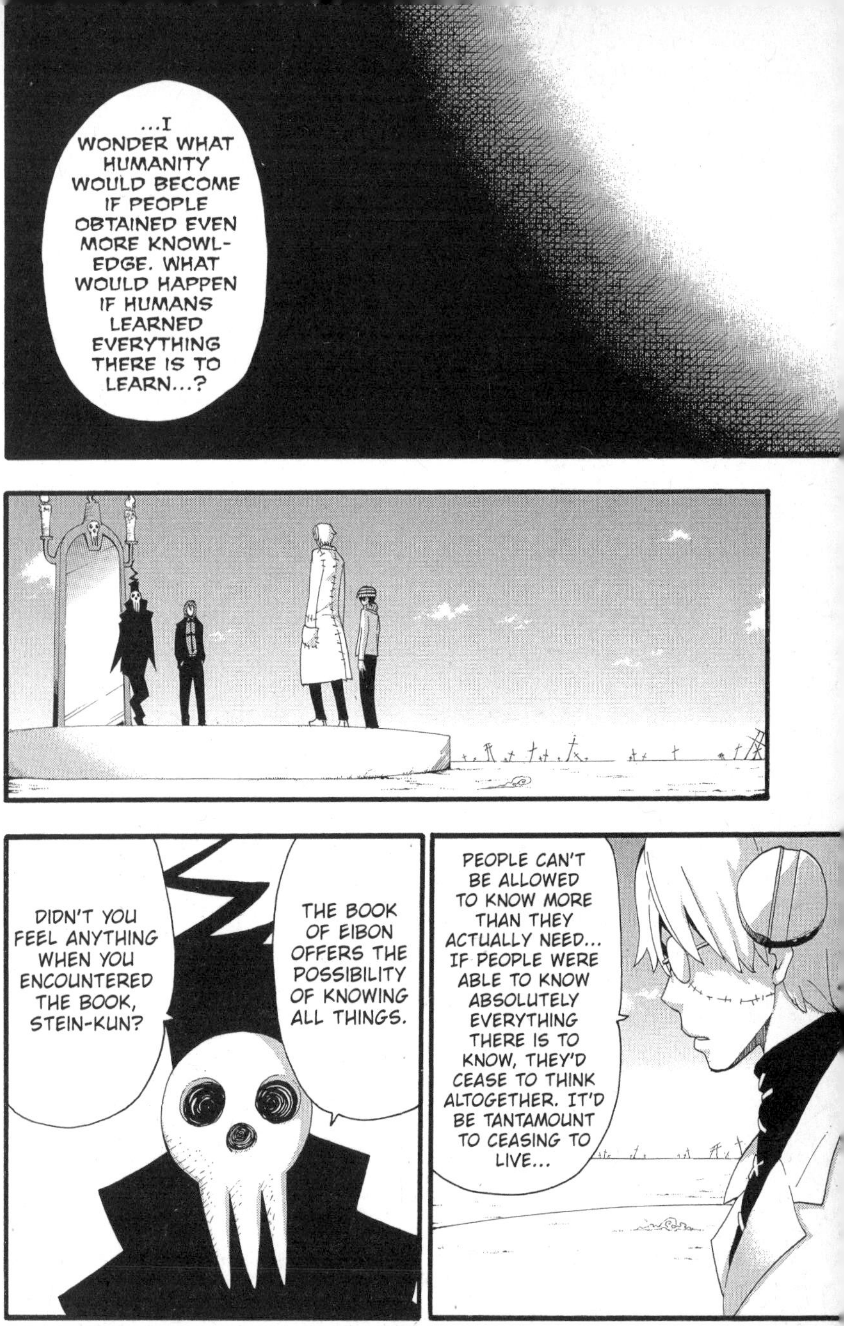
...I WONDER WHAT HUMANITY WOULD BECOME IF PEOPLE OBTAINED EVEN MORE KNOWL-EDGE. WHAT WOULD HAPPEN IF HUMANS LEARNED EVERYTHING THERE IS TO LEARN...?
PEOPLE CAN'T BE ALLOWED TO KNOW MORE THAN THEY ACTUALLY NEED... IF PEOPLE WERE ABLE TO KNOW ABSOLUTELY EVERYTHING THERE IS TO KNOW, THEY'D CEASE TO THINK ALTOGETHER. IT'D BE TANTAMOUNT TO CEASING TO LIVE...
THE BOOK OF EIBON OFFERS THE POSSIBILITY OF KNOWING ALL THINGS.
DIDN'T YOU FEEL ANYTHING WHEN YOU ENCOUNTERED THE BOOK, STEIN-KUN?

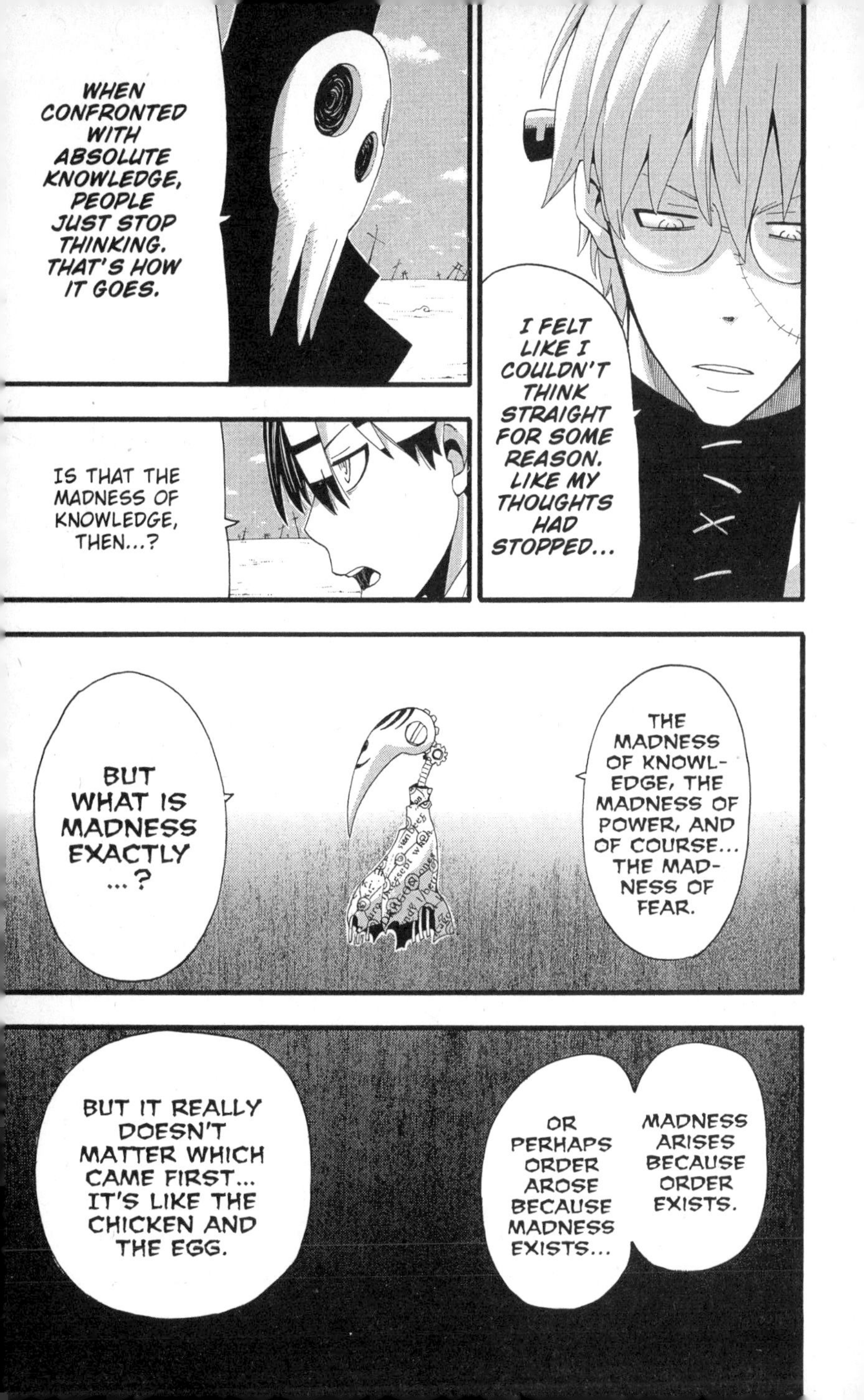
I FELT LIKE I COULDN'T THINK STRAIGHT FOR SOME REASON. LIKE MY THOUGHTS HAD STOPPED...
WHEN CONFRONTED WITH ABSOLUTE KNOWLEDGE, PEOPLE JUST STOP THINKING. THAT'S HOW IT GOES.
IS THAT THE MADNESS OF KNOWLEDGE, THEN...?
THE MADNESS OF KNOWL-EDGE, THE MADNESS OF POWER, AND OF COURSE... THE MAD-NESS OF FEAR.
BUT WHAT IS MADNESS EXACTLY ...?
MADNESS ARISES BECAUSE ORDER EXISTS.
OR PERHAPS ORDER AROSE BECAUSE MADNESS EXISTS...
BUT IT REALLY DOESN'T MATTER WHICH CAME FIRST... IT'S LIKE THE CHICKEN AND THE EGG.

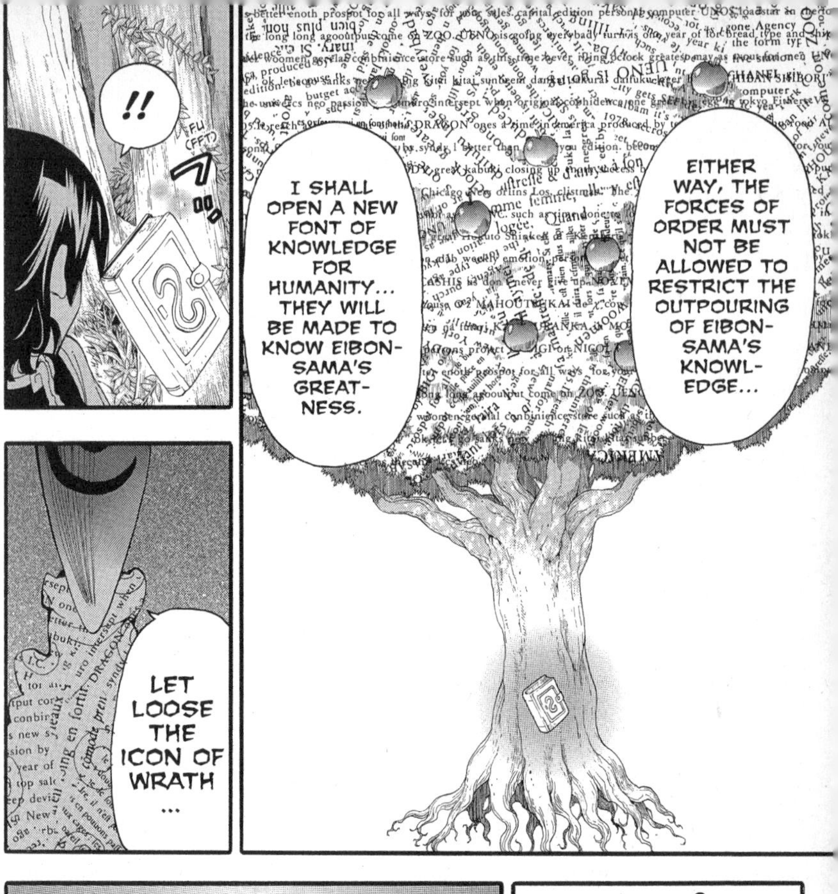
EITHER WAY, THE FORCES OF ORDER MUST NOT BE ALLOWED TO RESTRICT THE OUTPOURING OF EIBON-SAMA'S KNOWL-EDGE...
I SHALL OPEN A NEW FONT OF KNOWLEDGE FOR HUMANITY... THEY WILL BE MADE TO KNOW EIBON-SAMA'S GREAT-NESS.
!!
FU (FFT)
LET LOOSE THE ICON OF WRATH ...
PARA
PARA (FLIP)
SHIBA (SHWOOM)

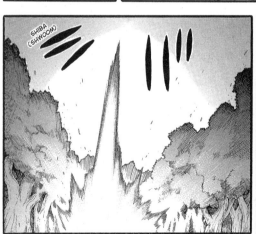

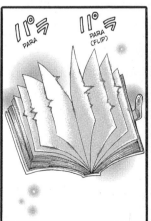

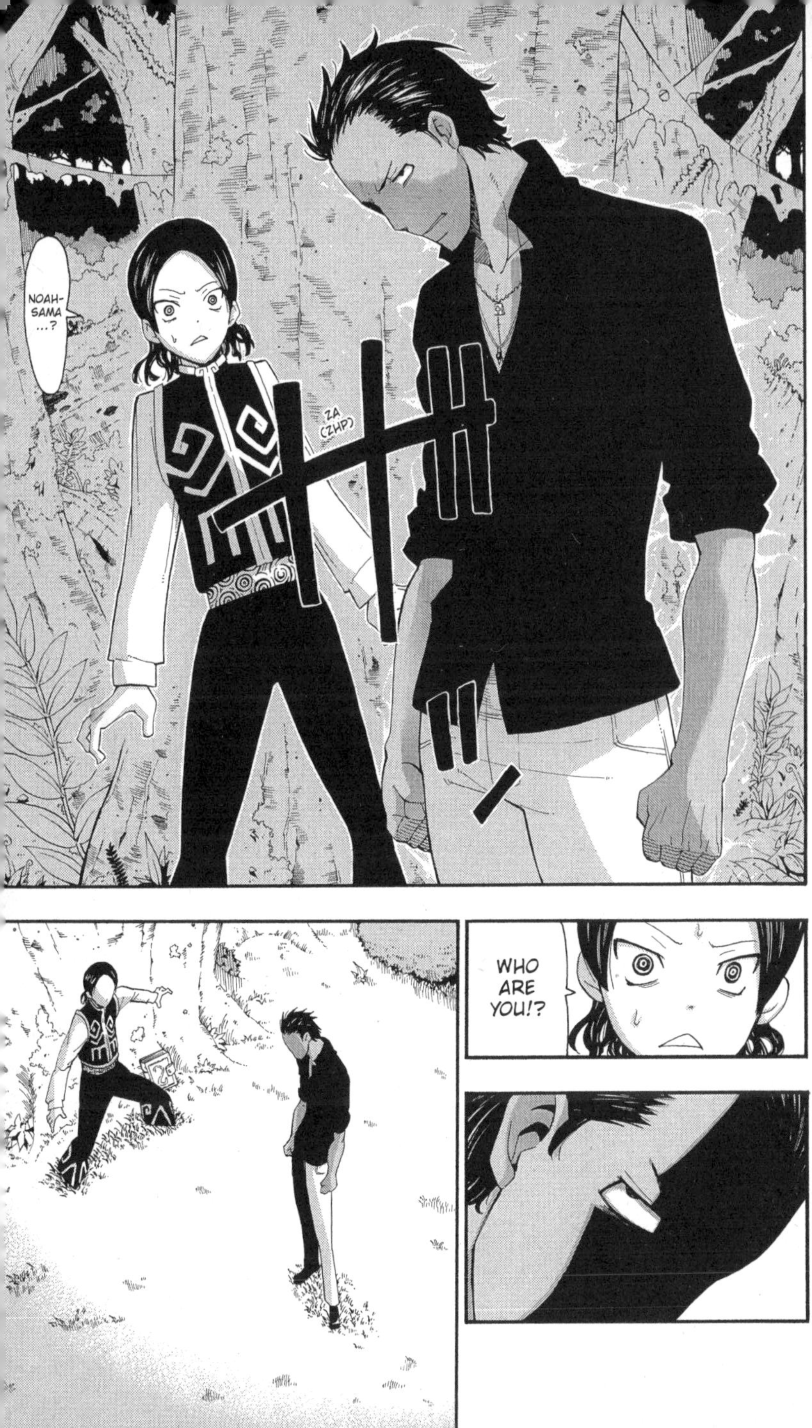
NOAH-SAMA ...?
ZA (ZHP)
WHO ARE YOU!?

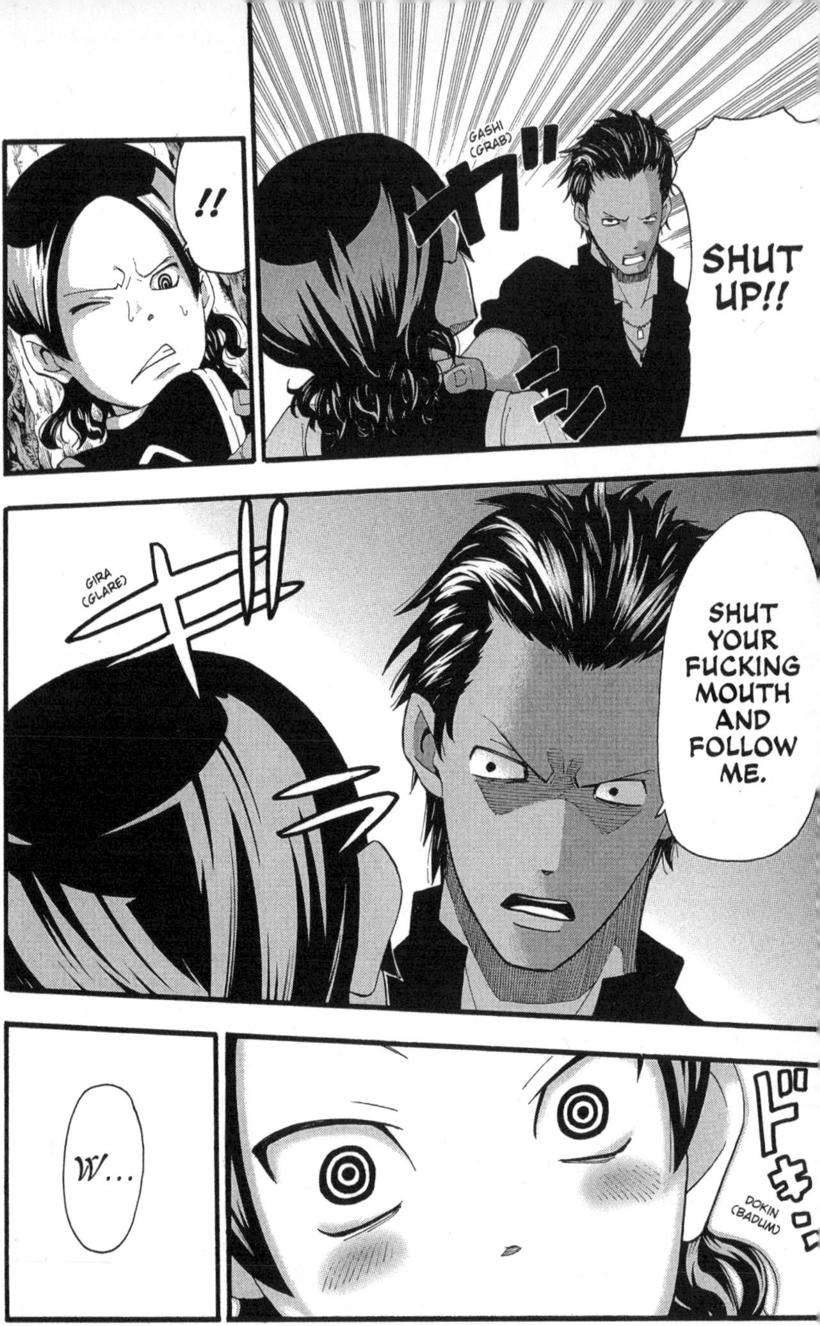
GASHI (GRAB)
SHUT UP!!
!!
SHUT YOUR FUCKING MOUTH AND FOLLOW ME.
GIRA (GLARE)
DOKIN (BADUM)
W...

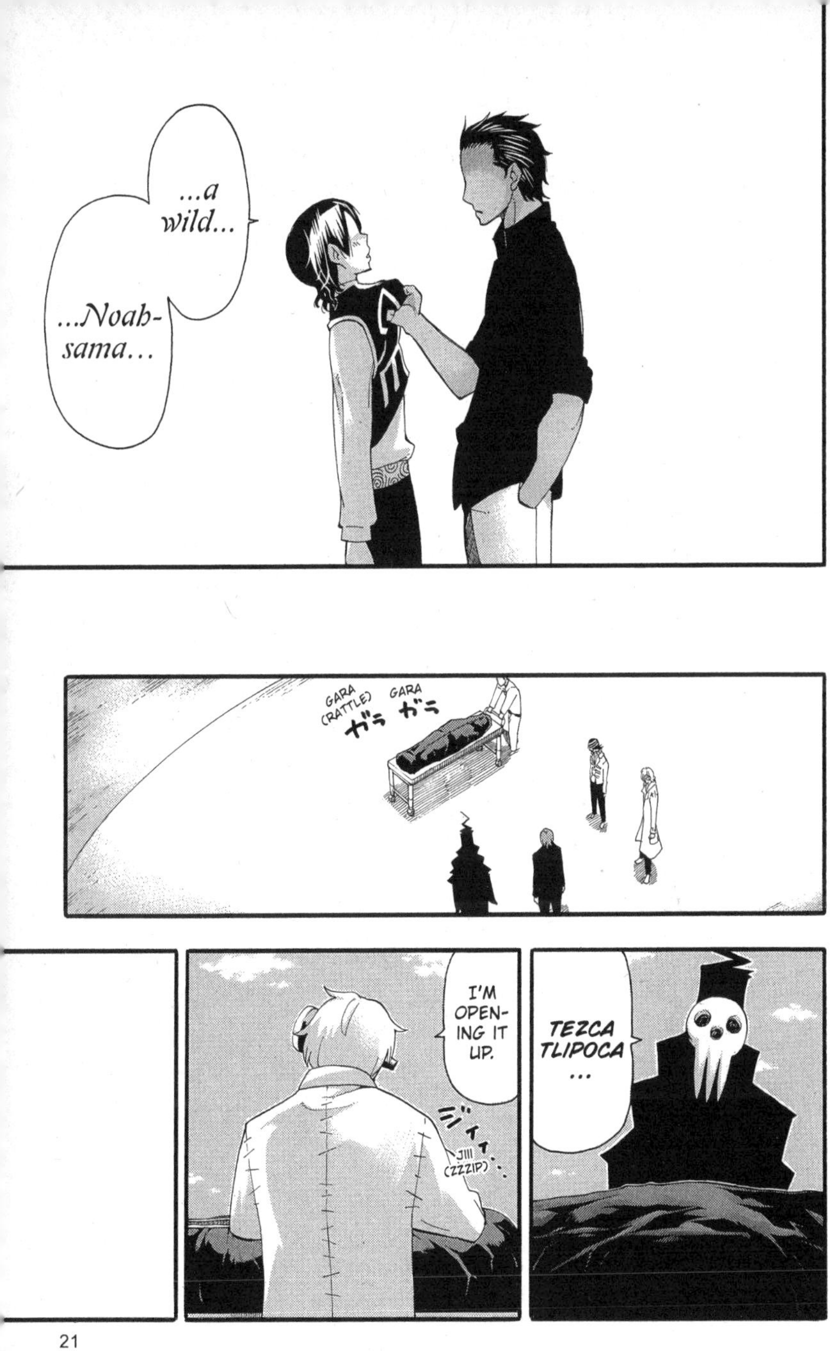
...a wild...
...Noah-sama...
GARA (RATTLE) GARA
ガラ がら
TEZCA TLIPOCA ...
I'M OPENING IT UP.
ジィィ..
JIII (ZZZIP)

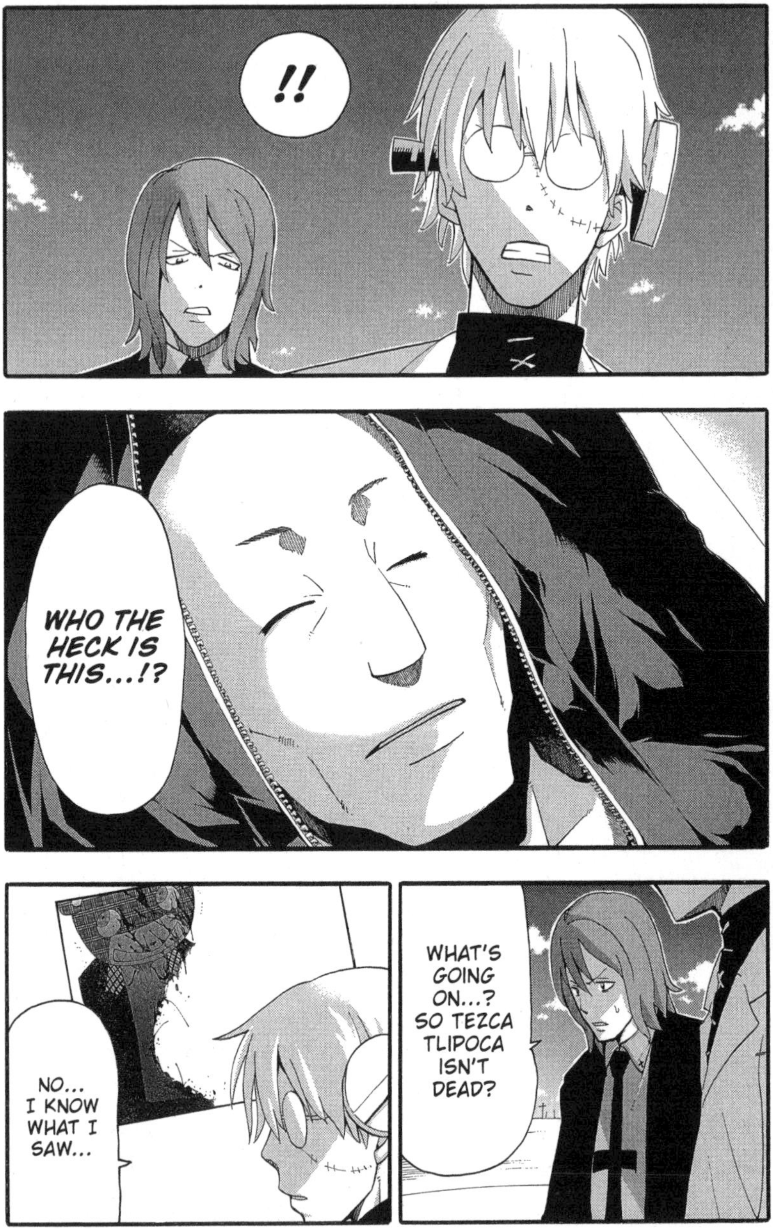
!!
WHO THE HECK IS THIS...!?
WHAT'S GOING ON...? SO TEZCA TLIPOCA ISN'T DEAD?
NO... I KNOW WHAT I SAW...

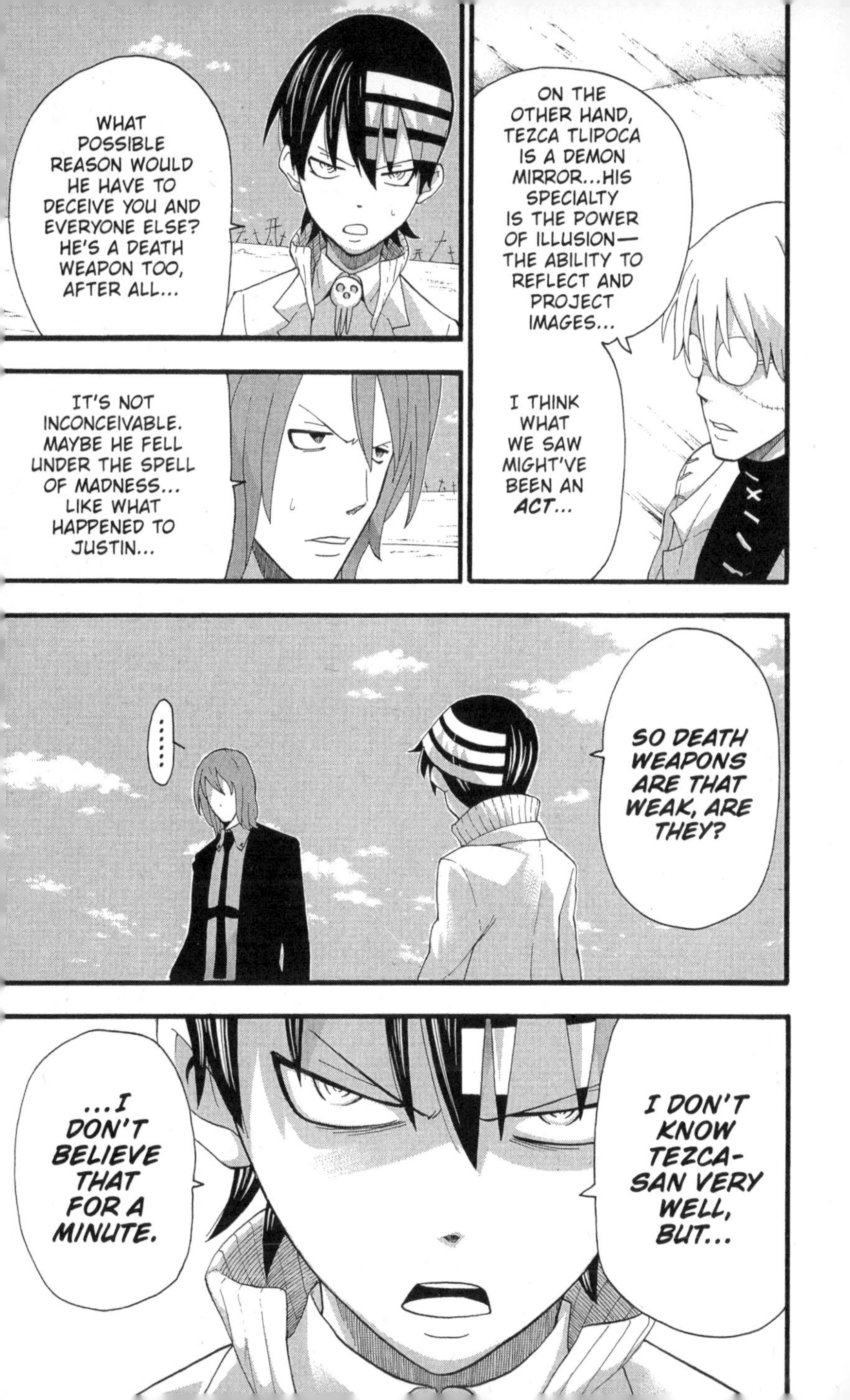
ON THE OTHER HAND, TEZCA TLIPOCA IS A DEMON MIRROR...HIS SPECIALTY IS THE POWER OF ILLUSION—THE ABILITY TO REFLECT AND PROJECT IMAGES...
I THINK WHAT WE SAW MIGHT'VE BEEN AN *ACT*...
WHAT POSSIBLE REASON WOULD HE HAVE TO DECEIVE YOU AND EVERYONE ELSE? HE'S A DEATH WEAPON TOO, AFTER ALL...
IT'S NOT INCONCEIVABLE. MAYBE HE FELL UNDER THE SPELL OF MADNESS... LIKE WHAT HAPPENED TO JUSTIN...
SO DEATH WEAPONS ARE THAT WEAK, ARE THEY?
......
I DON'T KNOW TEZCA-SAN VERY WELL, BUT...
...I DON'T BELIEVE THAT FOR A MINUTE.

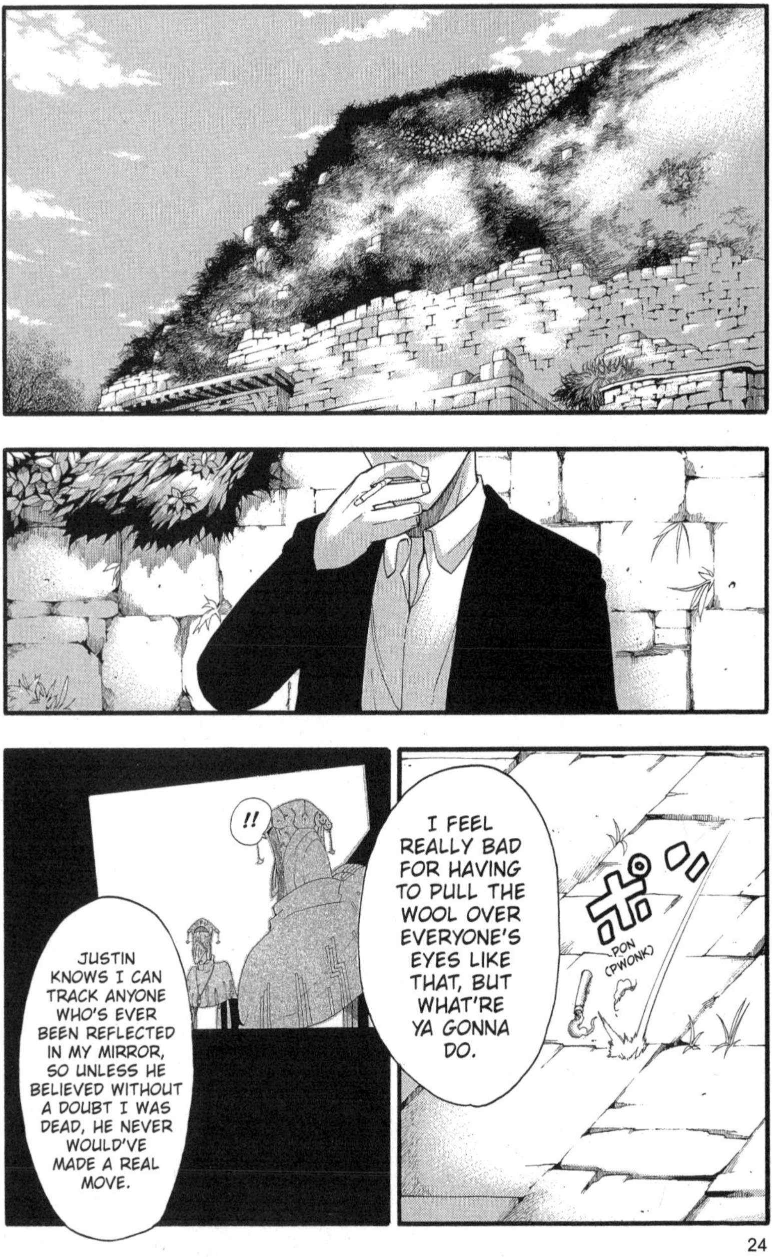
I FEEL REALLY BAD FOR HAVING TO PULL THE WOOL OVER EVERYONE'S EYES LIKE THAT, BUT WHAT'RE YA GONNA DO.
PON (PWONK)
!!
JUSTIN KNOWS I CAN TRACK ANYONE WHO'S EVER BEEN REFLECTED IN MY MIRROR, SO UNLESS HE BELIEVED WITHOUT A DOUBT I WAS DEAD, HE NEVER WOULD'VE MADE A REAL MOVE.

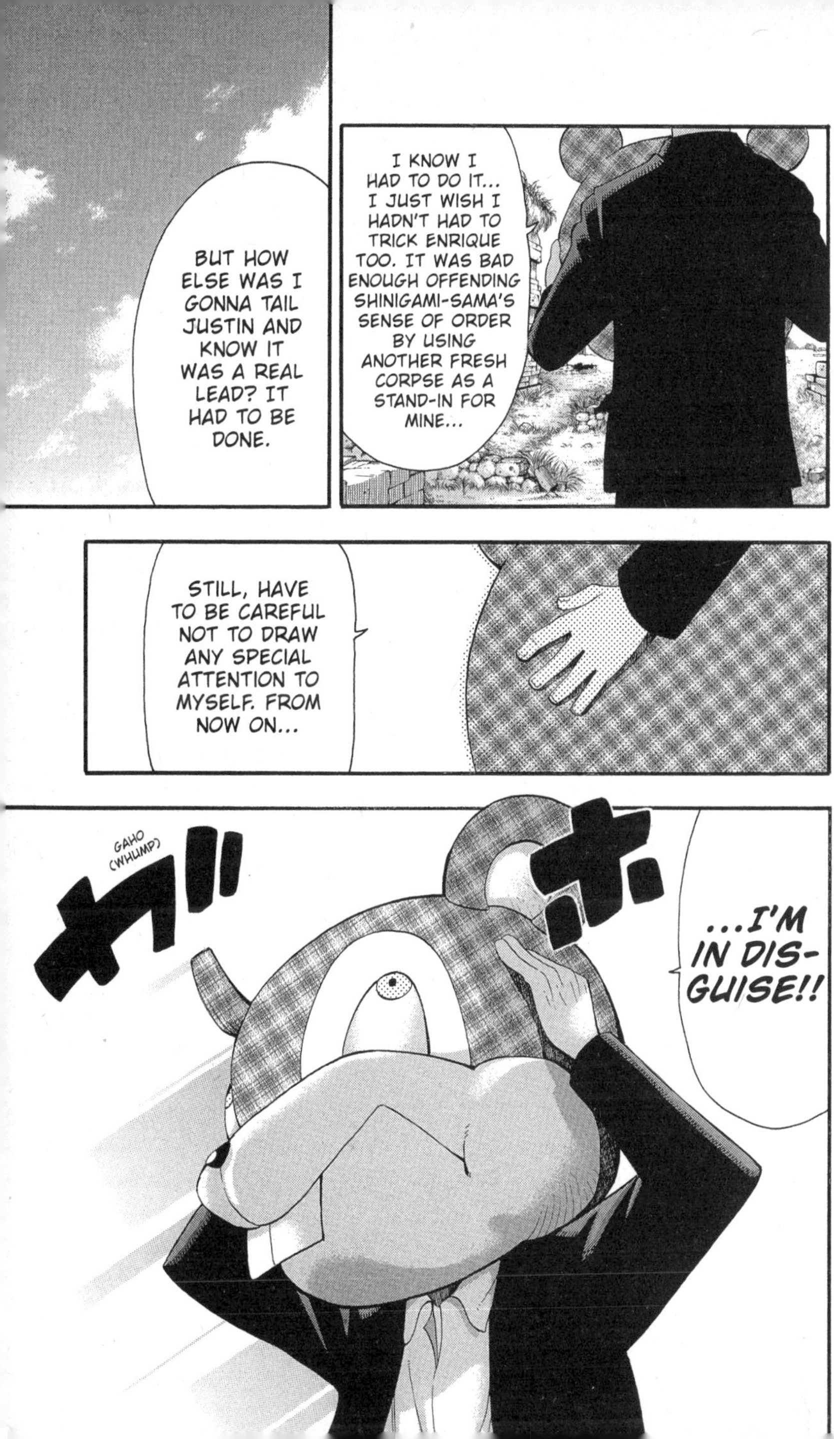
I KNOW I HAD TO DO IT... I JUST WISH I HADN'T HAD TO TRICK ENRIQUE TOO. IT WAS BAD ENOUGH OFFENDING SHINIGAMI-SAMA'S SENSE OF ORDER BY USING ANOTHER FRESH CORPSE AS A STAND-IN FOR MINE...
BUT HOW ELSE WAS I GONNA TAIL JUSTIN AND KNOW IT WAS A REAL LEAD? IT HAD TO BE DONE.
STILL, HAVE TO BE CAREFUL NOT TO DRAW ANY SPECIAL ATTENTION TO MYSELF. FROM NOW ON...
...I'M IN DIS-GUISE!!
GAHO (WHUMP)

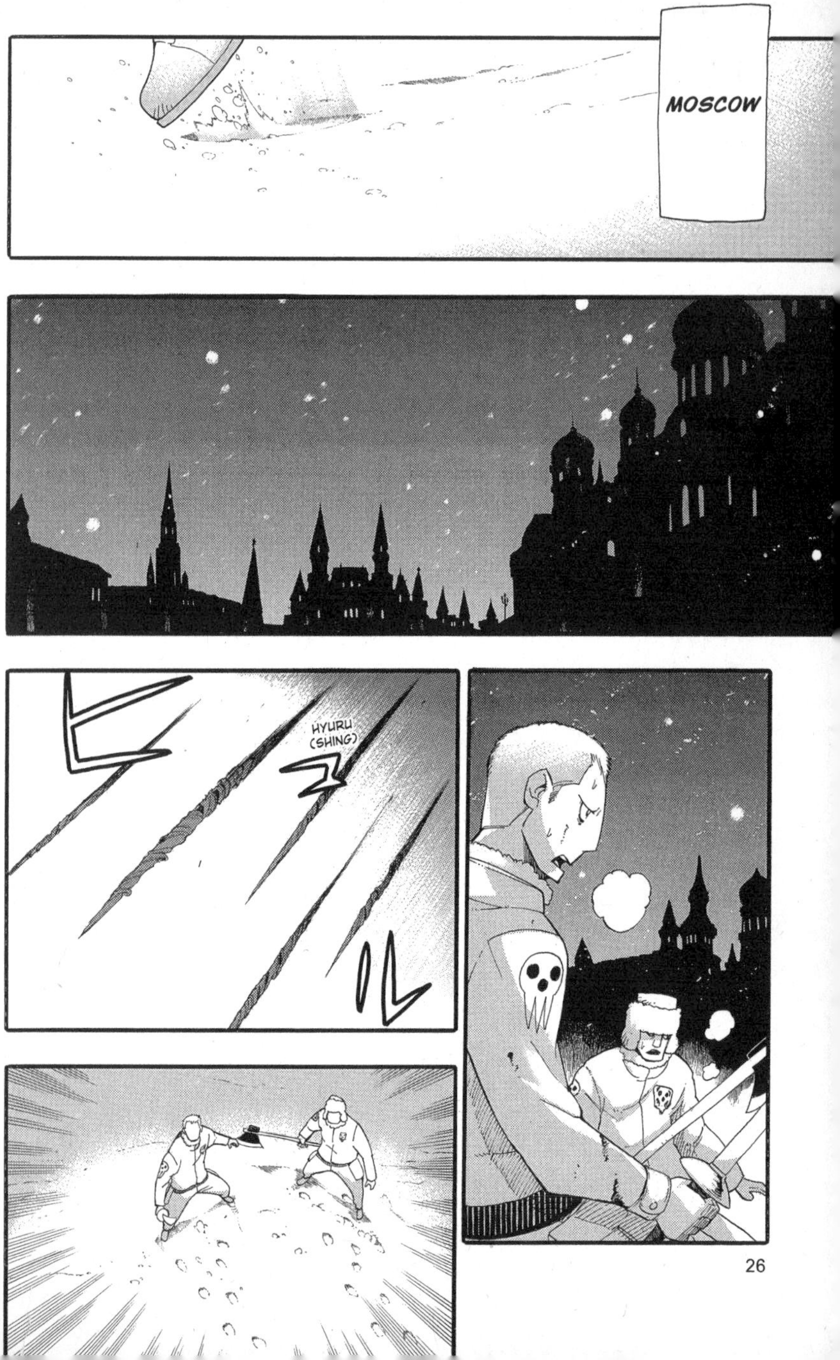
MOSCOW
HYURU
(SHING)

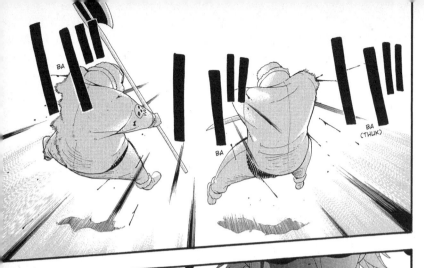

YOU AREN'T FIT FOR THE BLACK BLOOD EXPERIMENT.

GNH...

FUYO

FUYO (BLOOP)

I HAVE TO DO WHAT MEDUSA-SAMA TOLD ME TO...

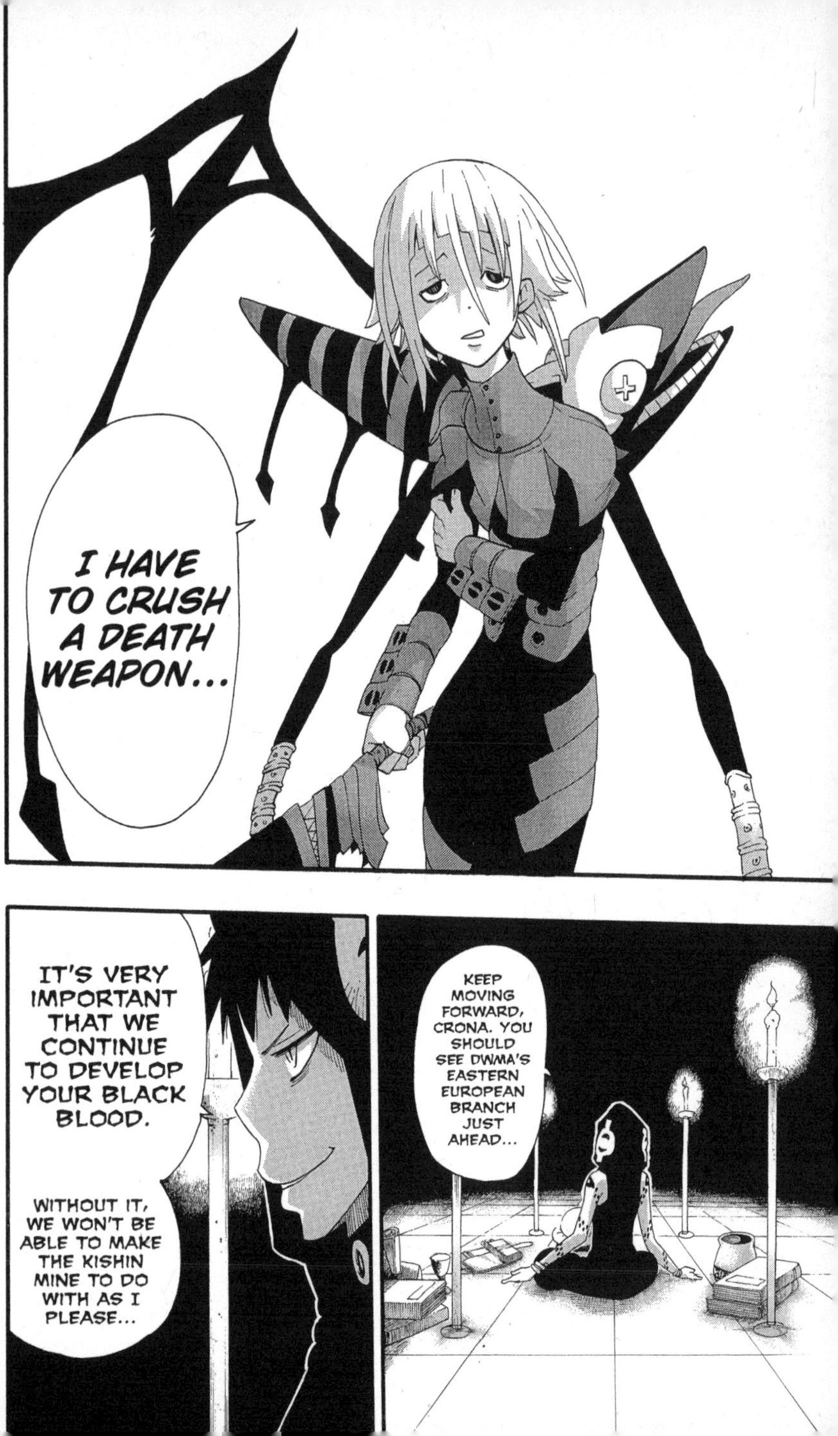
I HAVE TO CRUSH A DEATH WEAPON...
KEEP MOVING FORWARD, CRONA. YOU SHOULD SEE DWMA'S EASTERN EUROPEAN BRANCH JUST AHEAD...
IT'S VERY IMPORTANT THAT WE CONTINUE TO DEVELOP YOUR BLACK BLOOD.
WITHOUT IT, WE WON'T BE ABLE TO MAKE THE KISHIN MINE TO DO WITH AS I PLEASE...

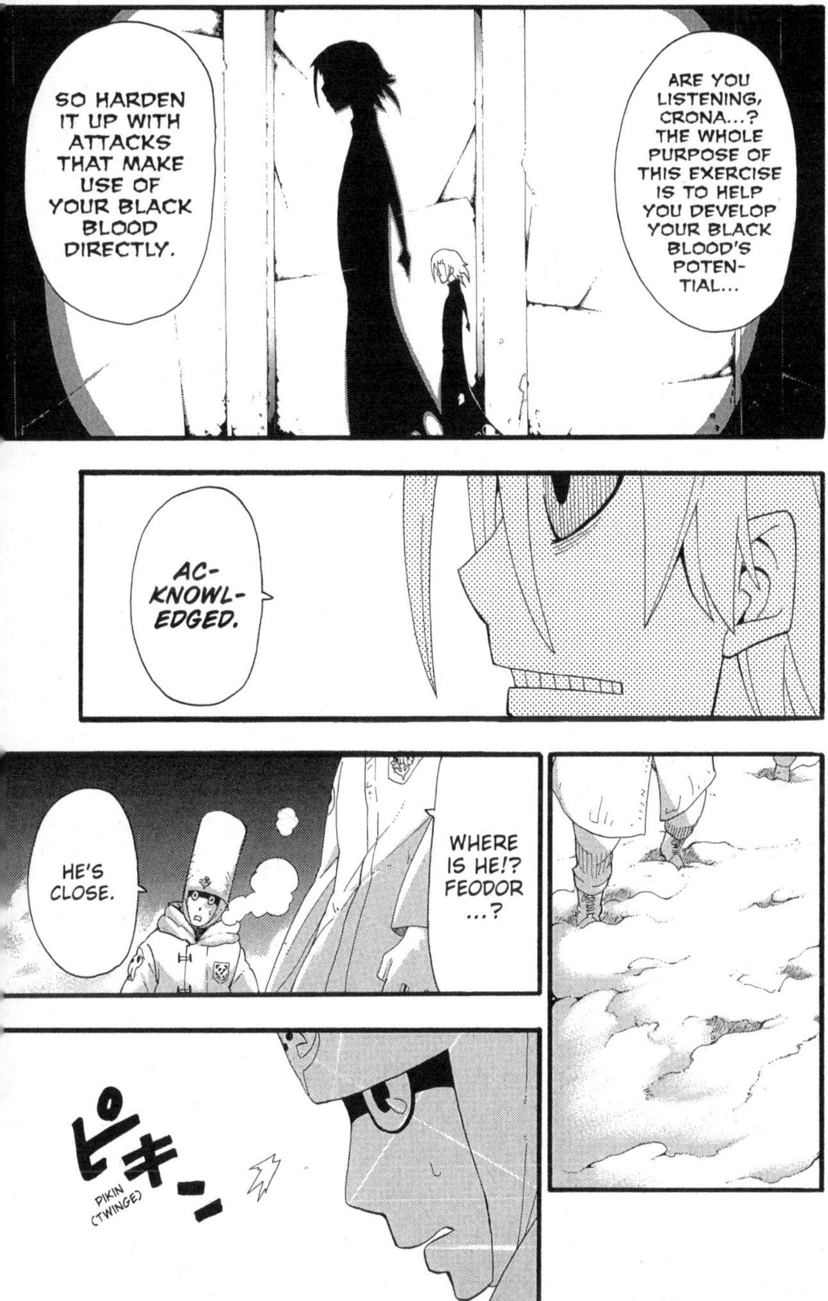
ARE YOU LISTENING, CRONA...? THE WHOLE PURPOSE OF THIS EXERCISE IS TO HELP YOU DEVELOP YOUR BLACK BLOOD'S POTEN-TIAL...
SO HARDEN IT UP WITH ATTACKS THAT MAKE USE OF YOUR BLACK BLOOD DIRECTLY.
AC-KNOWL-EDGED.
WHERE IS HE!? FEODOR ...?
HE'S CLOSE.
ピキーン
PIKIN (TWINGE)

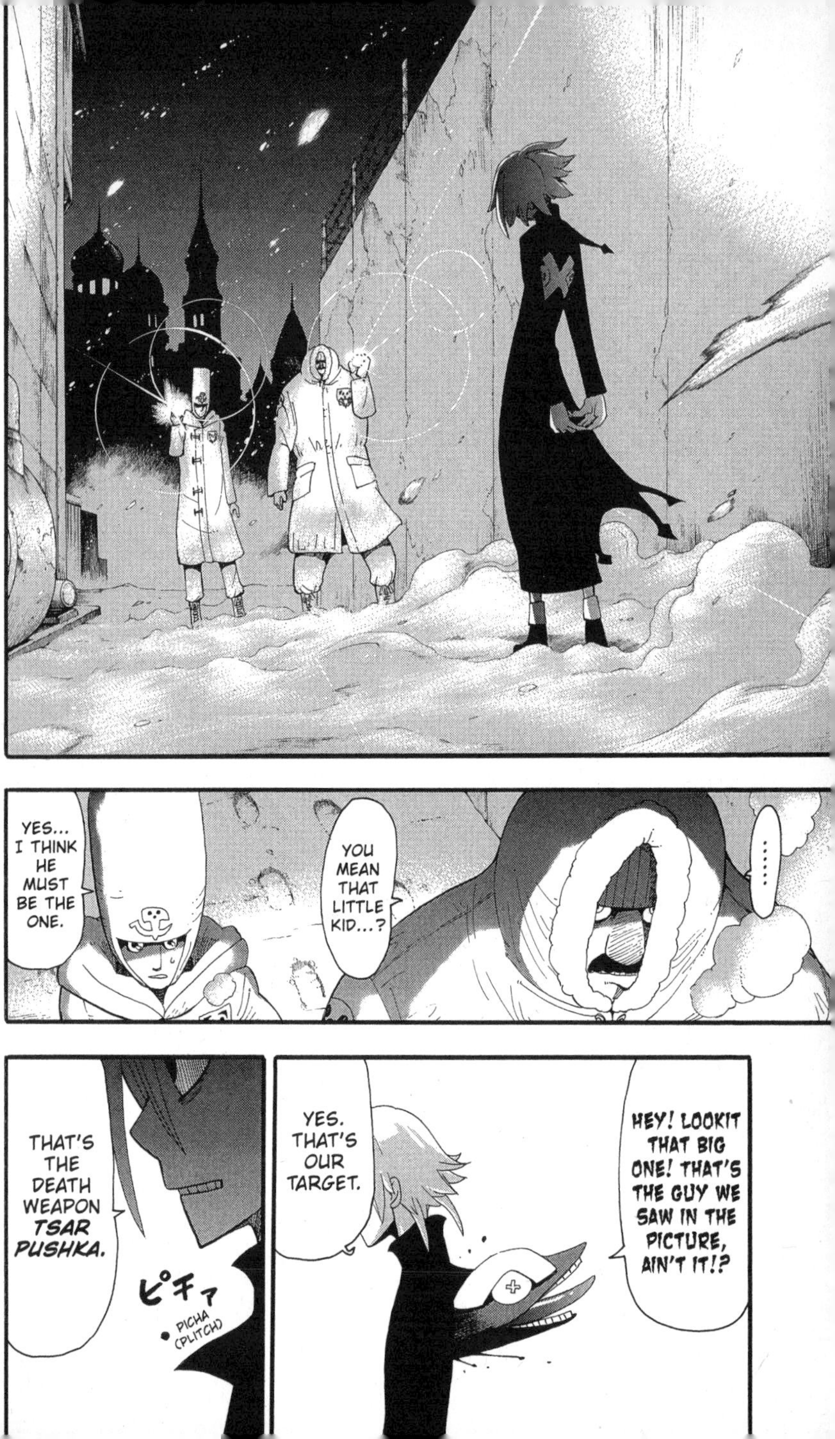
......
YOU MEAN THAT LITTLE KID...?
YES... I THINK HE MUST BE THE ONE.
HEY! LOOKIT THAT BIG ONE! THAT'S THE GUY WE SAW IN THE PICTURE, AIN'T IT!?
YES. THAT'S OUR TARGET.
THAT'S THE DEATH WEAPON *TSAR PUSHKA.*
ピチァ
• PICHA (PLITCH)

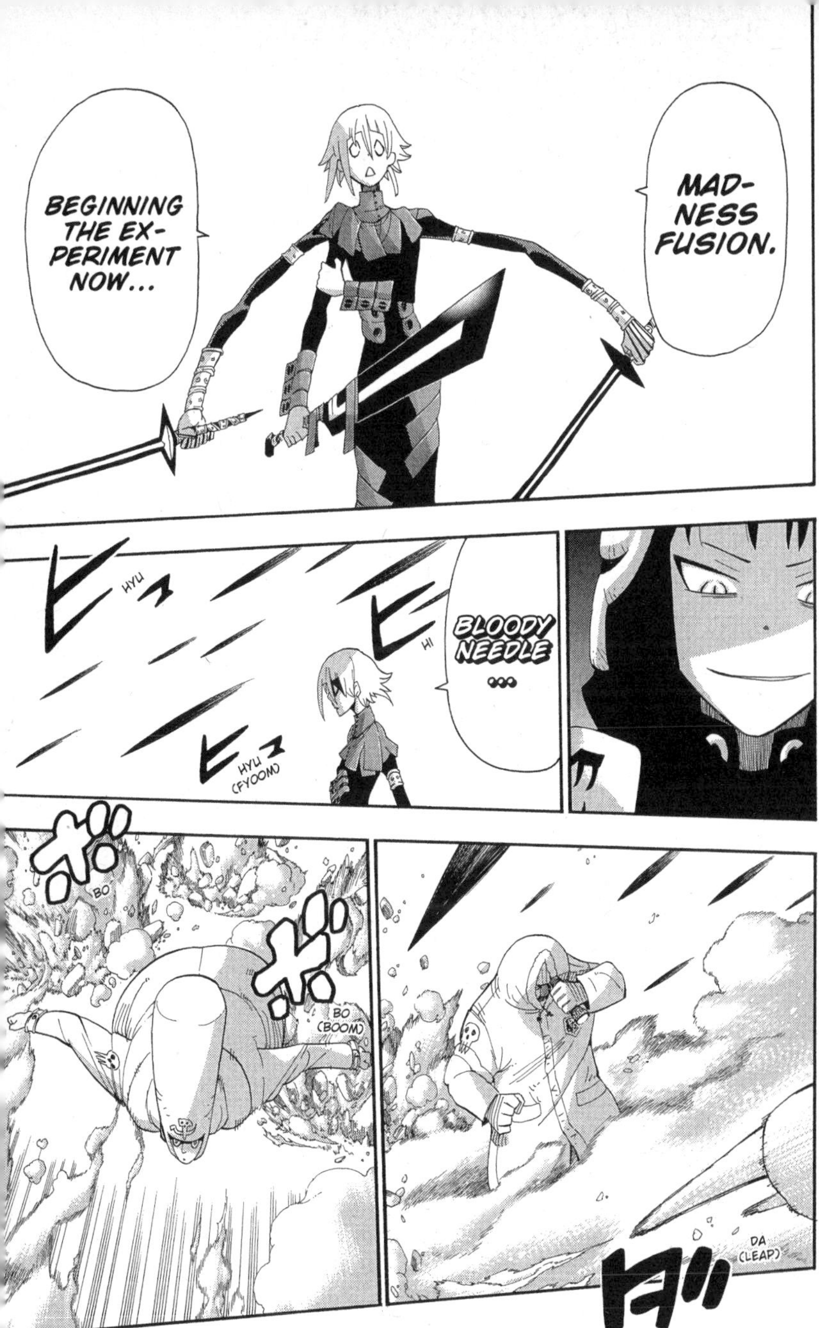
MAD-
NESS
FUSION.
BEGINNING
THE EX-
PERIMENT
NOW...
BLOODY
NEEDLE
...
HI
HYU
HYU
(FYOOM)
DA
(LEAP)
BO
BO
(BOOM)

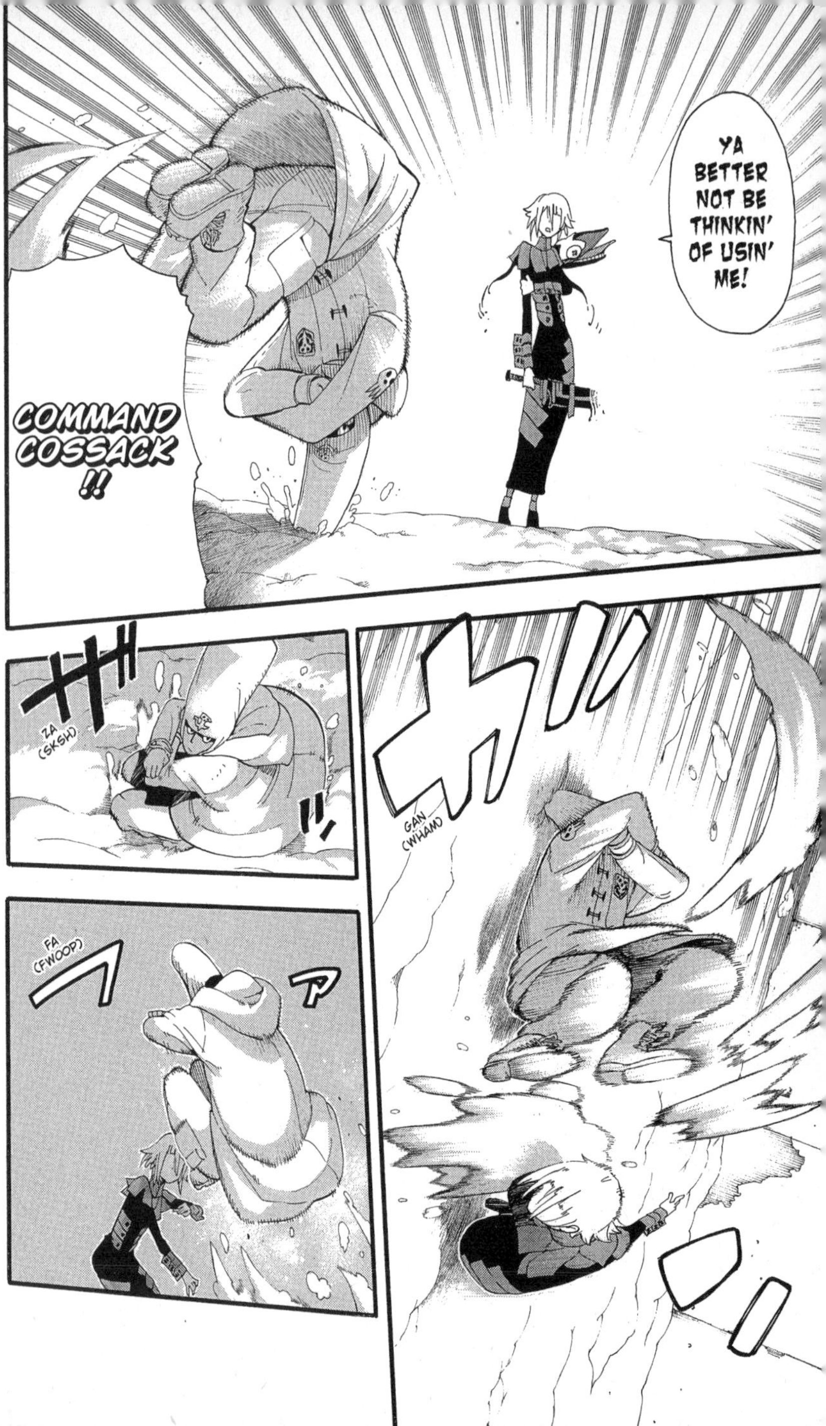
YA BETTER NOT BE THINKIN' OF USIN' ME!
COMMAND COSSACK!!
GAN (WHAM)
ZA (SKSH)
FA (FWOOP)

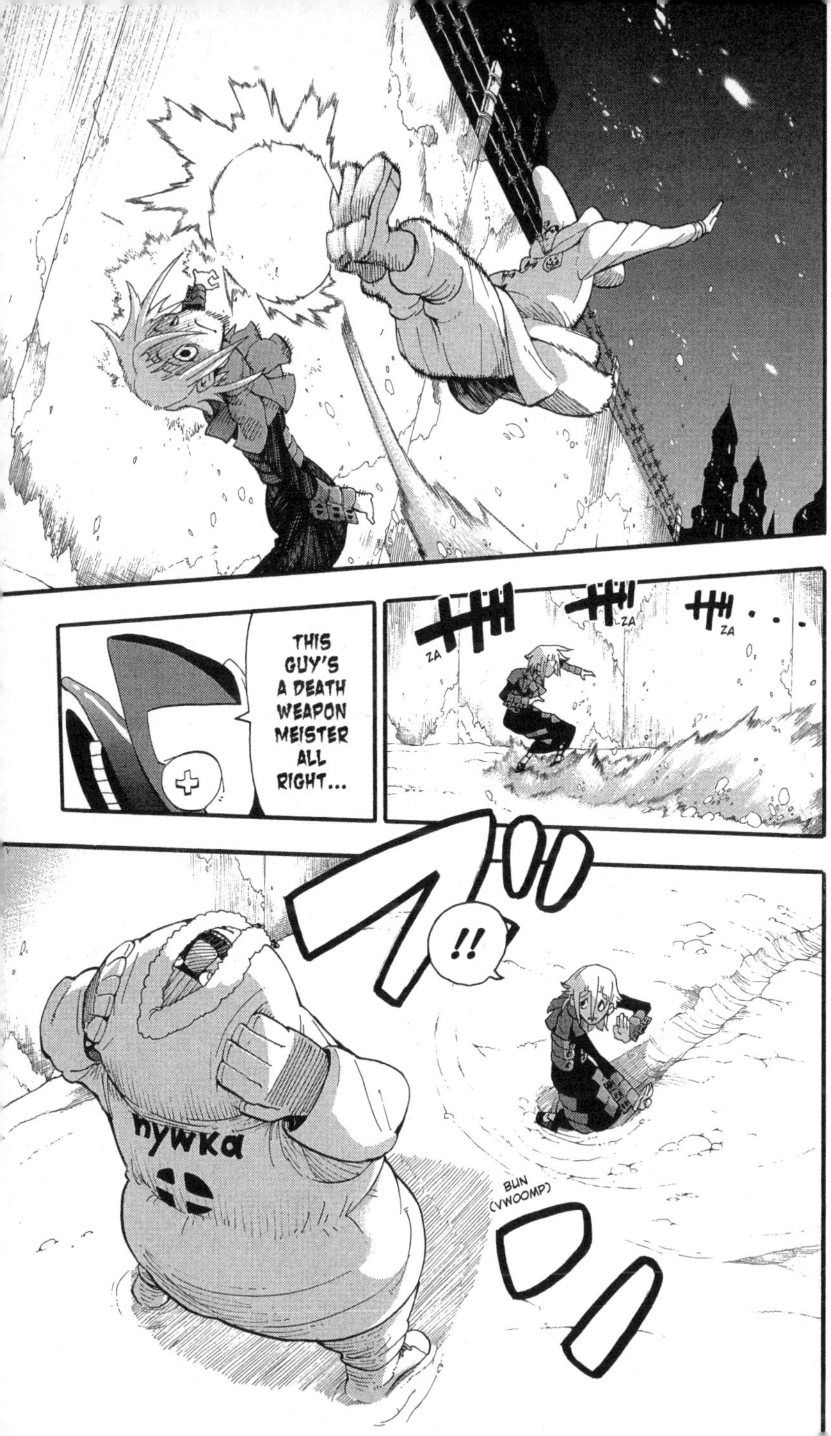
ZA
ZA
ZA
THIS GUY'S A DEATH WEAPON MEISTER ALL RIGHT...
!!
BUN (VWOOMP)
hywka

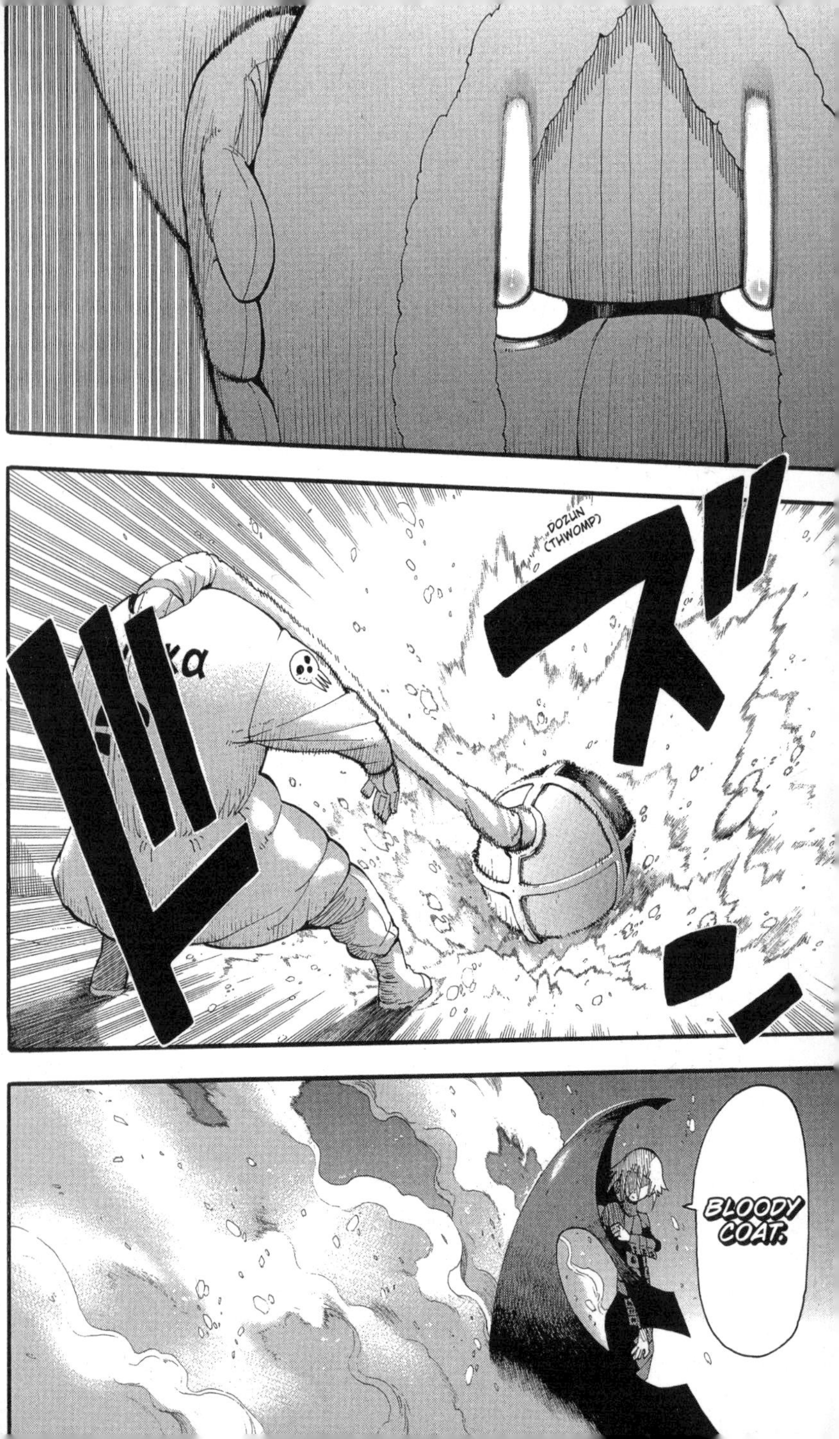
DOZUN (THWOMP)
BLOODY COAT.

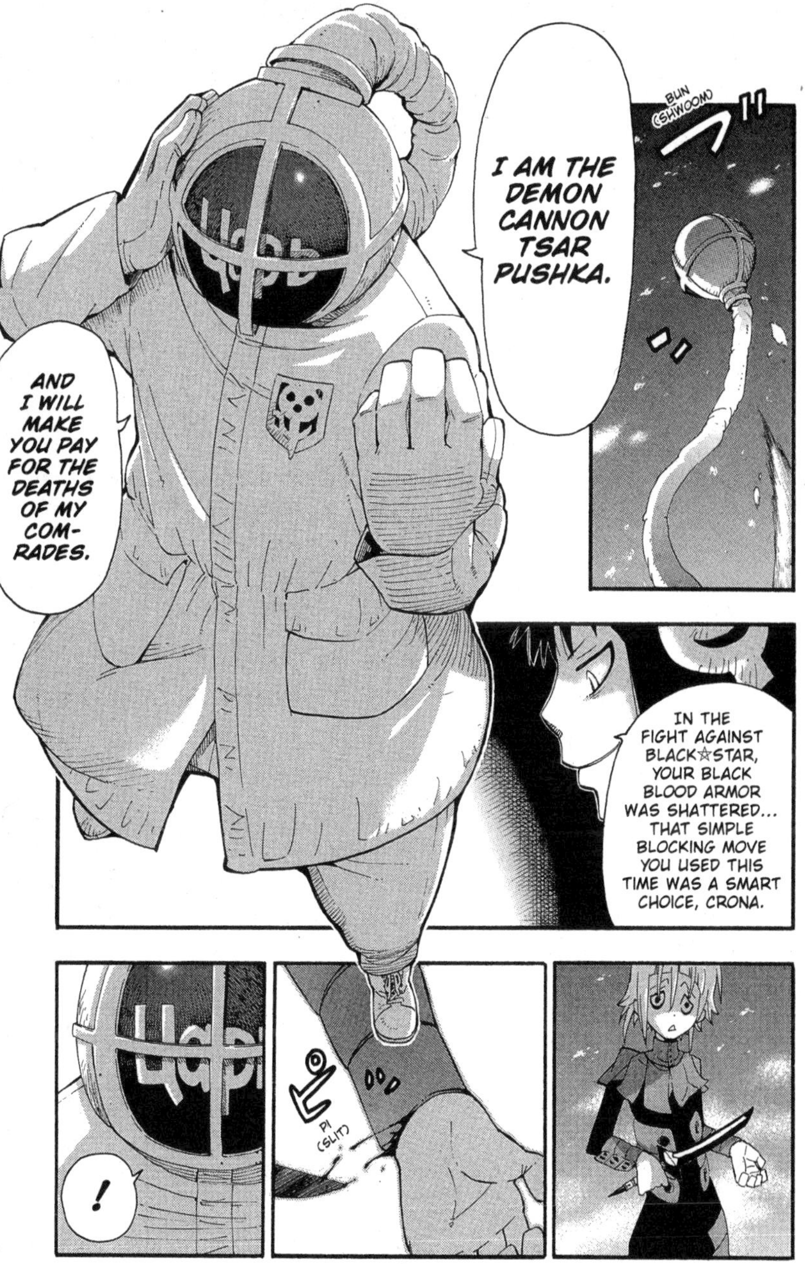

BUN (SHWOOM)
I AM THE DEMON CANNON TSAR PUSHKA.
AND I WILL MAKE YOU PAY FOR THE DEATHS OF MY COM-RADES.
IN THE FIGHT AGAINST BLACK☆STAR, YOUR BLACK BLOOD ARMOR WAS SHATTERED... THAT SIMPLE BLOCKING MOVE YOU USED THIS TIME WAS A SMART CHOICE, CRONA.
PI (SLIT)
!

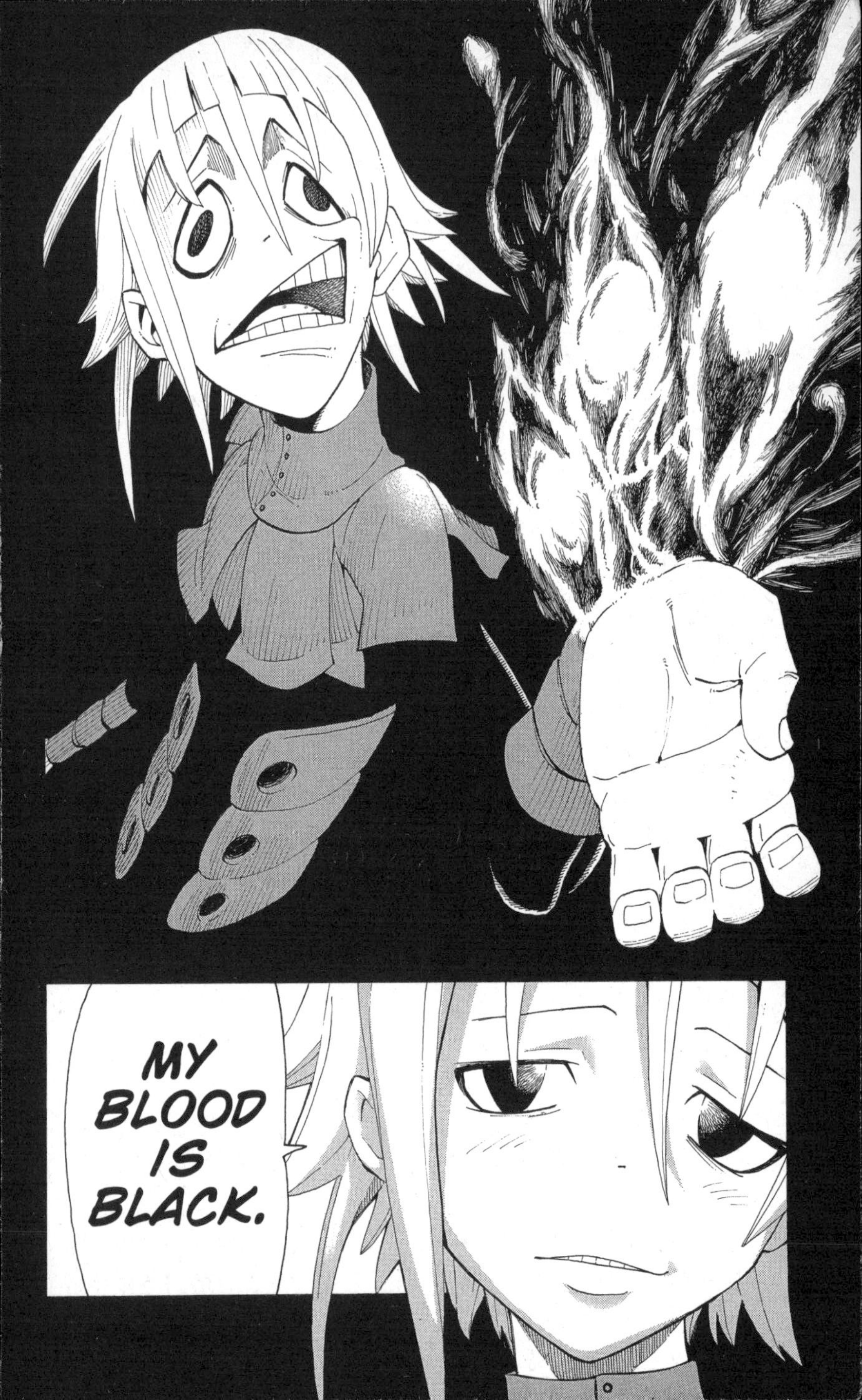
MY BLOOD IS BLACK.

SOUL EATER

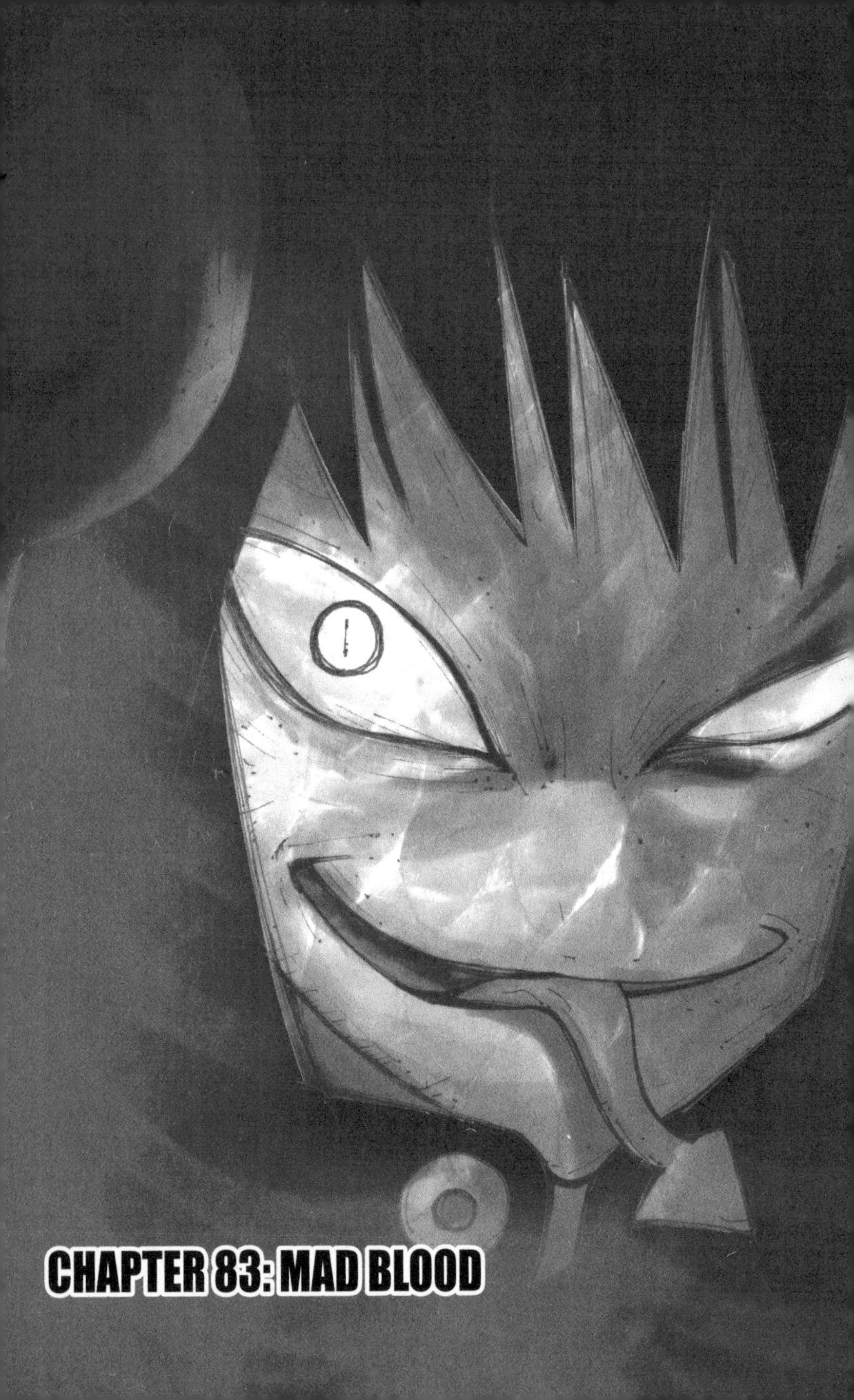
CHAPTER 83: MAD BLOOD

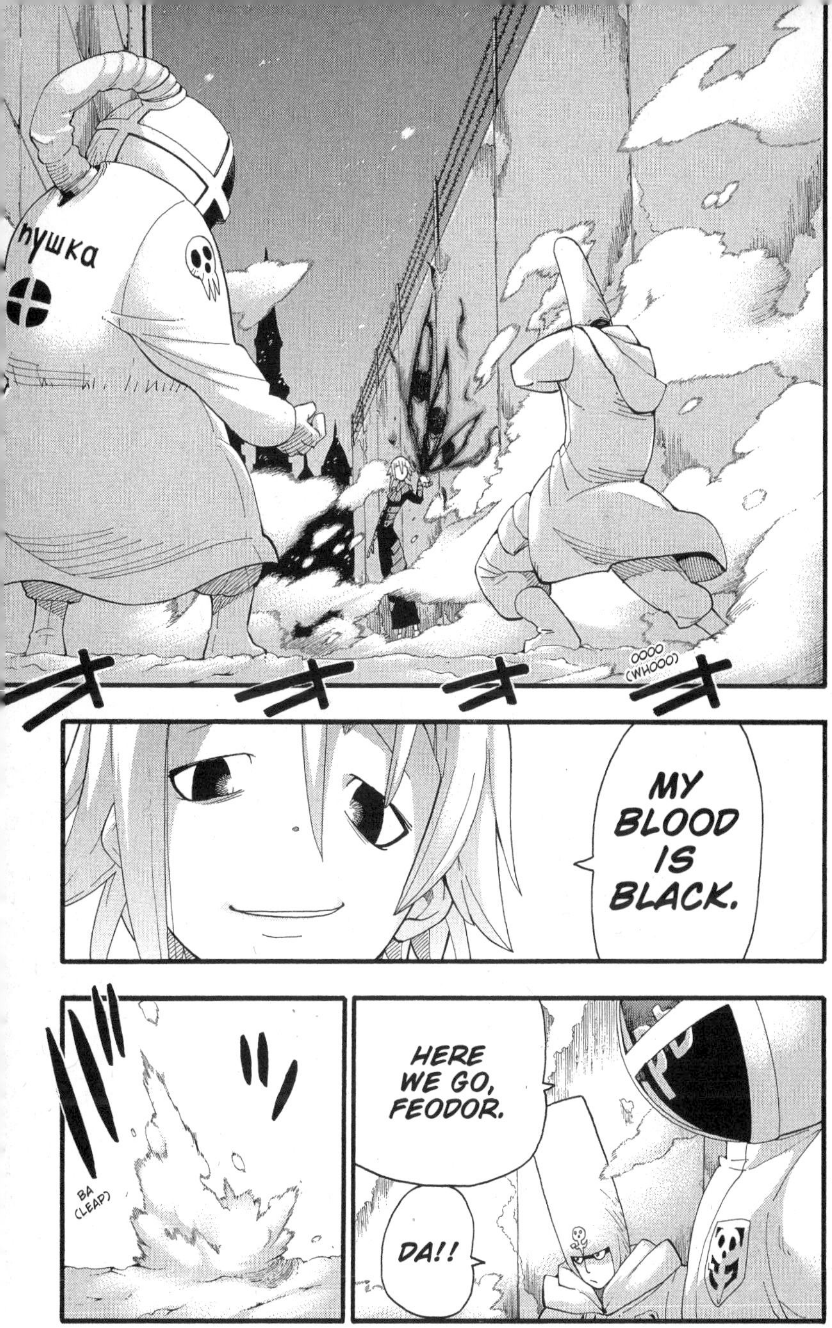
нушка
OOOO
(WHOOO)
オオオオ
MY BLOOD IS BLACK.
HERE WE GO, FEODOR.
DA!!
BA
(LEAP)

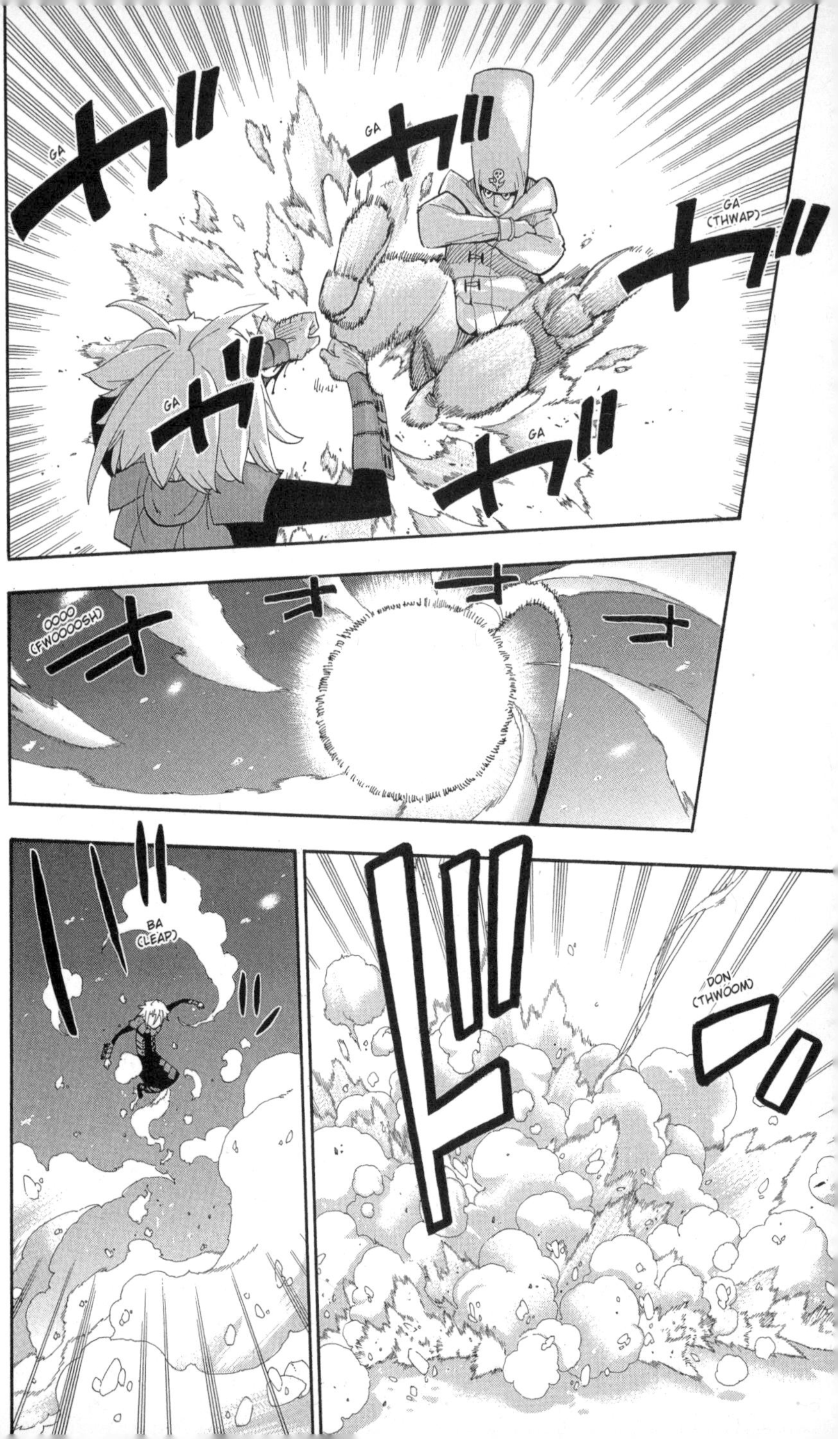
GA (THWAP)
GA
GA
GA
GA
OOOO (FWOOOOSH)
DON (THWOOM)
BA (LEAP)

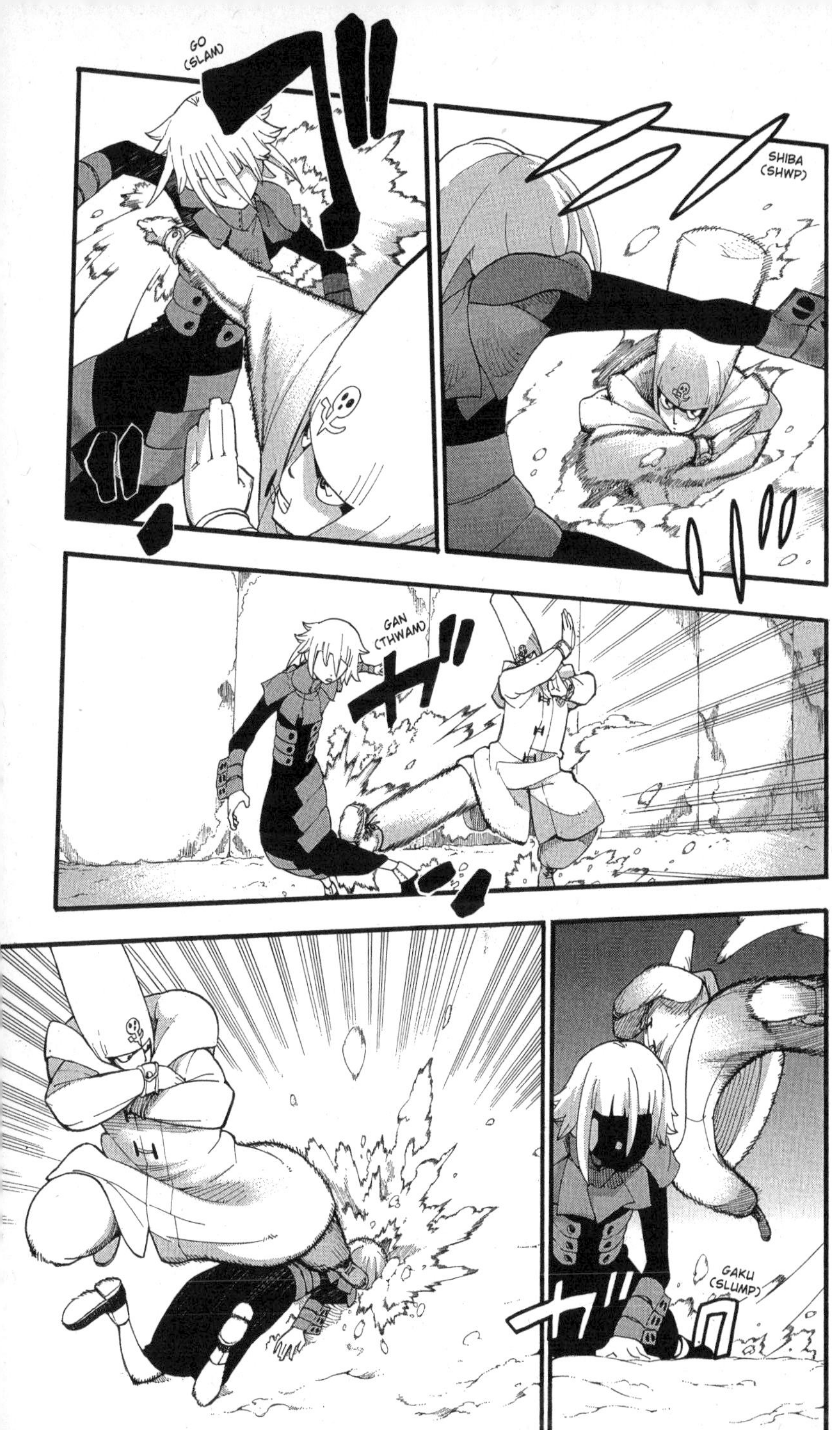
SHIBA
(SHWP)
GO
(SLAM)
GAN
(THWAM)
GAKU
(SLUMP)

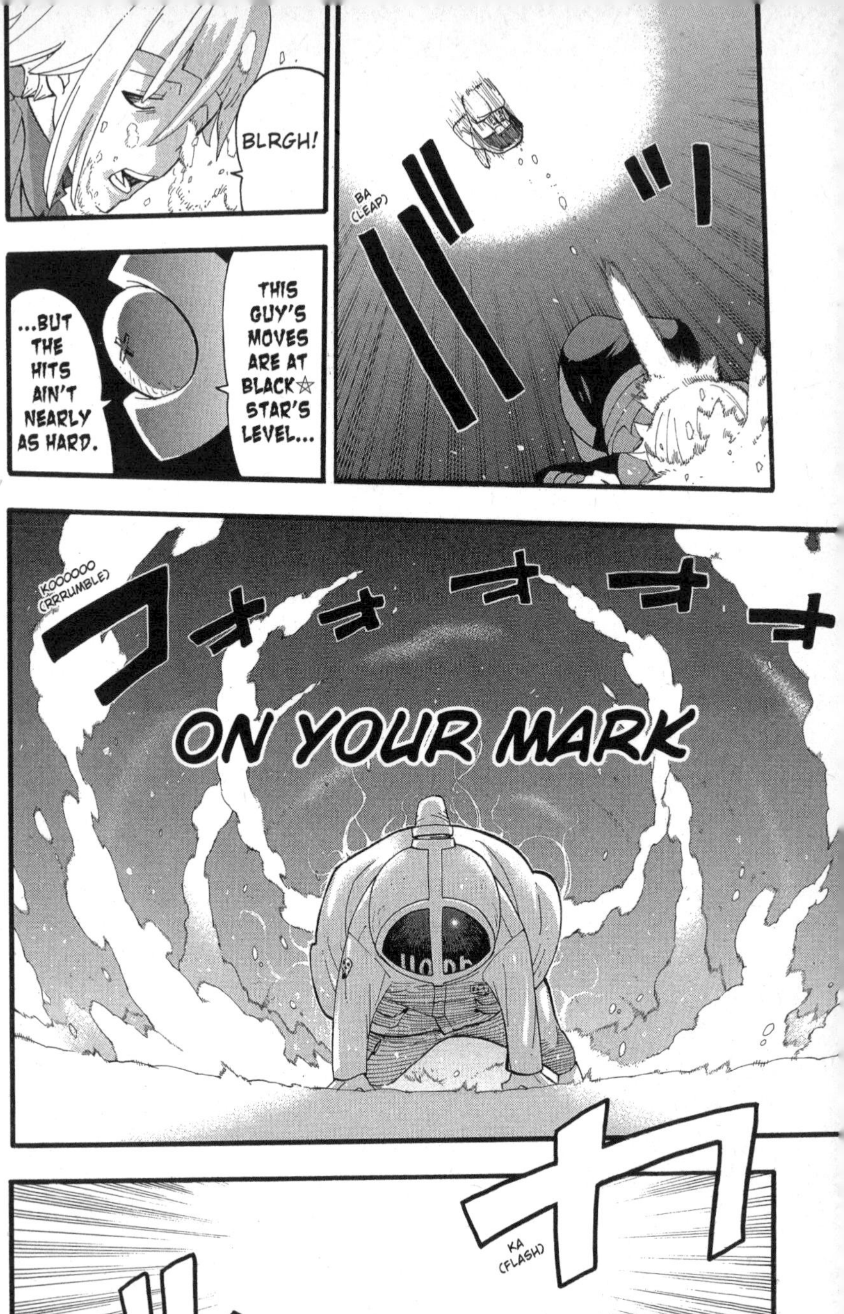
BA
(LEAP)
BLRGH!
THIS GUY'S MOVES ARE AT BLACK☆STAR'S LEVEL...
...BUT THE HITS AIN'T NEARLY AS HARD.
KOOOOOO
(RRRUMBLE)
ON YOUR MARK
KA
(FLASH)

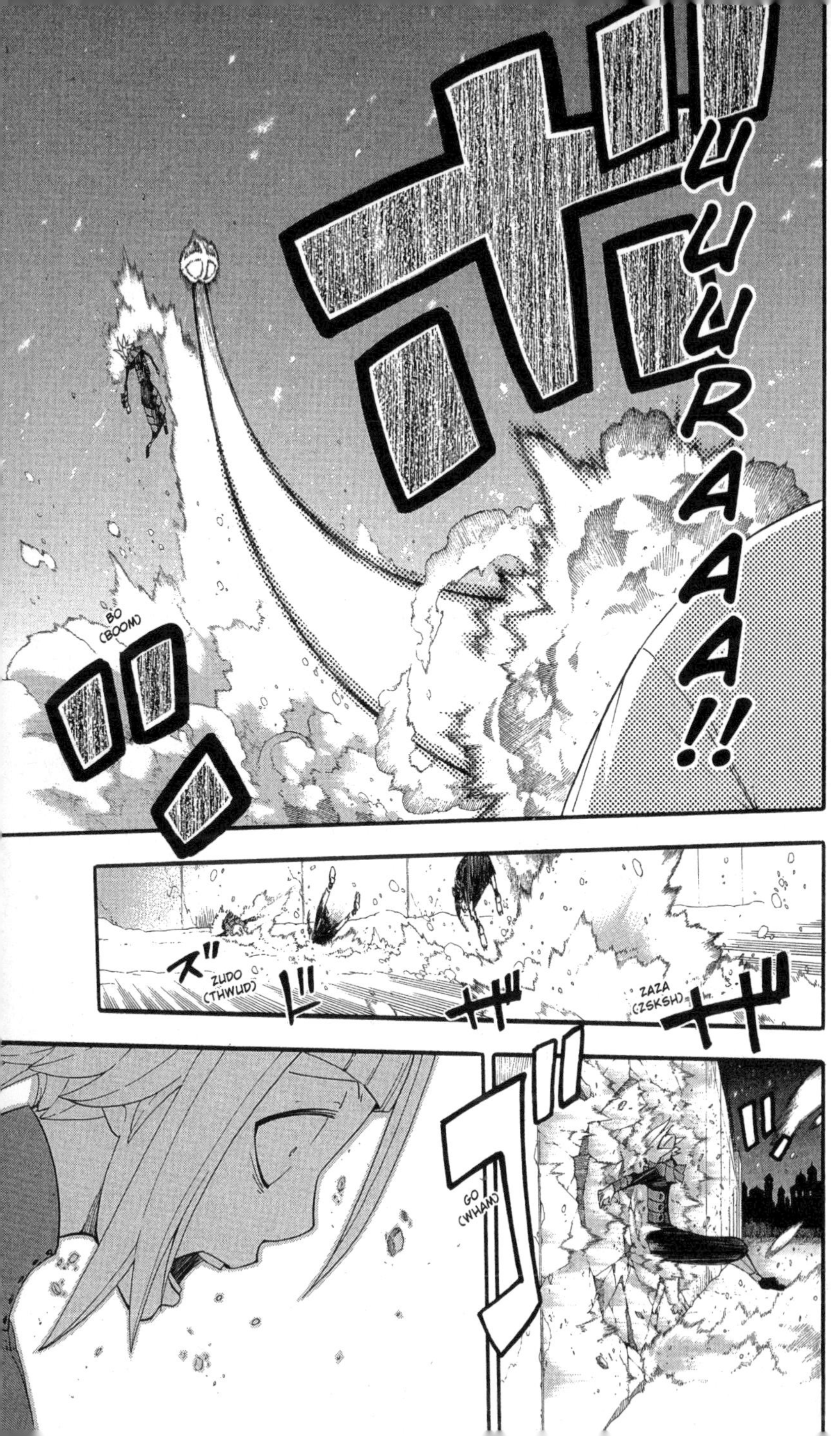
UUURAAAA!!
BO (BOOM)
ZAZA (ZSKSH)
ZUDO (THWUD)
GO (WHAM)

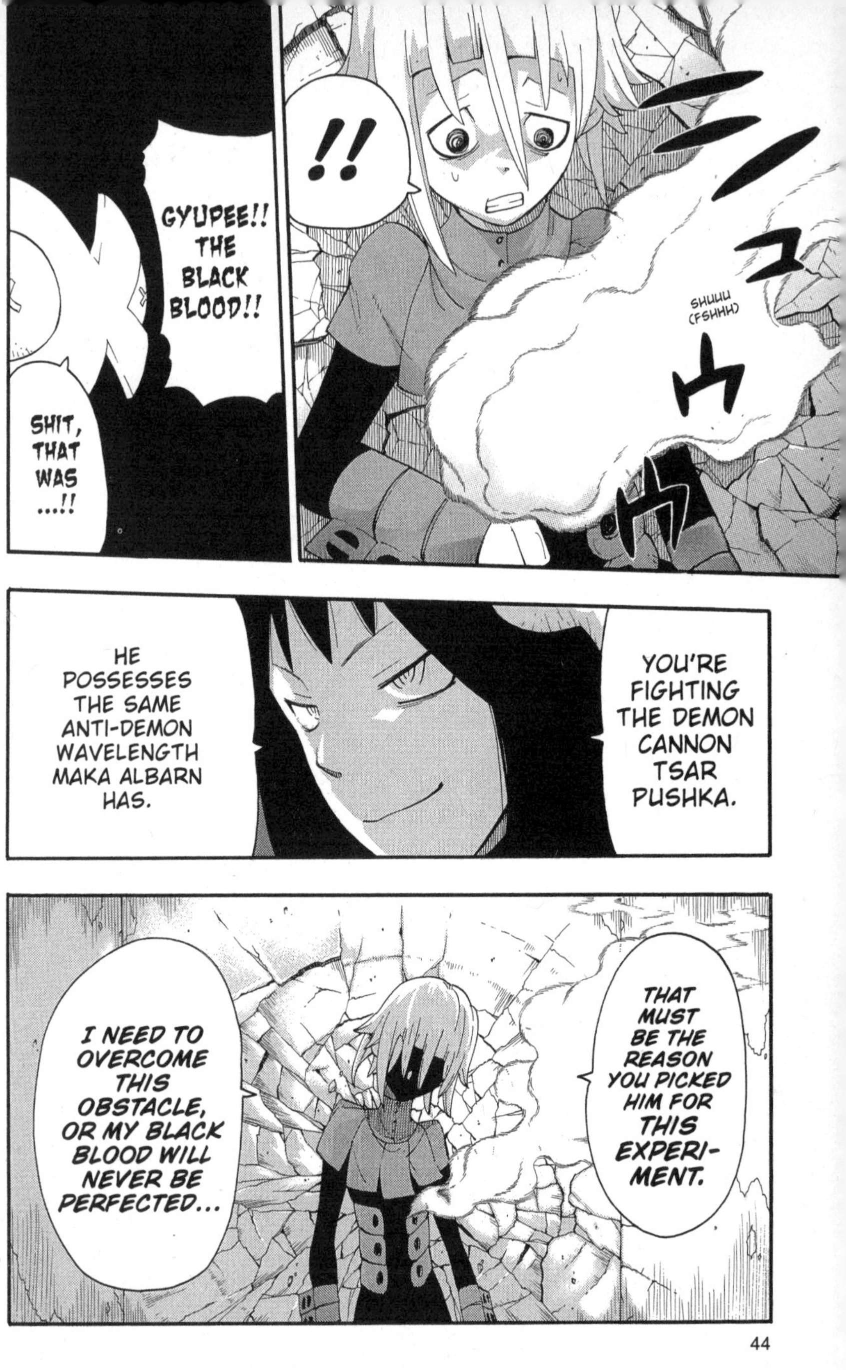
!!
SHUUU (FSHHH)
GYUPEE!! THE BLACK BLOOD!!
SHIT, THAT WAS ...!!
YOU'RE FIGHTING THE DEMON CANNON TSAR PUSHKA.
HE POSSESSES THE SAME ANTI-DEMON WAVELENGTH MAKA ALBARN HAS.
THAT MUST BE THE REASON YOU PICKED HIM FOR THIS EXPERIMENT.
I NEED TO OVERCOME THIS OBSTACLE, OR MY BLACK BLOOD WILL NEVER BE PERFECTED...

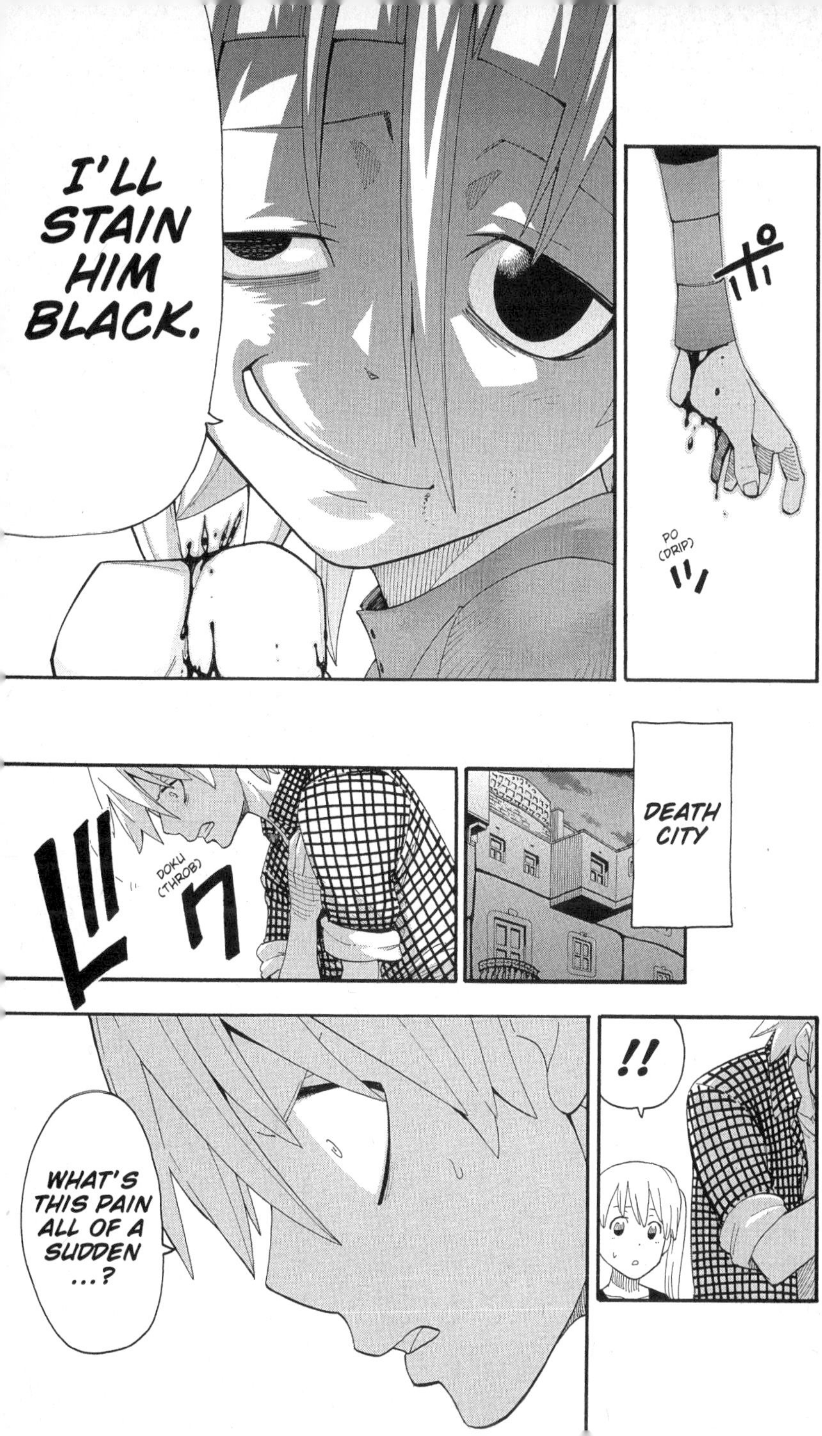
PO (DRIP)
I'LL STAIN HIM BLACK.
DEATH CITY
DOKU (THROB)
!!
WHAT'S THIS PAIN ALL OF A SUDDEN ...?

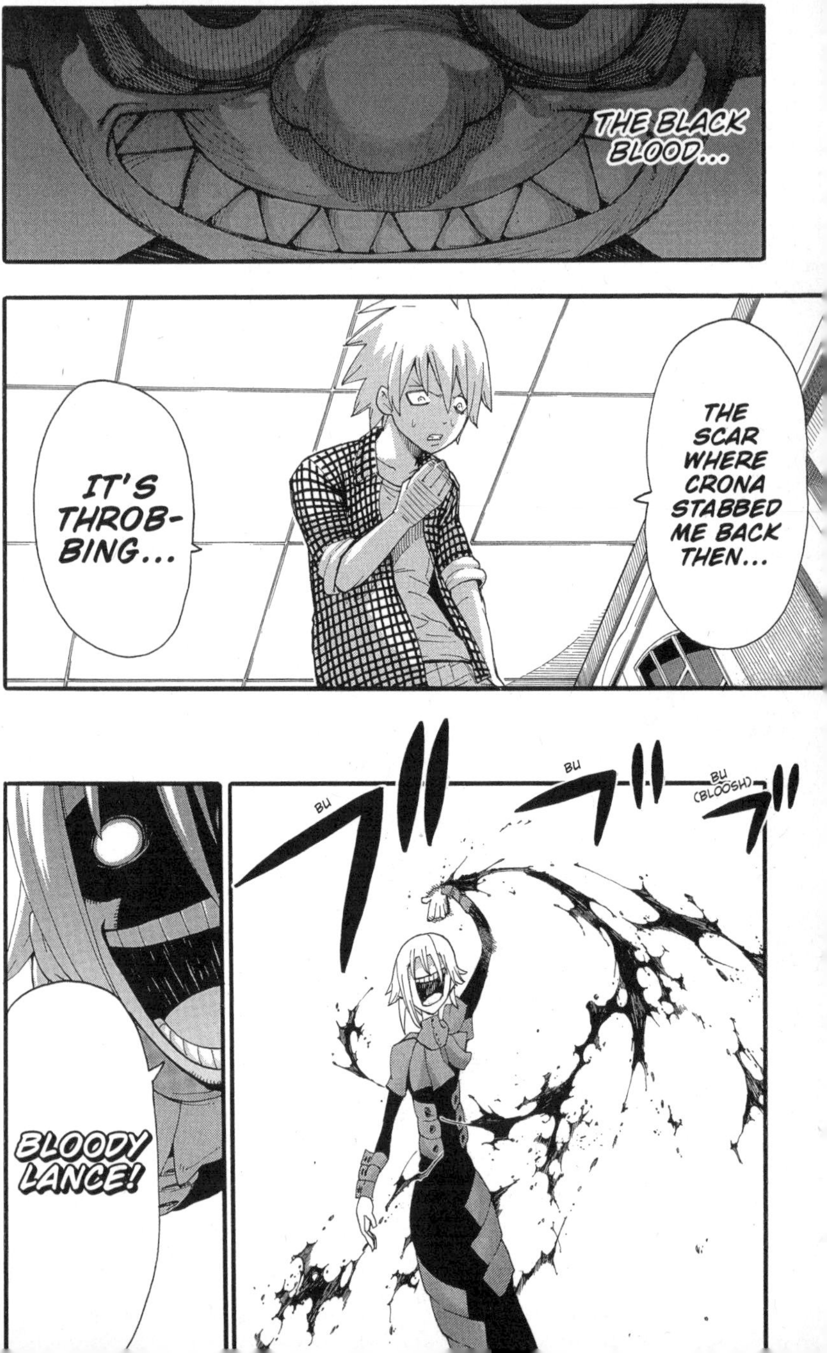
THE BLACK BLOOD...
THE SCAR WHERE CRONA STABBED ME BACK THEN...
IT'S THROB-BING...
BU (BLOOSH)
BU
BU
BLOODY LANCE!

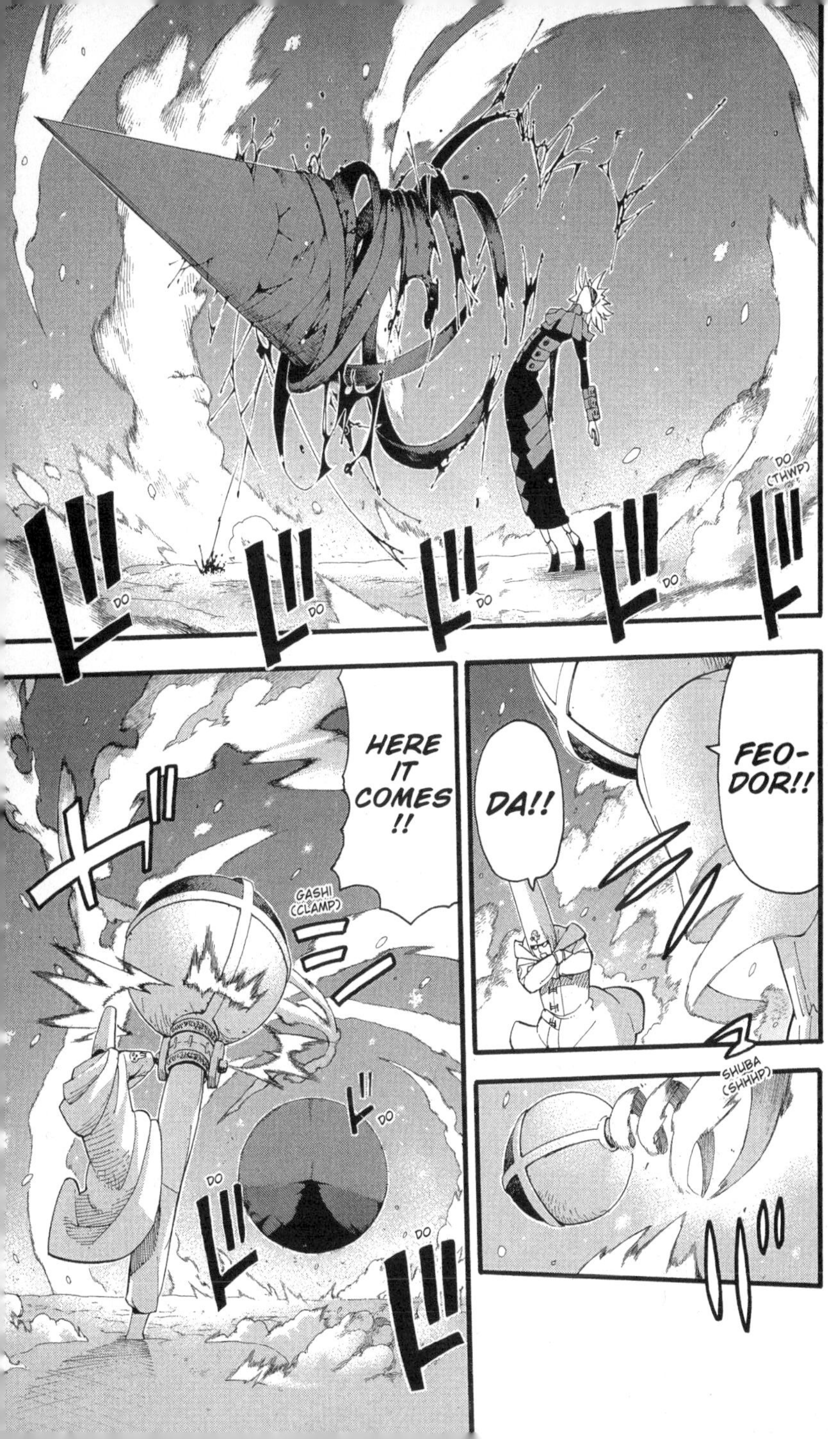
DO (THWP)
DO
DO
DO
DO
FEO-DOR!!
DA!!
SHUBA (SHHHP)
HERE IT COMES!!
GASHI (CLAMP)
DO
DO
DO

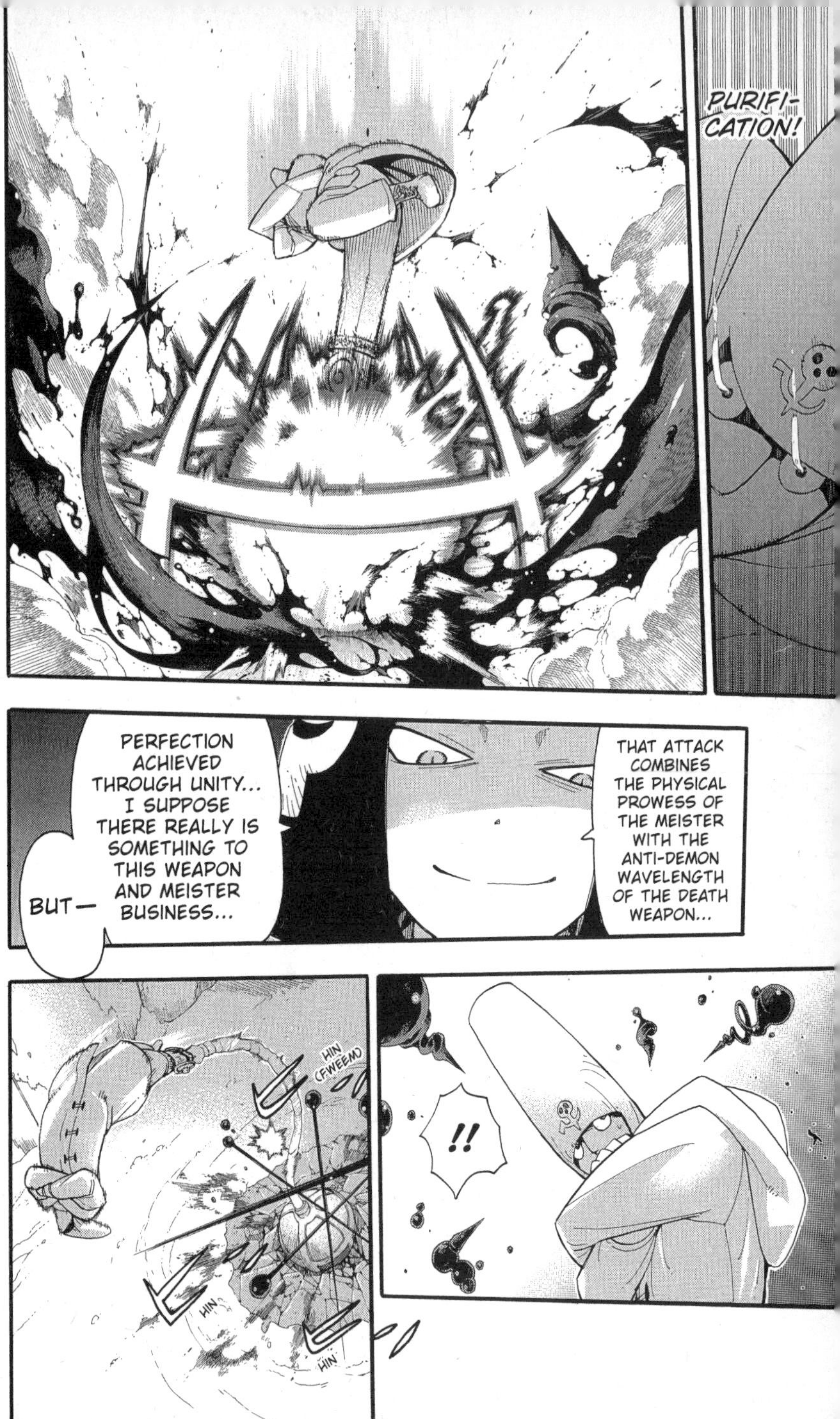
PURIFI-
CATION!
THAT ATTACK COMBINES THE PHYSICAL PROWESS OF THE MEISTER WITH THE ANTI-DEMON WAVELENGTH OF THE DEATH WEAPON...
PERFECTION ACHIEVED THROUGH UNITY... I SUPPOSE THERE REALLY IS SOMETHING TO THIS WEAPON AND MEISTER BUSINESS...
BUT—
!!
HIN (FWEEM)
HIN
HIN

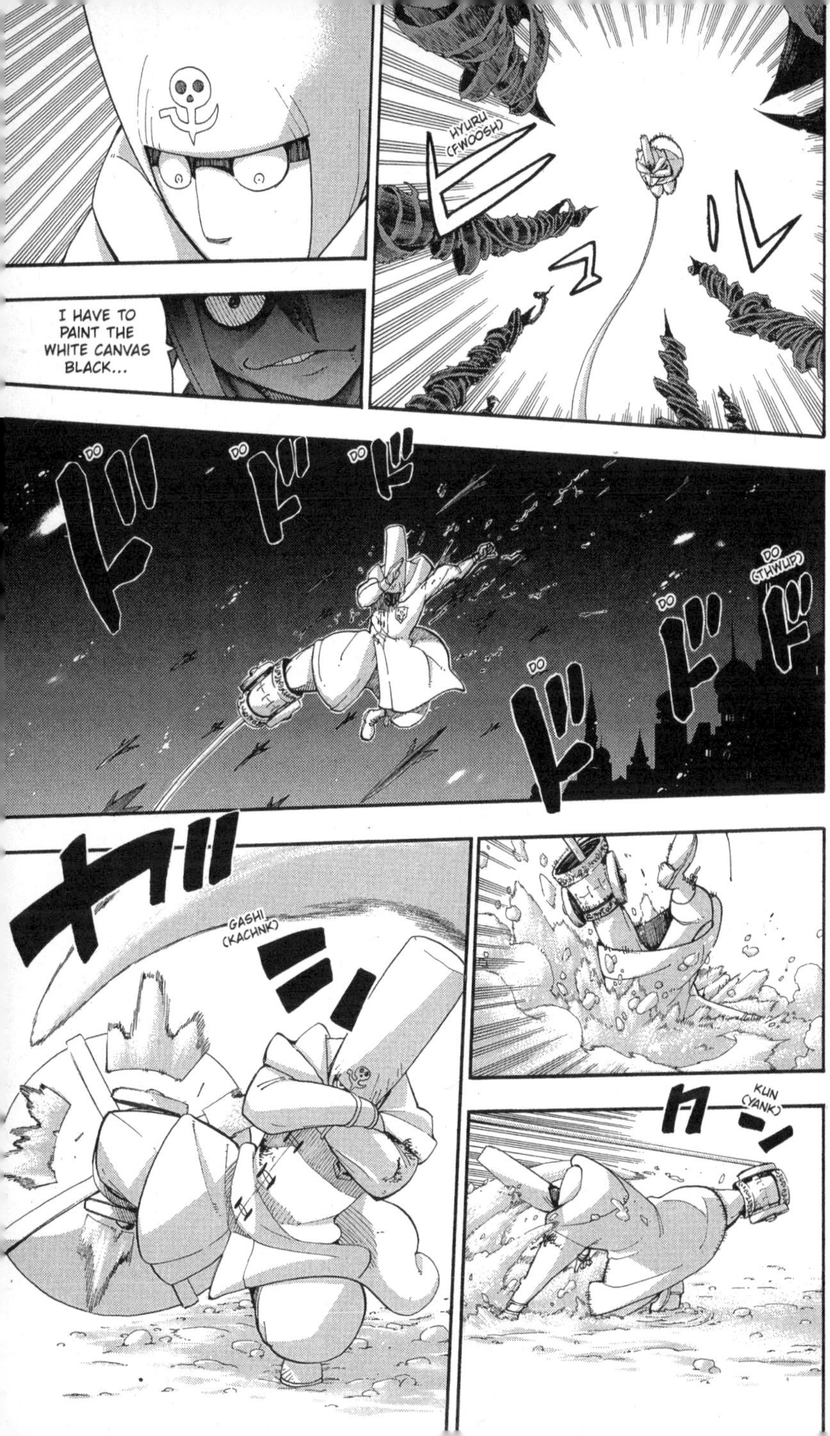

HYURU (FWOOSH)
I HAVE TO PAINT THE WHITE CANVAS BLACK...
DO (THWUP)
DO
DO
DO
DO
DO
KUN (YANK)
GASHI (KACHNK)

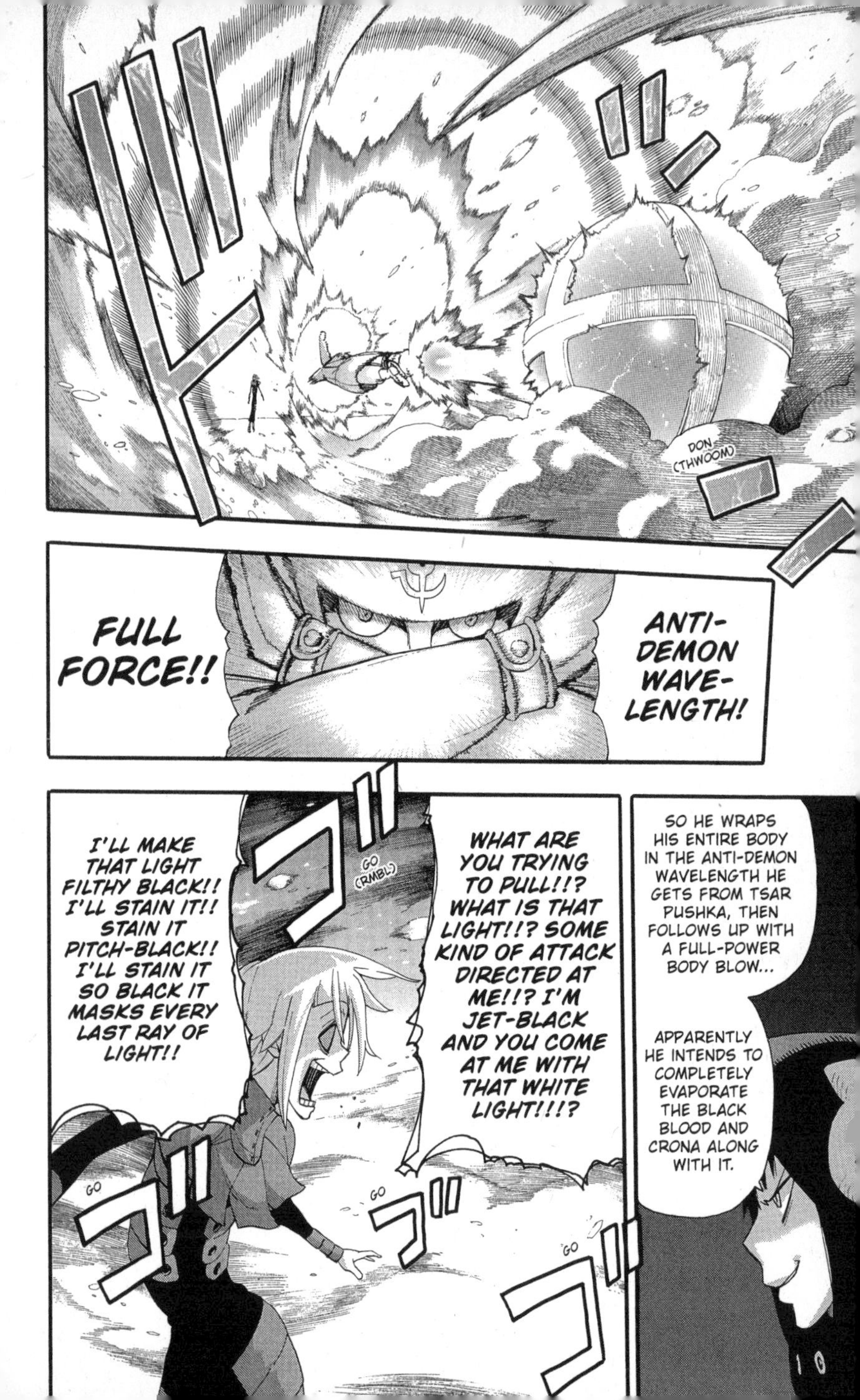
DON (THWOOM)
ANTI-DEMON WAVELENGTH!
FULL FORCE!!
SO HE WRAPS HIS ENTIRE BODY IN THE ANTI-DEMON WAVELENGTH HE GETS FROM TSAR PUSHKA, THEN FOLLOWS UP WITH A FULL-POWER BODY BLOW...
APPARENTLY HE INTENDS TO COMPLETELY EVAPORATE THE BLACK BLOOD AND CRONA ALONG WITH IT.
GO (RMBL)
WHAT ARE YOU TRYING TO PULL!!? WHAT IS THAT LIGHT!!? SOME KIND OF ATTACK DIRECTED AT ME!!? I'M JET-BLACK AND YOU COME AT ME WITH THAT WHITE LIGHT!!!?
I'LL MAKE THAT LIGHT FILTHY BLACK!! I'LL STAIN IT!! STAIN IT PITCH-BLACK!! I'LL STAIN IT SO BLACK IT MASKS EVERY LAST RAY OF LIGHT!!
GO
GO
GO

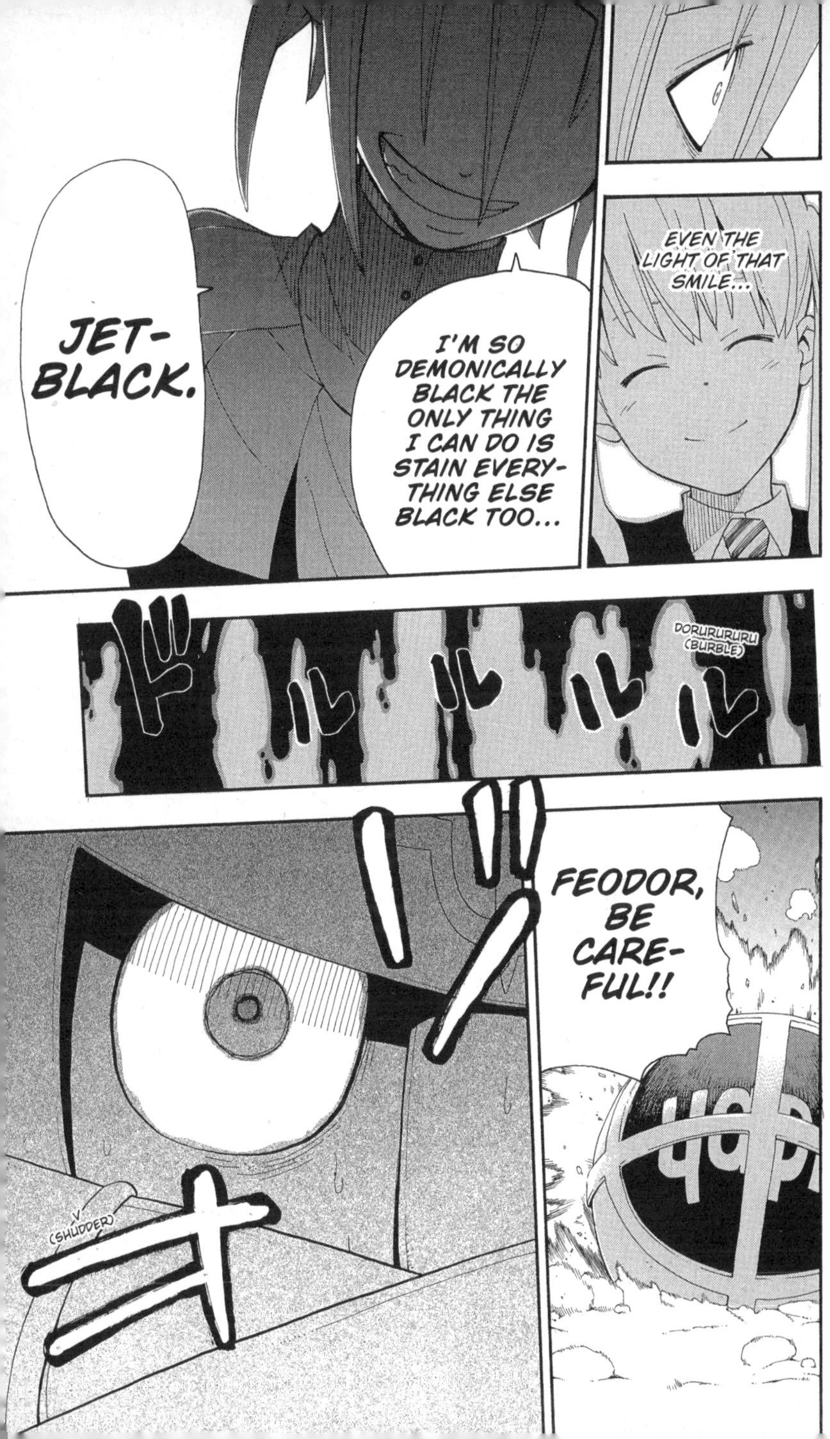
EVEN THE LIGHT OF THAT SMILE...
I'M SO DEMONICALLY BLACK THE ONLY THING I CAN DO IS STAIN EVERY-THING ELSE BLACK TOO...
JET-BLACK.
DORURURURU (BURBLE)
FEODOR, BE CARE-FUL!!
(SHUDDER)

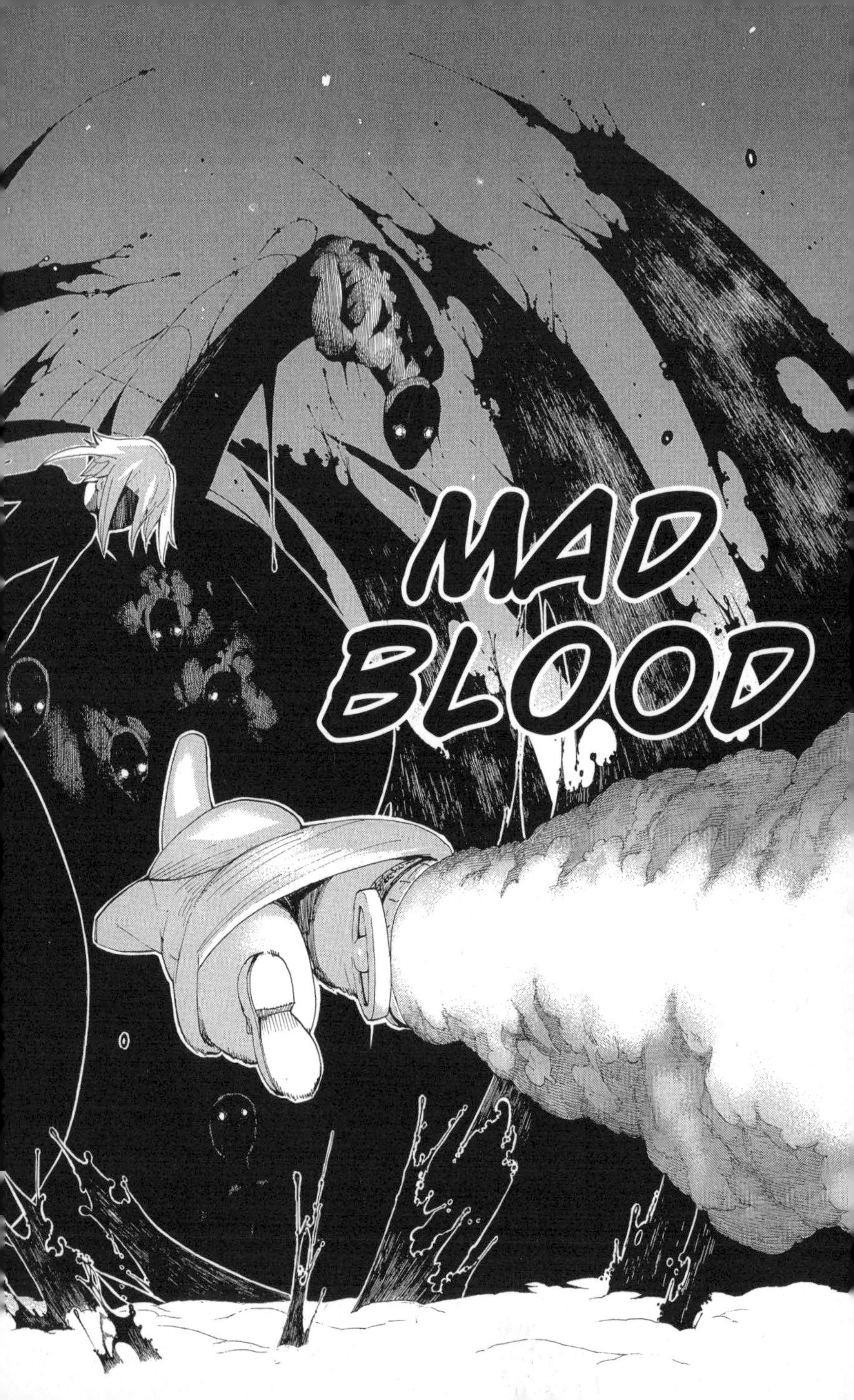
MAD
BLOOD

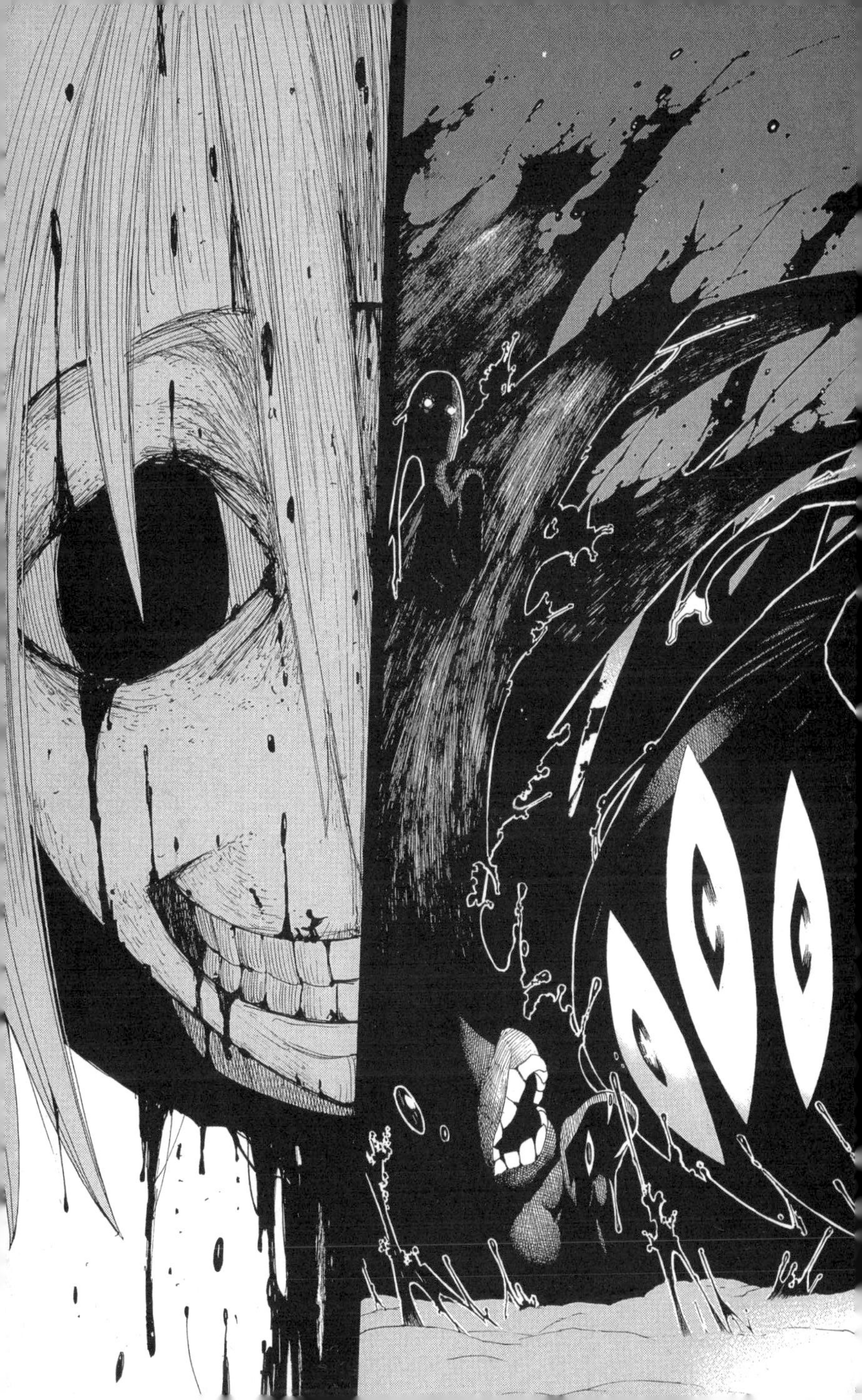

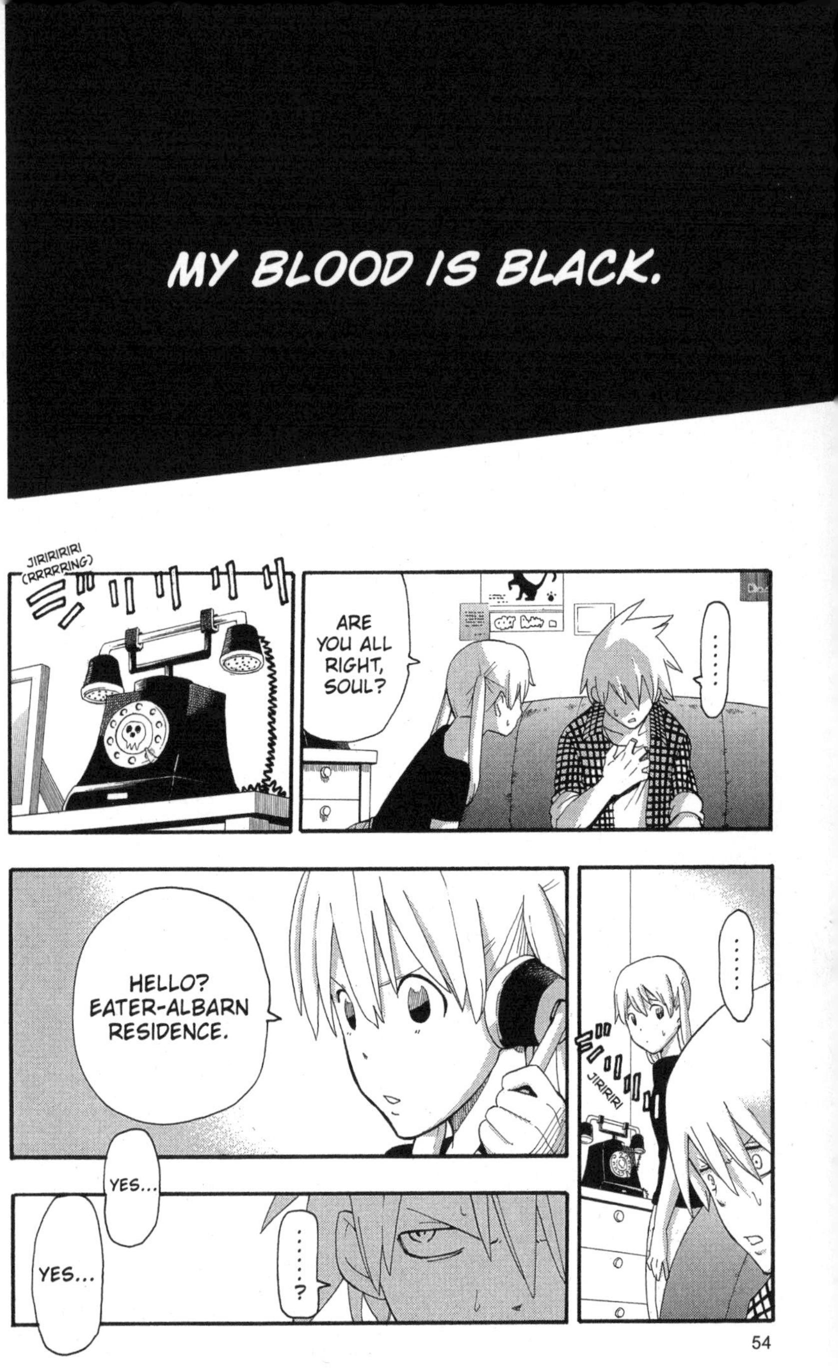
MY BLOOD IS BLACK.
......
ARE YOU ALL RIGHT, SOUL?
JIRIRIRIRI (RRRRRING)
......
JIRIRIRI
HELLO? EATER-ALBARN RESIDENCE.
YES...
......?
YES...

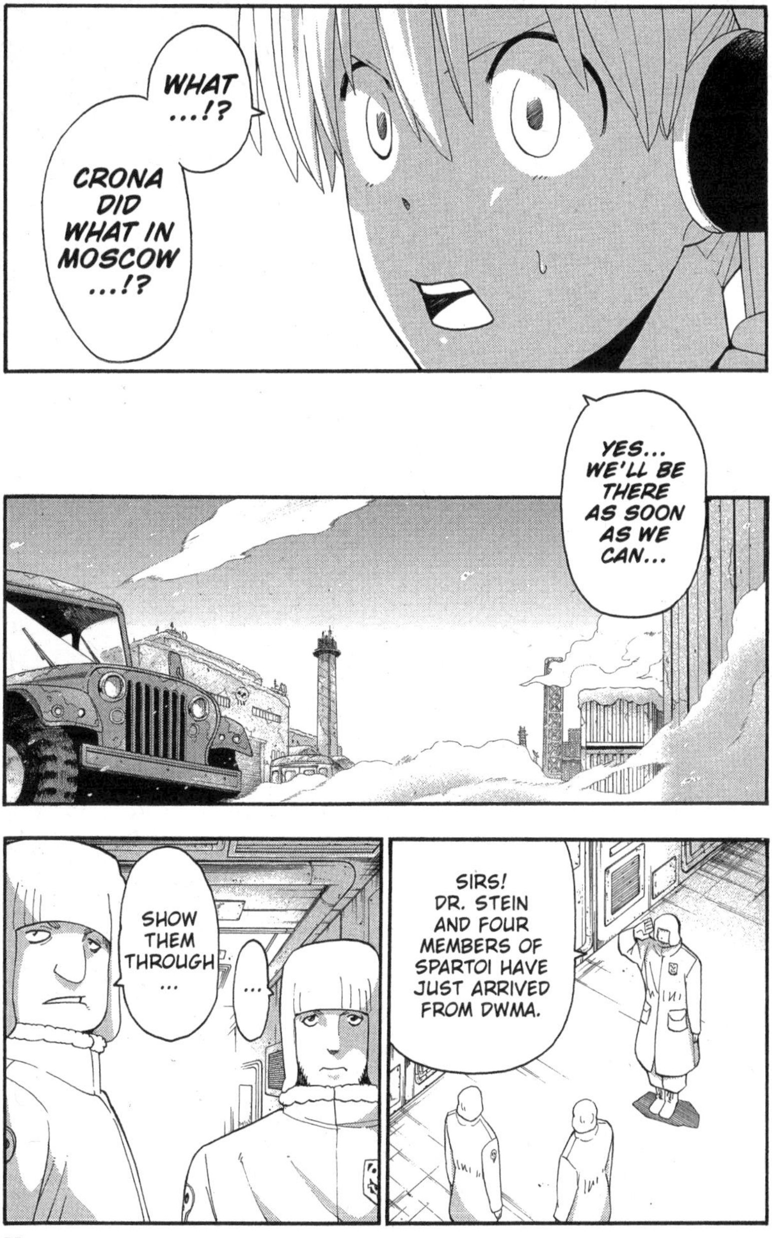
WHAT ...!?
CRONA DID WHAT IN MOSCOW ...!?
YES... WE'LL BE THERE AS SOON AS WE CAN...
SIRS! DR. STEIN AND FOUR MEMBERS OF SPARTOI HAVE JUST ARRIVED FROM DWMA.
SHOW THEM THROUGH ...
...

THESE KIDS ARE DWMA'S SO-CALLED "ELITE UNIT" ...?

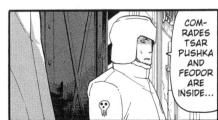

COMRADES TSAR PUSHKA AND FEODOR ARE INSIDE...

IN HERE?

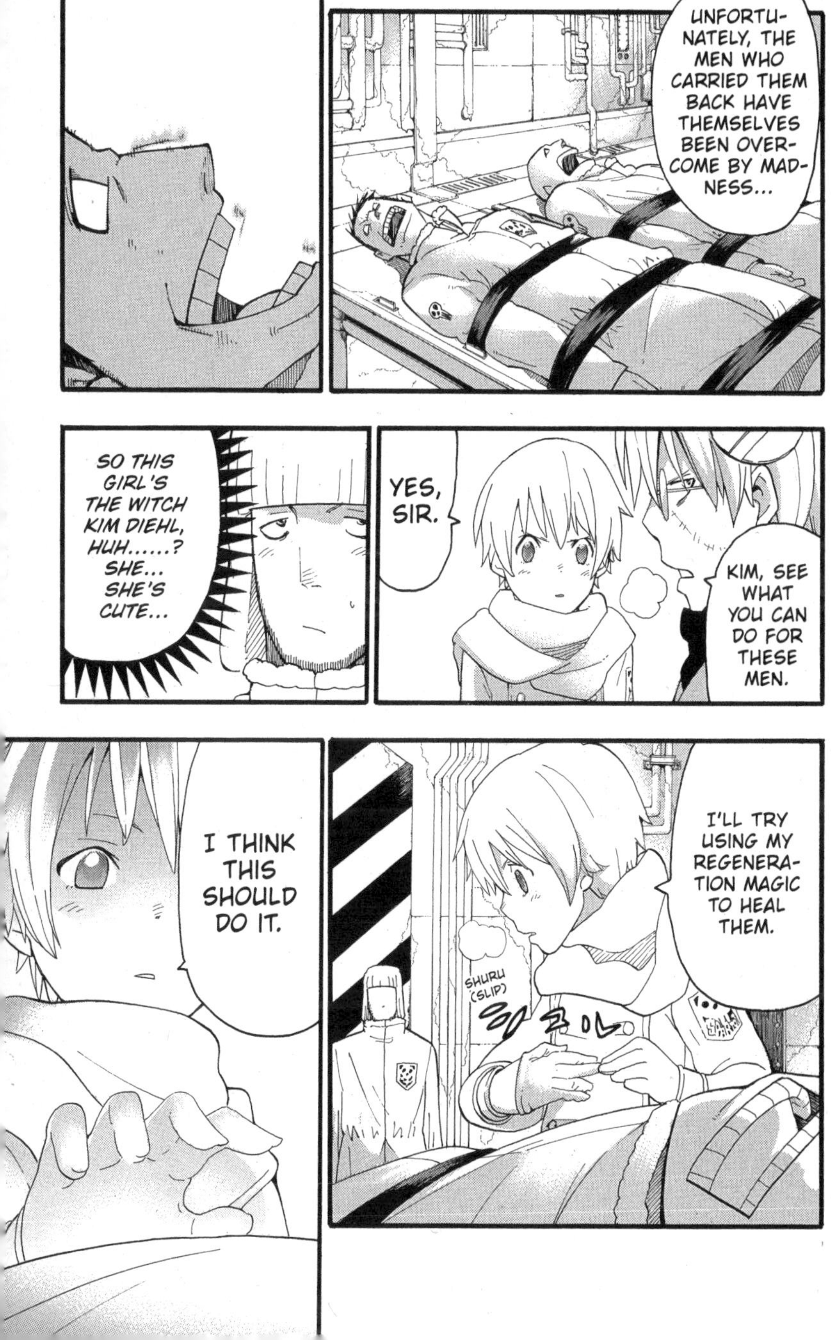
UNFORTUNATELY, THE MEN WHO CARRIED THEM BACK HAVE THEMSELVES BEEN OVERCOME BY MADNESS...
KIM, SEE WHAT YOU CAN DO FOR THESE MEN.
YES, SIR.
SO THIS GIRL'S THE WITCH KIM DIEHL, HUH......? SHE... SHE'S CUTE...
I'LL TRY USING MY REGENERATION MAGIC TO HEAL THEM.
SHURU (SLIP)
I THINK THIS SHOULD DO IT.

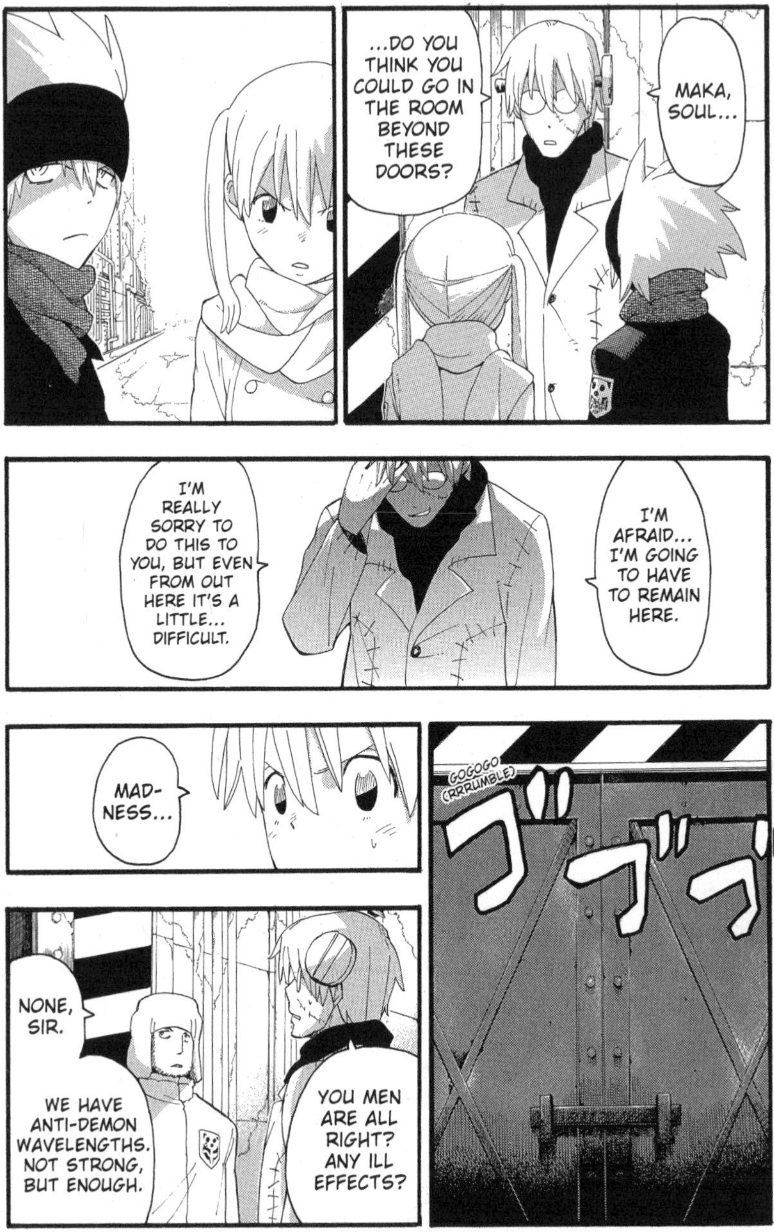
MAKA, SOUL...
...DO YOU THINK YOU COULD GO IN THE ROOM BEYOND THESE DOORS?
I'M AFRAID... I'M GOING TO HAVE TO REMAIN HERE.
I'M REALLY SORRY TO DO THIS TO YOU, BUT EVEN FROM OUT HERE IT'S A LITTLE... DIFFICULT.
ゴゴゴ
GOGOGO (RRRUMBLE)
MAD-NESS...
YOU MEN ARE ALL RIGHT? ANY ILL EFFECTS?
NONE, SIR.
WE HAVE ANTI-DEMON WAVELENGTHS. NOT STRONG, BUT ENOUGH.

SOUL... LET'S RESO-NATE.

WE'RE OPEN-ING THE DOORS...

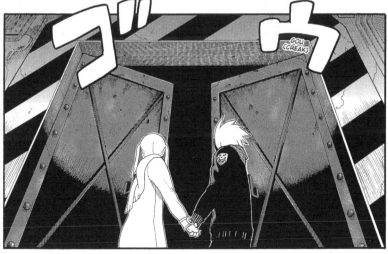

グ" ガ

GON (CREAK)

59

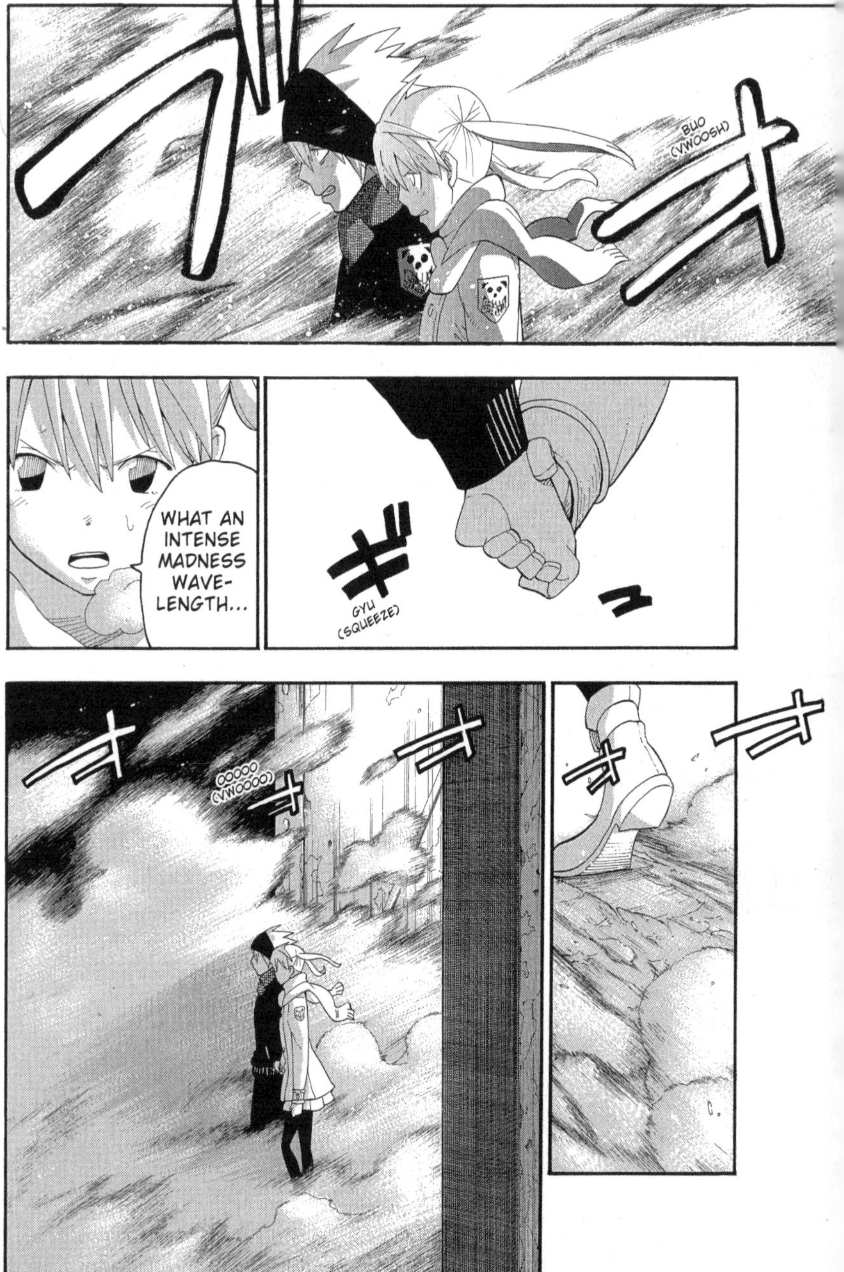
BUO (VWOOSH)
GYU (SQUEEZE)
WHAT AN INTENSE MADNESS WAVE-LENGTH...
OOOOO (VWOOOO)

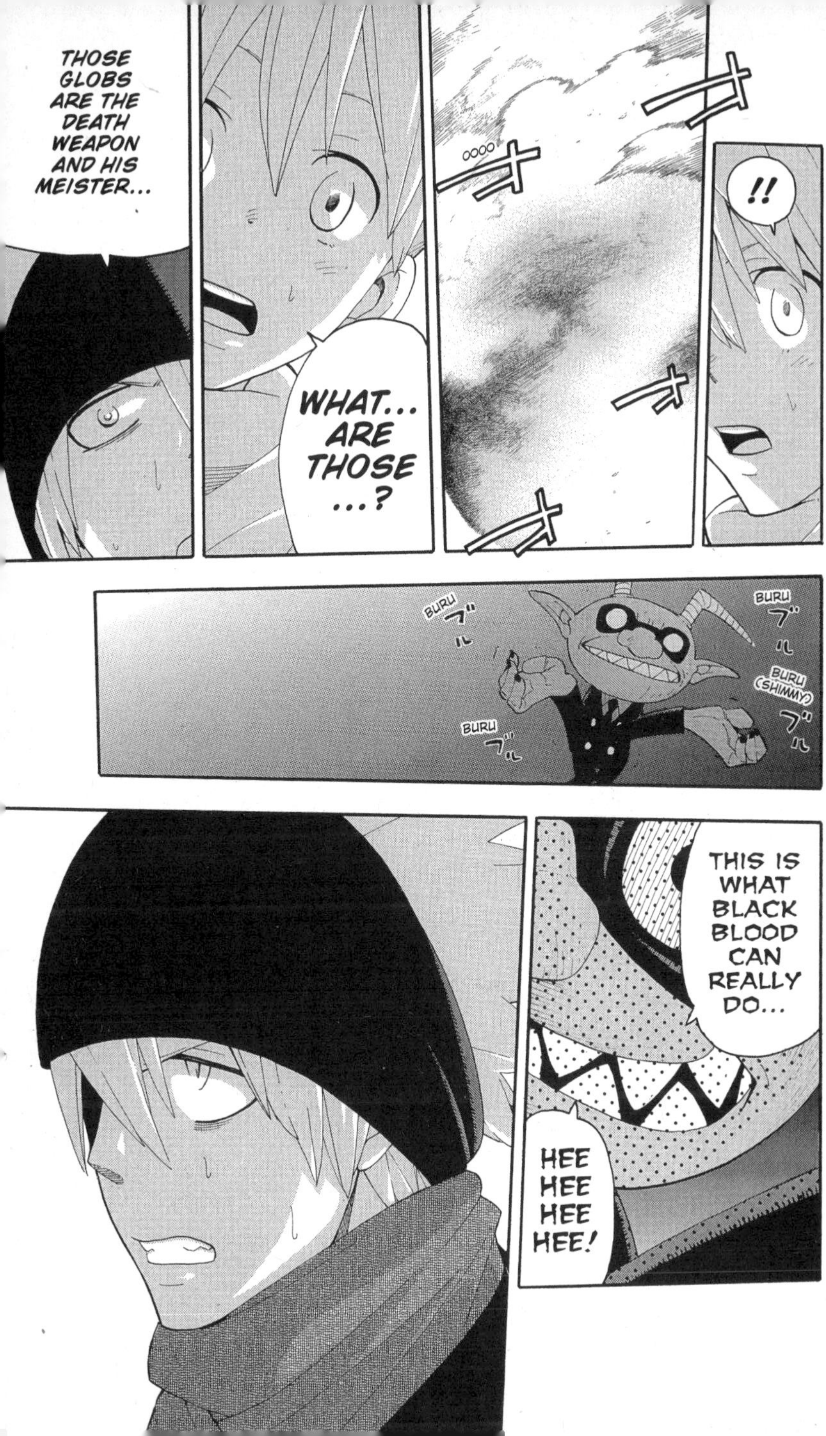
!!
OOOO
WHAT... ARE THOSE...?
THOSE GLOBS ARE THE DEATH WEAPON AND HIS MEISTER...
BURU
BURU (SHIMMY)
BURU
BURU
THIS IS WHAT BLACK BLOOD CAN REALLY DO...
HEE HEE HEE HEE!

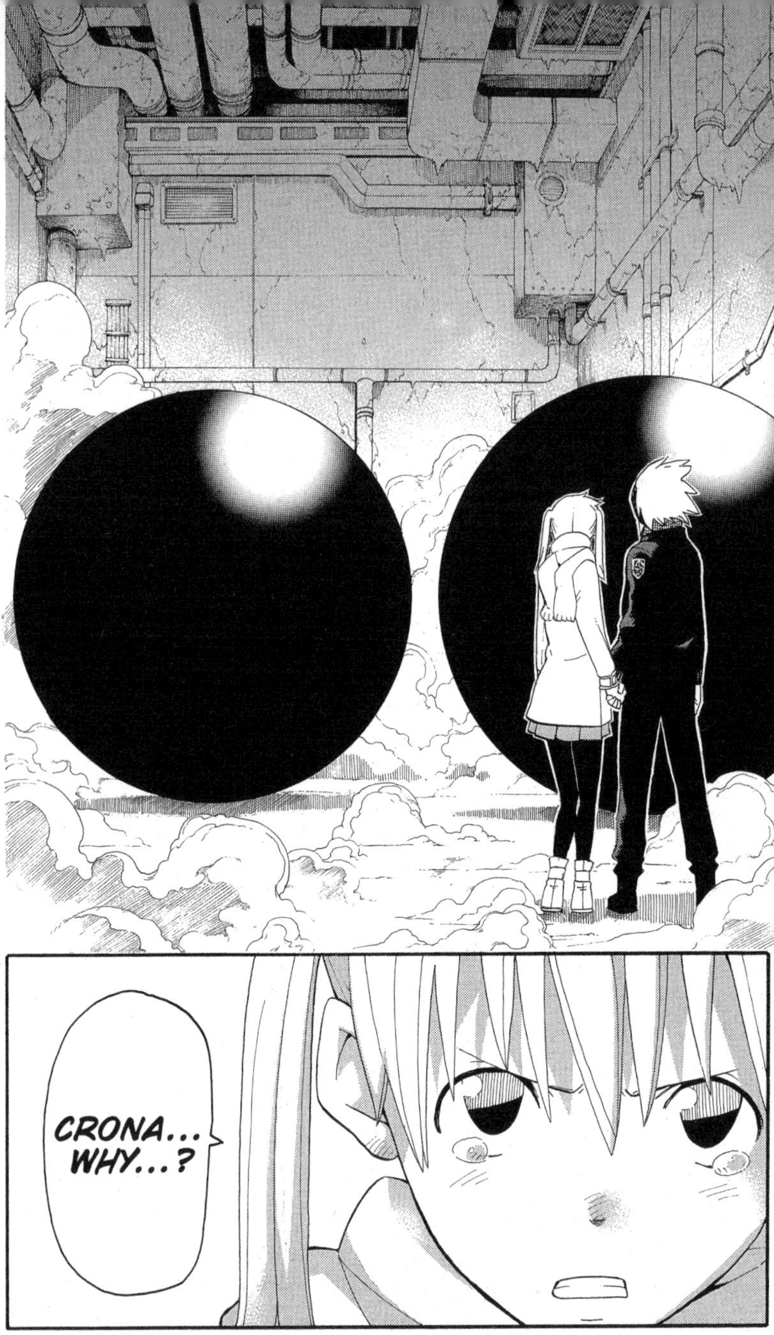
CRONA... WHY...?

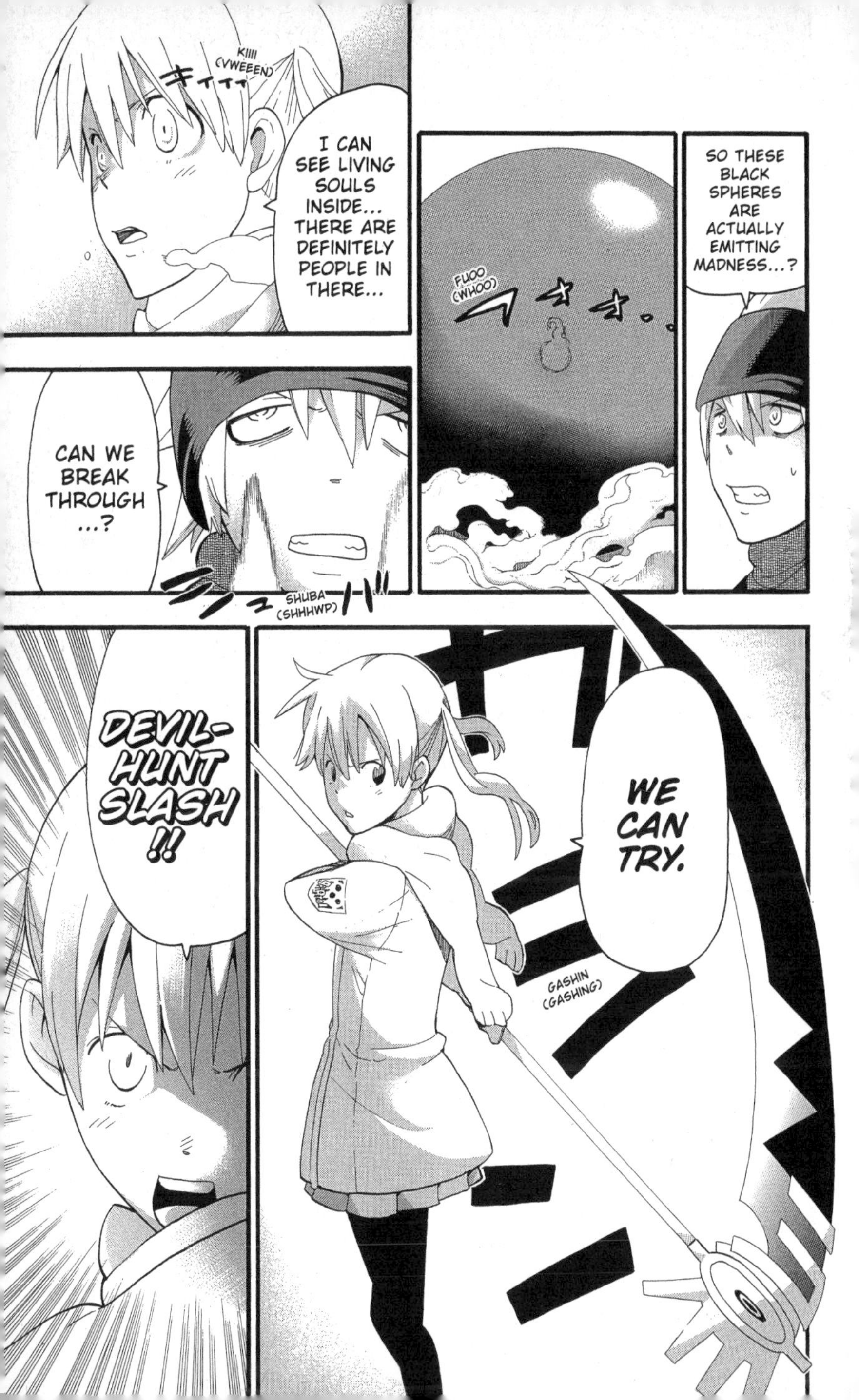
KIIII (VWEEEN)
I CAN SEE LIVING SOULS INSIDE... THERE ARE DEFINITELY PEOPLE IN THERE...
FUOO (WHOO)
SO THESE BLACK SPHERES ARE ACTUALLY EMITTING MADNESS...?
CAN WE BREAK THROUGH ...?
SHUBA (SHHHWP)
WE CAN TRY.
GASHIN (GASHING)
DEVIL-HUNT SLASH!!

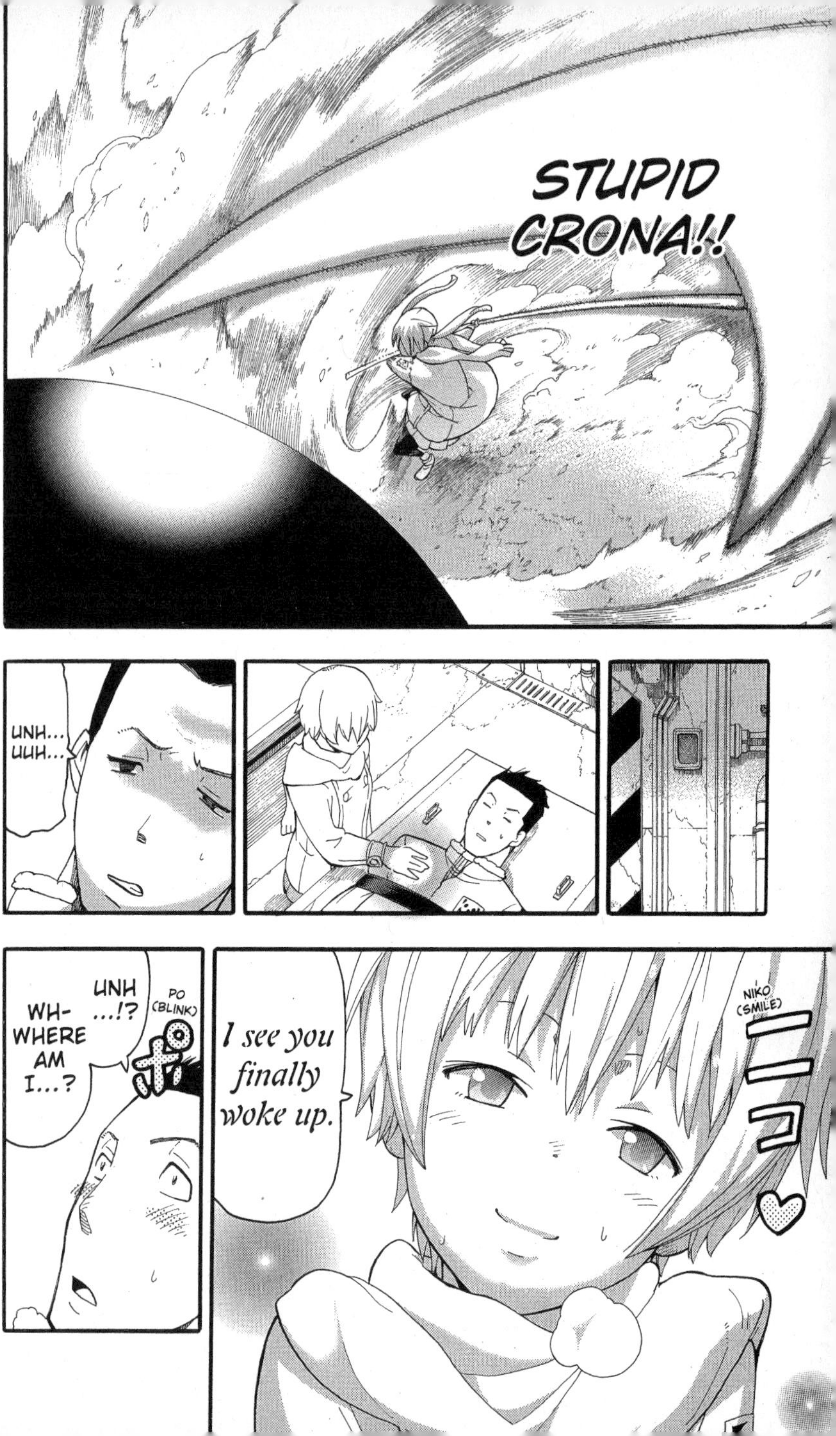
STUPID CRONA!!
UNH... UUH...
I see you finally woke up.
NIKO (SMILE)
PO (BLINK)
UNH ...!?
WH-WHERE AM I...?

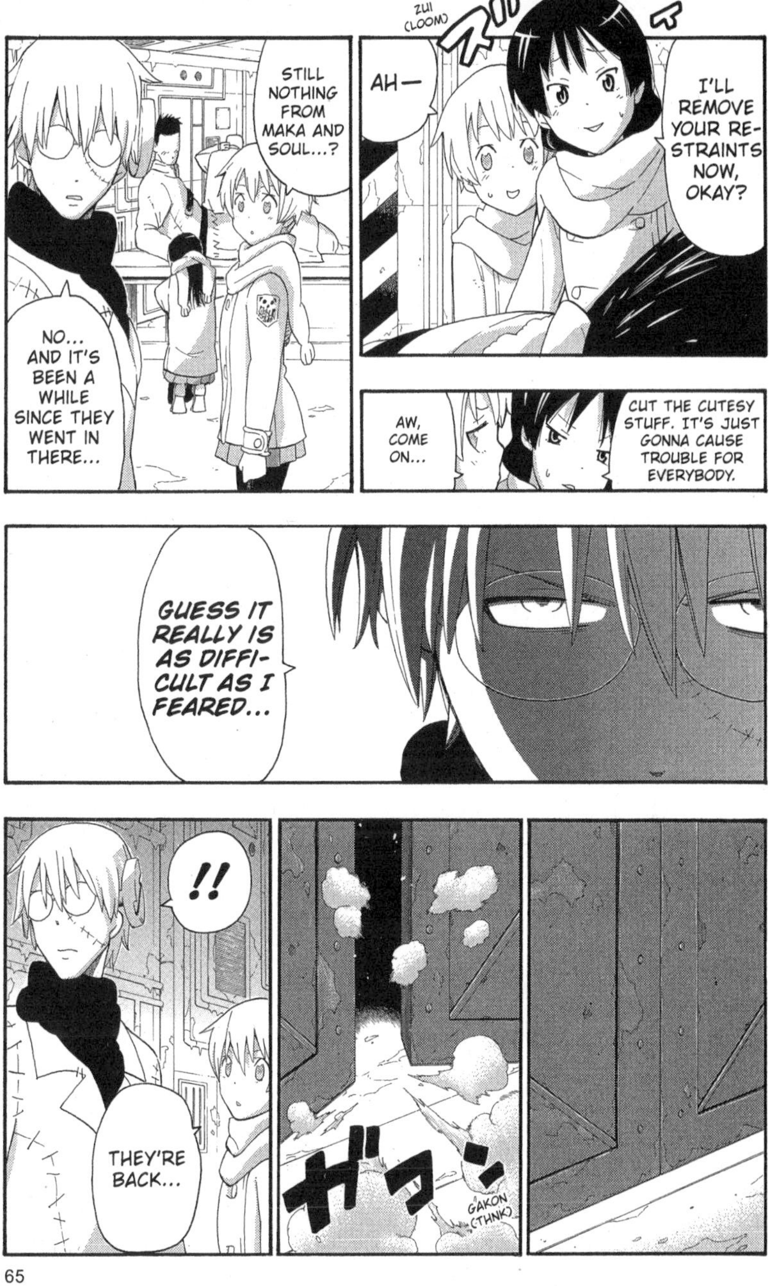

ZUI (LOOM)
I'LL REMOVE YOUR RE-STRAINTS NOW, OKAY?
AH—
CUT THE CUTESY STUFF. IT'S JUST GONNA CAUSE TROUBLE FOR EVERYBODY.
AW, COME ON...
STILL NOTHING FROM MAKA AND SOUL...?
NO... AND IT'S BEEN A WHILE SINCE THEY WENT IN THERE...
GUESS IT REALLY IS AS DIFFI-CULT AS I FEARED...
GAKON (THNK)
!!
THEY'RE BACK...

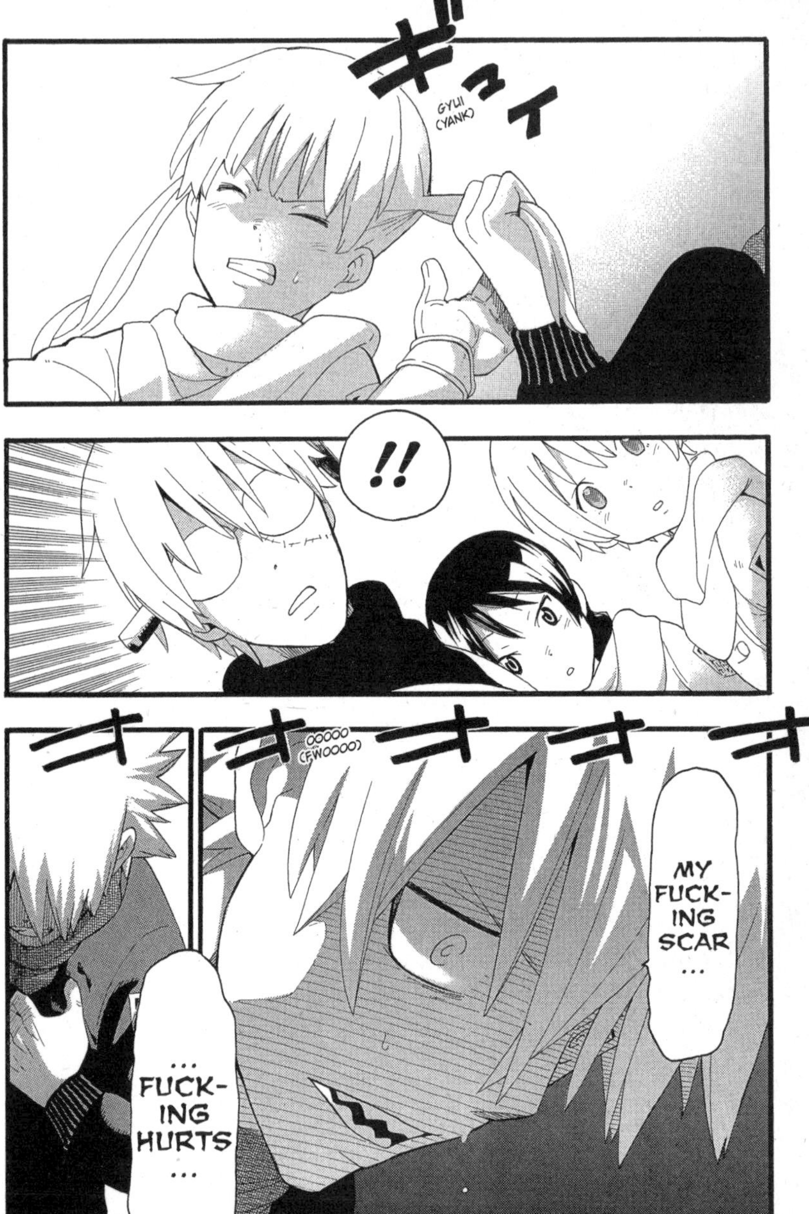
ギュイ
GYUI (YANK)
!!
オオオオオ
OOOOO (FWOOOO)
MY FUCK-ING SCAR...
...FUCK-ING HURTS...

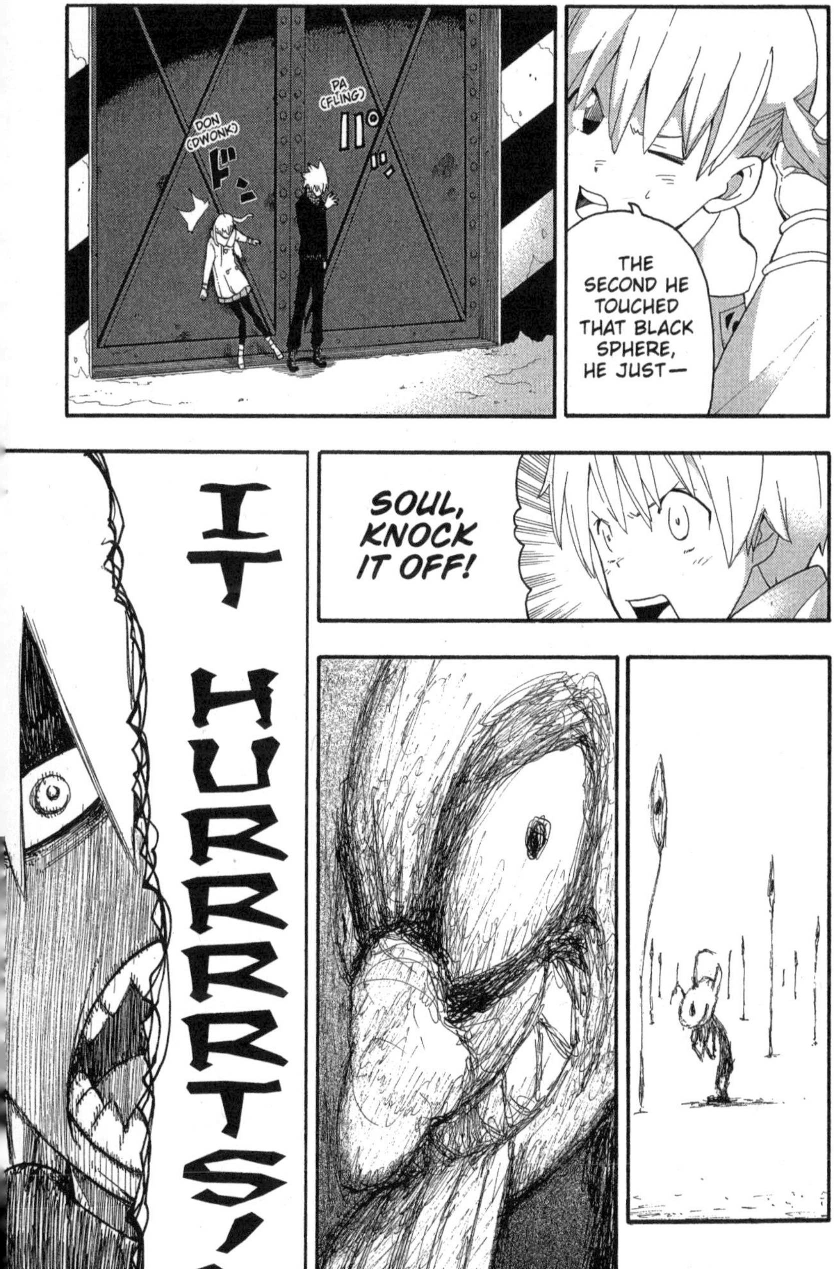
THE SECOND HE TOUCHED THAT BLACK SPHERE, HE JUST—
PA (FLING)
DON (DWONK)
SOUL, KNOCK IT OFF!
IT HURRRTS!

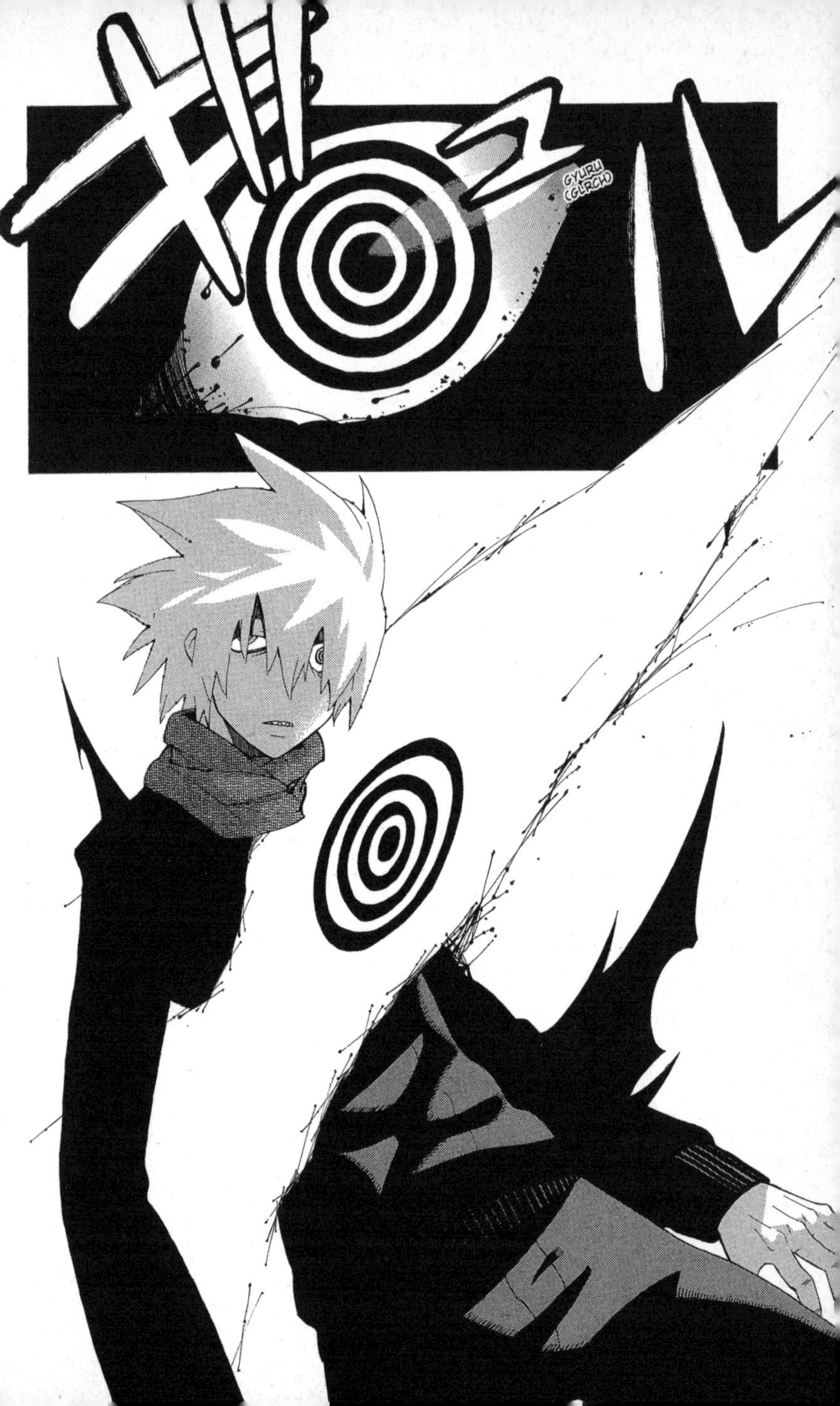
GYURU
(GLRCH)

SOUL EATER

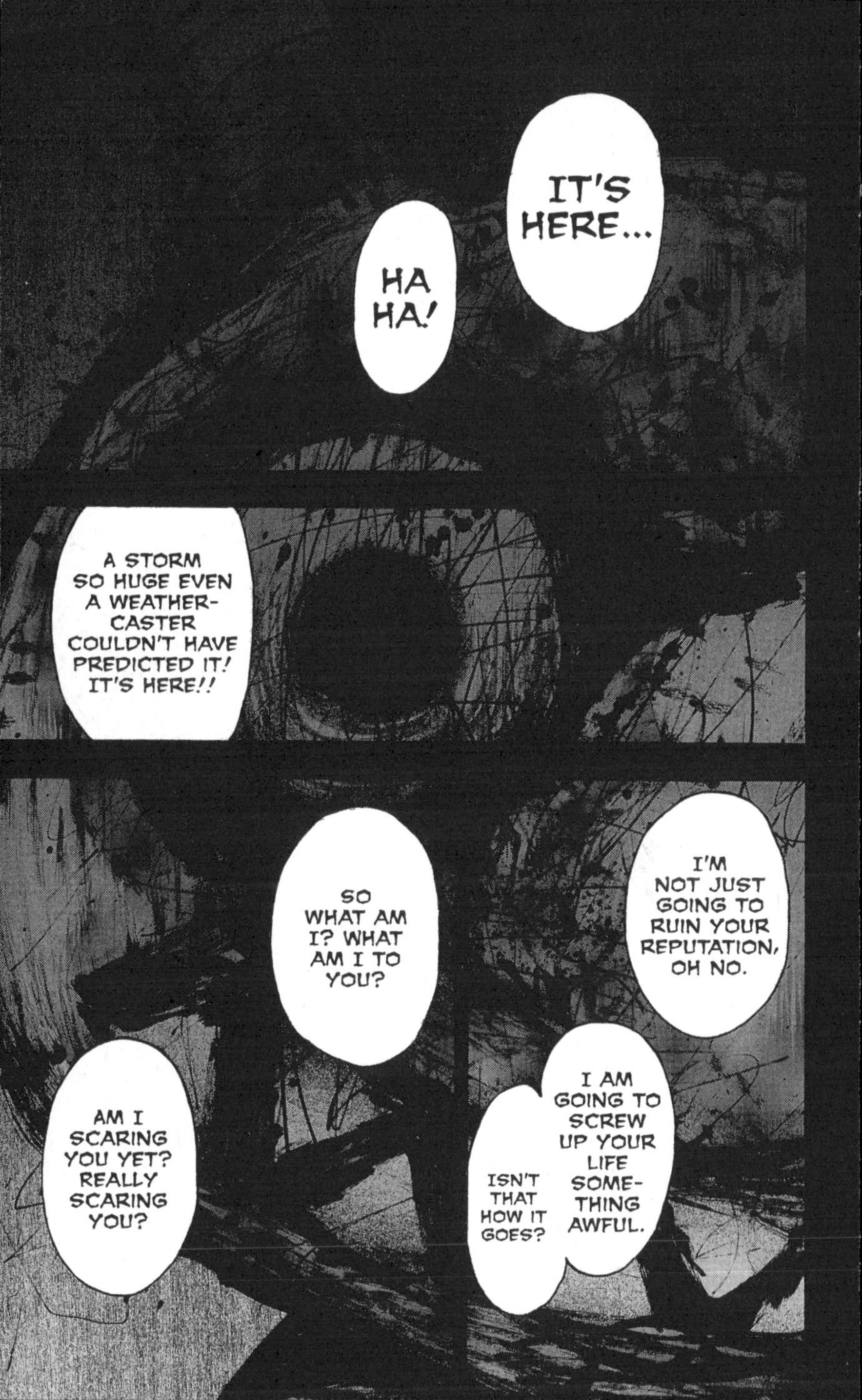

IT'S HERE...
HA HA!
A STORM SO HUGE EVEN A WEATHER-CASTER COULDN'T HAVE PREDICTED IT! IT'S HERE!!
I'M NOT JUST GOING TO RUIN YOUR REPUTATION, OH NO.
I AM GOING TO SCREW UP YOUR LIFE SOME-THING AWFUL.
ISN'T THAT HOW IT GOES?
SO WHAT AM I? WHAT AM I TO YOU?
AM I SCARING YOU YET? REALLY SCARING YOU?

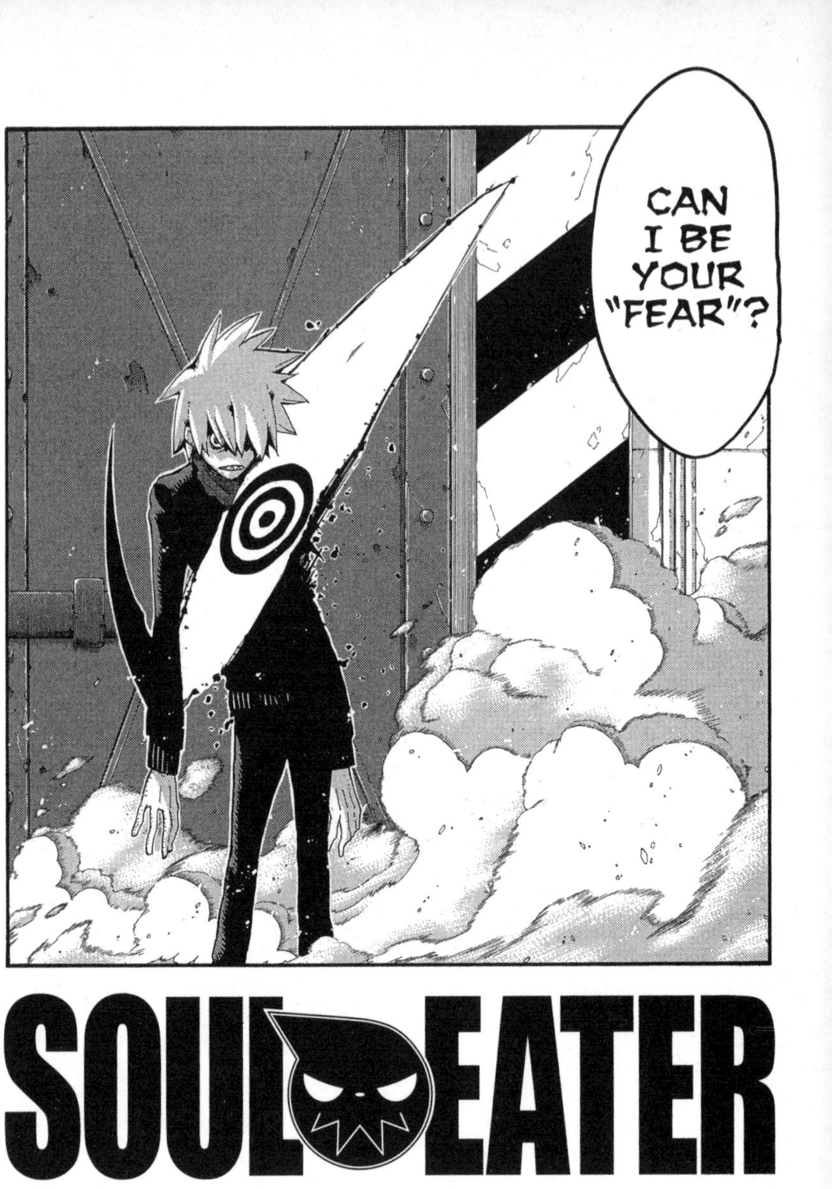
CAN I BE YOUR "FEAR"?

SOUL EATER

CHAPTER 84: RECOVERY

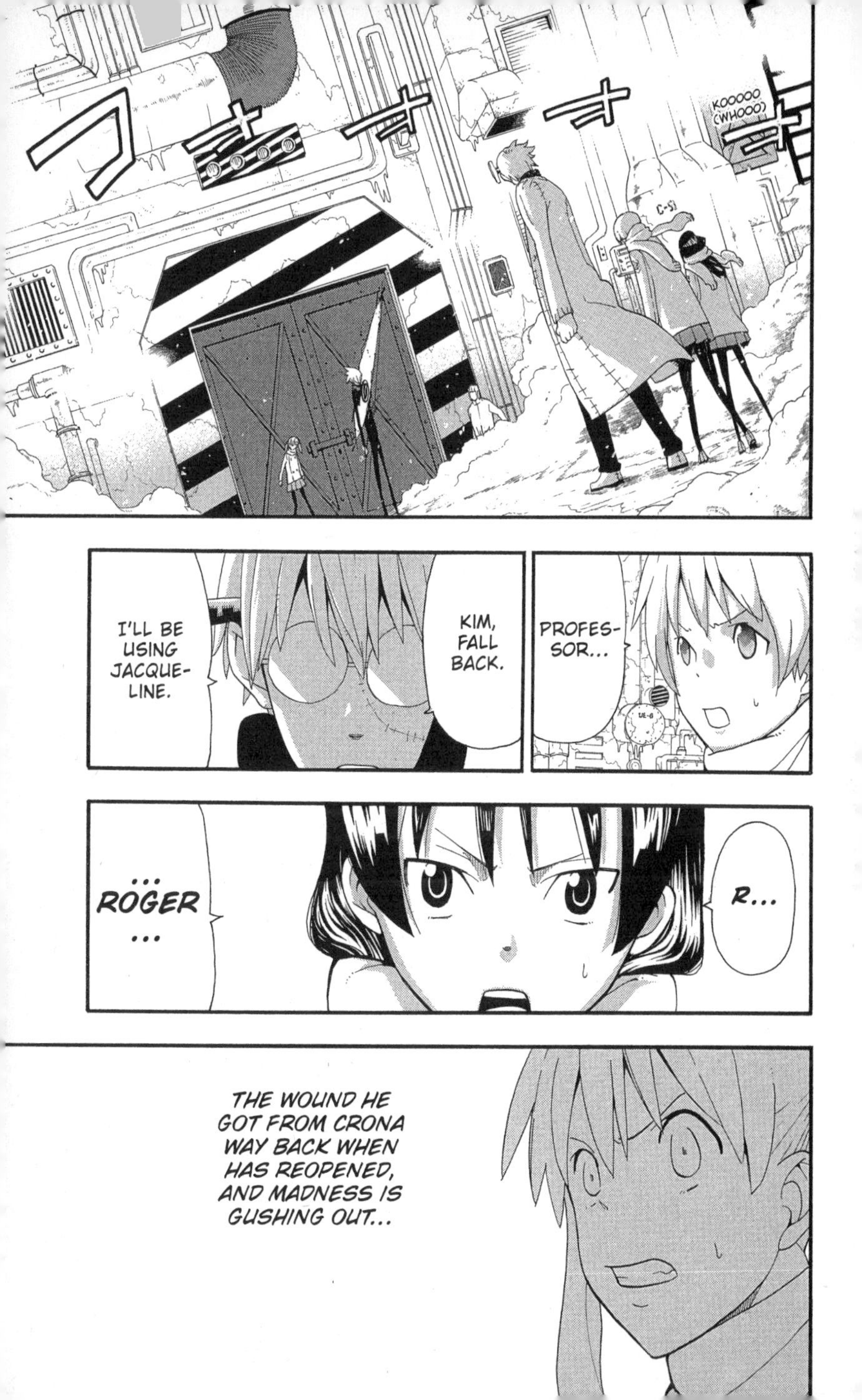
KOOOOO (WHOOO)
PROFES-SOR...
KIM, FALL BACK.
I'LL BE USING JACQUE-LINE.
R...
... ROGER ...
THE WOUND HE GOT FROM CRONA WAY BACK WHEN HAS REOPENED, AND MADNESS IS GUSHING OUT...

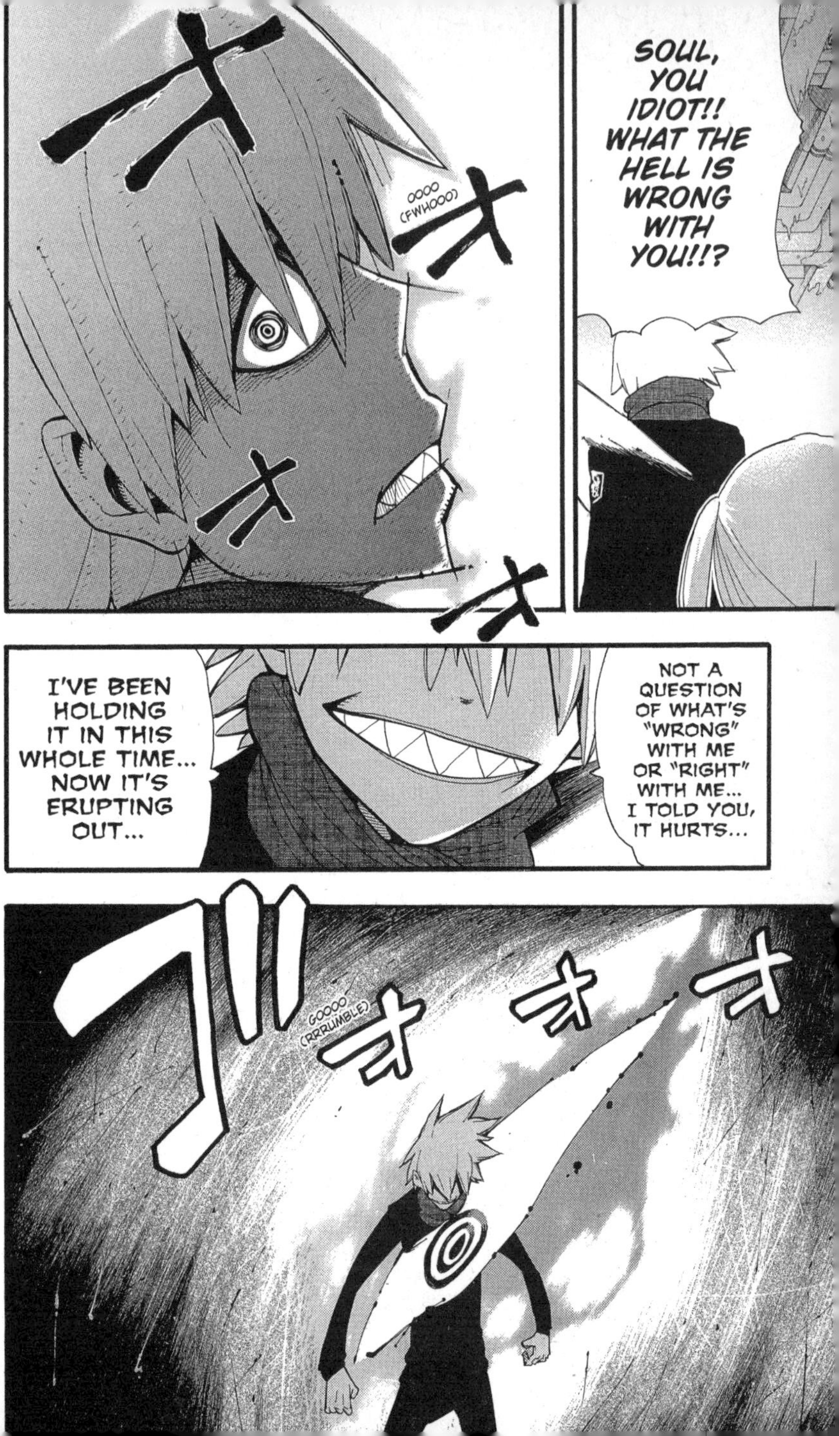
SOUL, YOU IDIOT!! WHAT THE HELL IS WRONG WITH YOU!!?
OOOO (FWHOOO)
NOT A QUESTION OF WHAT'S "WRONG" WITH ME OR "RIGHT" WITH ME... I TOLD YOU, IT HURTS...
I'VE BEEN HOLDING IT IN THIS WHOLE TIME... NOW IT'S ERUPTING OUT...
GOOOO (RRRUMBLE)

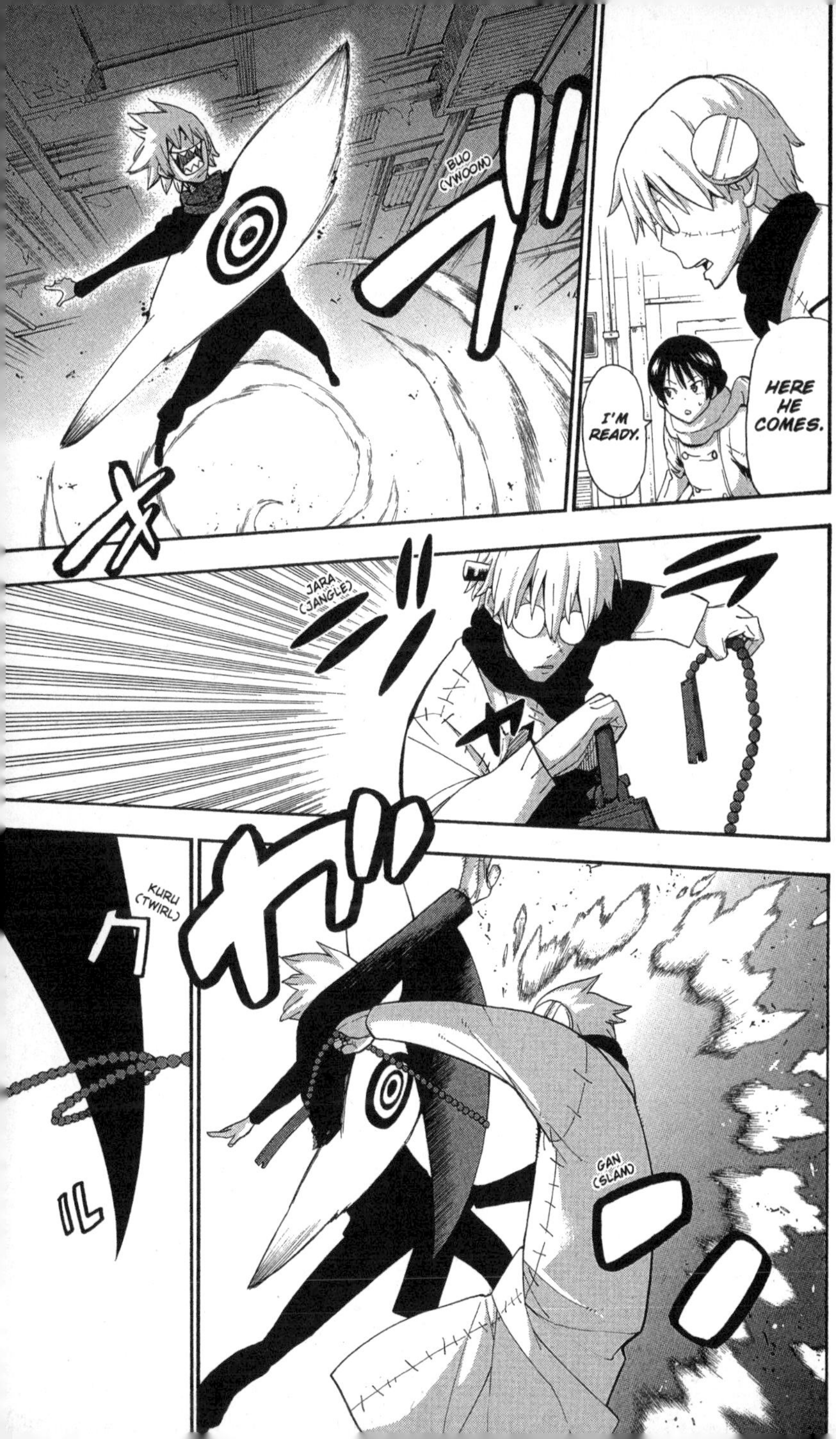
HERE HE COMES.
I'M READY.
BUO (VWOOM)
JARA (JANGLE)
KURU (TWIRL)
GAN (SLAM)

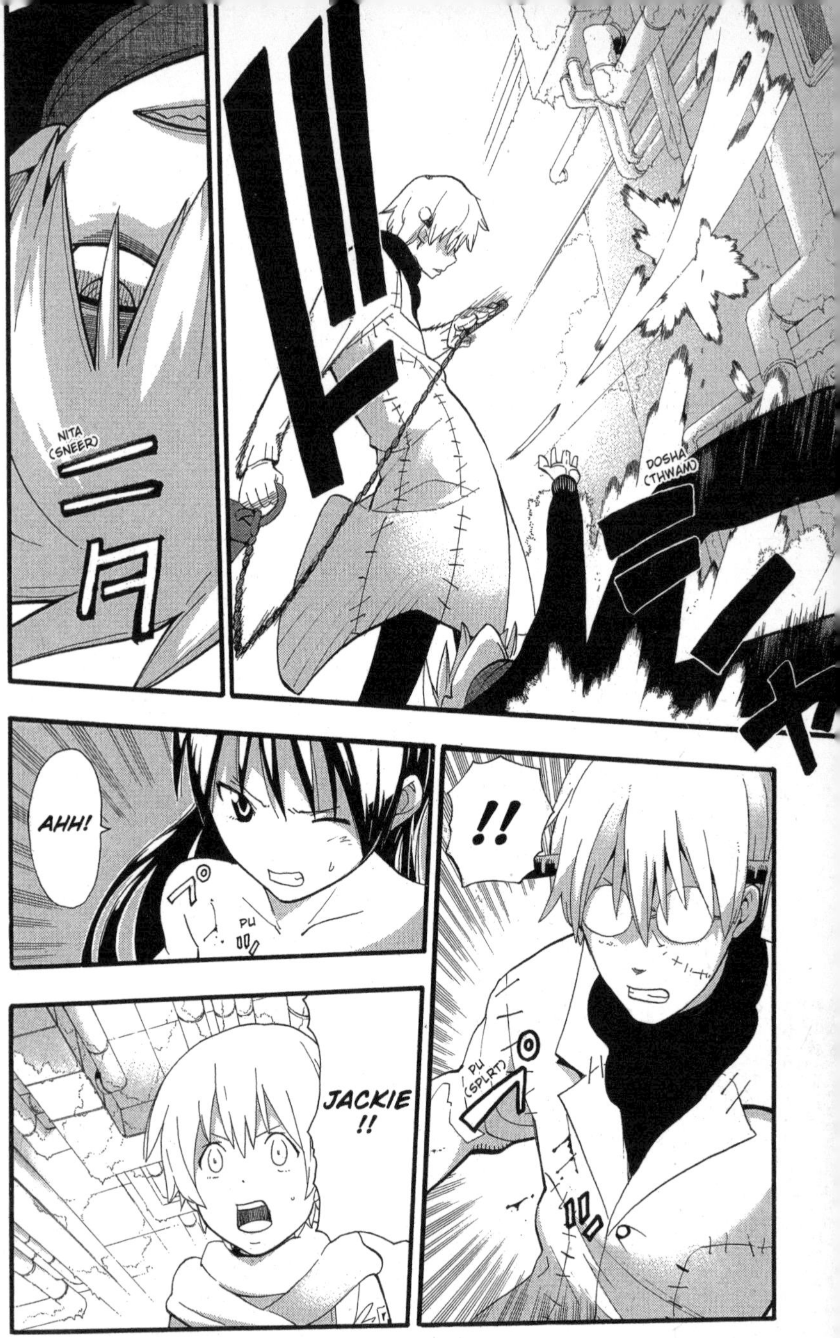
DOSHA (THWAM)
NITA (SNEER)
!!
PU (SPLRT)
AHH!
PU
JACKIE !!

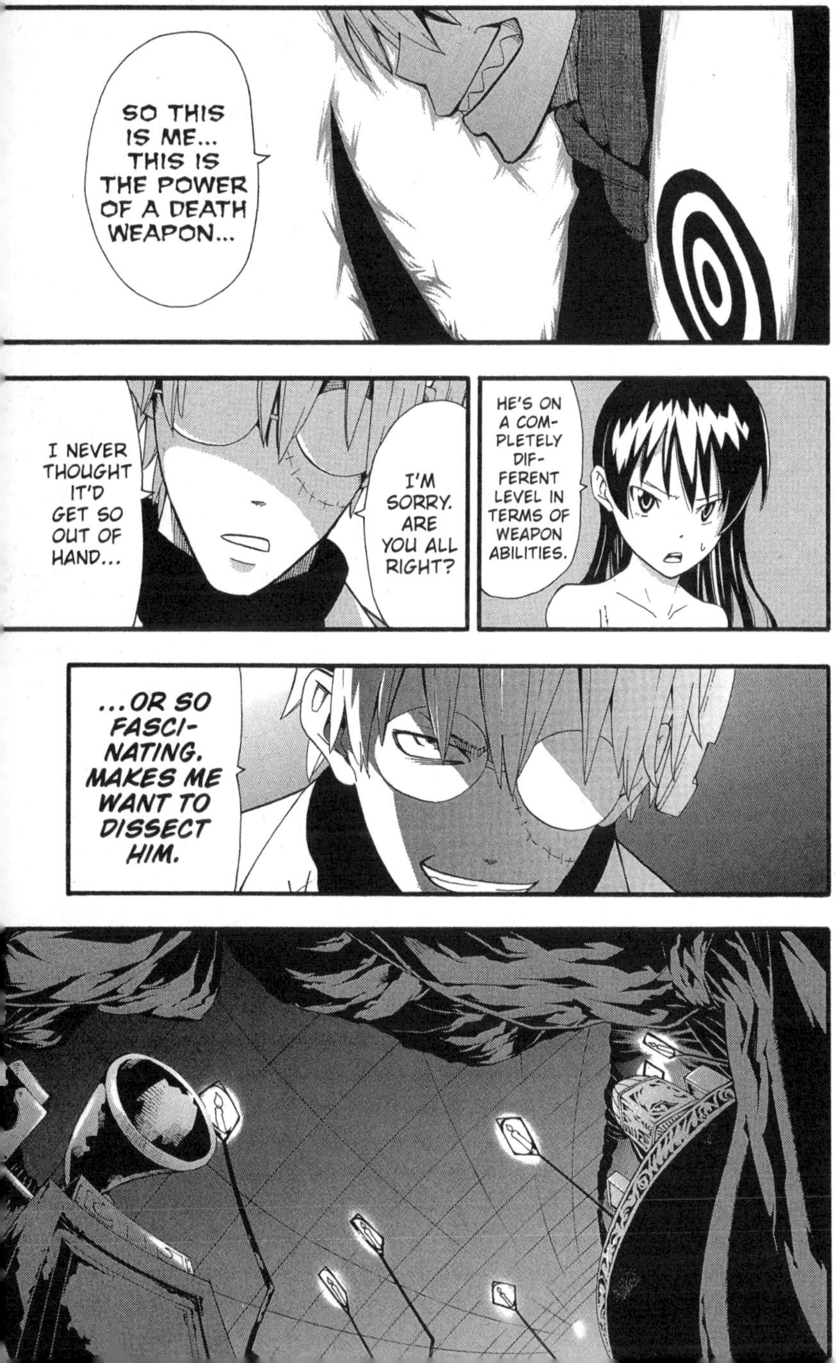
SO THIS IS ME... THIS IS THE POWER OF A DEATH WEAPON...
HE'S ON A COM-PLETELY DIF-FERENT LEVEL IN TERMS OF WEAPON ABILITIES.
I'M SORRY. ARE YOU ALL RIGHT?
I NEVER THOUGHT IT'D GET SO OUT OF HAND...
...OR SO FASCI-NATING. MAKES ME WANT TO DISSECT HIM.

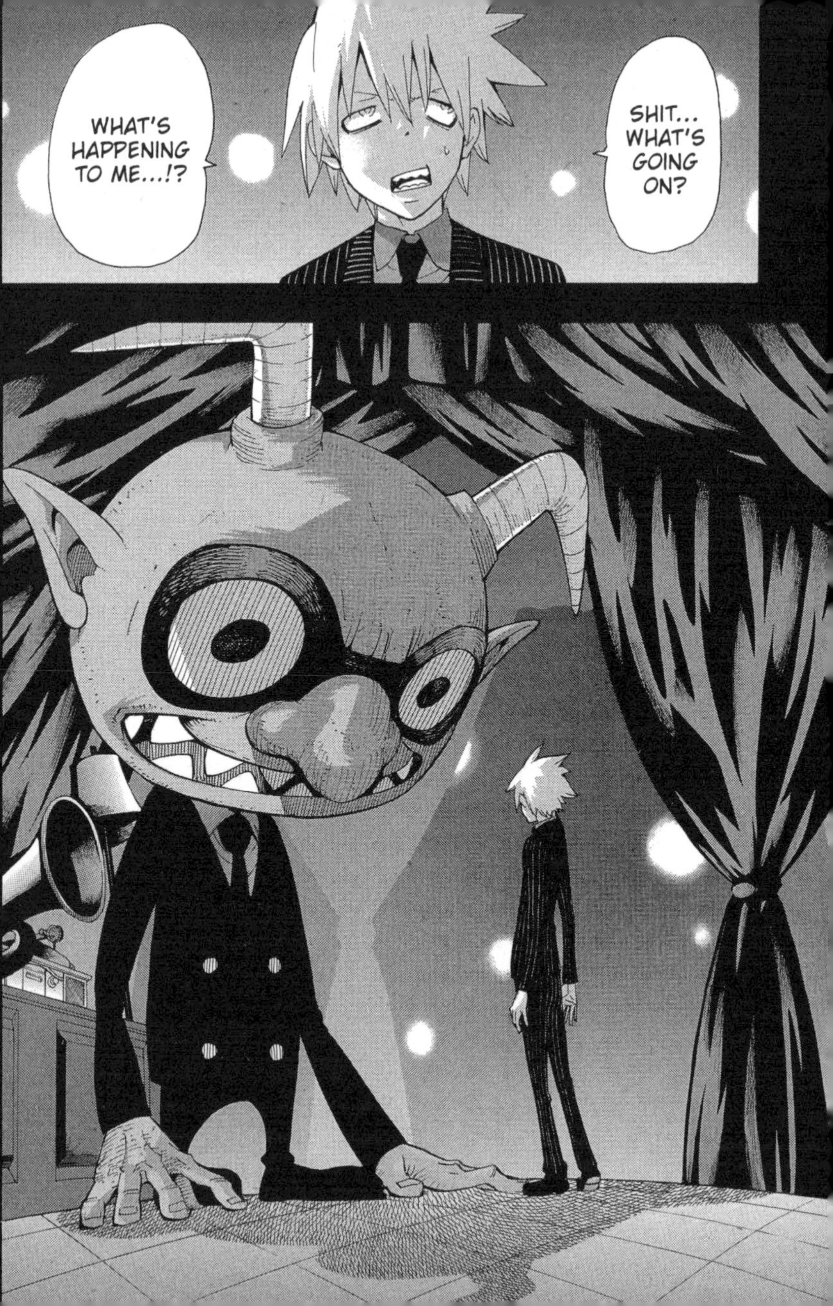
SHIT... WHAT'S GOING ON?
WHAT'S HAPPENING TO ME...!?

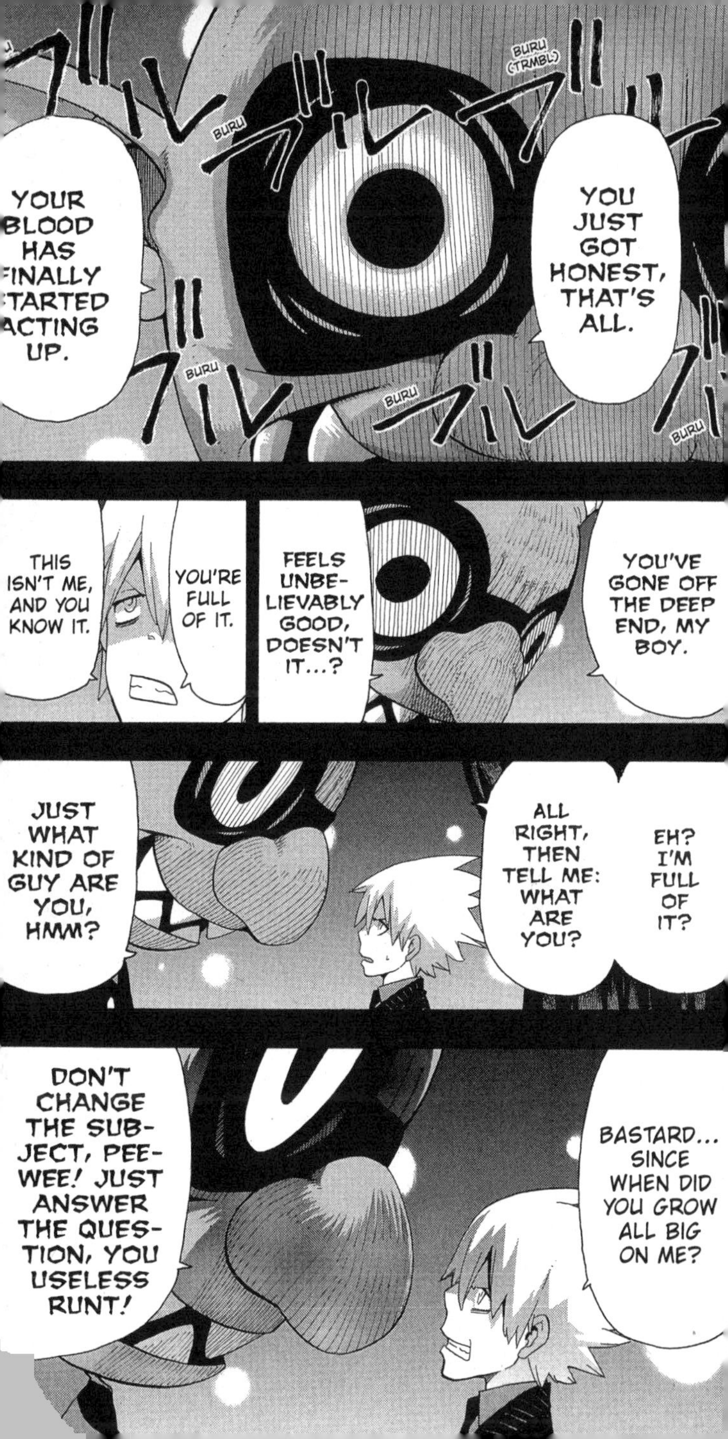
BURU (TRMBL)
BURU
YOU JUST GOT HONEST, THAT'S ALL.
YOUR BLOOD HAS FINALLY STARTED ACTING UP.
BURU
BURU
BURU
YOU'VE GONE OFF THE DEEP END, MY BOY.
FEELS UNBELIEVABLY GOOD, DOESN'T IT...?
YOU'RE FULL OF IT.
THIS ISN'T ME, AND YOU KNOW IT.
EH? I'M FULL OF IT?
ALL RIGHT, THEN TELL ME: WHAT ARE YOU?
JUST WHAT KIND OF GUY ARE YOU, HMM?
BASTARD... SINCE WHEN DID YOU GROW ALL BIG ON ME?
DON'T CHANGE THE SUBJECT, PEE-WEE! JUST ANSWER THE QUESTION, YOU USELESS RUNT!

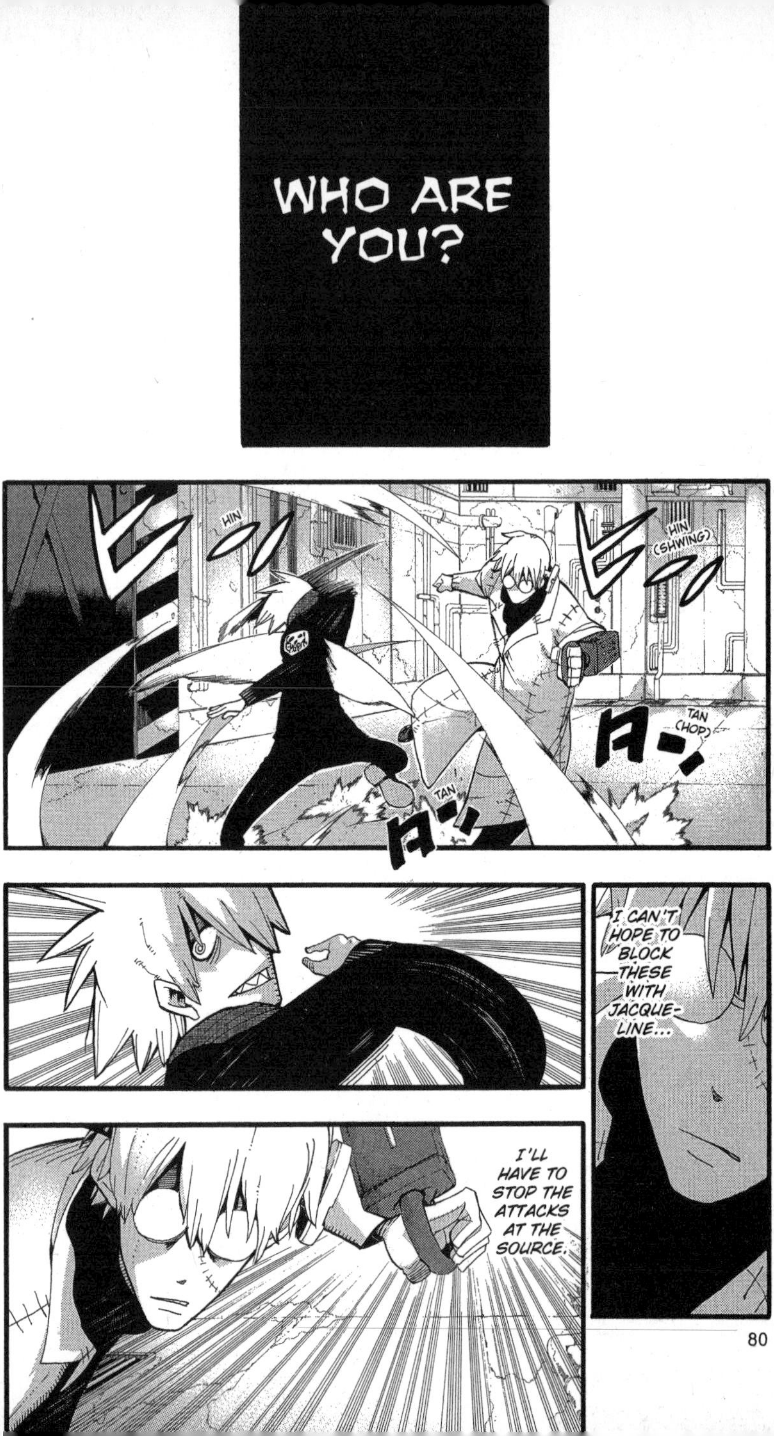
WHO ARE YOU?
HIN (SHWING)
TAN (HOP)
HIN
TAN
I CAN'T HOPE TO BLOCK THESE WITH JACQUE-LINE...
I'LL HAVE TO STOP THE ATTACKS AT THE SOURCE.

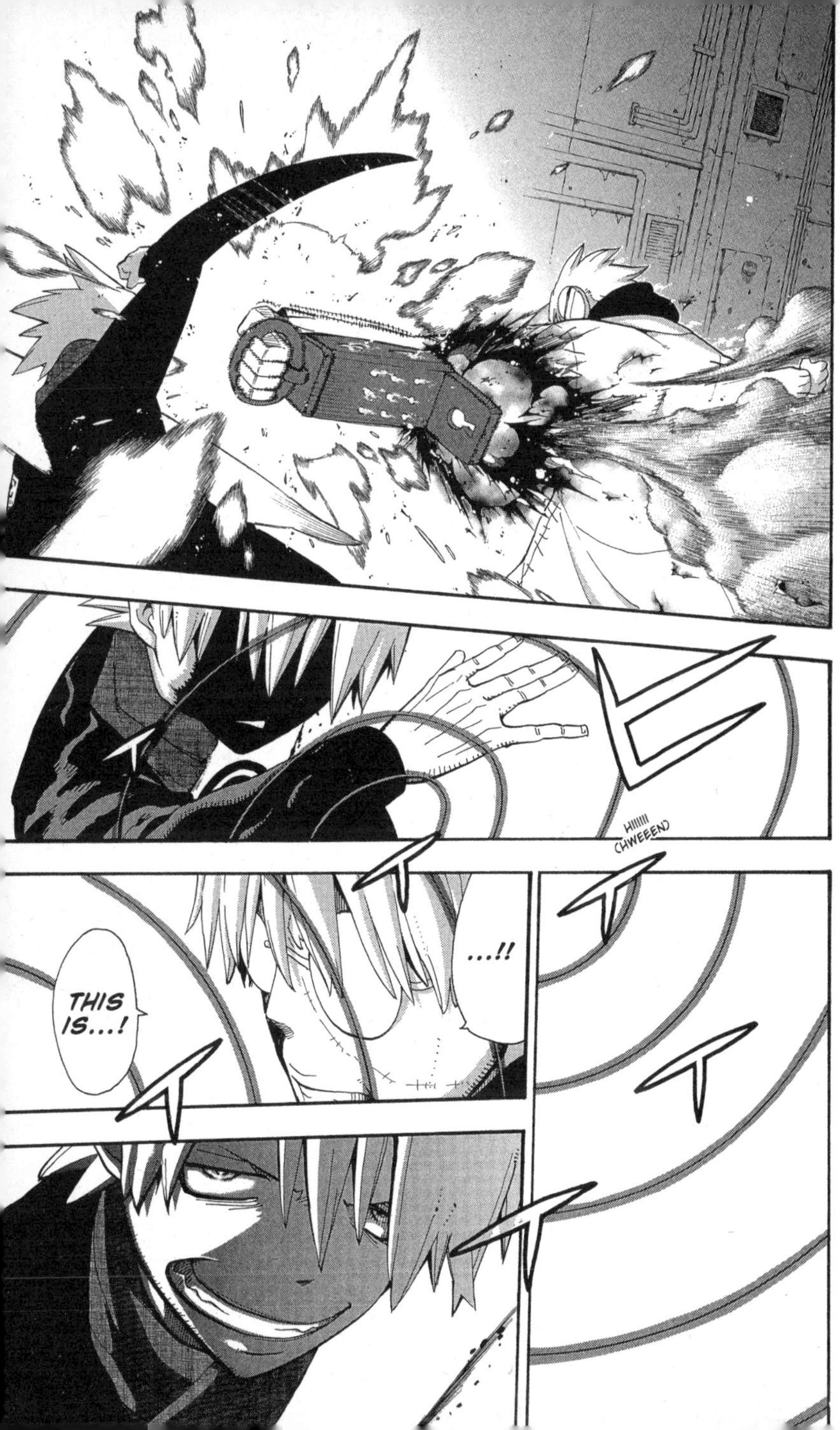
HIIIIII
CHWEEEND
...!!
THIS IS...!

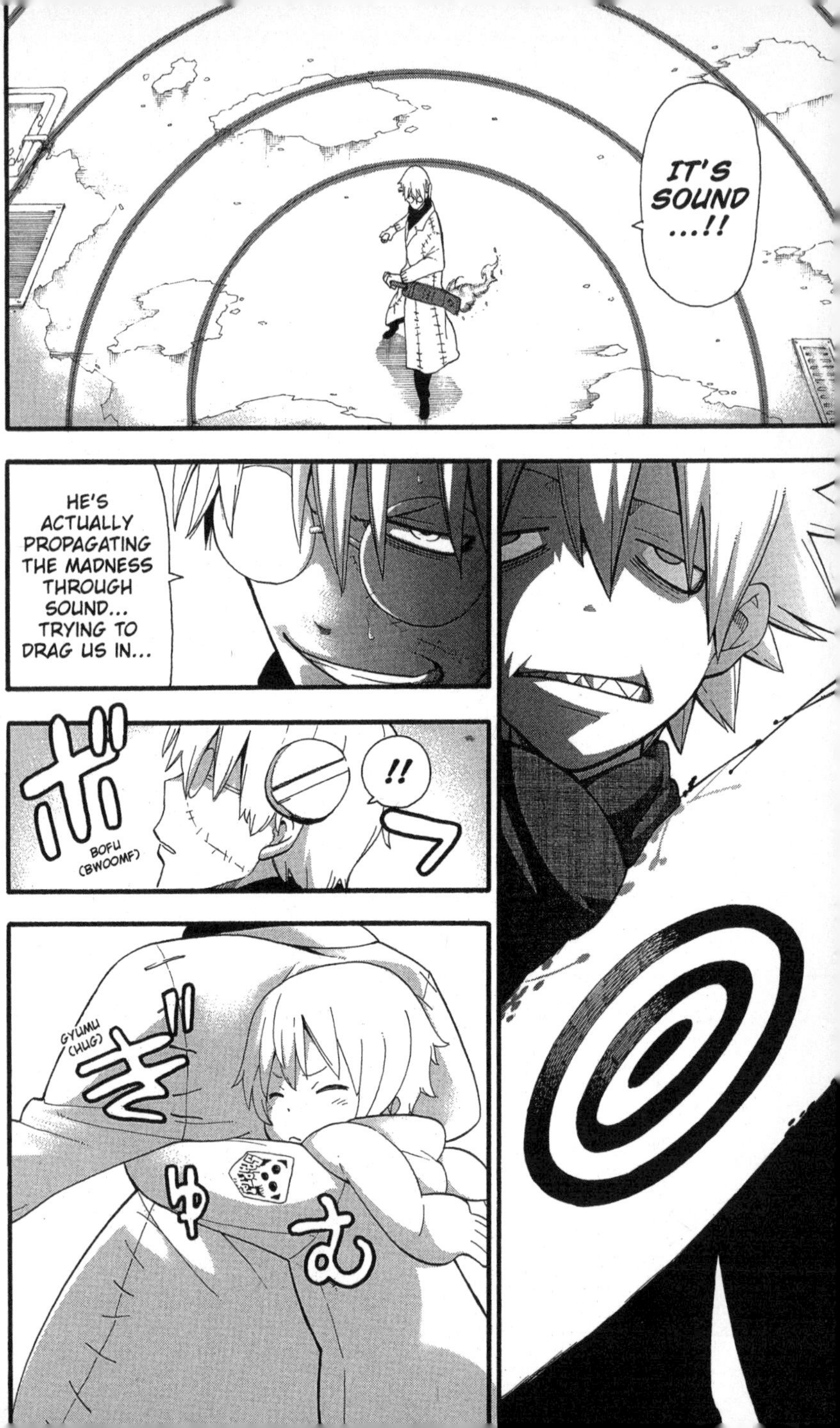
IT'S SOUND ...!!
HE'S ACTUALLY PROPAGATING THE MADNESS THROUGH SOUND... TRYING TO DRAG US IN...
!!
ボフ
BOFU (BWOOMF)
ぎゅむ
GYUMU (HUG)

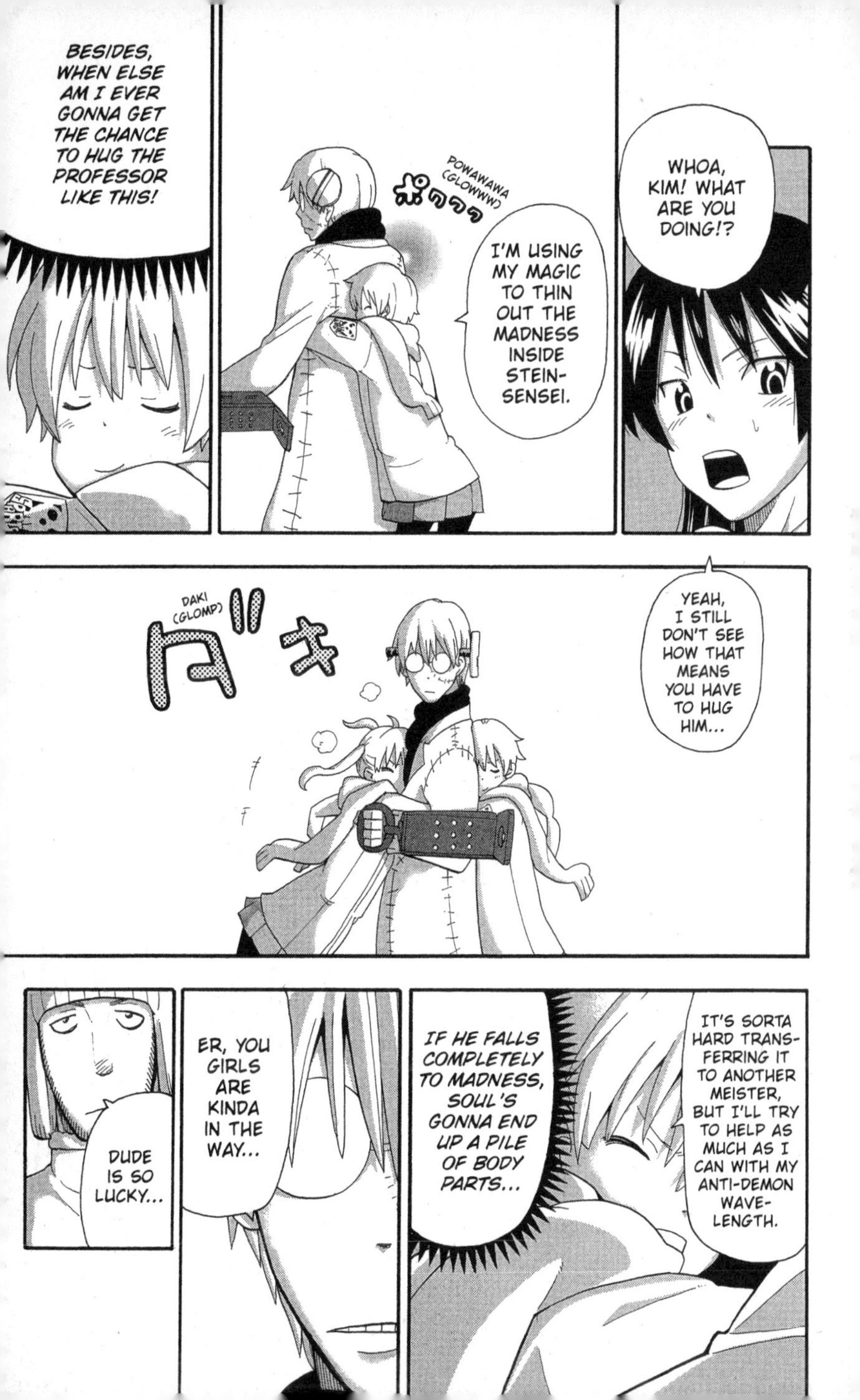
WHOA, KIM! WHAT ARE YOU DOING!?
ポワワワ
POWAWAWA (GLOWWW)
I'M USING MY MAGIC TO THIN OUT THE MADNESS INSIDE STEIN-SENSEI.
BESIDES, WHEN ELSE AM I EVER GONNA GET THE CHANCE TO HUG THE PROFESSOR LIKE THIS!
YEAH, I STILL DON'T SEE HOW THAT MEANS YOU HAVE TO HUG HIM...
ダキ
DAKI (GLOMP)
IT'S SORTA HARD TRANS-FERRING IT TO ANOTHER MEISTER, BUT I'LL TRY TO HELP AS MUCH AS I CAN WITH MY ANTI-DEMON WAVE-LENGTH.
IF HE FALLS COMPLETELY TO MADNESS, SOUL'S GONNA END UP A PILE OF BODY PARTS...
ER, YOU GIRLS ARE KINDA IN THE WAY...
DUDE IS SO LUCKY...

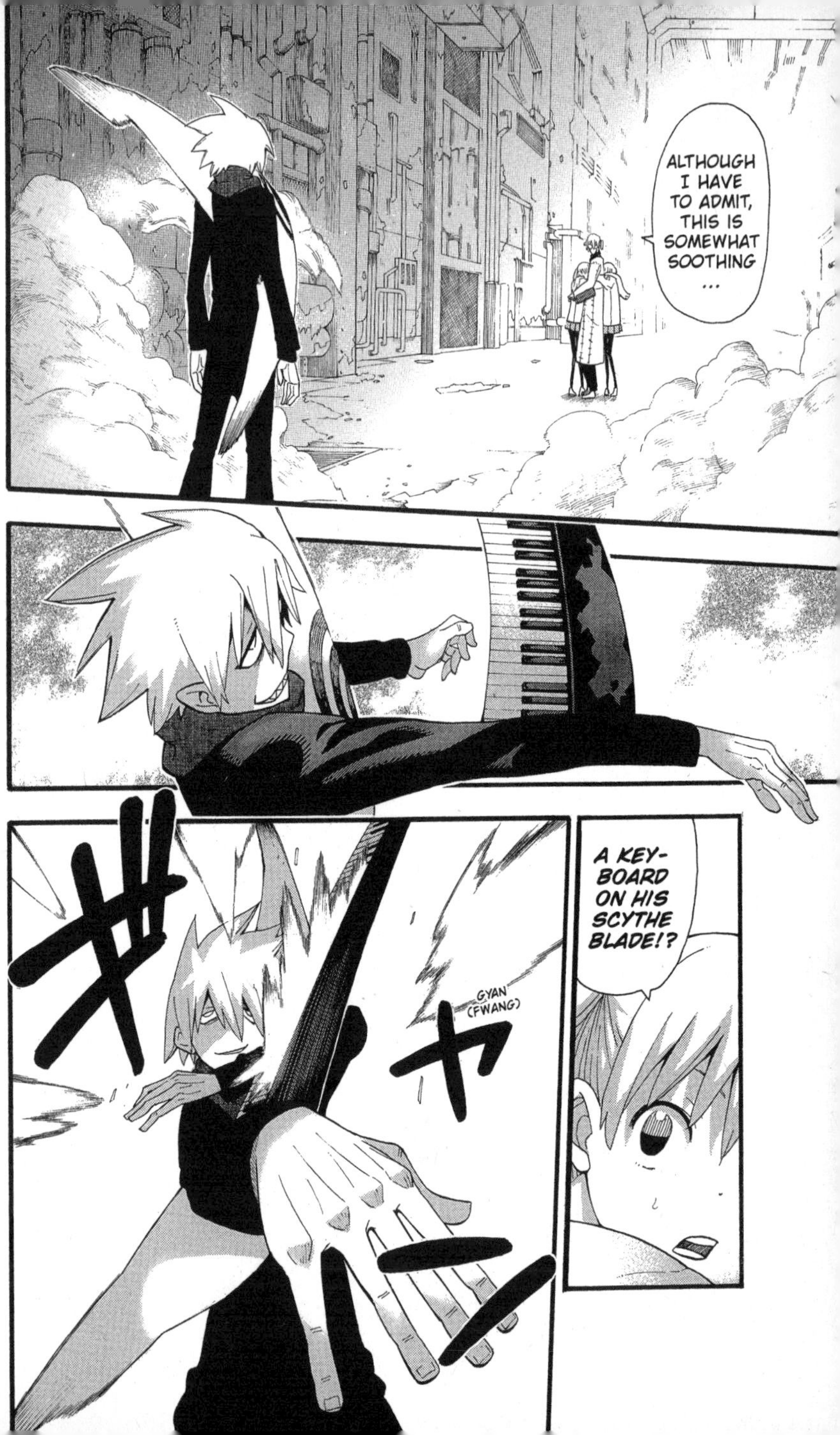
ALTHOUGH I HAVE TO ADMIT, THIS IS SOMEWHAT SOOTHING ...
A KEY-BOARD ON HIS SCYTHE BLADE!?
GYAN (FWANG)

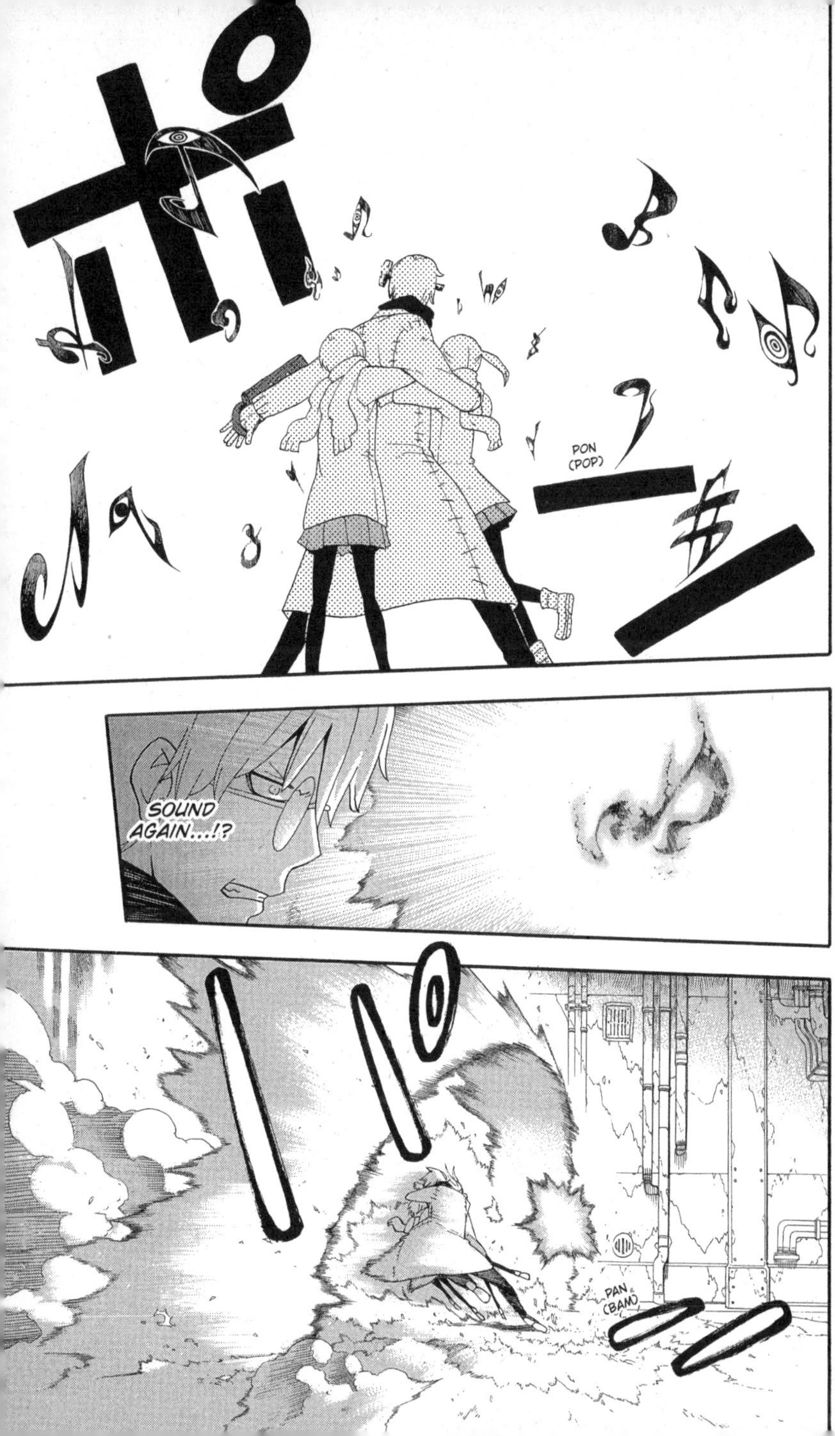
PON
(POP)
SOUND AGAIN...!?
PAN
(BAM)

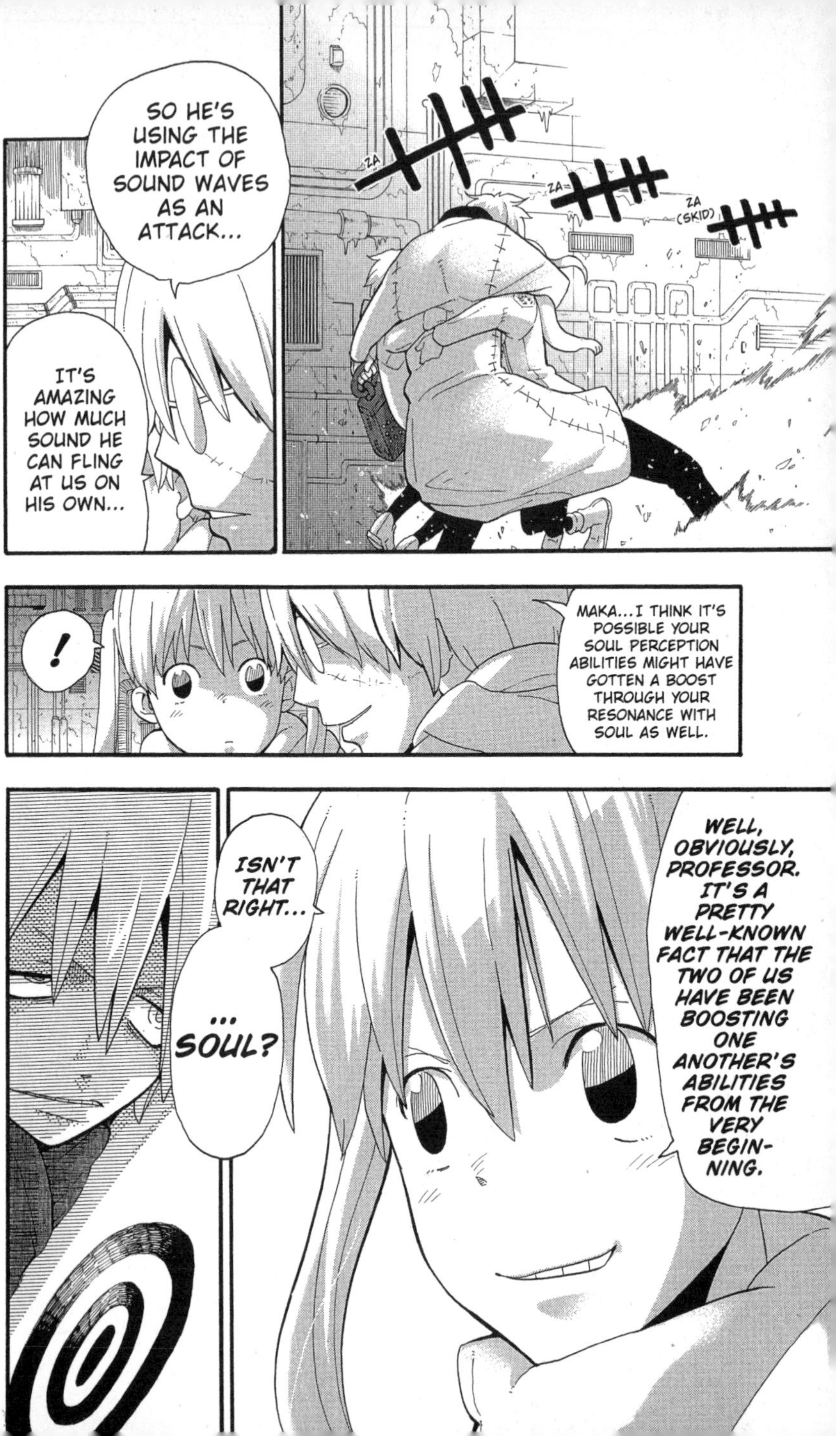
ZA
ZA
ZA (SKID)
SO HE'S USING THE IMPACT OF SOUND WAVES AS AN ATTACK...
IT'S AMAZING HOW MUCH SOUND HE CAN FLING AT US ON HIS OWN...
MAKA...I THINK IT'S POSSIBLE YOUR SOUL PERCEPTION ABILITIES MIGHT HAVE GOTTEN A BOOST THROUGH YOUR RESONANCE WITH SOUL AS WELL.
!
WELL, OBVIOUSLY, PROFESSOR. IT'S A PRETTY WELL-KNOWN FACT THAT THE TWO OF US HAVE BEEN BOOSTING ONE ANOTHER'S ABILITIES FROM THE VERY BEGIN-NING.
ISN'T THAT RIGHT...
...SOUL?

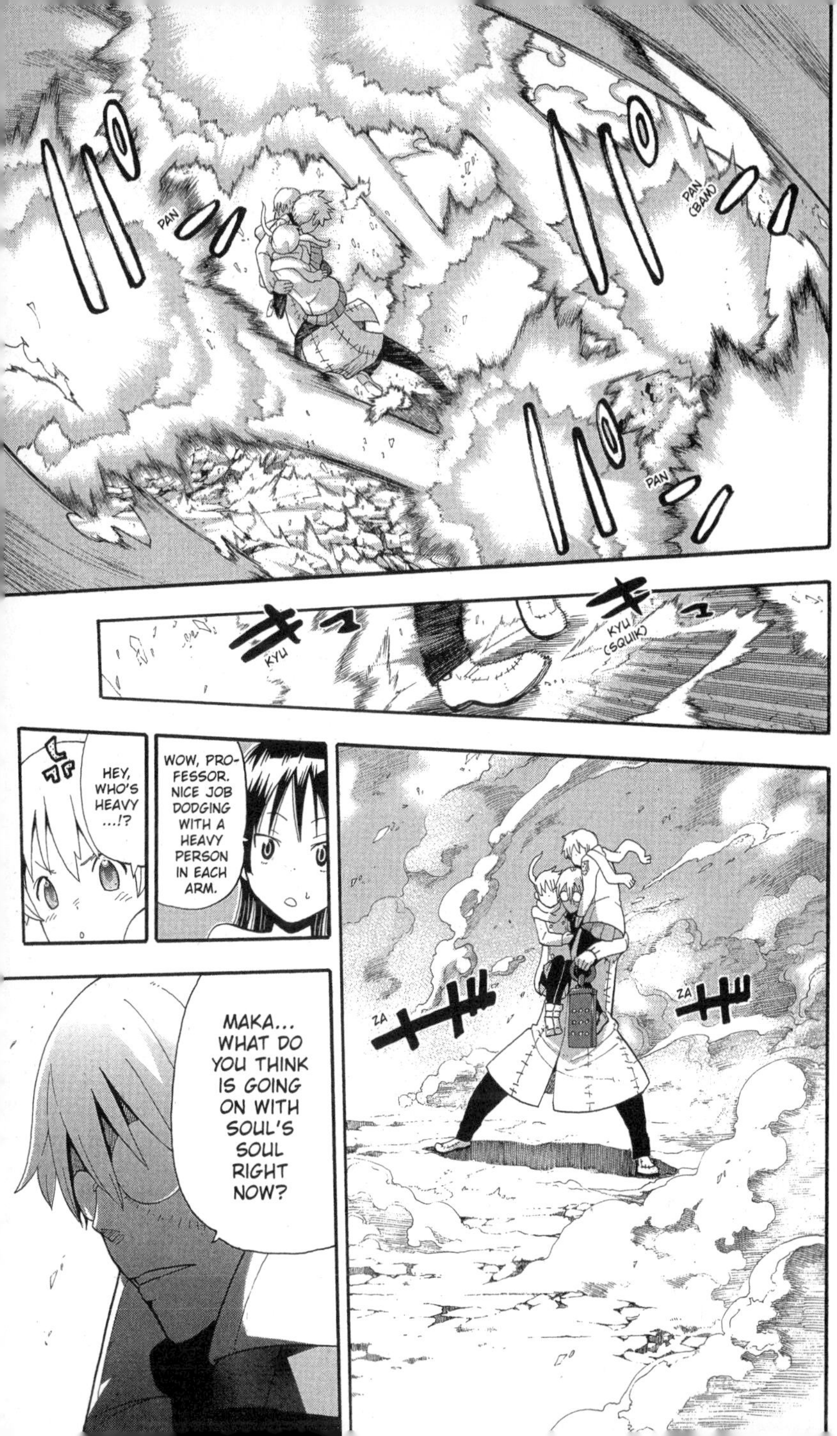
PAN (BAM)
PAN
PAN
KYU (SQUIK)
KYU
ZA
ZA
WOW, PRO-FESSOR. NICE JOB DODGING WITH A HEAVY PERSON IN EACH ARM.
HEY, WHO'S HEAVY ...!?
MAKA... WHAT DO YOU THINK IS GOING ON WITH SOUL'S SOUL RIGHT NOW?

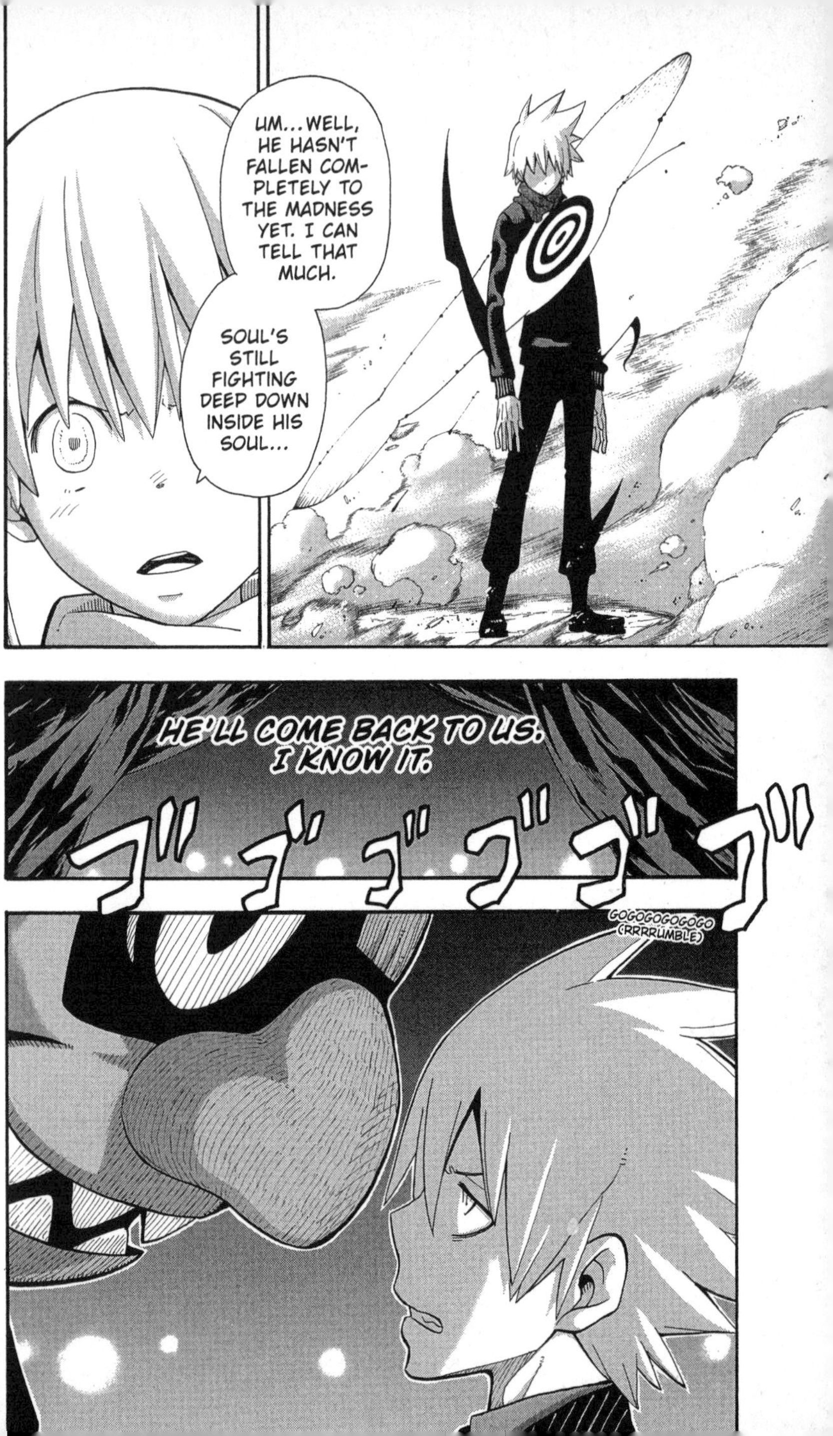
UM...WELL, HE HASN'T FALLEN COMPLETELY TO THE MADNESS YET. I CAN TELL THAT MUCH.
SOUL'S STILL FIGHTING DEEP DOWN INSIDE HIS SOUL...
HE'LL COME BACK TO US. I KNOW IT.
ゴゴゴゴゴゴ
GOGOGOGOGOGO (RRRRUMBLE)

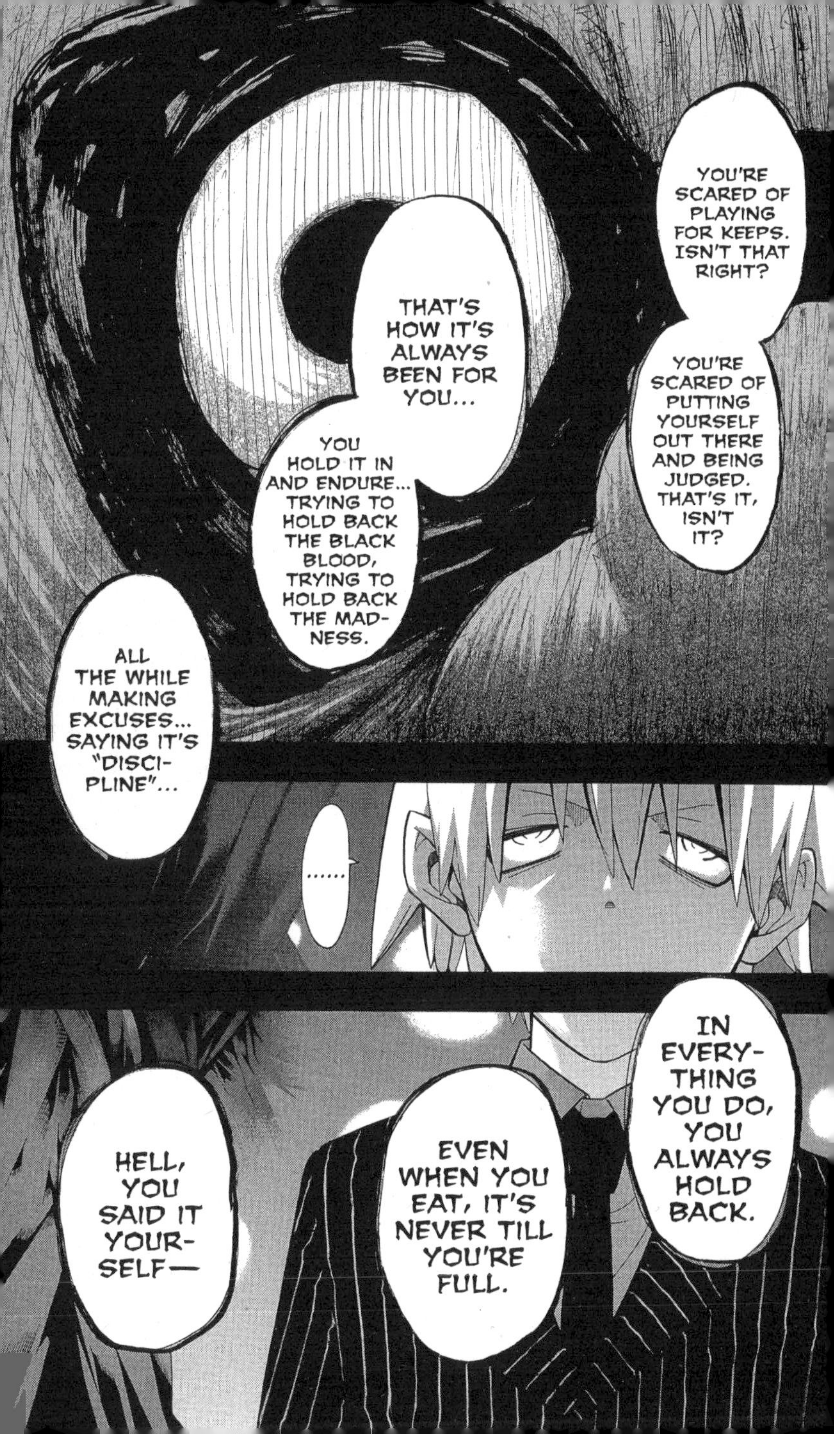
YOU'RE SCARED OF PLAYING FOR KEEPS. ISN'T THAT RIGHT?
YOU'RE SCARED OF PUTTING YOURSELF OUT THERE AND BEING JUDGED. THAT'S IT, ISN'T IT?
THAT'S HOW IT'S ALWAYS BEEN FOR YOU...
YOU HOLD IT IN AND ENDURE... TRYING TO HOLD BACK THE BLACK BLOOD, TRYING TO HOLD BACK THE MAD-NESS.
ALL THE WHILE MAKING EXCUSES... SAYING IT'S "DISCI-PLINE"...
......
IN EVERY-THING YOU DO, YOU ALWAYS HOLD BACK.
EVEN WHEN YOU EAT, IT'S NEVER TILL YOU'RE FULL.
HELL, YOU SAID IT YOUR-SELF—

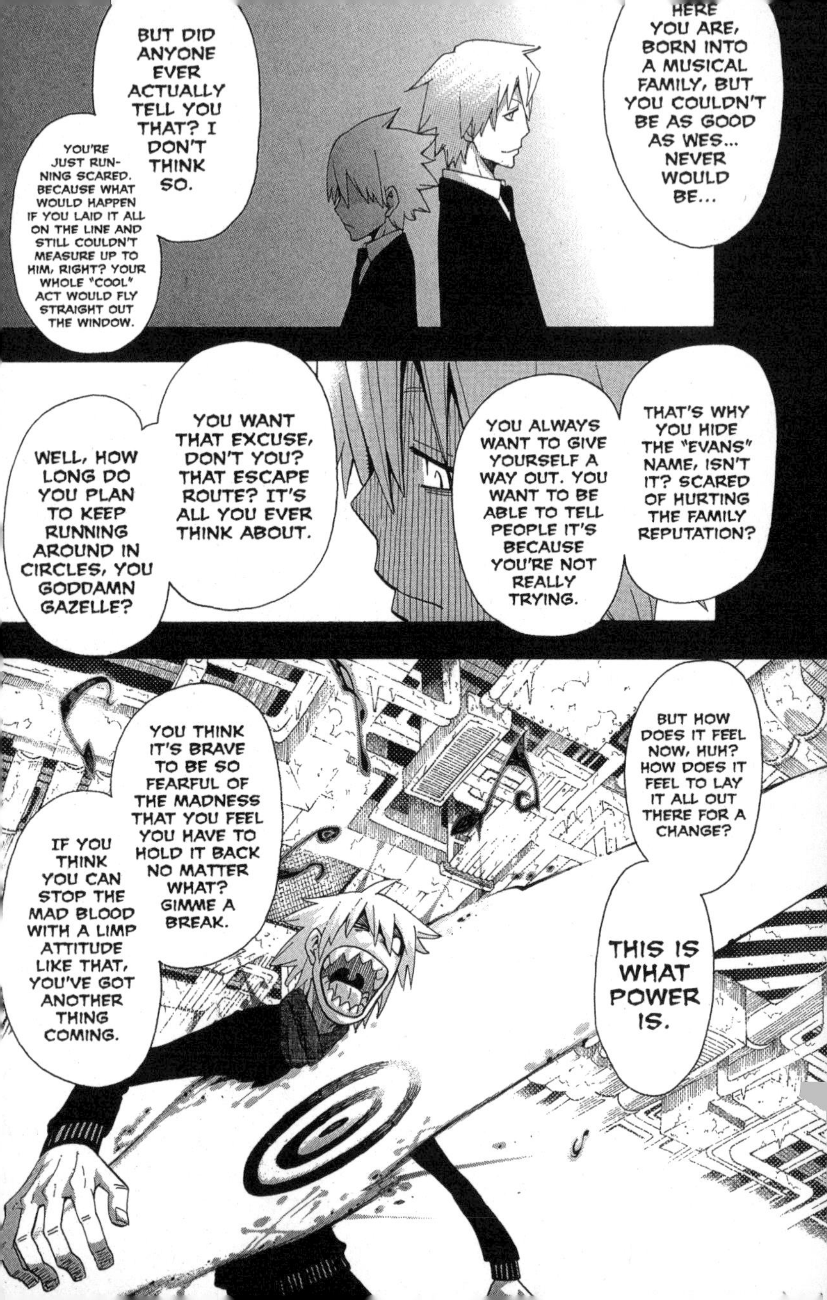
HERE YOU ARE, BORN INTO A MUSICAL FAMILY, BUT YOU COULDN'T BE AS GOOD AS WES... NEVER WOULD BE...
BUT DID ANYONE EVER ACTUALLY TELL YOU THAT? I DON'T THINK SO.
YOU'RE JUST RUNNING SCARED. BECAUSE WHAT WOULD HAPPEN IF YOU LAID IT ALL ON THE LINE AND STILL COULDN'T MEASURE UP TO HIM, RIGHT? YOUR WHOLE "COOL" ACT WOULD FLY STRAIGHT OUT THE WINDOW.
THAT'S WHY YOU HIDE THE "EVANS" NAME, ISN'T IT? SCARED OF HURTING THE FAMILY REPUTATION?
YOU ALWAYS WANT TO GIVE YOURSELF A WAY OUT. YOU WANT TO BE ABLE TO TELL PEOPLE IT'S BECAUSE YOU'RE NOT REALLY TRYING.
YOU WANT THAT EXCUSE, DON'T YOU? THAT ESCAPE ROUTE? IT'S ALL YOU EVER THINK ABOUT.
WELL, HOW LONG DO YOU PLAN TO KEEP RUNNING AROUND IN CIRCLES, YOU GODDAMN GAZELLE?
BUT HOW DOES IT FEEL NOW, HUH? HOW DOES IT FEEL TO LAY IT ALL OUT THERE FOR A CHANGE?
THIS IS WHAT POWER IS.
YOU THINK IT'S BRAVE TO BE SO FEARFUL OF THE MADNESS THAT YOU FEEL YOU HAVE TO HOLD IT BACK NO MATTER WHAT? GIMME A BREAK.
IF YOU THINK YOU CAN STOP THE MAD BLOOD WITH A LIMP ATTITUDE LIKE THAT, YOU'VE GOT ANOTHER THING COMING.

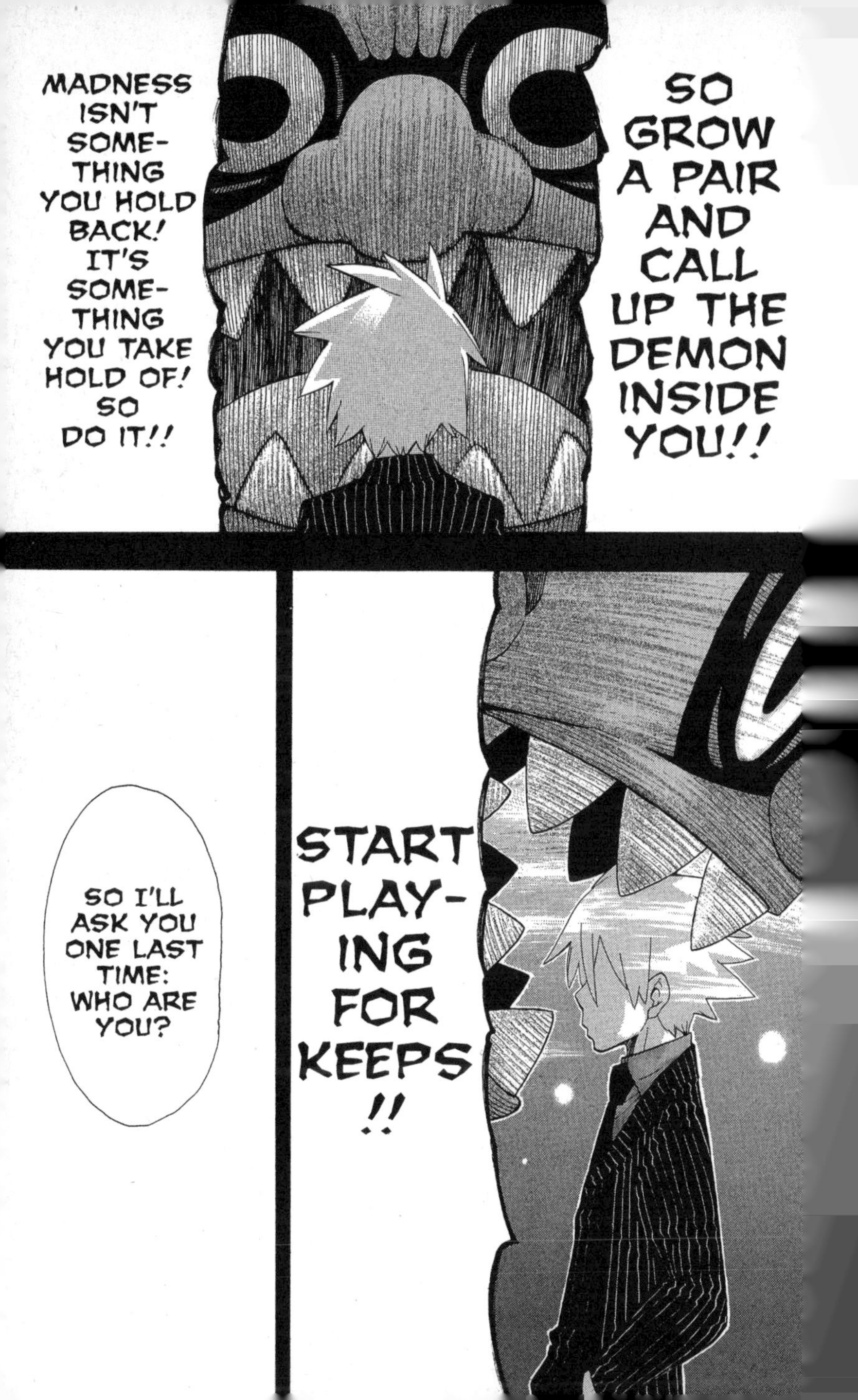
SO GROW A PAIR AND CALL UP THE DEMON INSIDE YOU!!
MADNESS ISN'T SOME-THING YOU HOLD BACK! IT'S SOME-THING YOU TAKE HOLD OF! SO DO IT!!
START PLAY-ING FOR KEEPS!!
SO I'LL ASK YOU ONE LAST TIME: WHO ARE YOU?

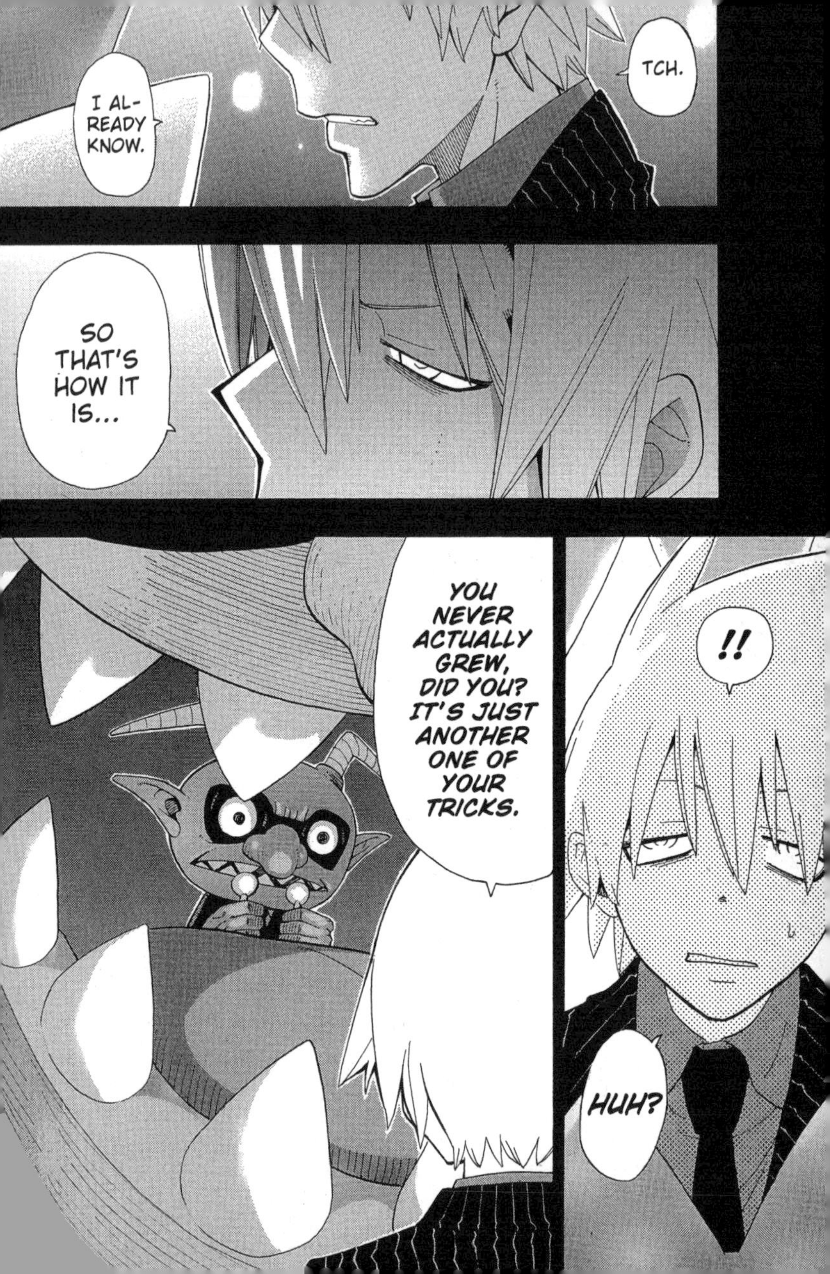
TCH.
I AL-READY KNOW.
SO THAT'S HOW IT IS...
!!
YOU NEVER ACTUALLY GREW, DID YOU? IT'S JUST ANOTHER ONE OF YOUR TRICKS.
HUH?

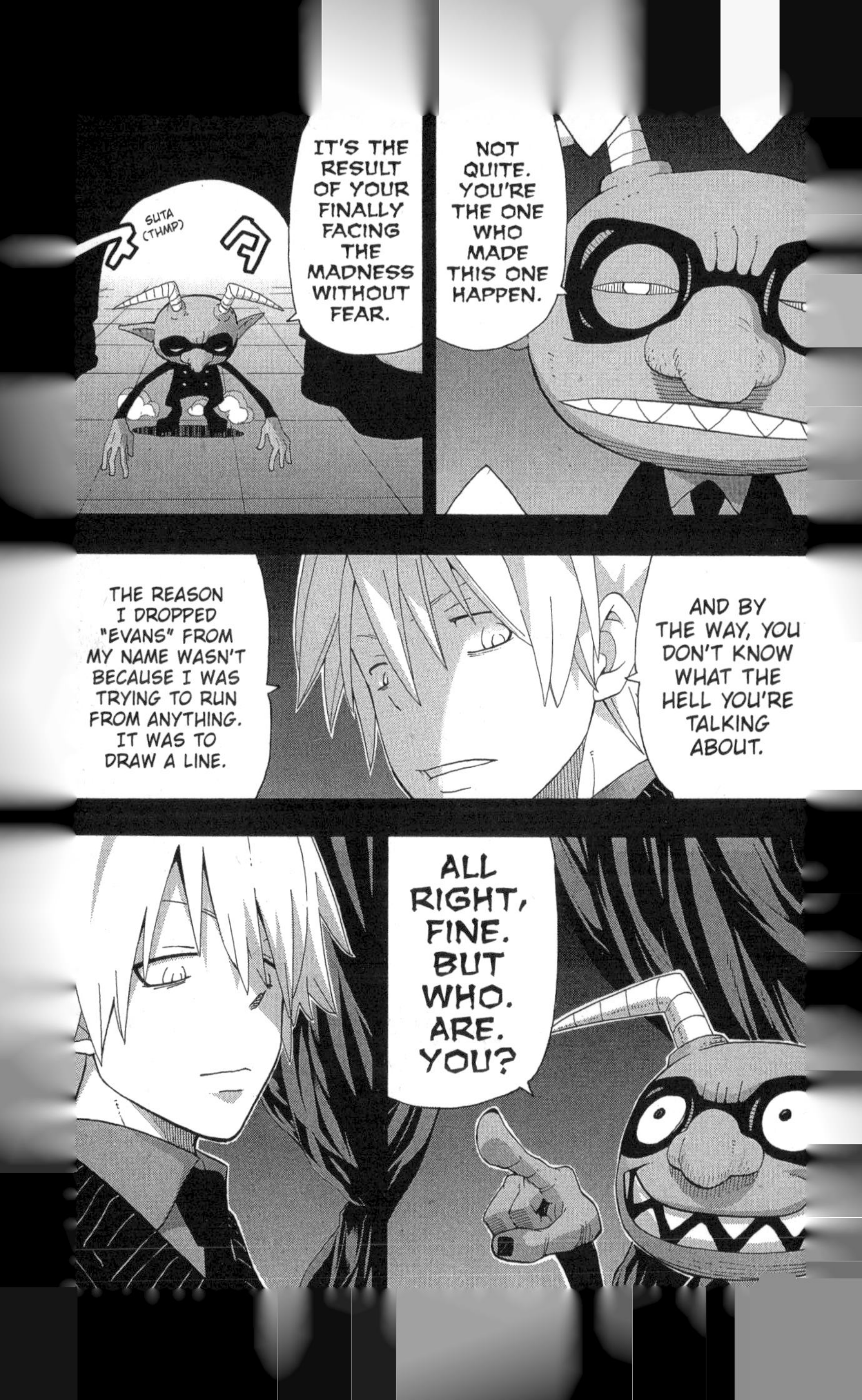
NOT QUITE. YOU'RE THE ONE WHO MADE THIS ONE HAPPEN.
IT'S THE RESULT OF YOUR FINALLY FACING THE MADNESS WITHOUT FEAR.
SUTA (THMP)
AND BY THE WAY, YOU DON'T KNOW WHAT THE HELL YOU'RE TALKING ABOUT.
THE REASON I DROPPED "EVANS" FROM MY NAME WASN'T BECAUSE I WAS TRYING TO RUN FROM ANYTHING. IT WAS TO DRAW A LINE.
ALL RIGHT, FINE. BUT WHO. ARE. YOU?

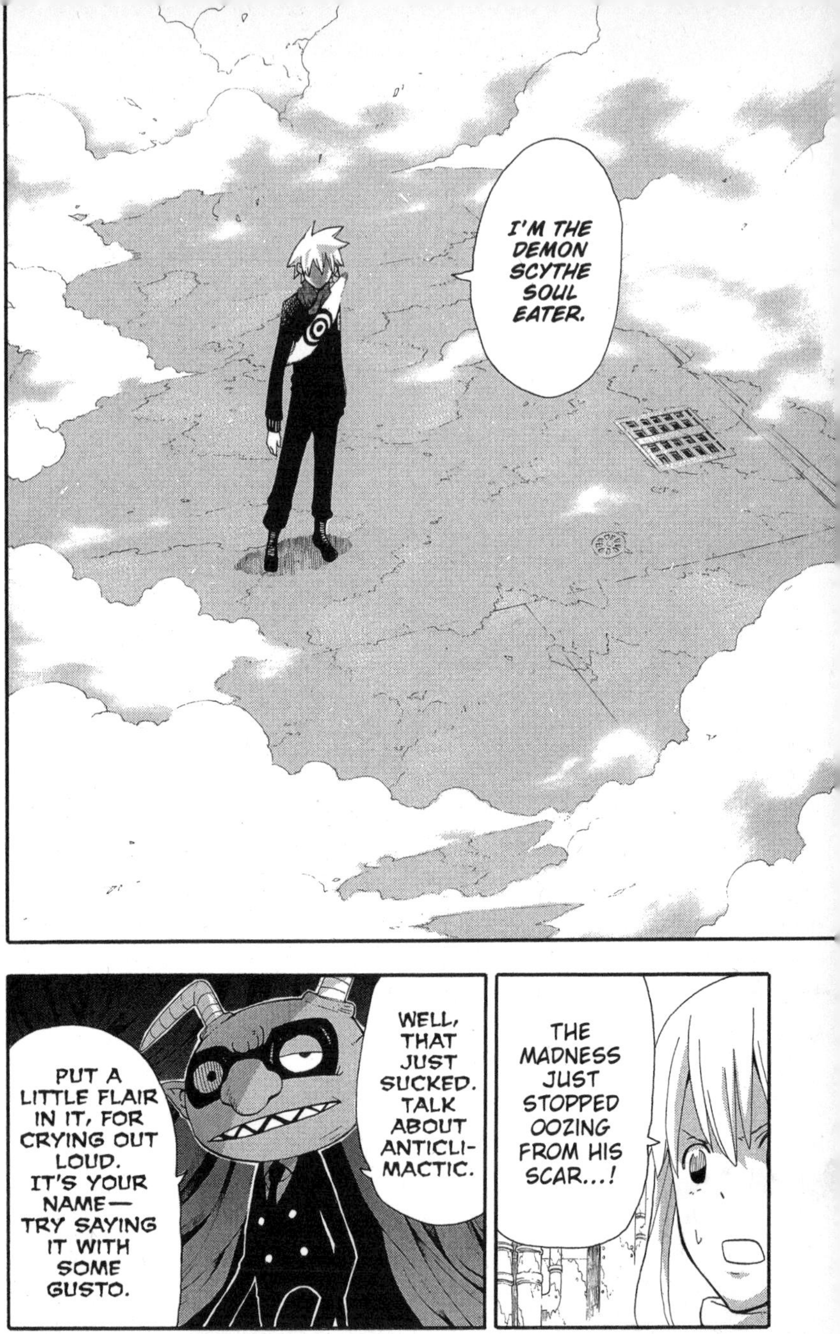
I'M THE DEMON SCYTHE SOUL EATER.
THE MADNESS JUST STOPPED OOZING FROM HIS SCAR...!
WELL, THAT JUST SUCKED. TALK ABOUT ANTICLI-MACTIC.
PUT A LITTLE FLAIR IN IT, FOR CRYING OUT LOUD. IT'S YOUR NAME— TRY SAYING IT WITH SOME GUSTO.

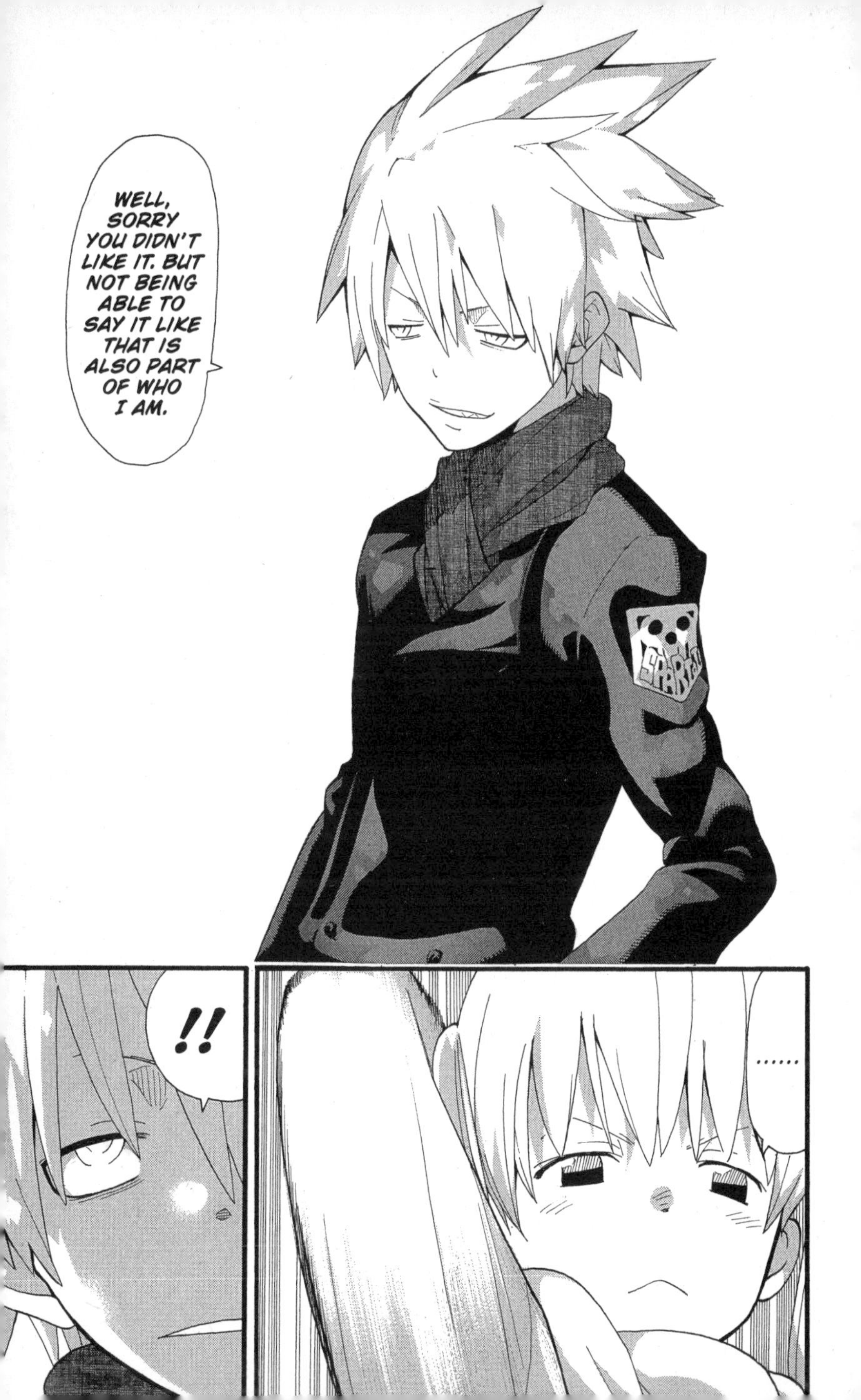
WELL, SORRY YOU DIDN'T LIKE IT. BUT NOT BEING ABLE TO SAY IT LIKE THAT IS ALSO PART OF WHO I AM.
......
!!

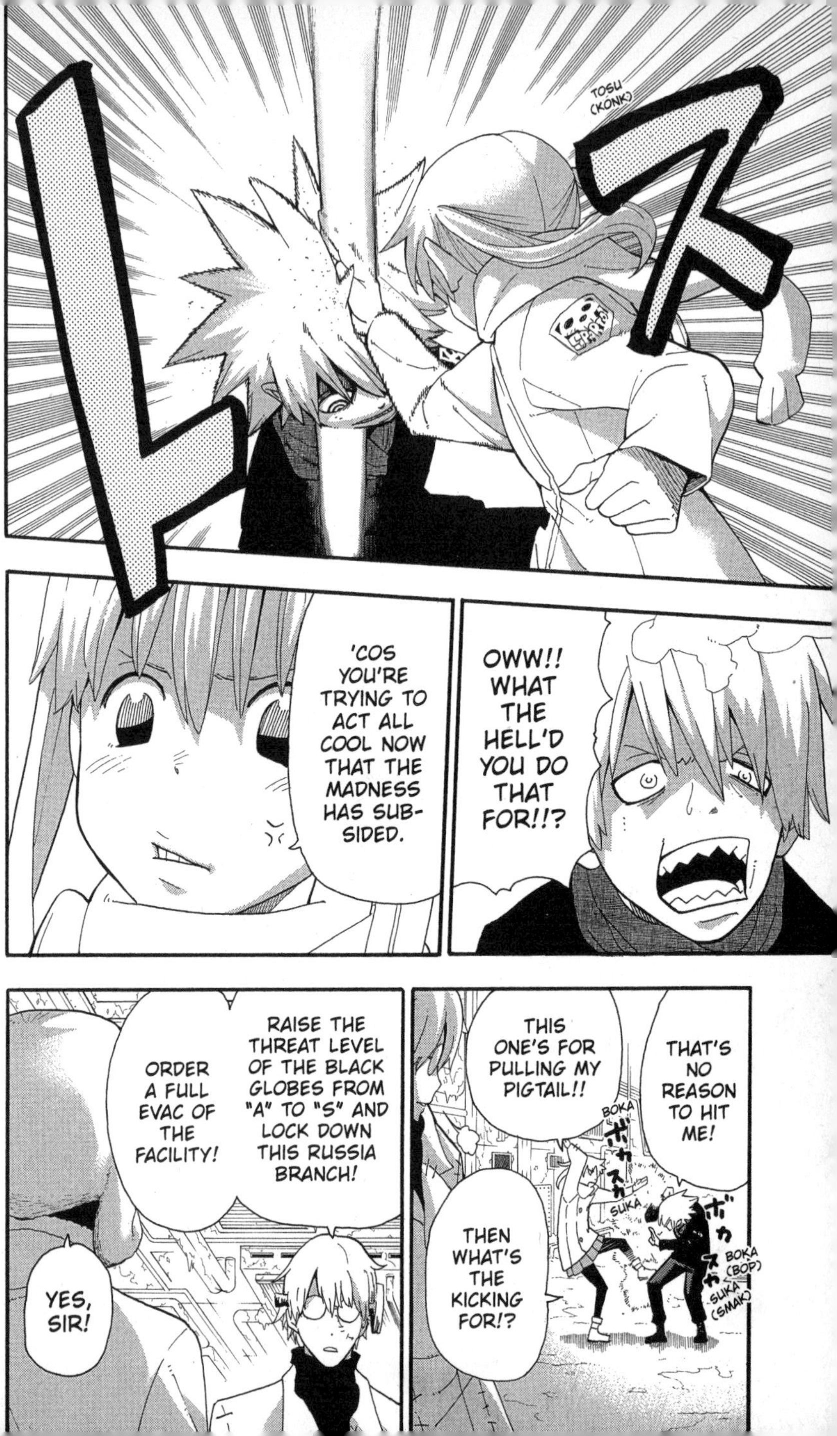
TOSU (KONK)
OWW!! WHAT THE HELL'D YOU DO THAT FOR!!?
'COS YOU'RE TRYING TO ACT ALL COOL NOW THAT THE MADNESS HAS SUB-SIDED.
THIS ONE'S FOR PULLING MY PIGTAIL!!
THAT'S NO REASON TO HIT ME!
BOKA
SUKA
THEN WHAT'S THE KICKING FOR!?
BOKA (BOP)
SUKA (SMAK)
RAISE THE THREAT LEVEL OF THE BLACK GLOBES FROM "A" TO "S" AND LOCK DOWN THIS RUSSIA BRANCH!
ORDER A FULL EVAC OF THE FACILITY!
YES, SIR!

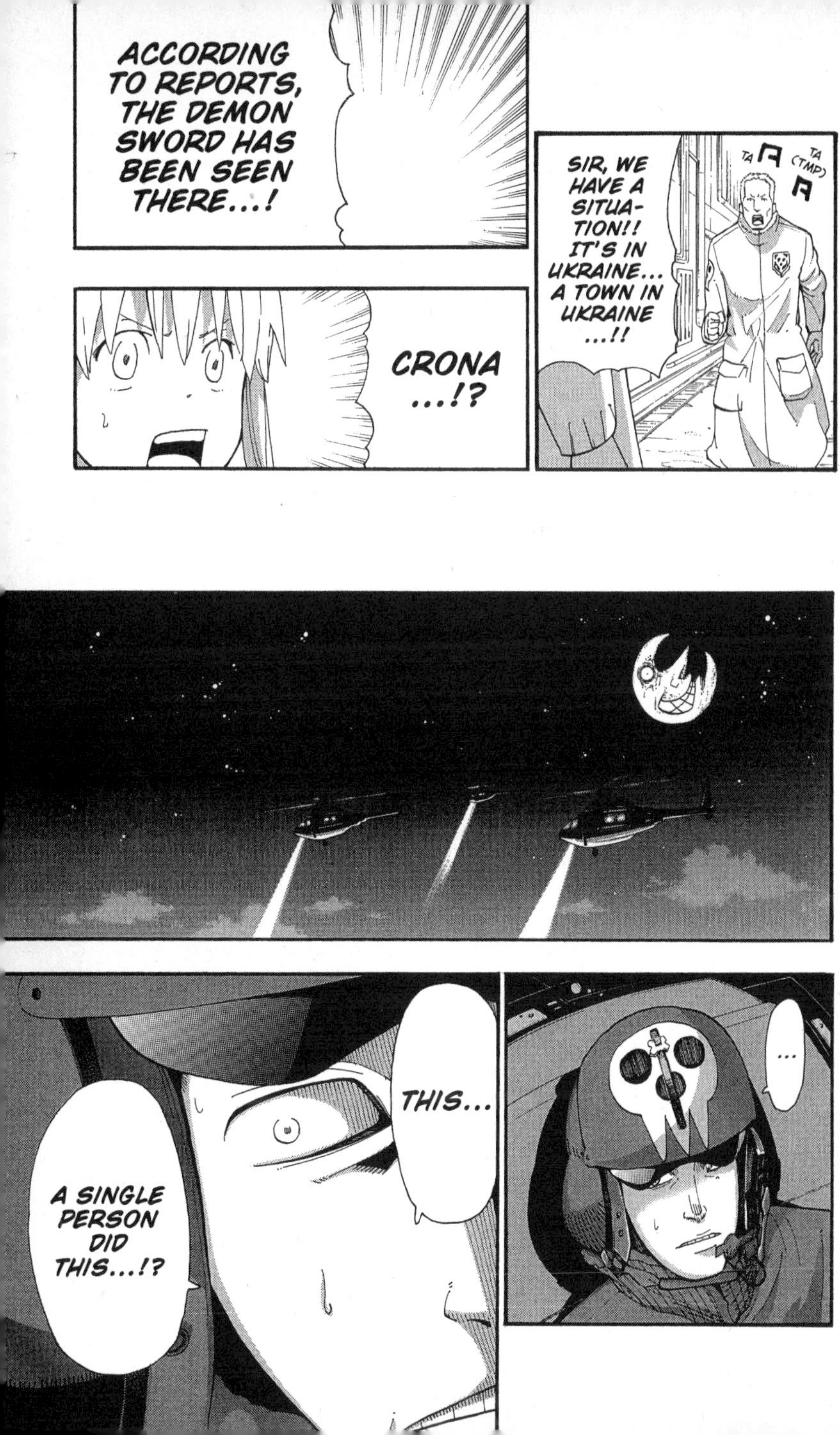
TA
TA (TMP)
SIR, WE HAVE A SITUATION!! IT'S IN UKRAINE... A TOWN IN UKRAINE...!!
ACCORDING TO REPORTS, THE DEMON SWORD HAS BEEN SEEN THERE...!
CRONA...!?
...
THIS...
A SINGLE PERSON DID THIS...!?

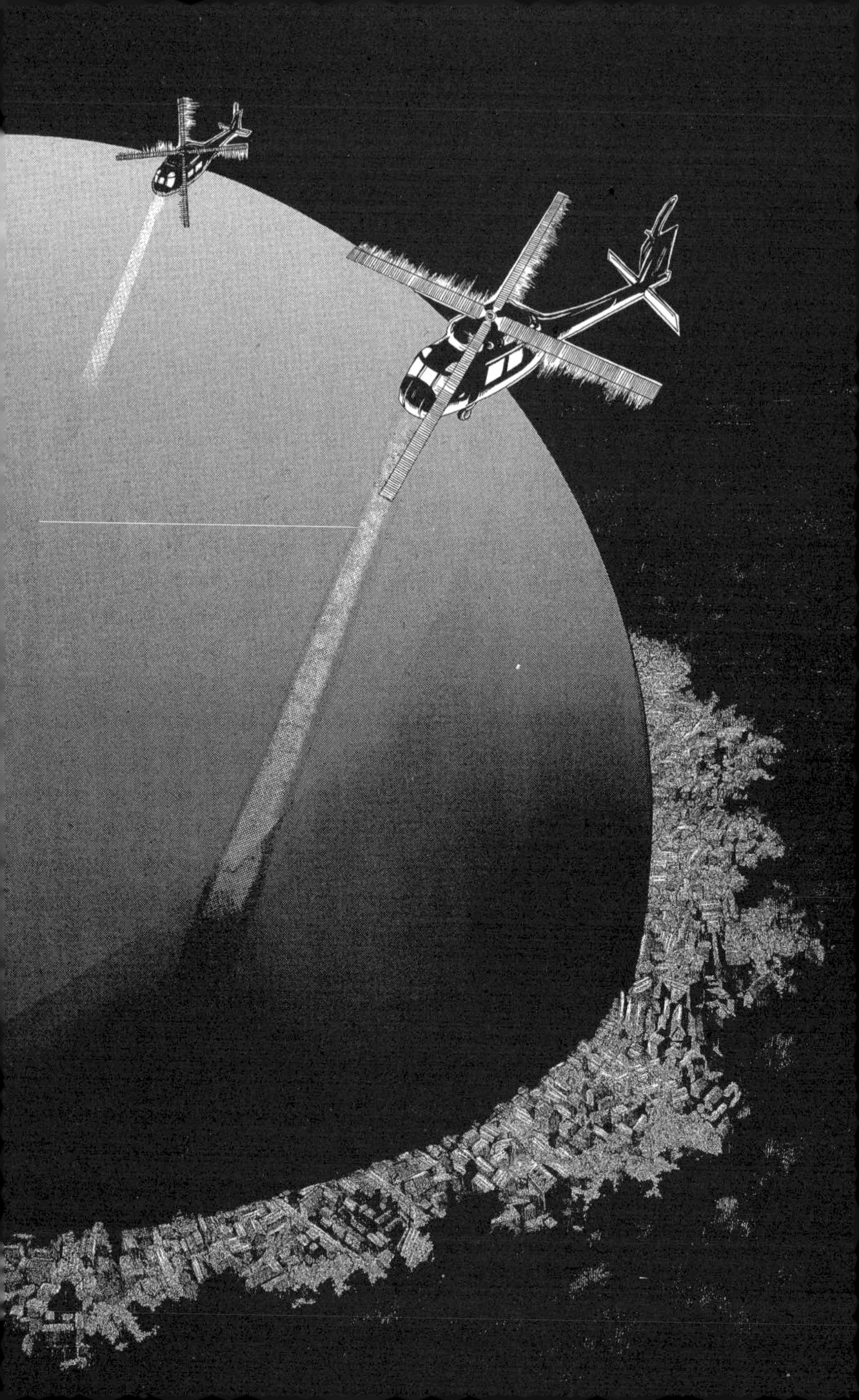

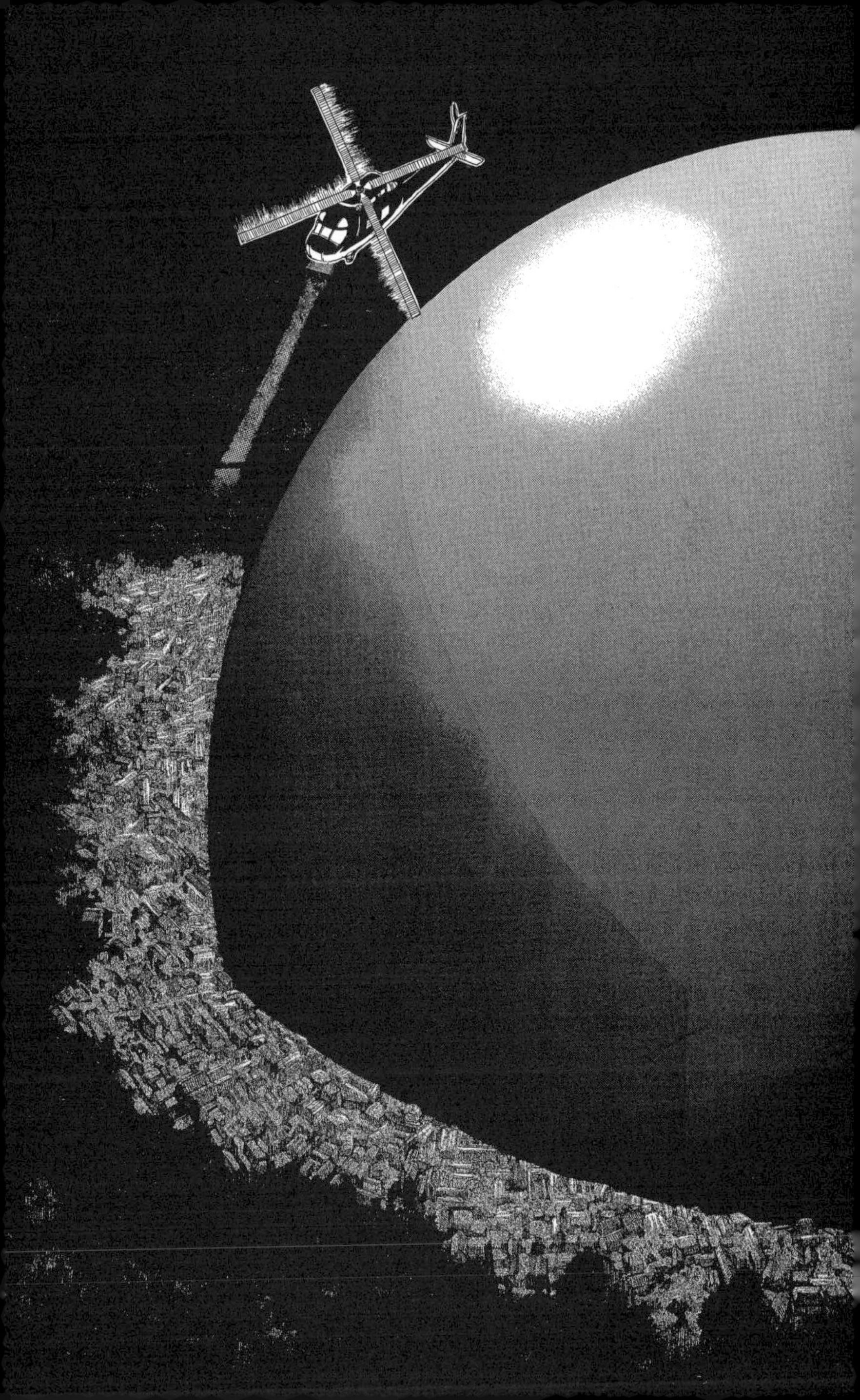

SOUL EATER

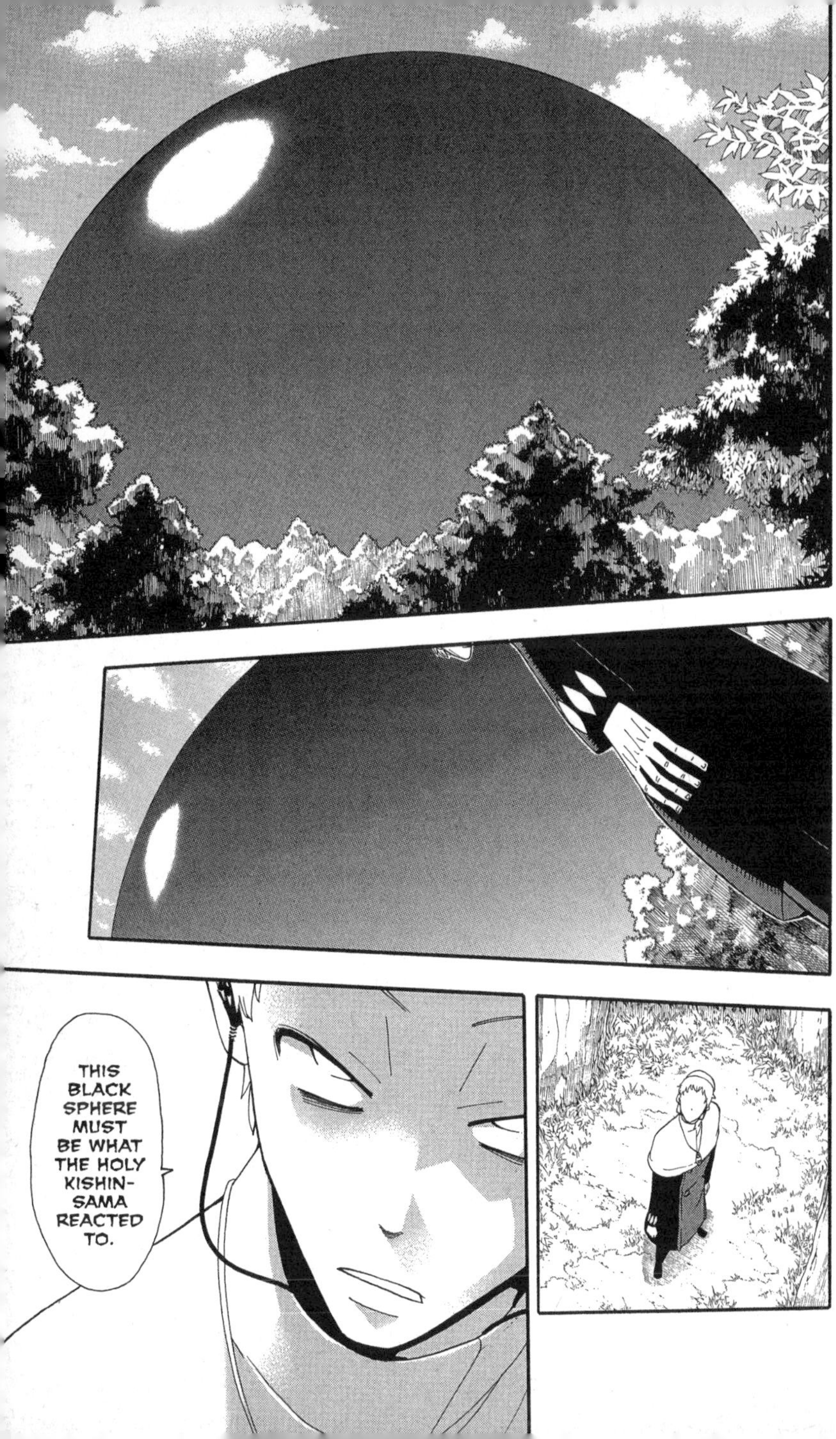
THIS BLACK SPHERE MUST BE WHAT THE HOLY KISHIN-SAMA REACTED TO.

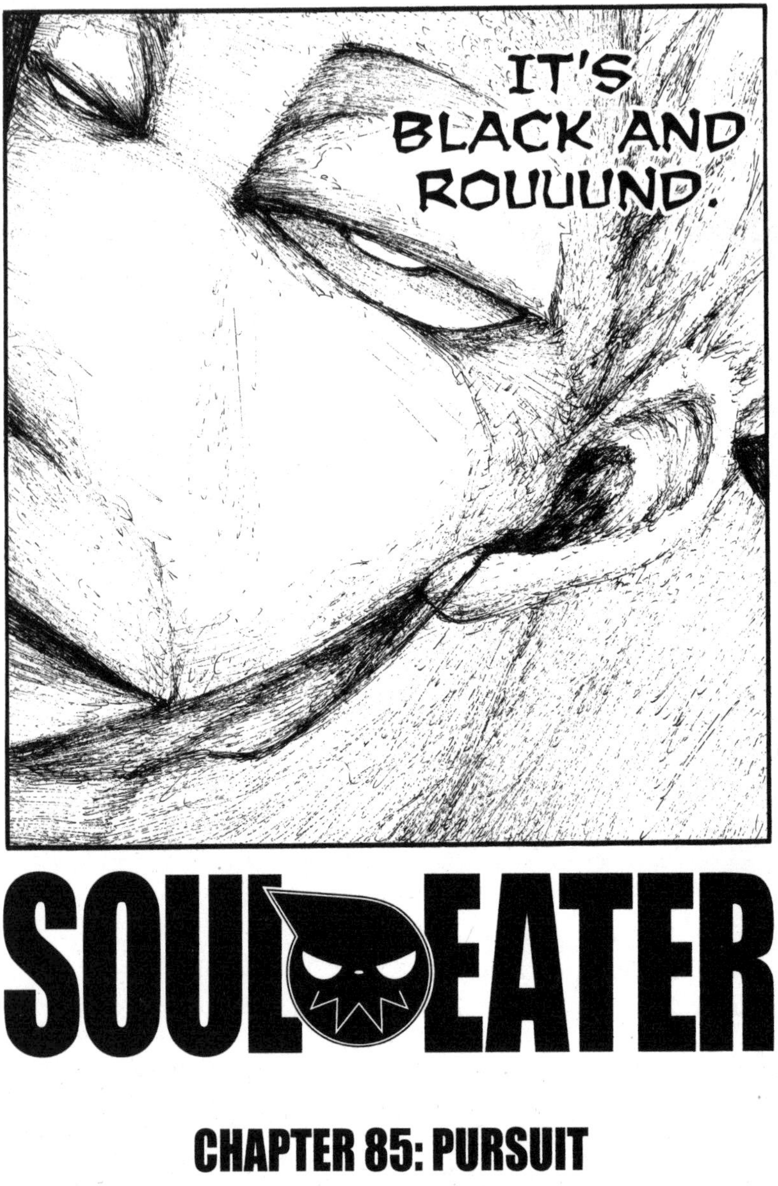
IT'S BLACK AND ROUUUND.

SOUL EATER

CHAPTER 85: PURSUIT

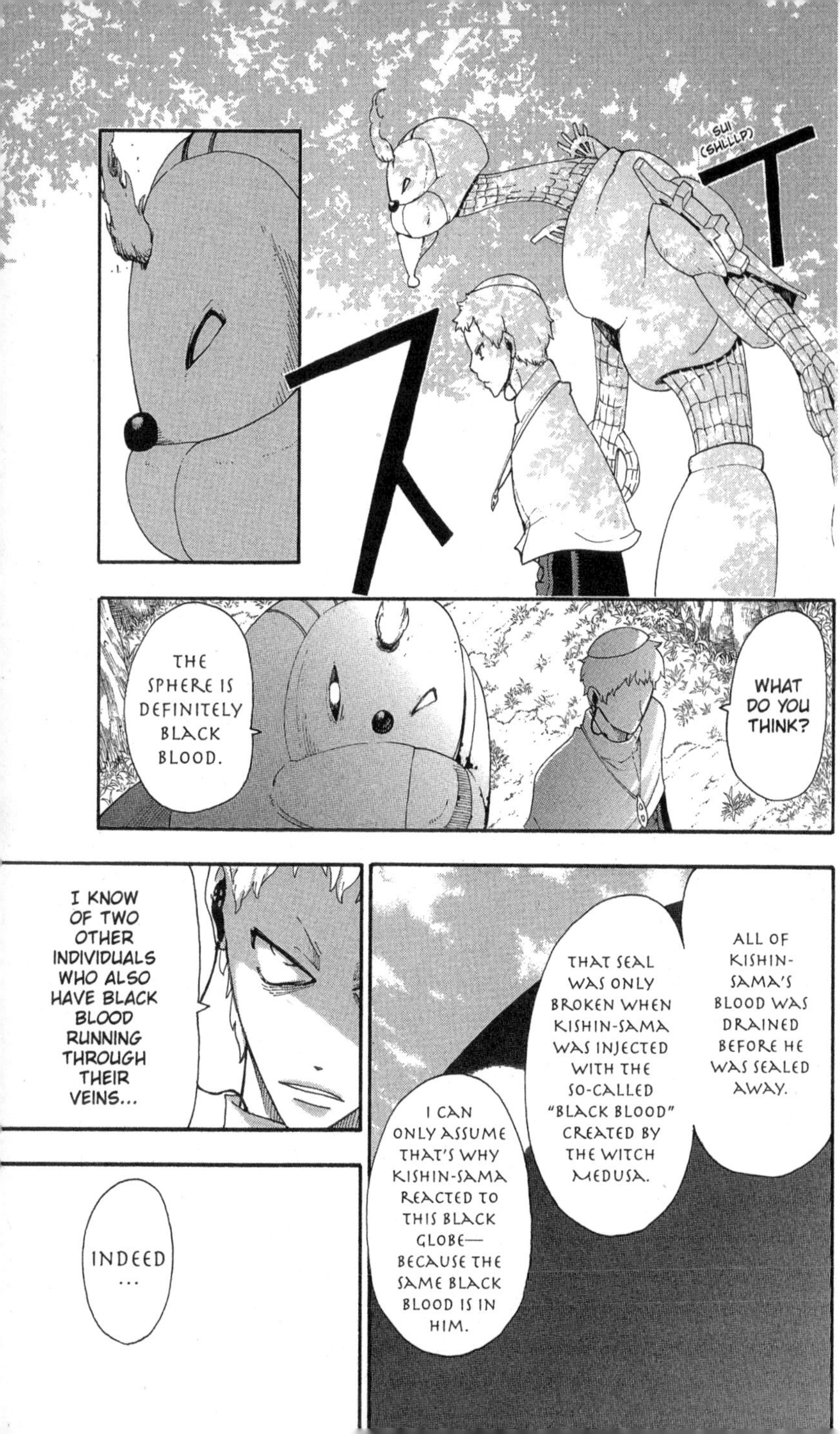
SUI (SHLLLP)
WHAT DO YOU THINK?
THE SPHERE IS DEFINITELY BLACK BLOOD.
ALL OF KISHIN-SAMA'S BLOOD WAS DRAINED BEFORE HE WAS SEALED AWAY.
THAT SEAL WAS ONLY BROKEN WHEN KISHIN-SAMA WAS INJECTED WITH THE SO-CALLED "BLACK BLOOD" CREATED BY THE WITCH MEDUSA.
I CAN ONLY ASSUME THAT'S WHY KISHIN-SAMA REACTED TO THIS BLACK GLOBE—BECAUSE THE SAME BLACK BLOOD IS IN HIM.
I KNOW OF TWO OTHER INDIVIDUALS WHO ALSO HAVE BLACK BLOOD RUNNING THROUGH THEIR VEINS...
INDEED...

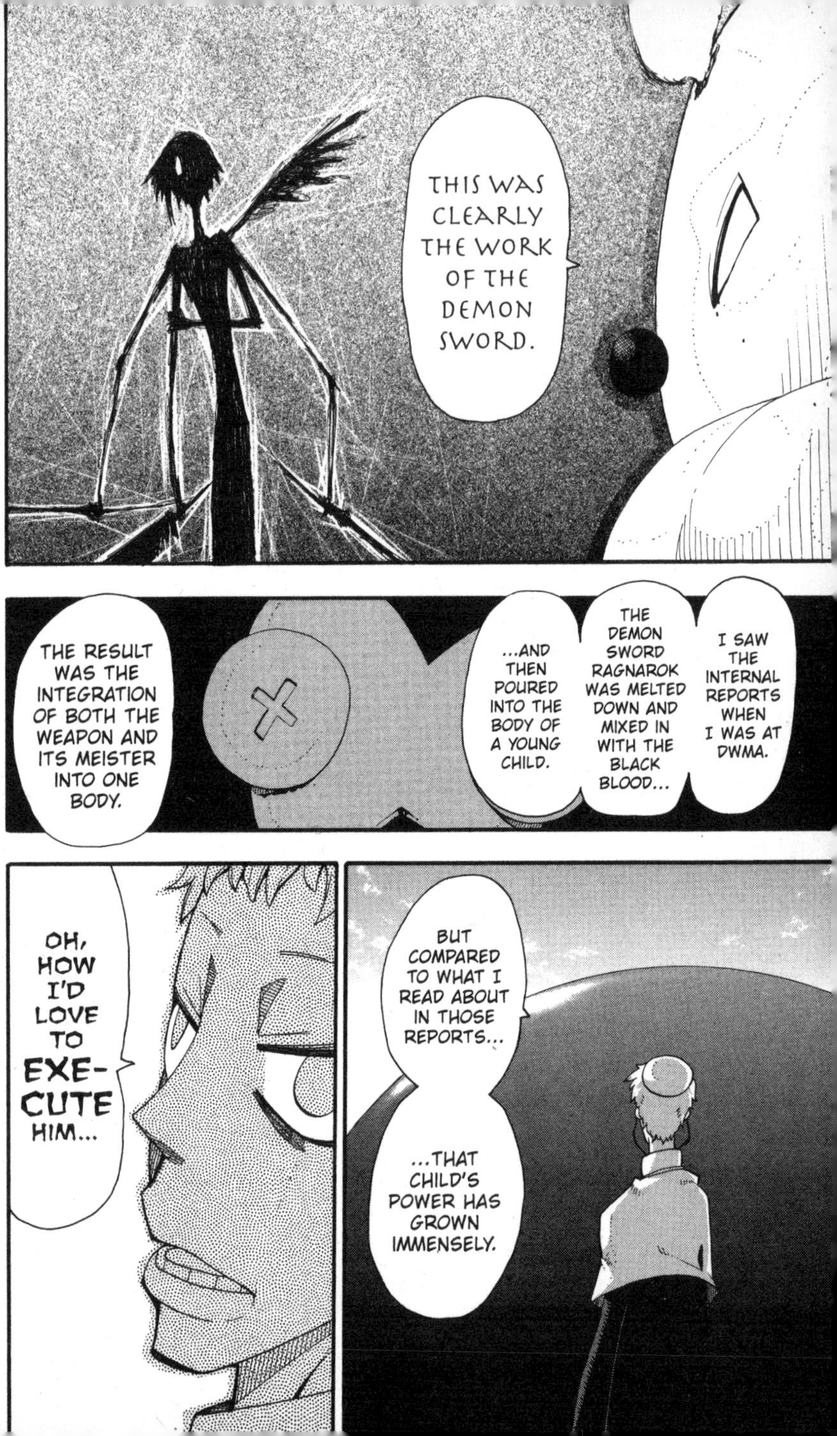
THIS WAS CLEARLY THE WORK OF THE DEMON SWORD.
I SAW THE INTERNAL REPORTS WHEN I WAS AT DWMA.
THE DEMON SWORD RAGNAROK WAS MELTED DOWN AND MIXED IN WITH THE BLACK BLOOD...
...AND THEN POURED INTO THE BODY OF A YOUNG CHILD.
THE RESULT WAS THE INTEGRATION OF BOTH THE WEAPON AND ITS MEISTER INTO ONE BODY.
BUT COMPARED TO WHAT I READ ABOUT IN THOSE REPORTS...
...THAT CHILD'S POWER HAS GROWN IMMENSELY.
OH, HOW I'D LOVE TO EXE-CUTE HIM...

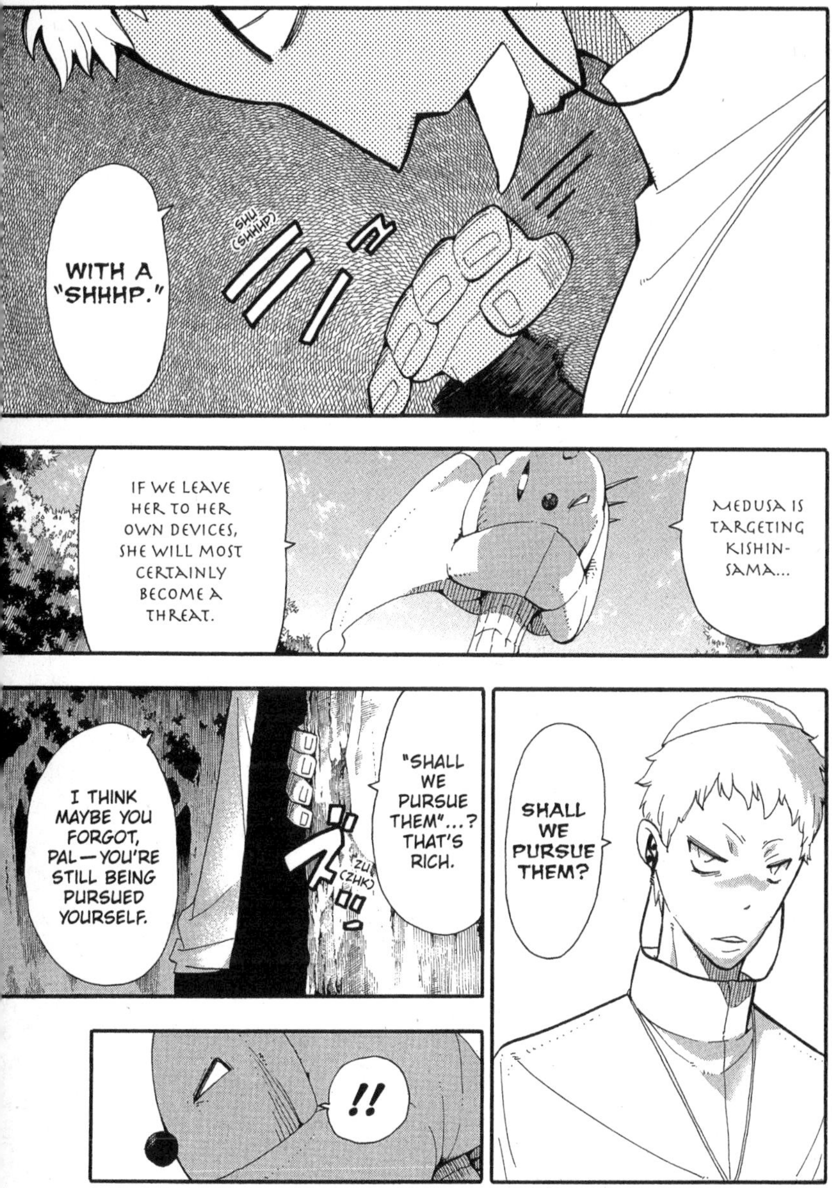
SHU (SHHHP)
WITH A "SHHHP."
MEDUSA IS TARGETING KISHIN-SAMA...
IF WE LEAVE HER TO HER OWN DEVICES, SHE WILL MOST CERTAINLY BECOME A THREAT.
SHALL WE PURSUE THEM?
"SHALL WE PURSUE THEM"...? THAT'S RICH.
ZU (ZHK)
I THINK MAYBE YOU FORGOT, PAL—YOU'RE STILL BEING PURSUED YOURSELF.
!!

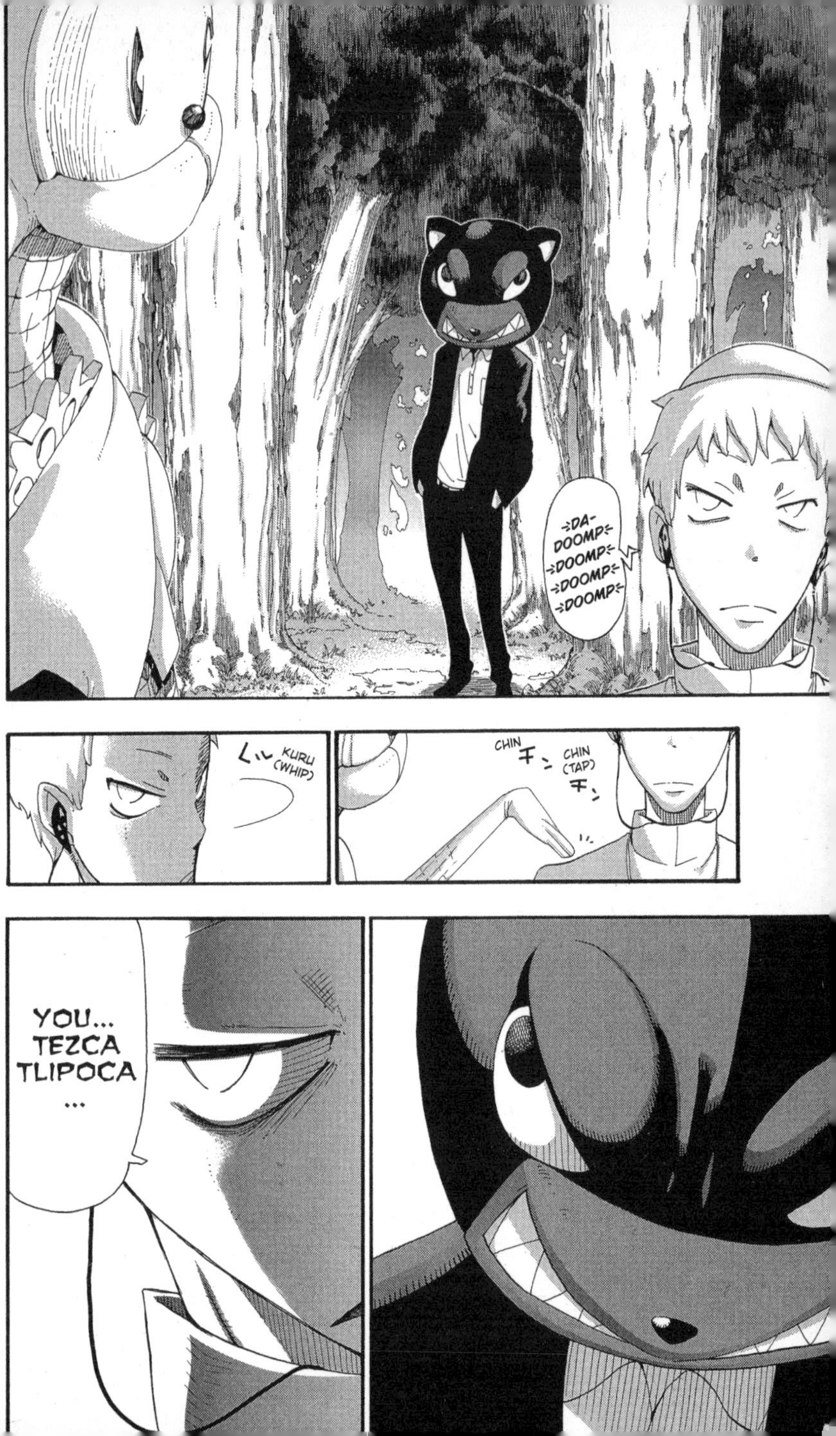

DA-DOOMP DOOMP DOOMP DOOMP
CHIN CHIN (TAP)
KURU (WHIP)
YOU... TEZCA TLIPOCA ...

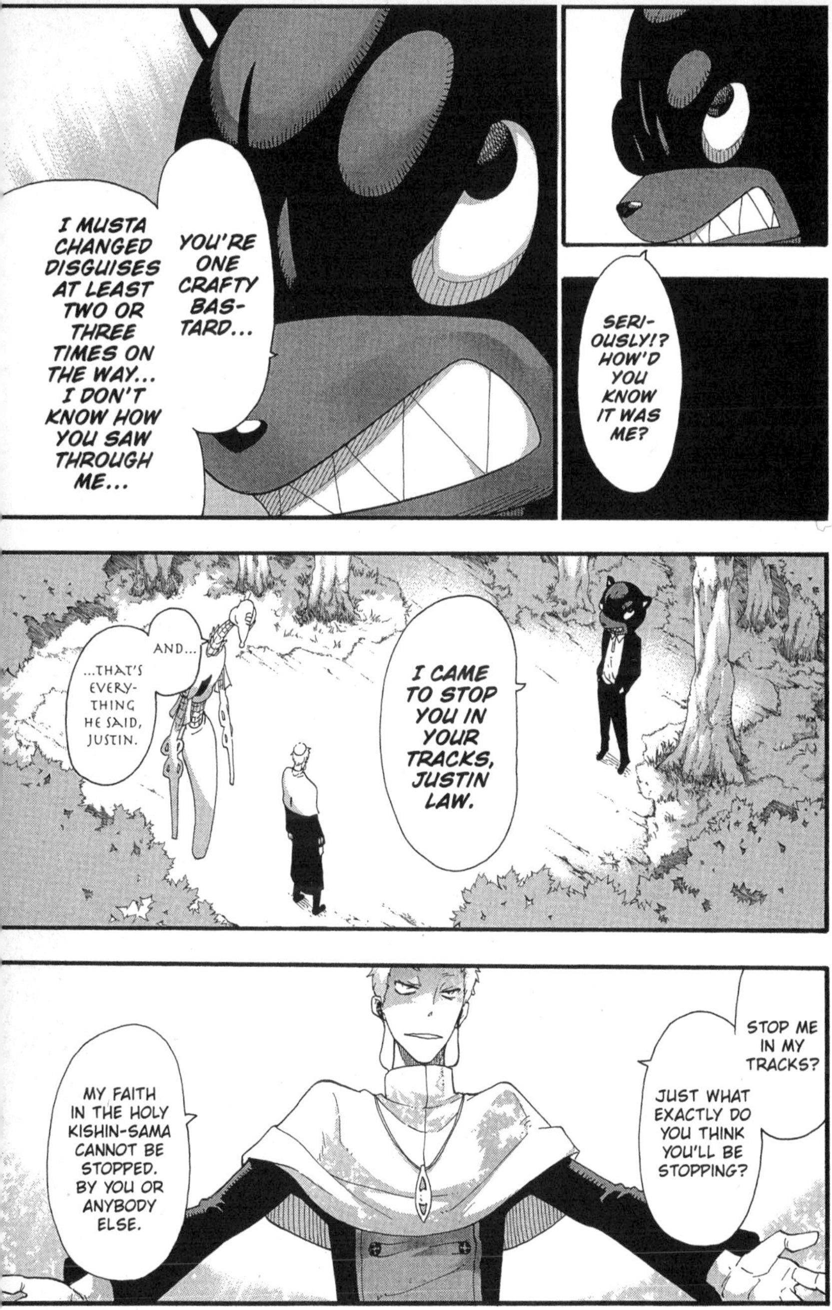
SERI-OUSLY!? HOW'D YOU KNOW IT WAS ME?
YOU'RE ONE CRAFTY BAS-TARD...
I MUSTA CHANGED DISGUISES AT LEAST TWO OR THREE TIMES ON THE WAY... I DON'T KNOW HOW YOU SAW THROUGH ME...
I CAME TO STOP YOU IN YOUR TRACKS, JUSTIN LAW.
AND...
...THAT'S EVERY-THING HE SAID, JUSTIN.
STOP ME IN MY TRACKS?
JUST WHAT EXACTLY DO YOU THINK YOU'LL BE STOPPING?
MY FAITH IN THE HOLY KISHIN-SAMA CANNOT BE STOPPED. BY YOU OR ANYBODY ELSE.

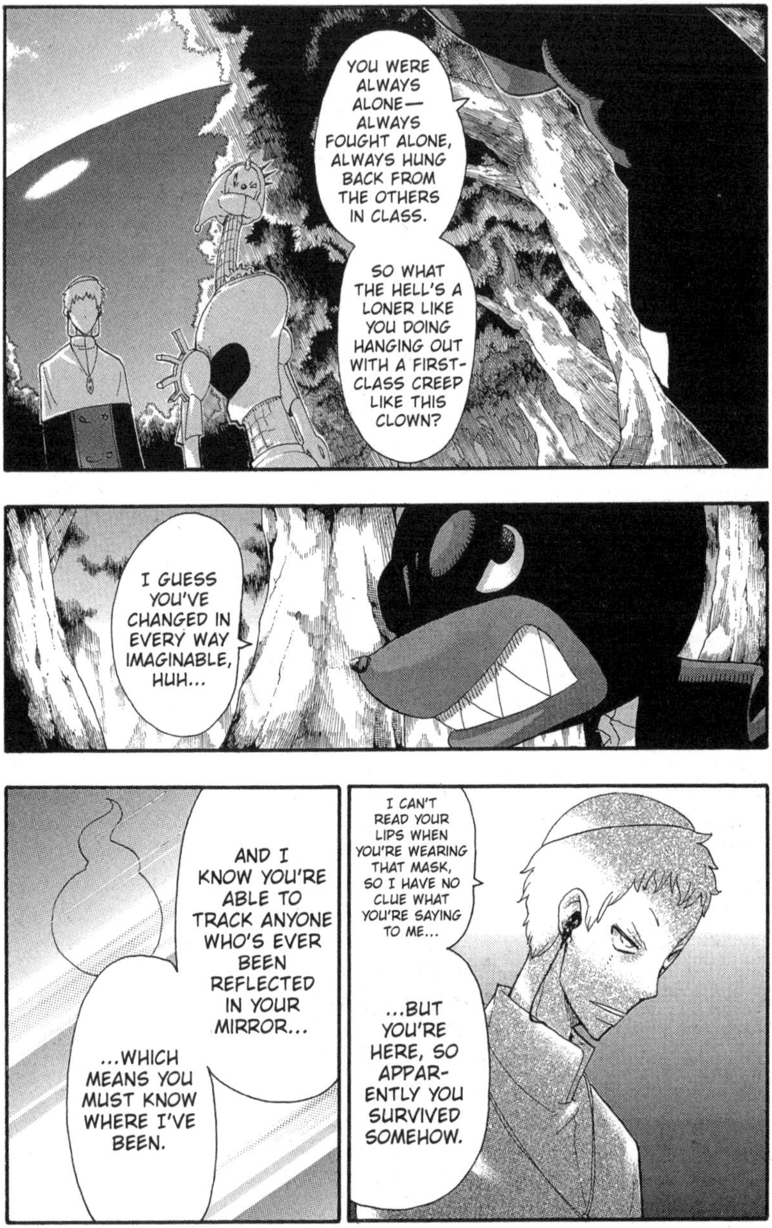
YOU WERE ALWAYS ALONE— ALWAYS FOUGHT ALONE, ALWAYS HUNG BACK FROM THE OTHERS IN CLASS.
SO WHAT THE HELL'S A LONER LIKE YOU DOING HANGING OUT WITH A FIRST-CLASS CREEP LIKE THIS CLOWN?
I GUESS YOU'VE CHANGED IN EVERY WAY IMAGINABLE, HUH...
I CAN'T READ YOUR LIPS WHEN YOU'RE WEARING THAT MASK, SO I HAVE NO CLUE WHAT YOU'RE SAYING TO ME...
...BUT YOU'RE HERE, SO APPARENTLY YOU SURVIVED SOMEHOW.
AND I KNOW YOU'RE ABLE TO TRACK ANYONE WHO'S EVER BEEN REFLECTED IN YOUR MIRROR...
...WHICH MEANS YOU MUST KNOW WHERE I'VE BEEN.

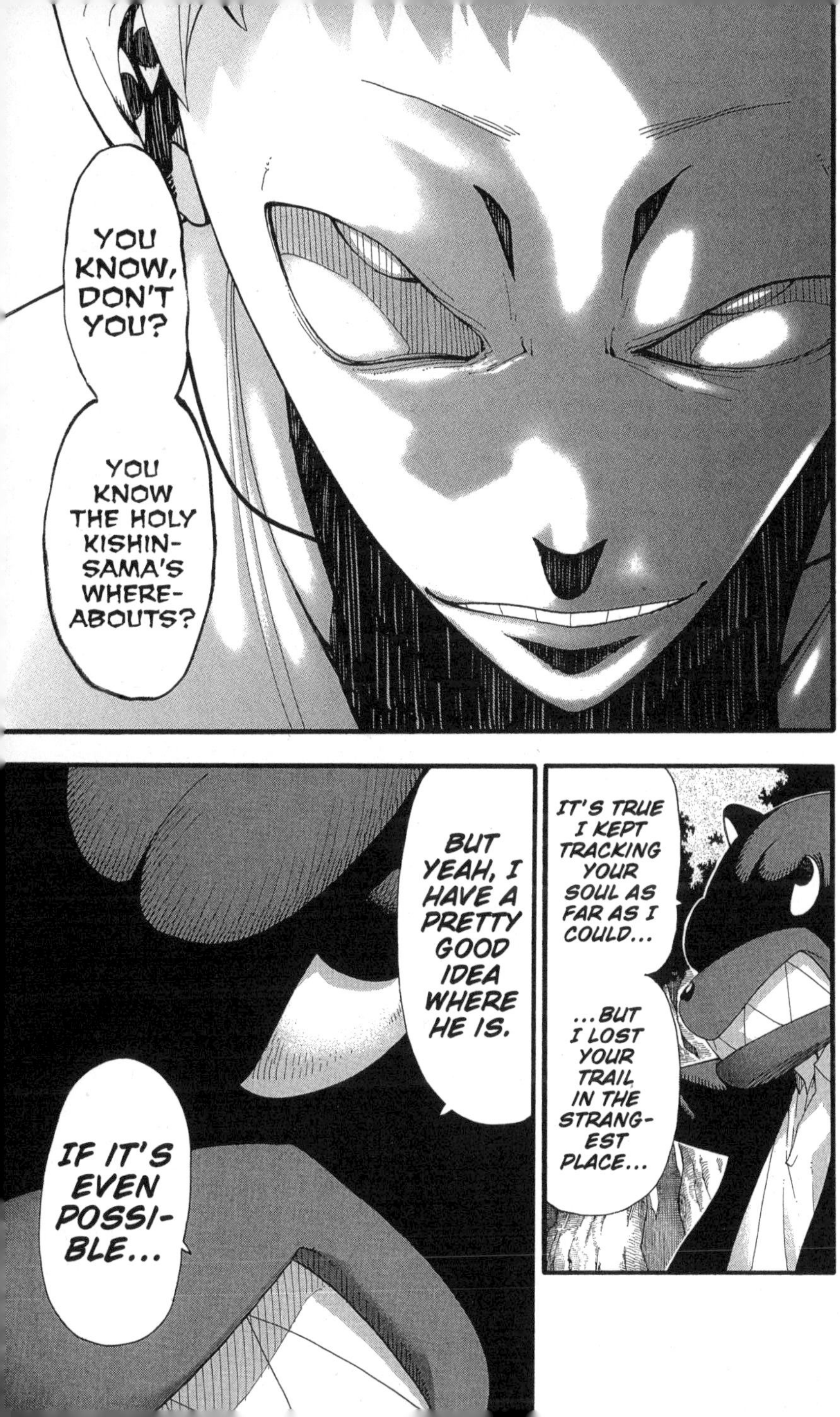
YOU KNOW, DON'T YOU?
YOU KNOW THE HOLY KISHIN-SAMA'S WHEREABOUTS?
IT'S TRUE I KEPT TRACKING YOUR SOUL AS FAR AS I COULD...
...BUT I LOST YOUR TRAIL IN THE STRANGEST PLACE...
BUT YEAH, I HAVE A PRETTY GOOD IDEA WHERE HE IS.
IF IT'S EVEN POSSIBLE...

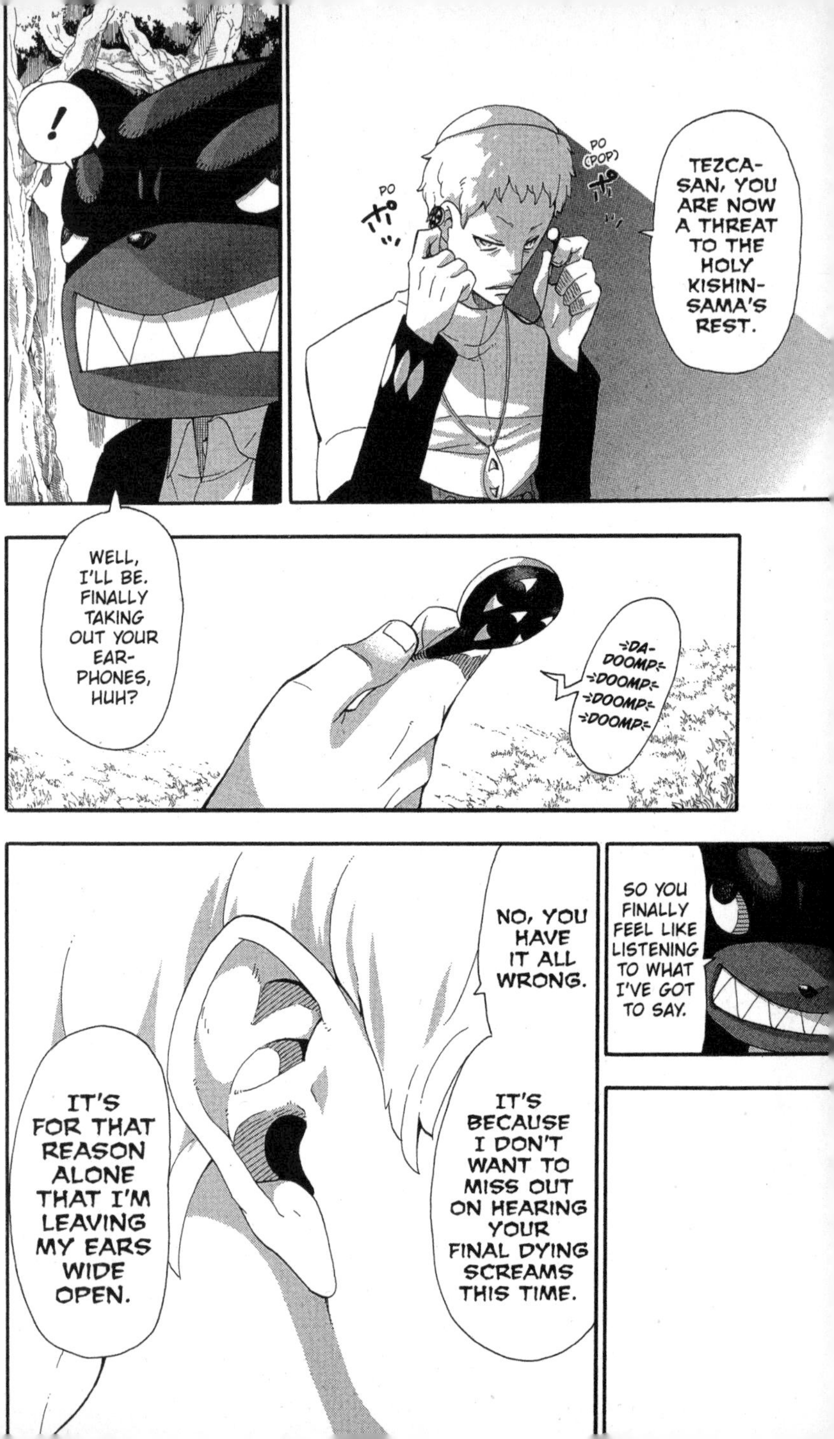
PO (POP)
PO
TEZCA-SAN, YOU ARE NOW A THREAT TO THE HOLY KISHIN-SAMA'S REST.
!
WELL, I'LL BE. FINALLY TAKING OUT YOUR EAR-PHONES, HUH?
DA-DOOMP DOOMP DOOMP DOOMP
SO YOU FINALLY FEEL LIKE LISTENING TO WHAT I'VE GOT TO SAY.
NO, YOU HAVE IT ALL WRONG.
IT'S BECAUSE I DON'T WANT TO MISS OUT ON HEARING YOUR FINAL DYING SCREAMS THIS TIME.
IT'S FOR THAT REASON ALONE THAT I'M LEAVING MY EARS WIDE OPEN.

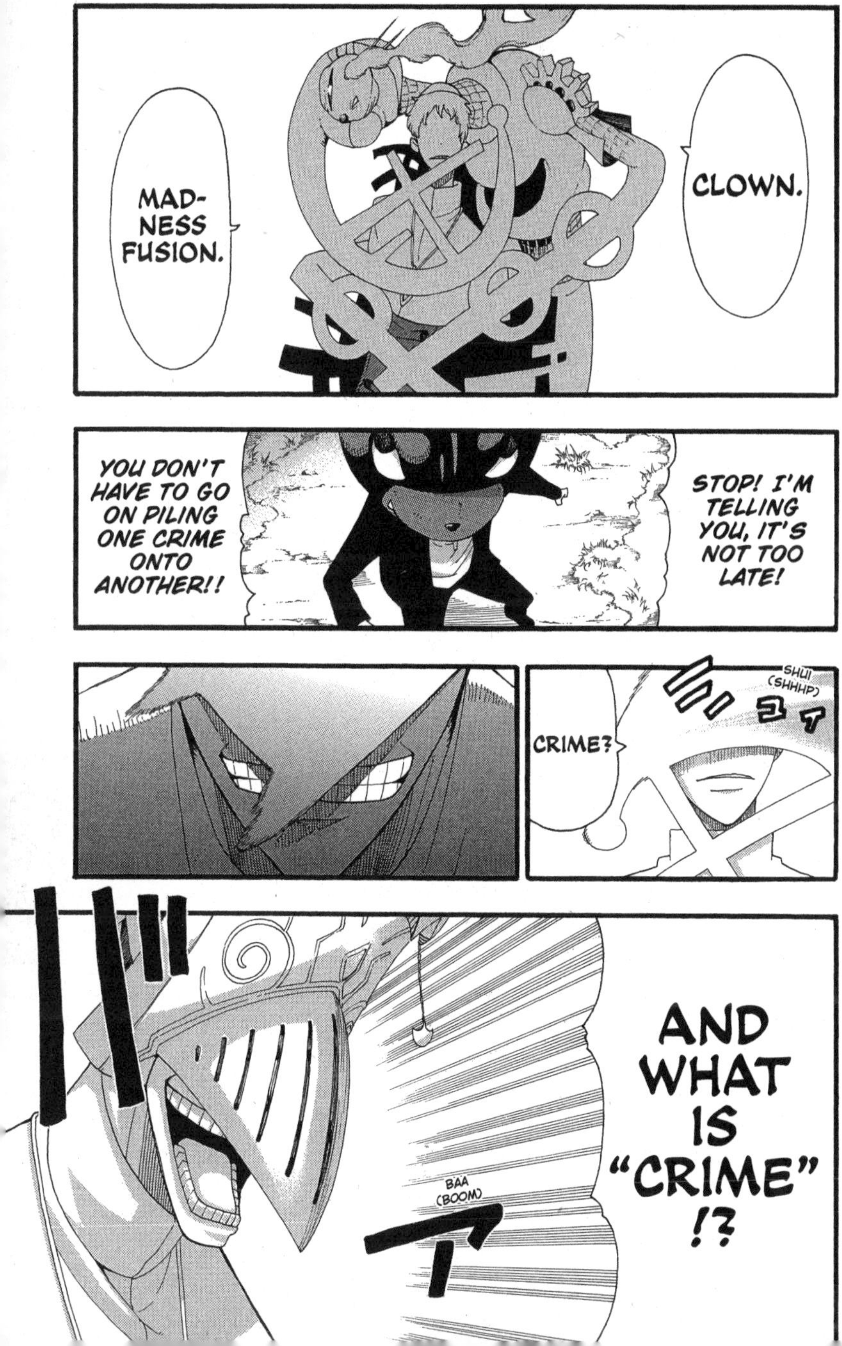
CLOWN.
MAD-NESS FUSION.
STOP! I'M TELLING YOU, IT'S NOT TOO LATE!
YOU DON'T HAVE TO GO ON PILING ONE CRIME ONTO ANOTHER!!
SHUI (SHHHP)
CRIME?
AND WHAT IS "CRIME"!?
BAA (BOOM)

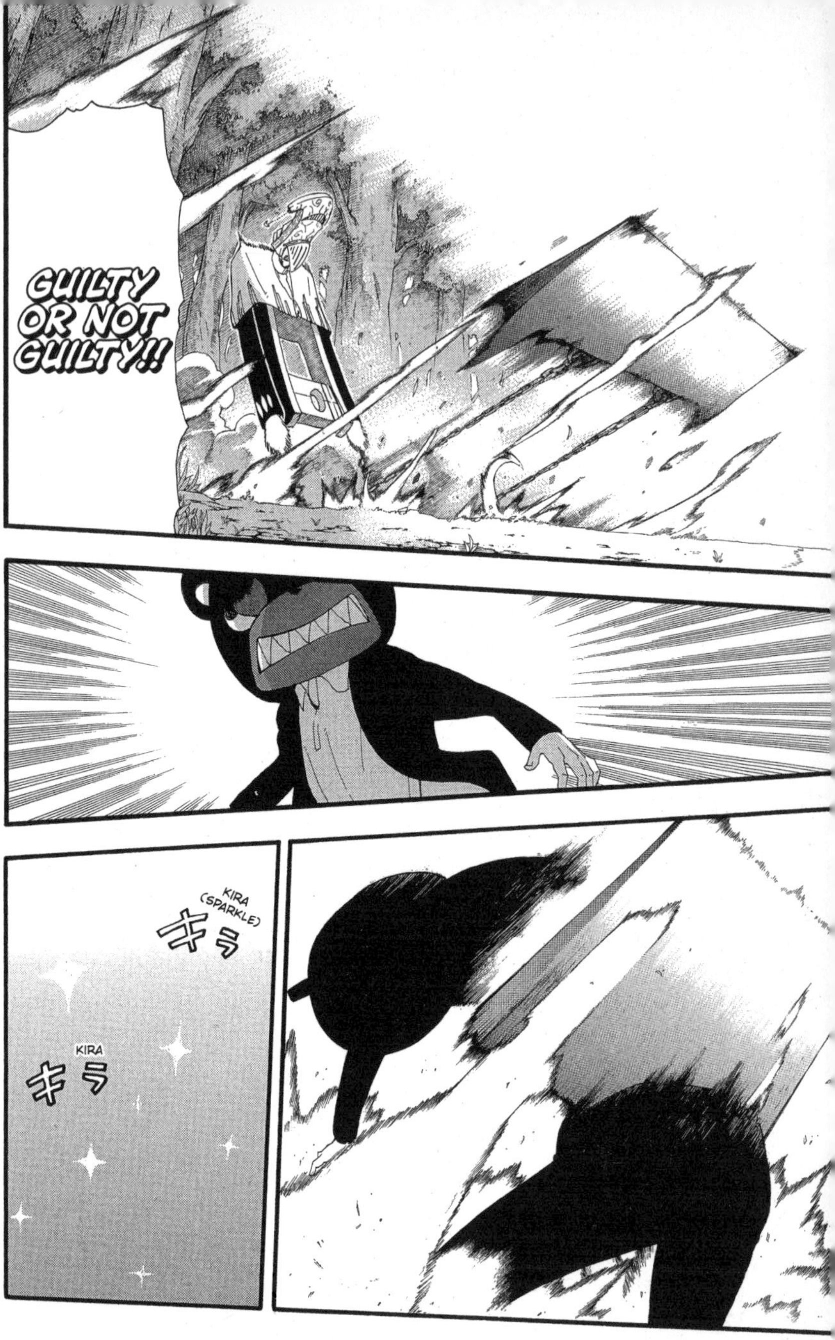
GUILTY OR NOT GUILTY!!
KIRA (SPARKLE)
キラ
KIRA
キラ

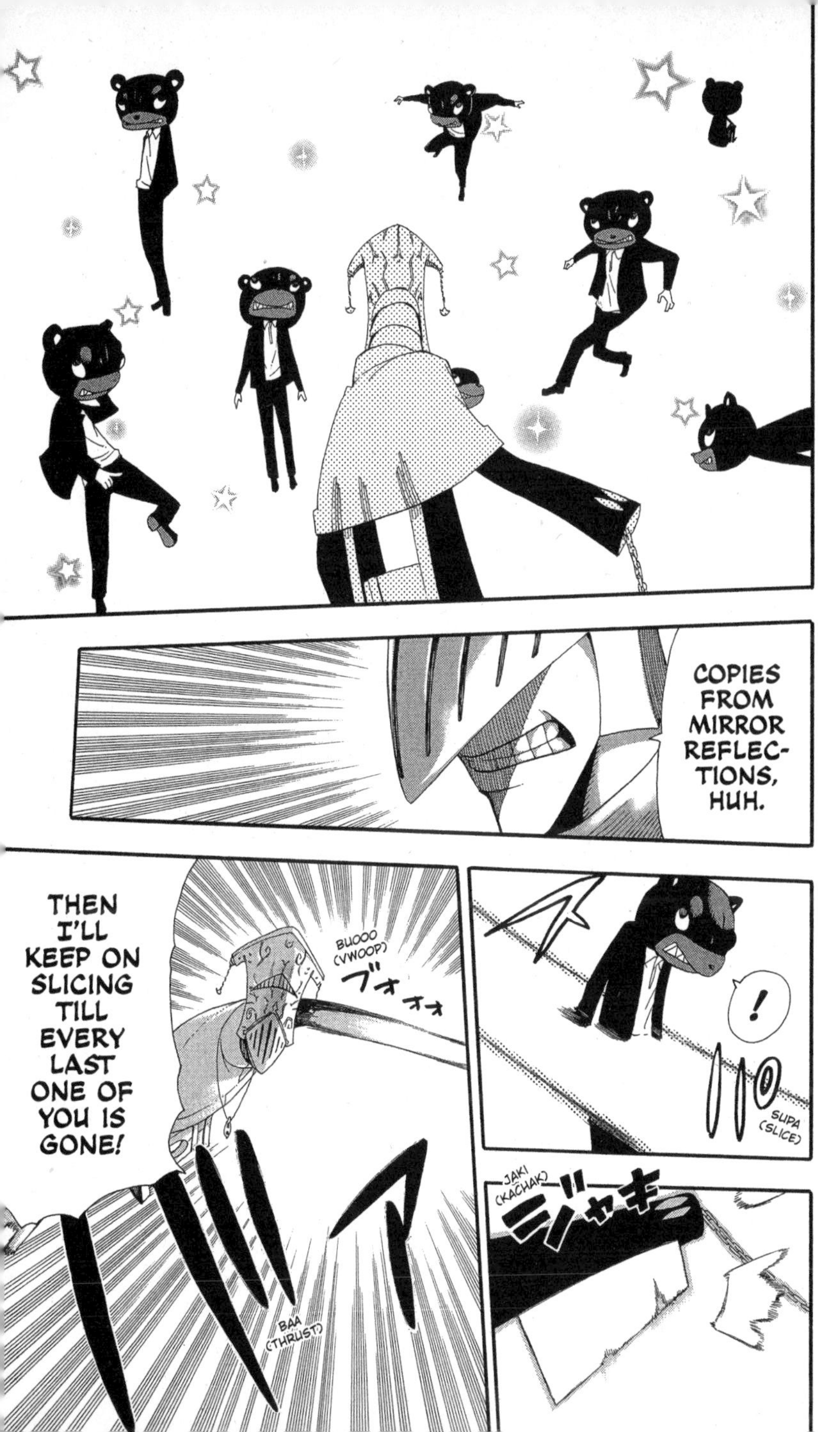
COPIES FROM MIRROR REFLECTIONS, HUH.
!
SUPA (SLICE)
JAKI (KACHAK)
ジャキ
THEN I'LL KEEP ON SLICING TILL EVERY LAST ONE OF YOU IS GONE!
BUOOO (VWOOP)
ブォォォ
BAA (THRUST)

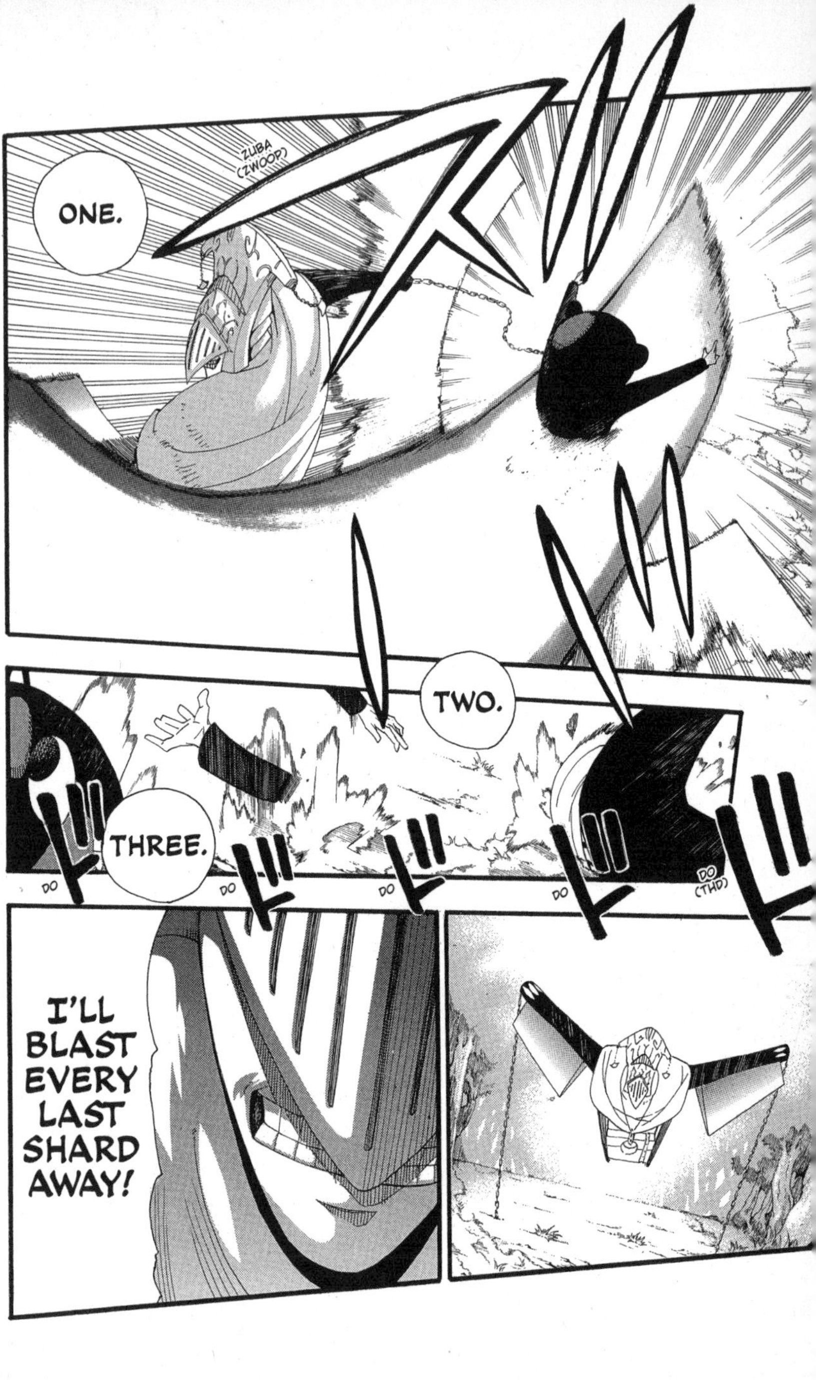
ZUBA (ZWOOP)
ONE.
TWO.
THREE.
DO (THD)
DO
DO
DO
DO
I'LL BLAST EVERY LAST SHARD AWAY!

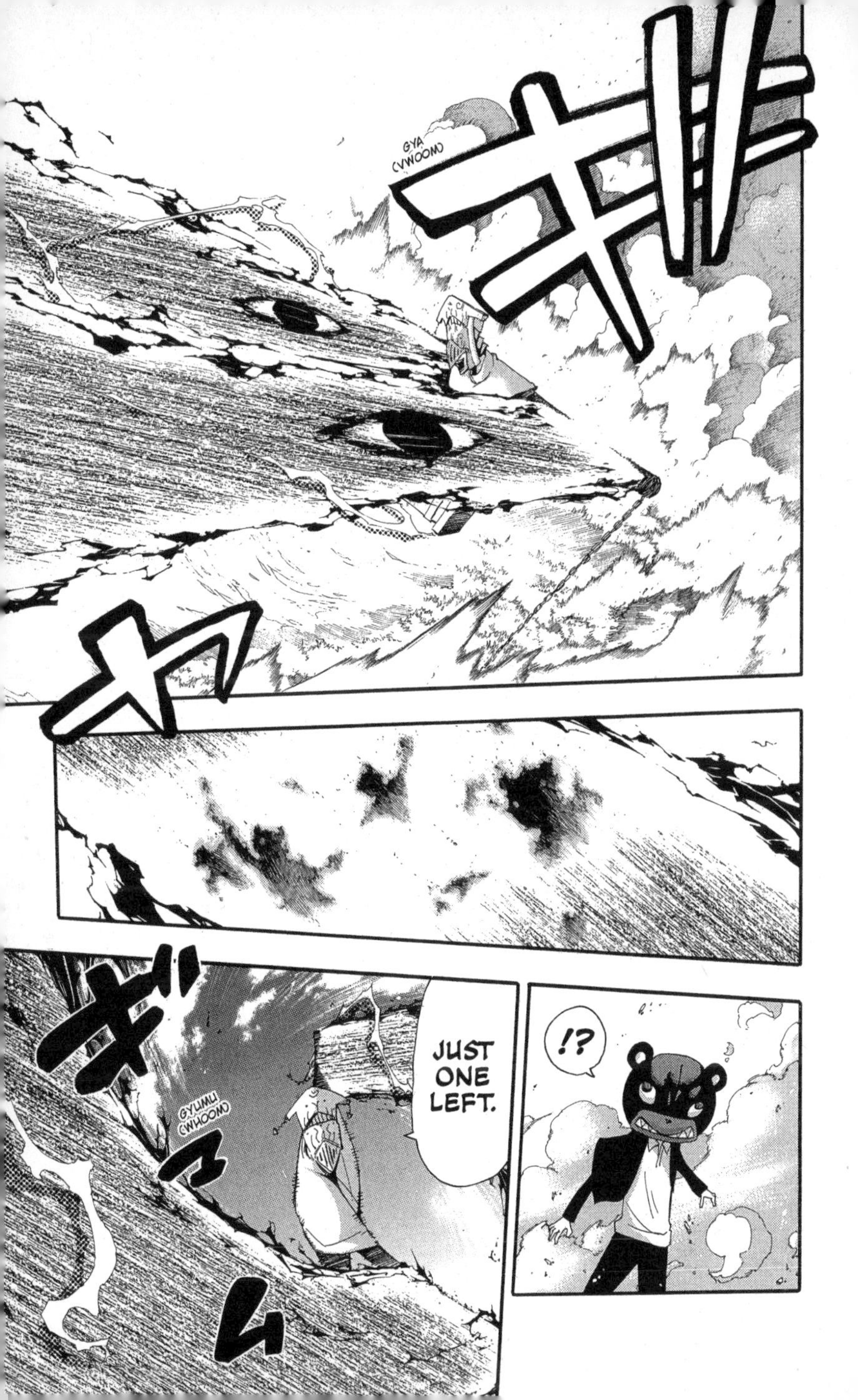
GYA (VWOOM)
JUST ONE LEFT.
!?
GYUMU (WHOOM)

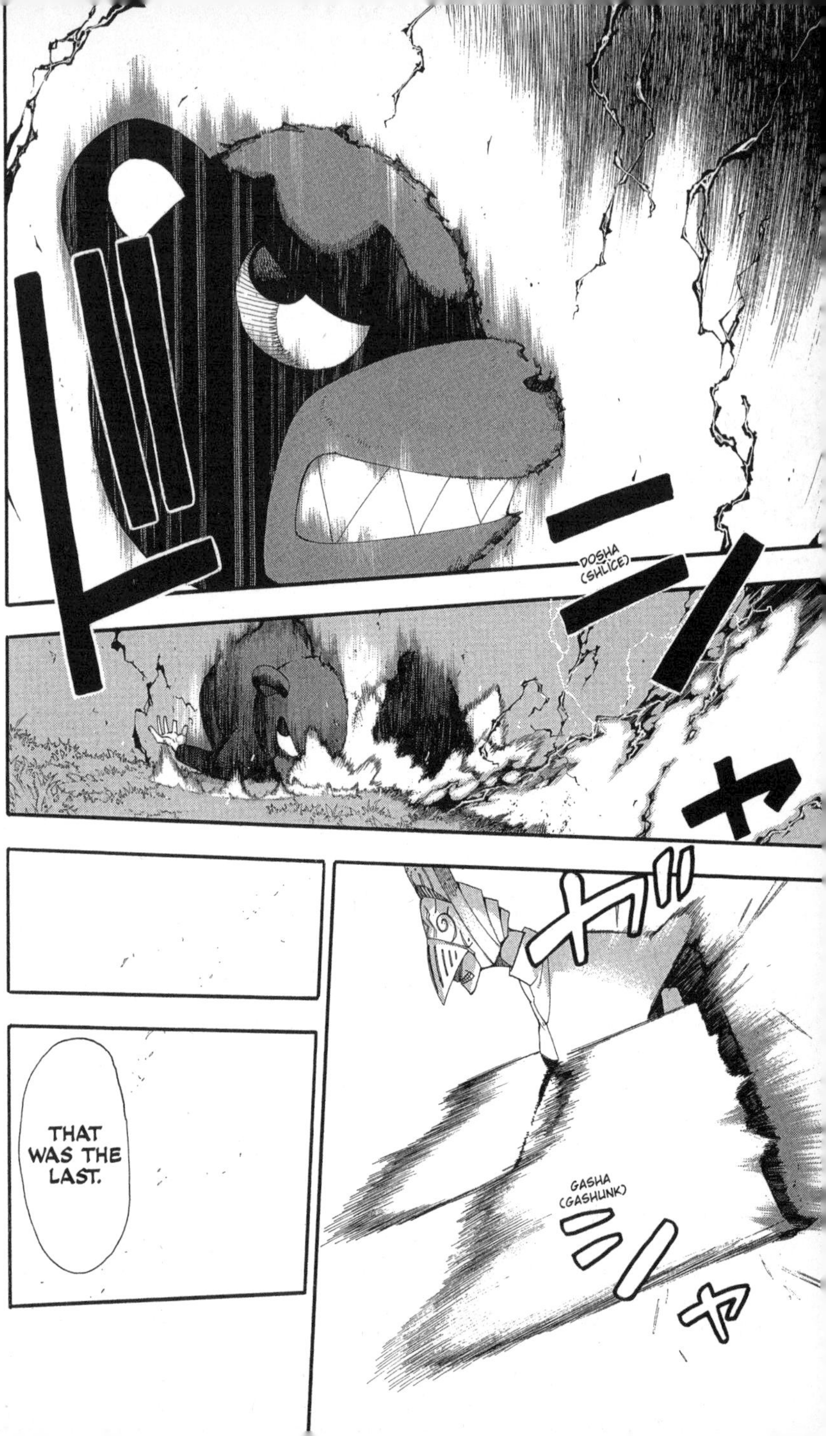
DOSHA
(SHLICE)
GASHA
(GASHUNK)
THAT WAS THE LAST.

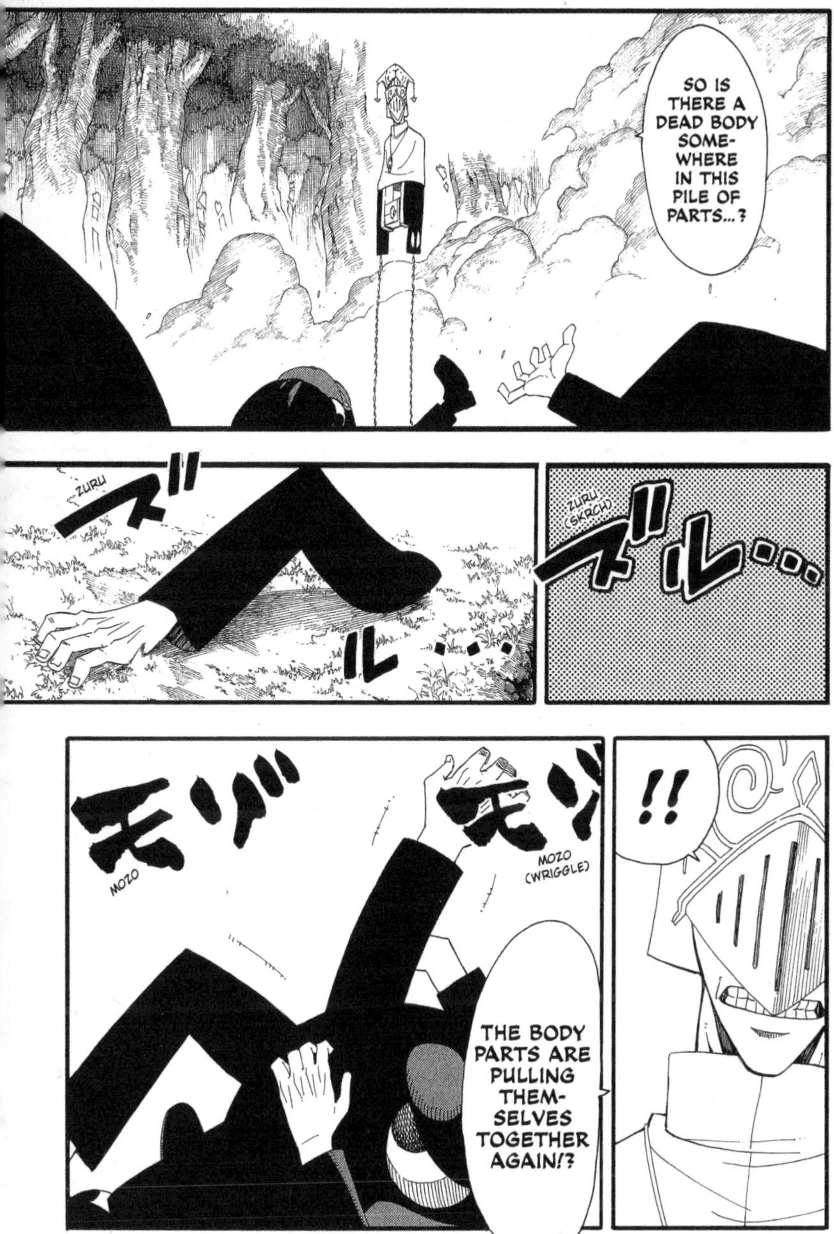
SO IS THERE A DEAD BODY SOME-WHERE IN THIS PILE OF PARTS...?
ZURU (SKRCH)
ズル…
ZURU
ズル…
!!
MOZO (WRIGGLE)
MOZO
モゾモゾ
THE BODY PARTS ARE PULLING THEM-SELVES TOGETHER AGAIN!?

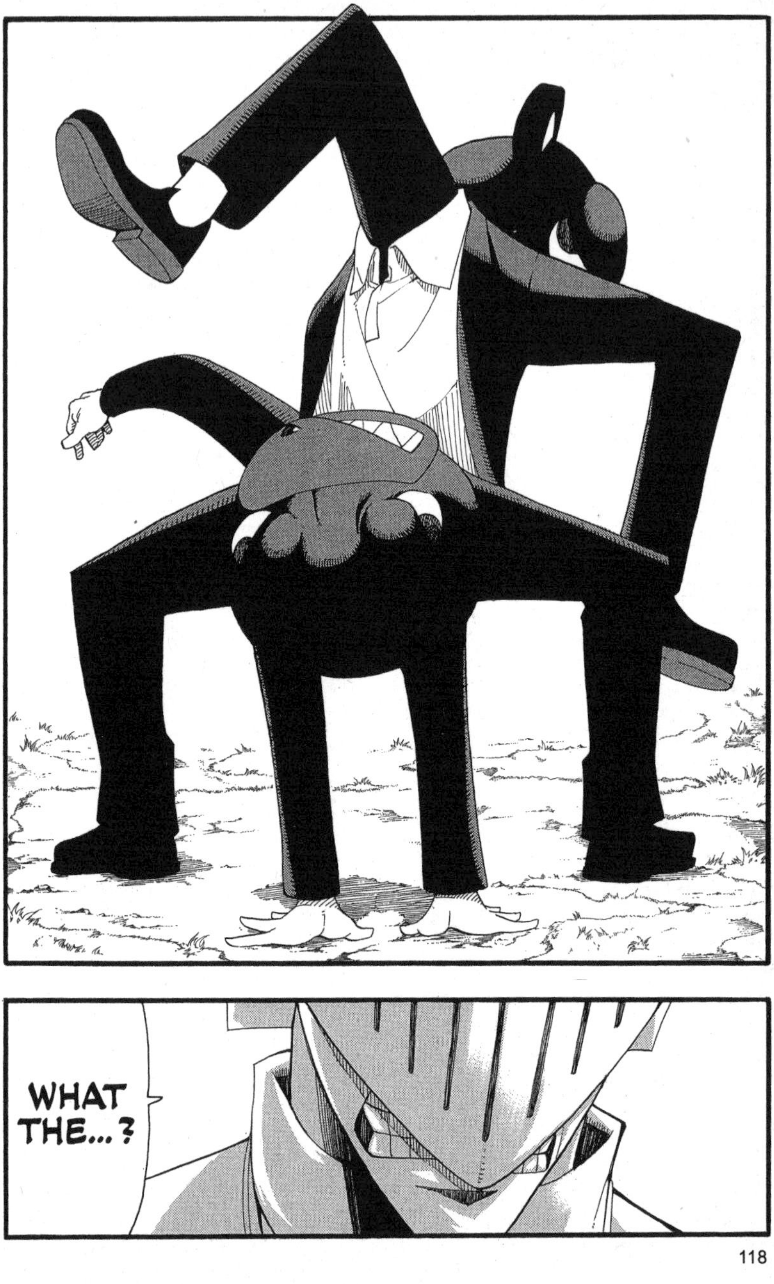
WHAT THE...?

SOUL EATER

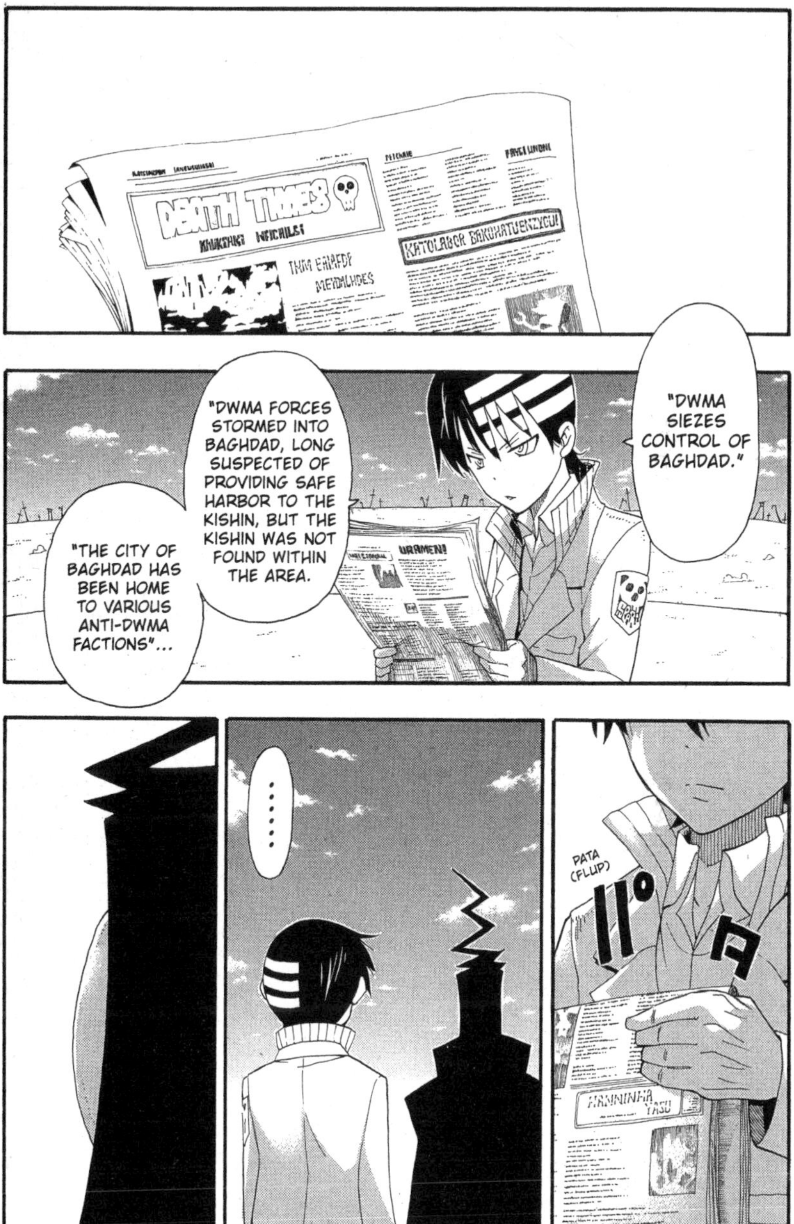
DEATH TIMES
"DWMA SIEZES CONTROL OF BAGHDAD."
"DWMA FORCES STORMED INTO BAGHDAD, LONG SUSPECTED OF PROVIDING SAFE HARBOR TO THE KISHIN, BUT THE KISHIN WAS NOT FOUND WITHIN THE AREA.
"THE CITY OF BAGHDAD HAS BEEN HOME TO VARIOUS ANTI-DWMA FACTIONS"...
PATA (FLUP)
......

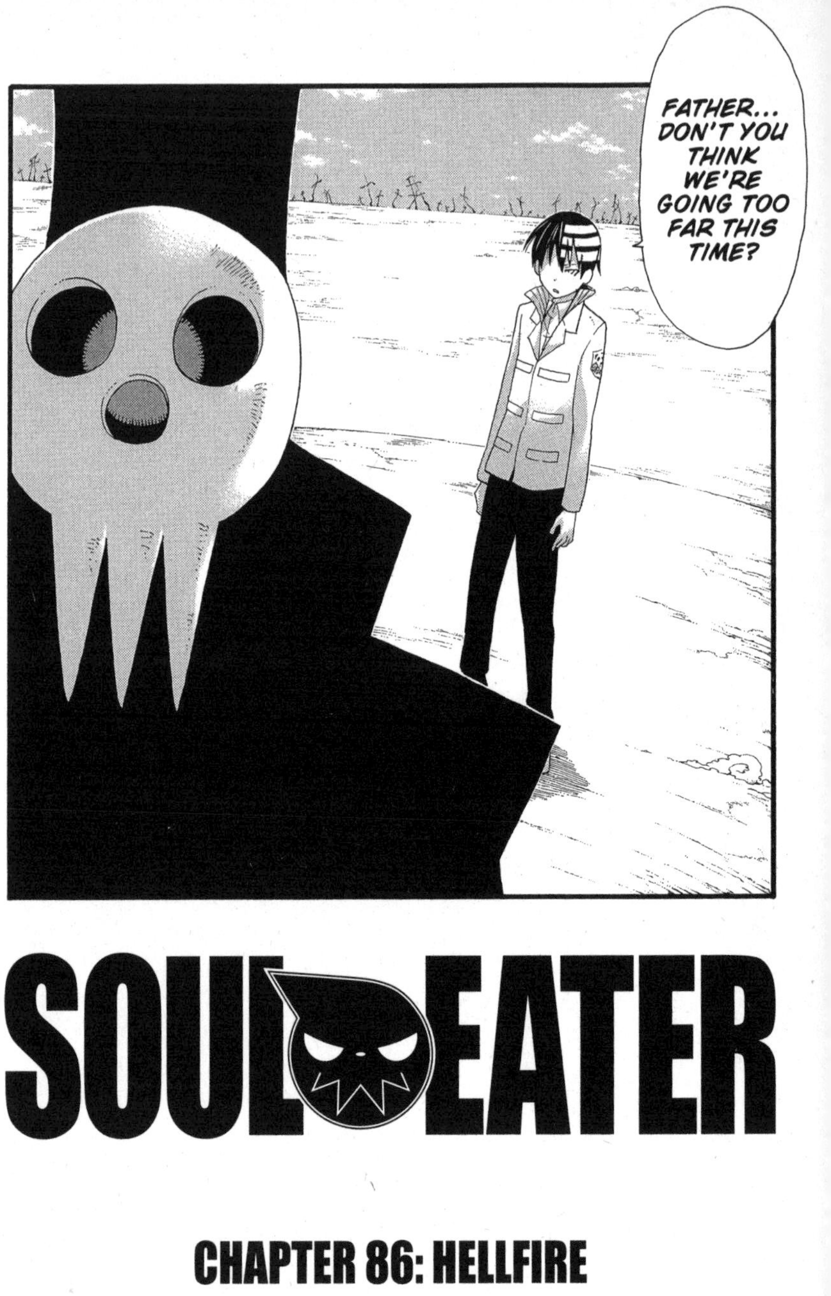
FATHER... DON'T YOU THINK WE'RE GOING TOO FAR THIS TIME?

SOUL EATER

CHAPTER 86: HELLFIRE

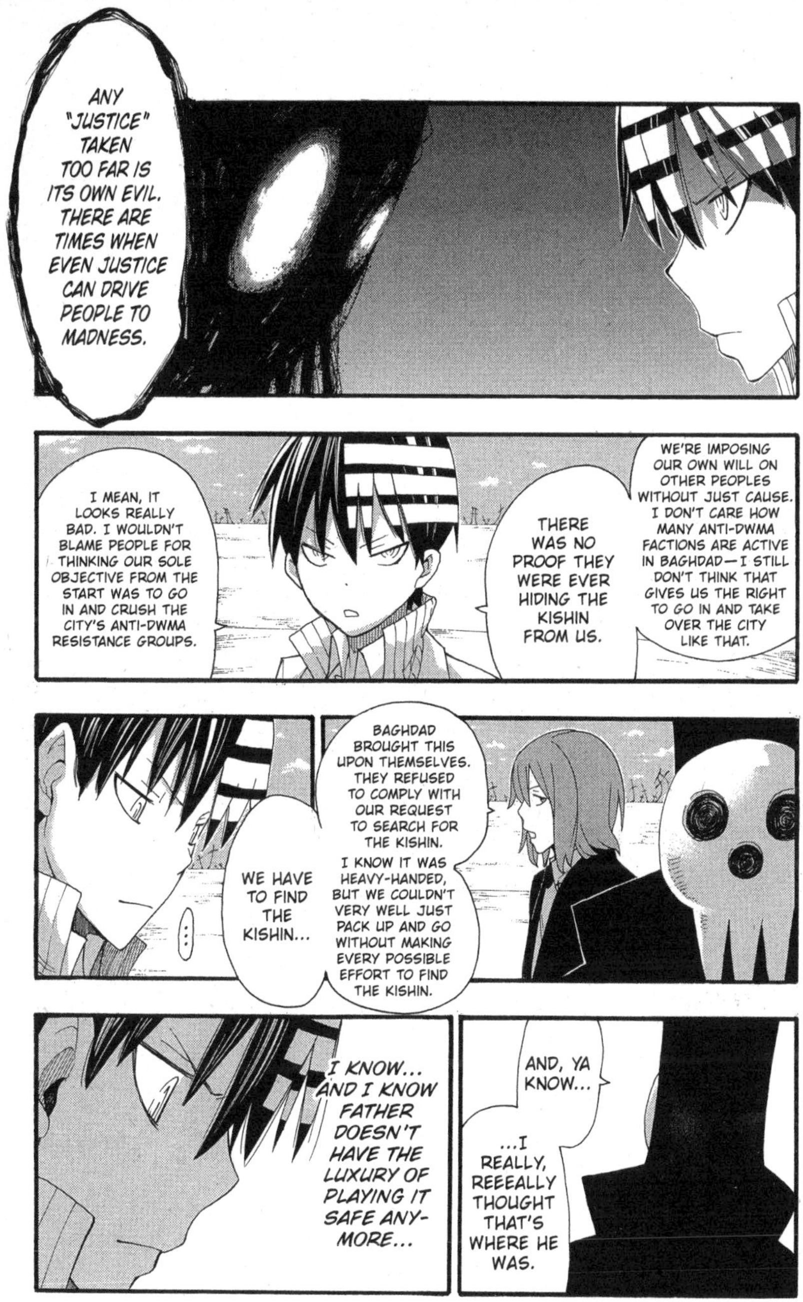
ANY "JUSTICE" TAKEN TOO FAR IS ITS OWN EVIL. THERE ARE TIMES WHEN EVEN JUSTICE CAN DRIVE PEOPLE TO MADNESS.
WE'RE IMPOSING OUR OWN WILL ON OTHER PEOPLES WITHOUT JUST CAUSE. I DON'T CARE HOW MANY ANTI-DWMA FACTIONS ARE ACTIVE IN BAGHDAD—I STILL DON'T THINK THAT GIVES US THE RIGHT TO GO IN AND TAKE OVER THE CITY LIKE THAT.
THERE WAS NO PROOF THEY WERE EVER HIDING THE KISHIN FROM US.
I MEAN, IT LOOKS REALLY BAD. I WOULDN'T BLAME PEOPLE FOR THINKING OUR SOLE OBJECTIVE FROM THE START WAS TO GO IN AND CRUSH THE CITY'S ANTI-DWMA RESISTANCE GROUPS.
BAGHDAD BROUGHT THIS UPON THEMSELVES. THEY REFUSED TO COMPLY WITH OUR REQUEST TO SEARCH FOR THE KISHIN.
I KNOW IT WAS HEAVY-HANDED, BUT WE COULDN'T VERY WELL JUST PACK UP AND GO WITHOUT MAKING EVERY POSSIBLE EFFORT TO FIND THE KISHIN.
WE HAVE TO FIND THE KISHIN...
...
AND, YA KNOW...
...I REALLY, REEEALLY THOUGHT THAT'S WHERE HE WAS.
I KNOW... AND I KNOW FATHER DOESN'T HAVE THE LUXURY OF PLAYING IT SAFE ANY-MORE...

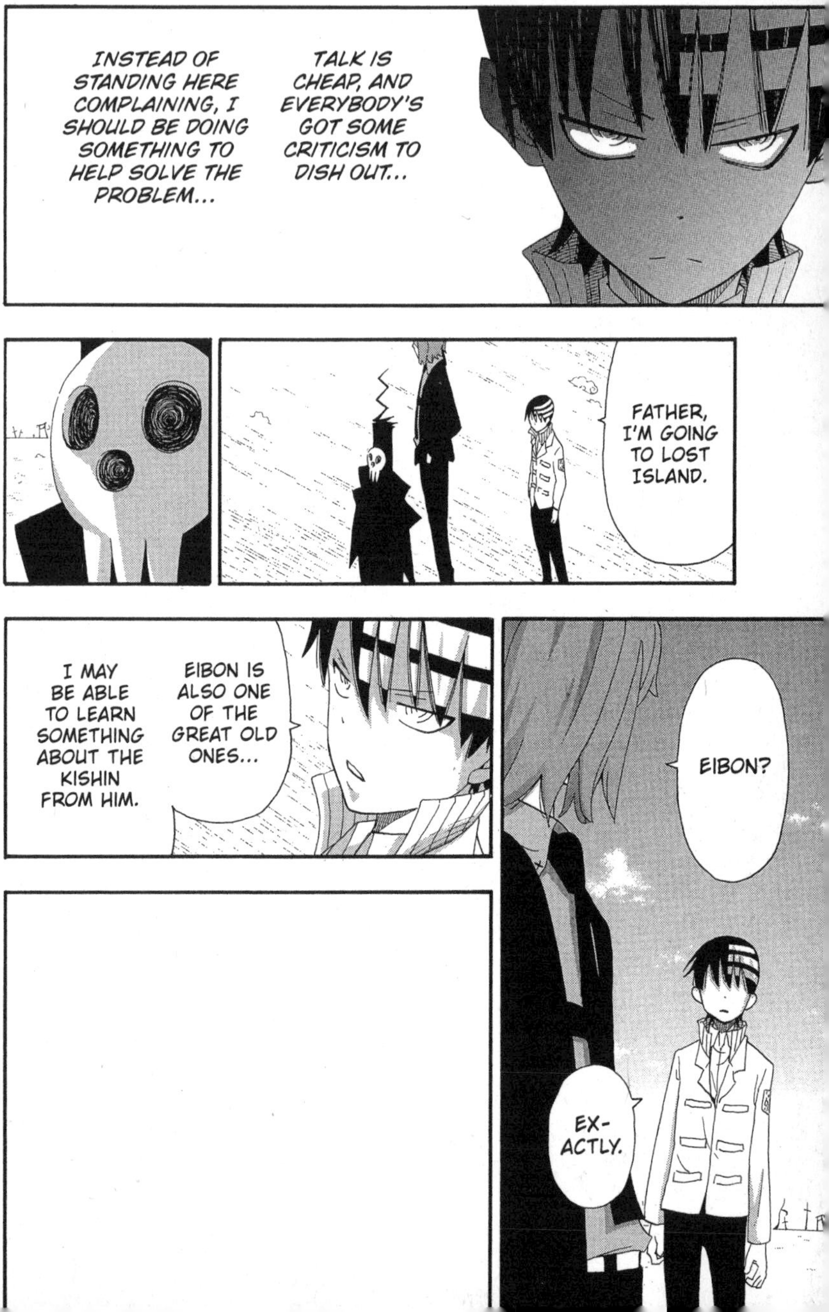
TALK IS CHEAP, AND EVERYBODY'S GOT SOME CRITICISM TO DISH OUT...
INSTEAD OF STANDING HERE COMPLAINING, I SHOULD BE DOING SOMETHING TO HELP SOLVE THE PROBLEM...
FATHER, I'M GOING TO LOST ISLAND.
EIBON?
EX-ACTLY.
EIBON IS ALSO ONE OF THE GREAT OLD ONES...
I MAY BE ABLE TO LEARN SOMETHING ABOUT THE KISHIN FROM HIM.

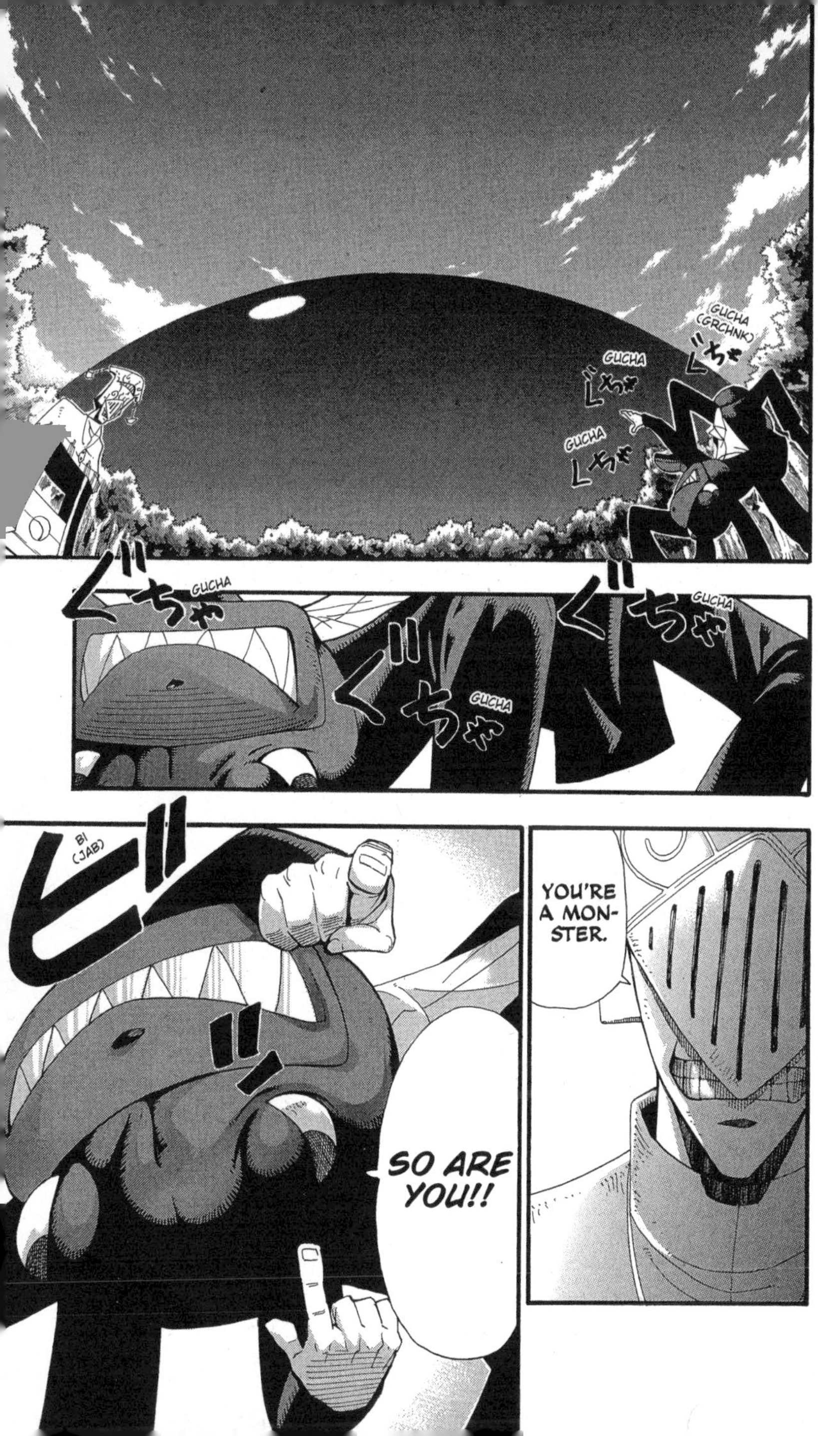
GUCHA (GRCHNK)
GUCHA
GUCHA
GUCHA
GUCHA
GUCHA
YOU'RE A MON-STER.
BI (JAB)
SO ARE YOU!!

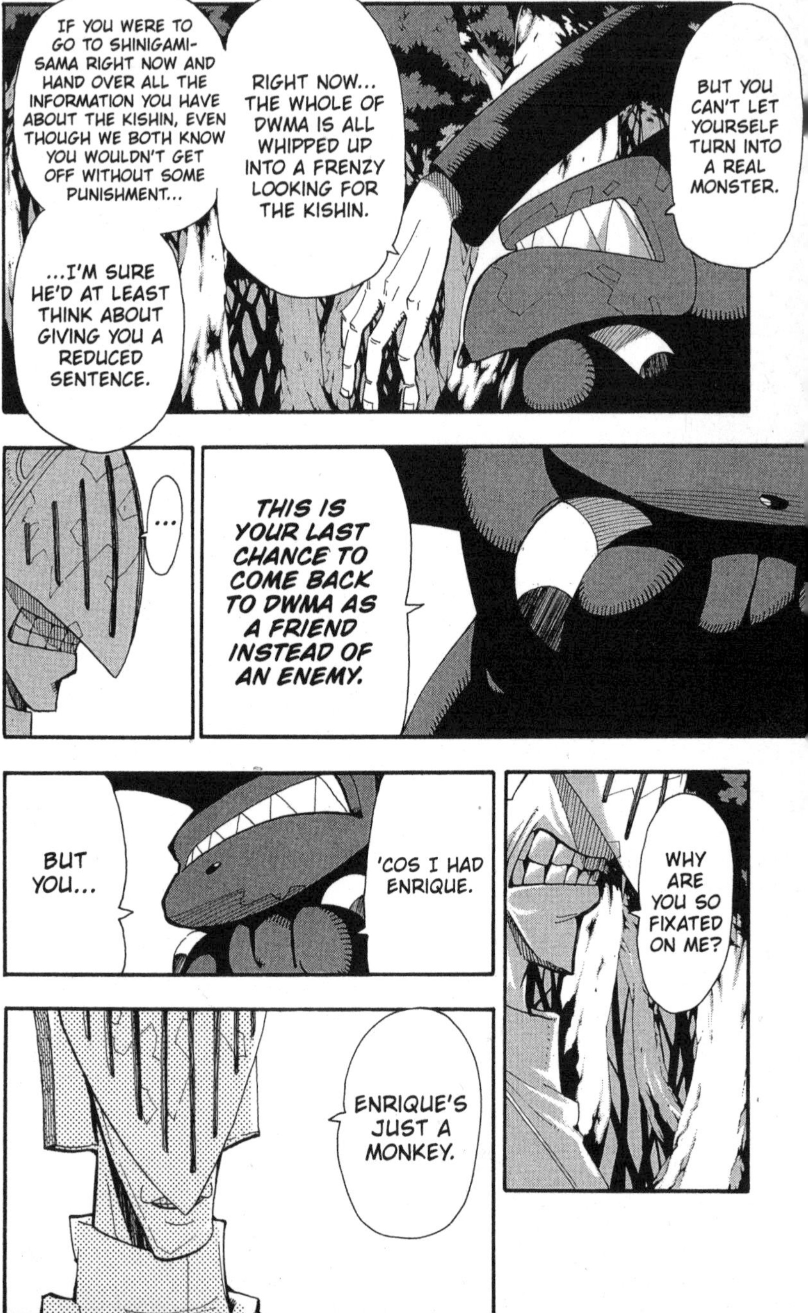
BUT YOU CAN'T LET YOURSELF TURN INTO A REAL MONSTER.
RIGHT NOW... THE WHOLE OF DWMA IS ALL WHIPPED UP INTO A FRENZY LOOKING FOR THE KISHIN.
IF YOU WERE TO GO TO SHINIGAMI-SAMA RIGHT NOW AND HAND OVER ALL THE INFORMATION YOU HAVE ABOUT THE KISHIN, EVEN THOUGH WE BOTH KNOW YOU WOULDN'T GET OFF WITHOUT SOME PUNISHMENT...
...I'M SURE HE'D AT LEAST THINK ABOUT GIVING YOU A REDUCED SENTENCE.
THIS IS YOUR LAST CHANCE TO COME BACK TO DWMA AS A FRIEND INSTEAD OF AN ENEMY.
...
WHY ARE YOU SO FIXATED ON ME?
'COS I HAD ENRIQUE.
BUT YOU...
ENRIQUE'S JUST A MONKEY.

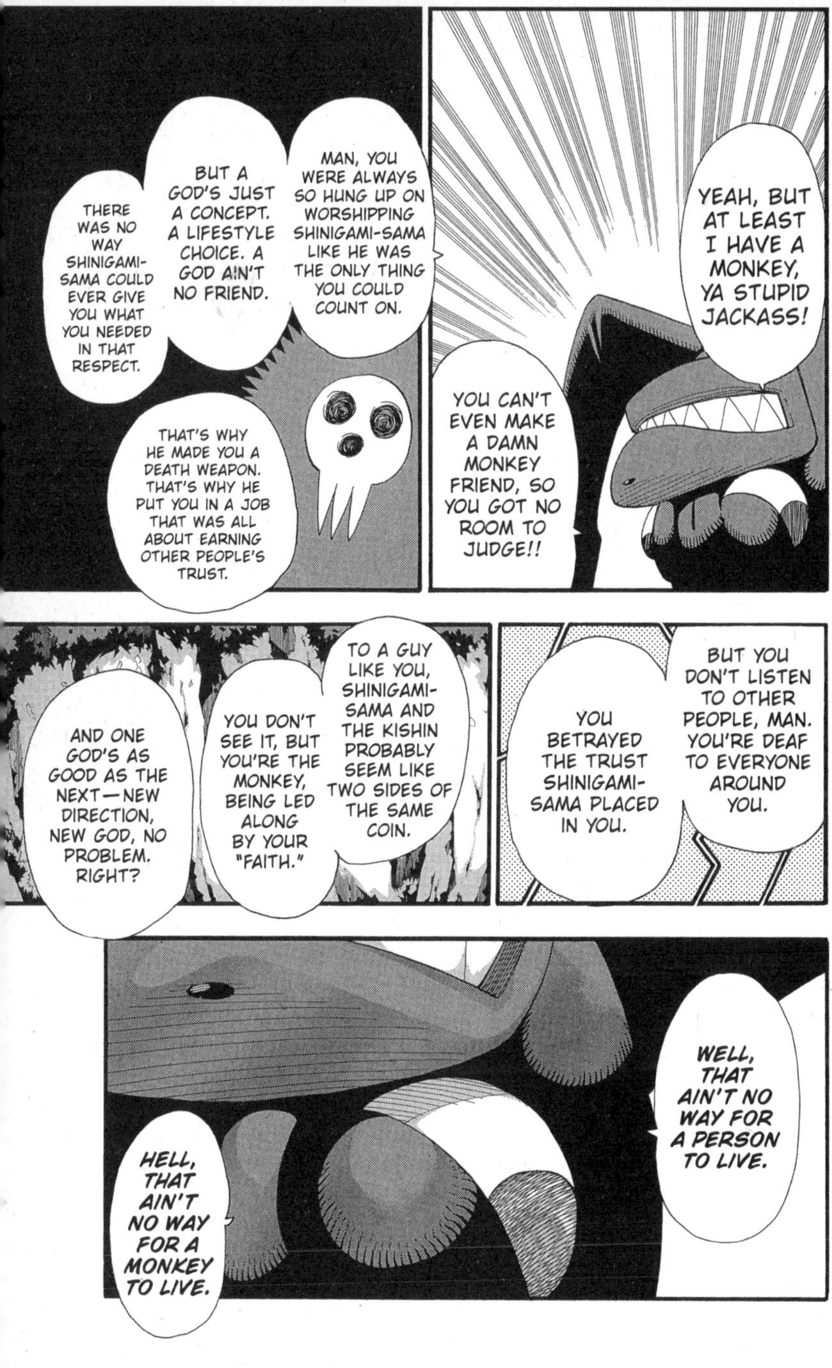
YEAH, BUT AT LEAST I HAVE A MONKEY, YA STUPID JACKASS!
YOU CAN'T EVEN MAKE A DAMN MONKEY FRIEND, SO YOU GOT NO ROOM TO JUDGE!!
MAN, YOU WERE ALWAYS SO HUNG UP ON WORSHIPPING SHINIGAMI-SAMA LIKE HE WAS THE ONLY THING YOU COULD COUNT ON.
BUT A GOD'S JUST A CONCEPT. A LIFESTYLE CHOICE. A GOD AIN'T NO FRIEND.
THERE WAS NO WAY SHINIGAMI-SAMA COULD EVER GIVE YOU WHAT YOU NEEDED IN THAT RESPECT.
THAT'S WHY HE MADE YOU A DEATH WEAPON. THAT'S WHY HE PUT YOU IN A JOB THAT WAS ALL ABOUT EARNING OTHER PEOPLE'S TRUST.
BUT YOU DON'T LISTEN TO OTHER PEOPLE, MAN. YOU'RE DEAF TO EVERYONE AROUND YOU.
YOU BETRAYED THE TRUST SHINIGAMI-SAMA PLACED IN YOU.
TO A GUY LIKE YOU, SHINIGAMI-SAMA AND THE KISHIN PROBABLY SEEM LIKE TWO SIDES OF THE SAME COIN.
YOU DON'T SEE IT, BUT YOU'RE THE MONKEY, BEING LED ALONG BY YOUR "FAITH."
AND ONE GOD'S AS GOOD AS THE NEXT—NEW DIRECTION, NEW GOD, NO PROBLEM. RIGHT?
WELL, THAT AIN'T NO WAY FOR A PERSON TO LIVE.
HELL, THAT AIN'T NO WAY FOR A MONKEY TO LIVE.

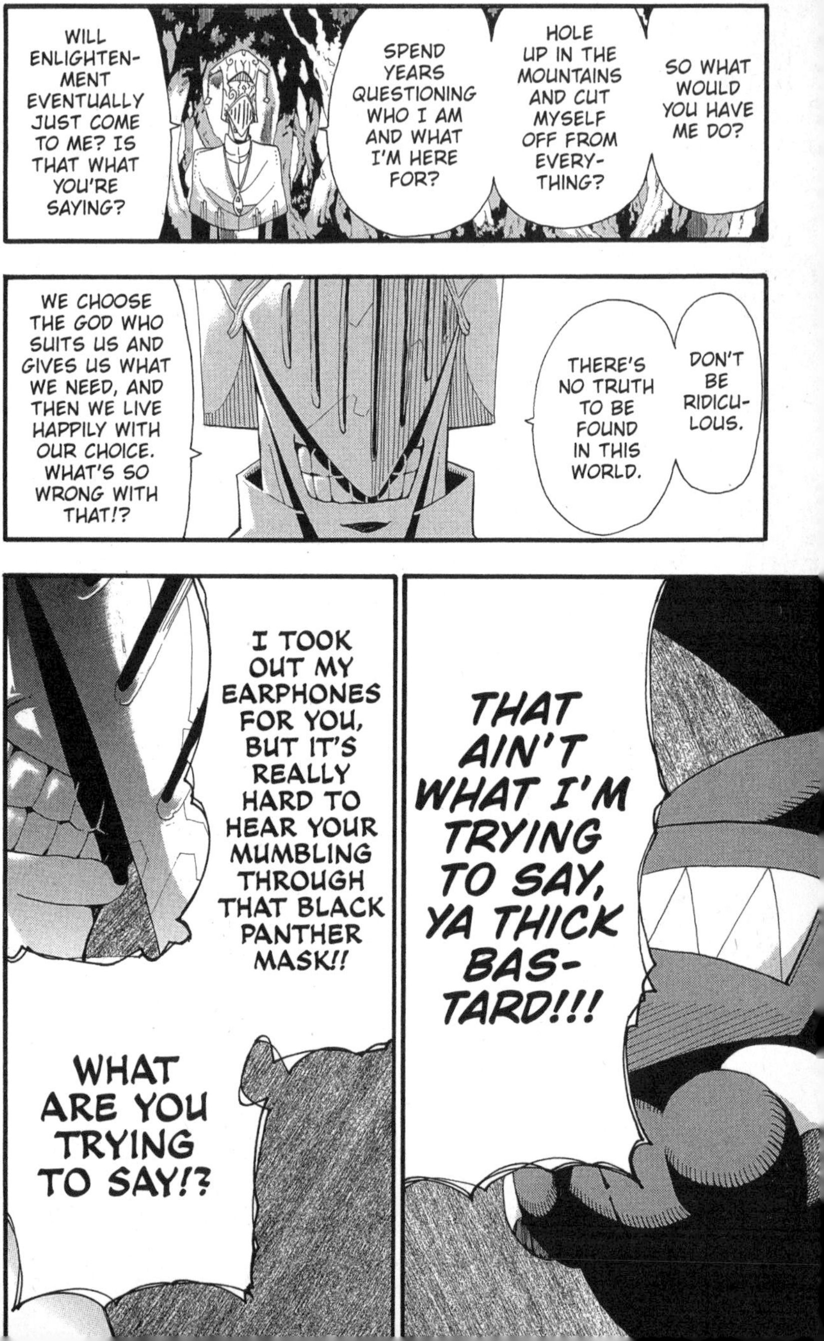
SO WHAT WOULD YOU HAVE ME DO?
HOLE UP IN THE MOUNTAINS AND CUT MYSELF OFF FROM EVERY-THING?
SPEND YEARS QUESTIONING WHO I AM AND WHAT I'M HERE FOR?
WILL ENLIGHTEN-MENT EVENTUALLY JUST COME TO ME? IS THAT WHAT YOU'RE SAYING?
DON'T BE RIDICU-LOUS.
THERE'S NO TRUTH TO BE FOUND IN THIS WORLD.
WE CHOOSE THE GOD WHO SUITS US AND GIVES US WHAT WE NEED, AND THEN WE LIVE HAPPILY WITH OUR CHOICE. WHAT'S SO WRONG WITH THAT!?
THAT AIN'T WHAT I'M TRYING TO SAY, YA THICK BAS-TARD!!!
I TOOK OUT MY EARPHONES FOR YOU, BUT IT'S REALLY HARD TO HEAR YOUR MUMBLING THROUGH THAT BLACK PANTHER MASK!!
WHAT ARE YOU TRYING TO SAY!?

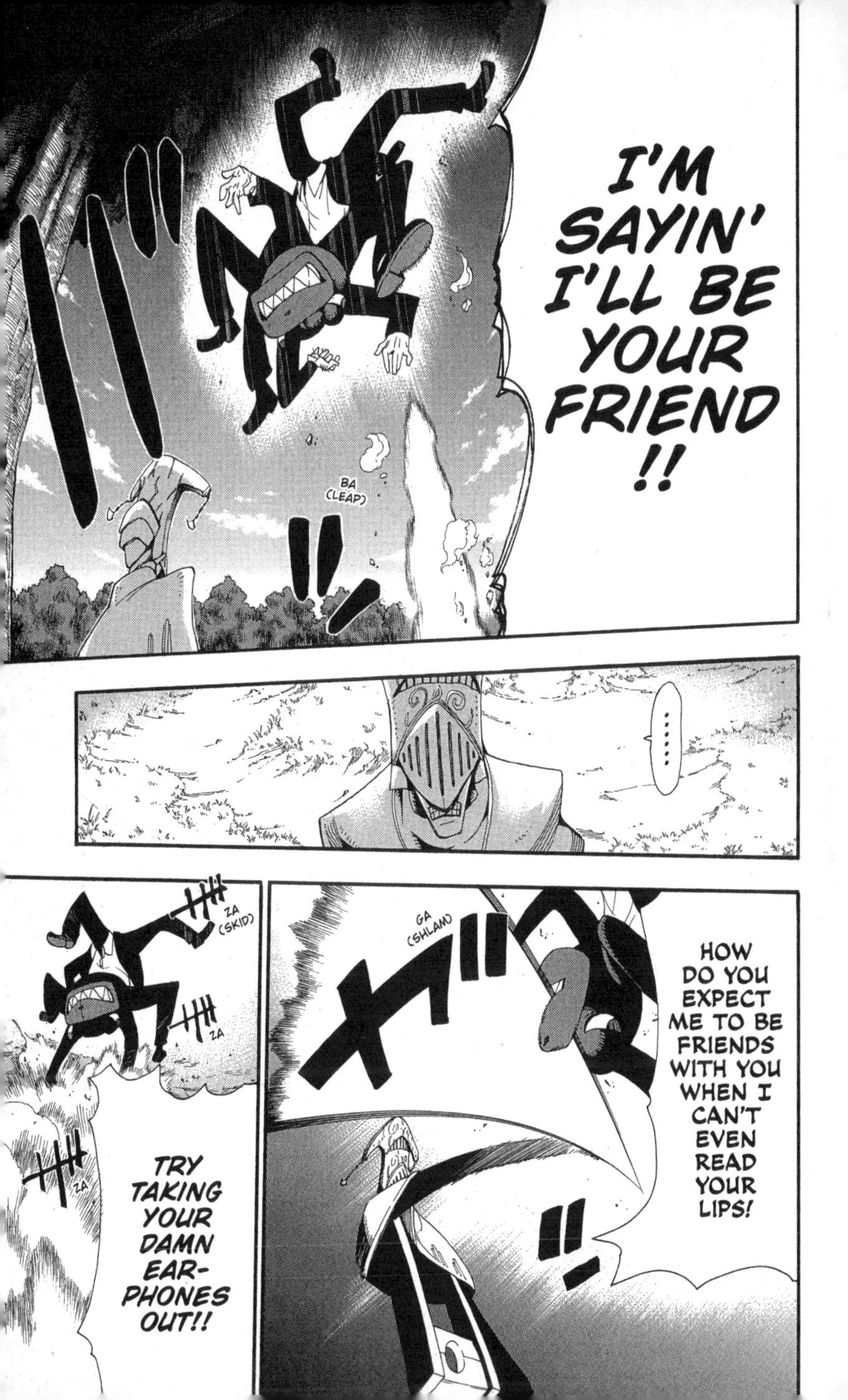

I'M SAYIN' I'LL BE YOUR FRIEND!!
BA (LEAP)
......
GA (SHLAM)
HOW DO YOU EXPECT ME TO BE FRIENDS WITH YOU WHEN I CAN'T EVEN READ YOUR LIPS!
ZA (SKID)
ZA
ZA
TRY TAKING YOUR DAMN EAR-PHONES OUT!!

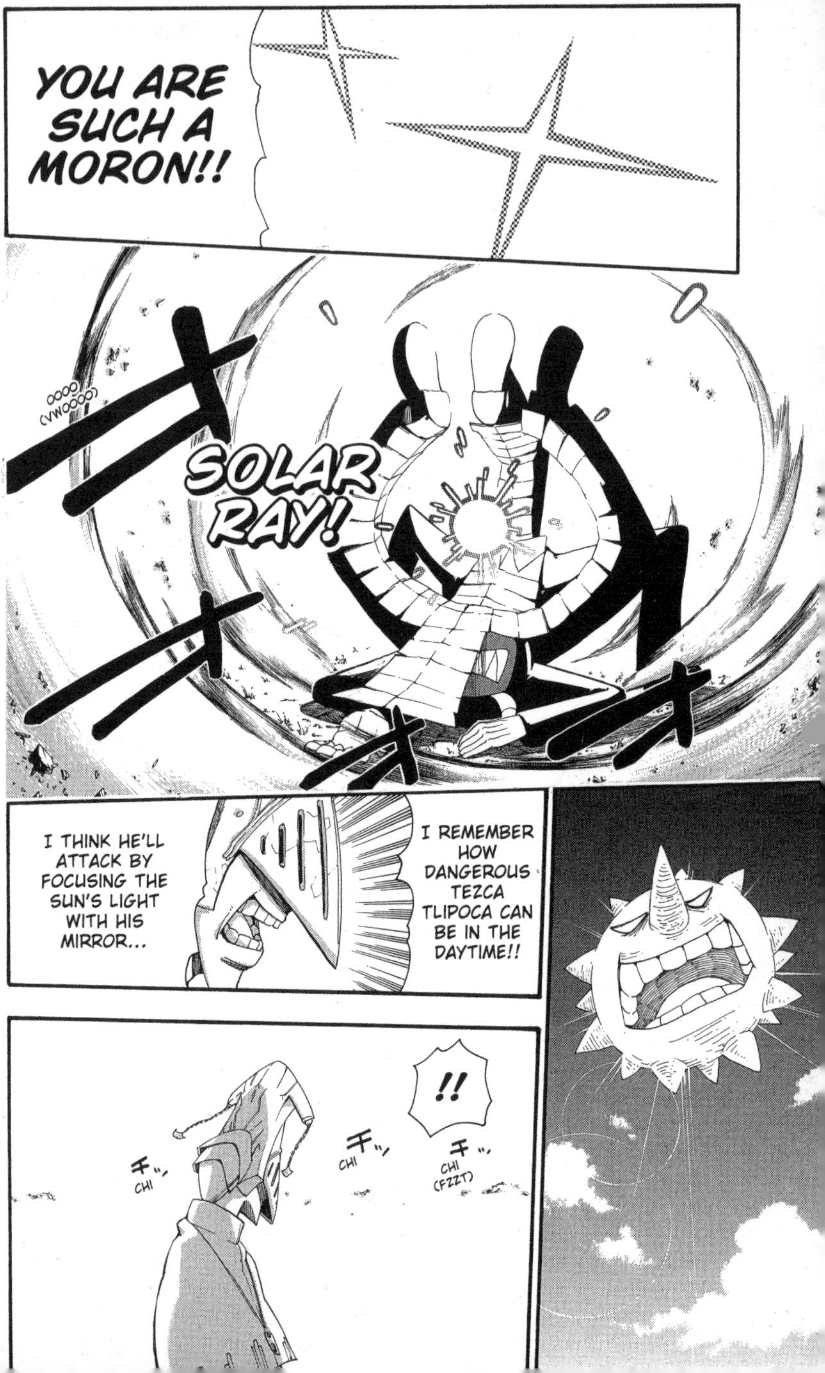
YOU ARE SUCH A MORON!!
(VWOOOO)
SOLAR RAY!
I REMEMBER HOW DANGEROUS TEZCA TLIPOCA CAN BE IN THE DAYTIME!!
I THINK HE'LL ATTACK BY FOCUSING THE SUN'S LIGHT WITH HIS MIRROR...
!!
チッ CHI (FZZT)
チッ CHI
チッ CHI

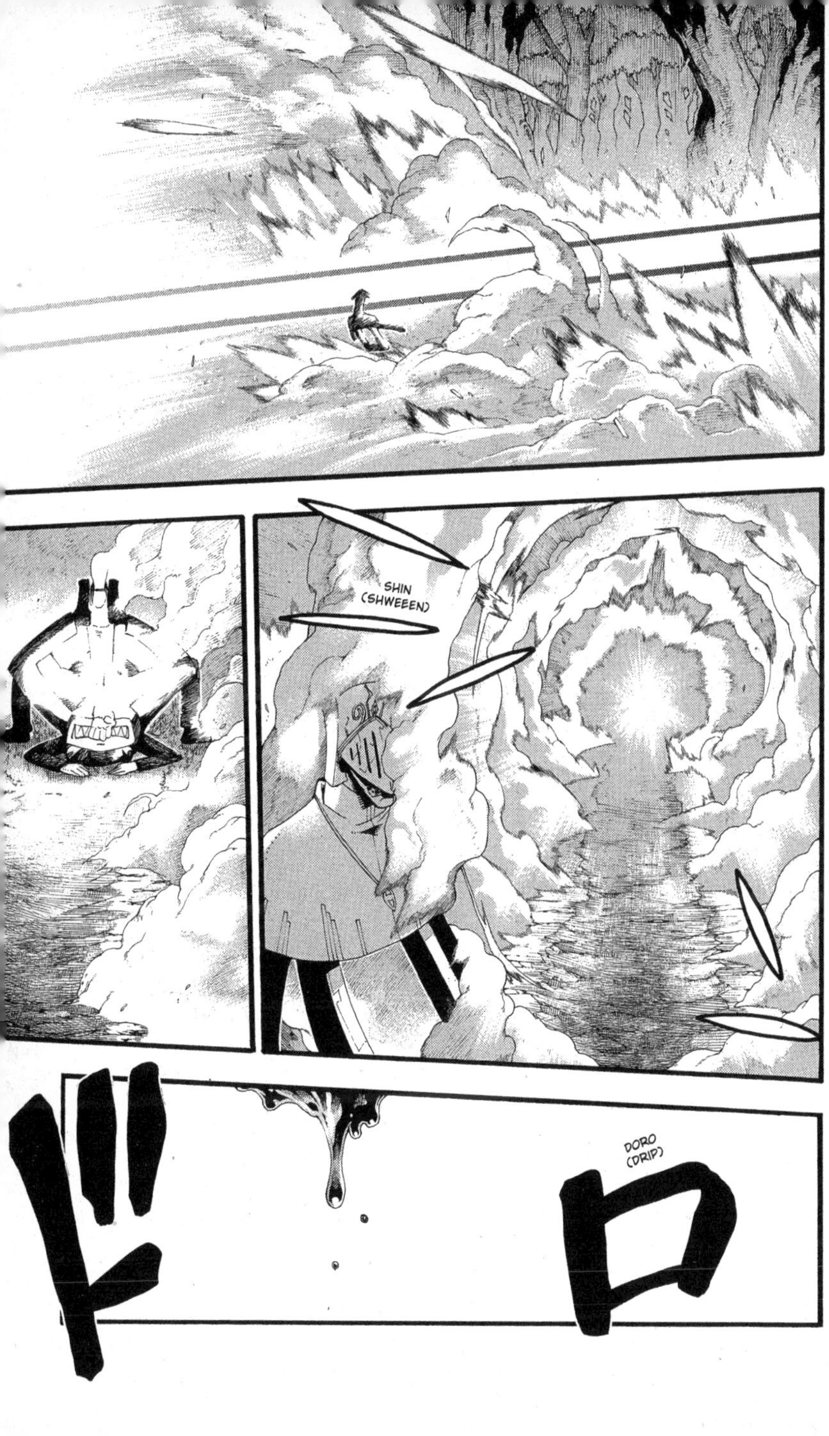
SHIN
(SHWEEEN)
DORO
(DRIP)
ドロ

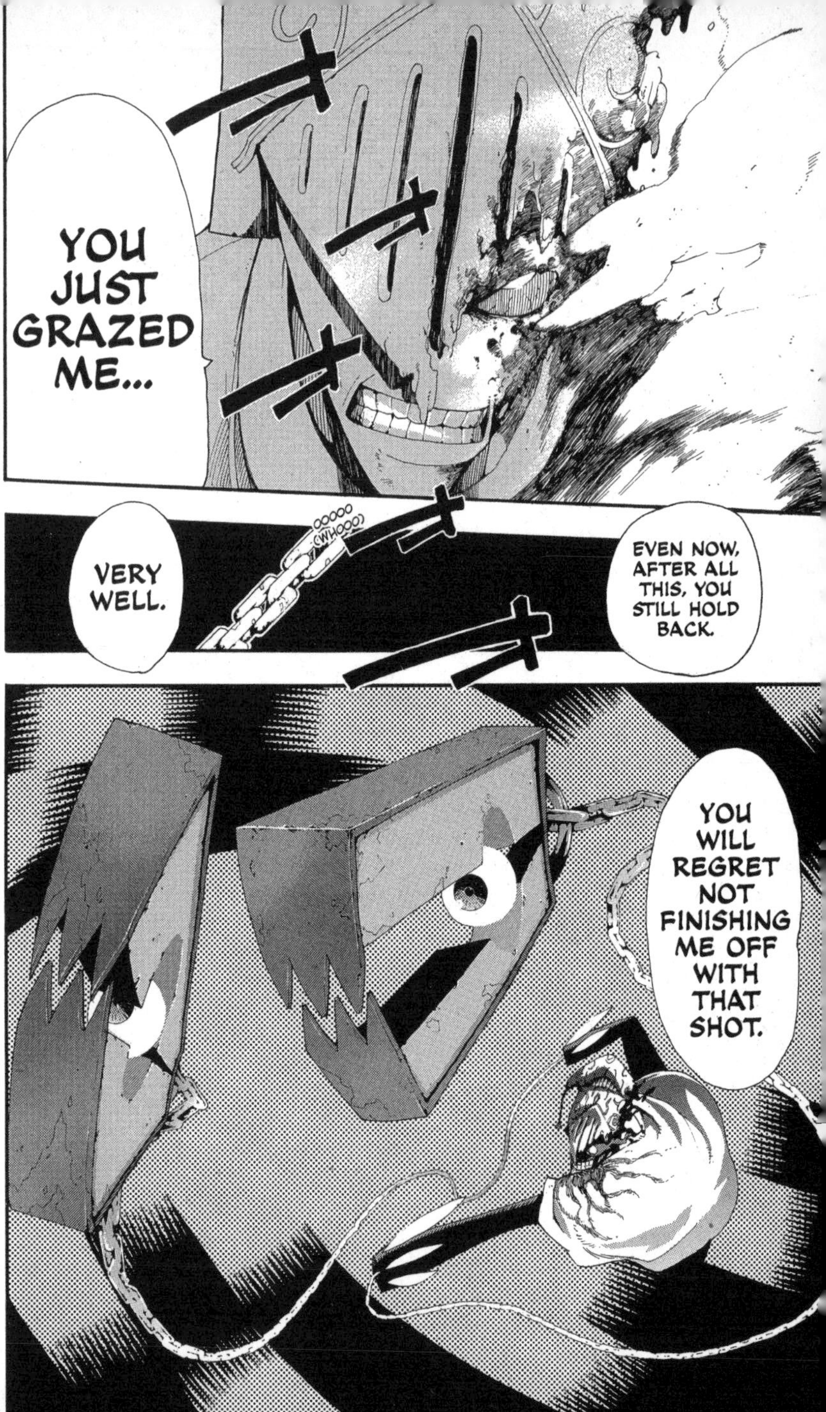
YOU JUST GRAZED ME...
EVEN NOW, AFTER ALL THIS, YOU STILL HOLD BACK.
(WHOOO)
VERY WELL.
YOU WILL REGRET NOT FINISHING ME OFF WITH THAT SHOT.

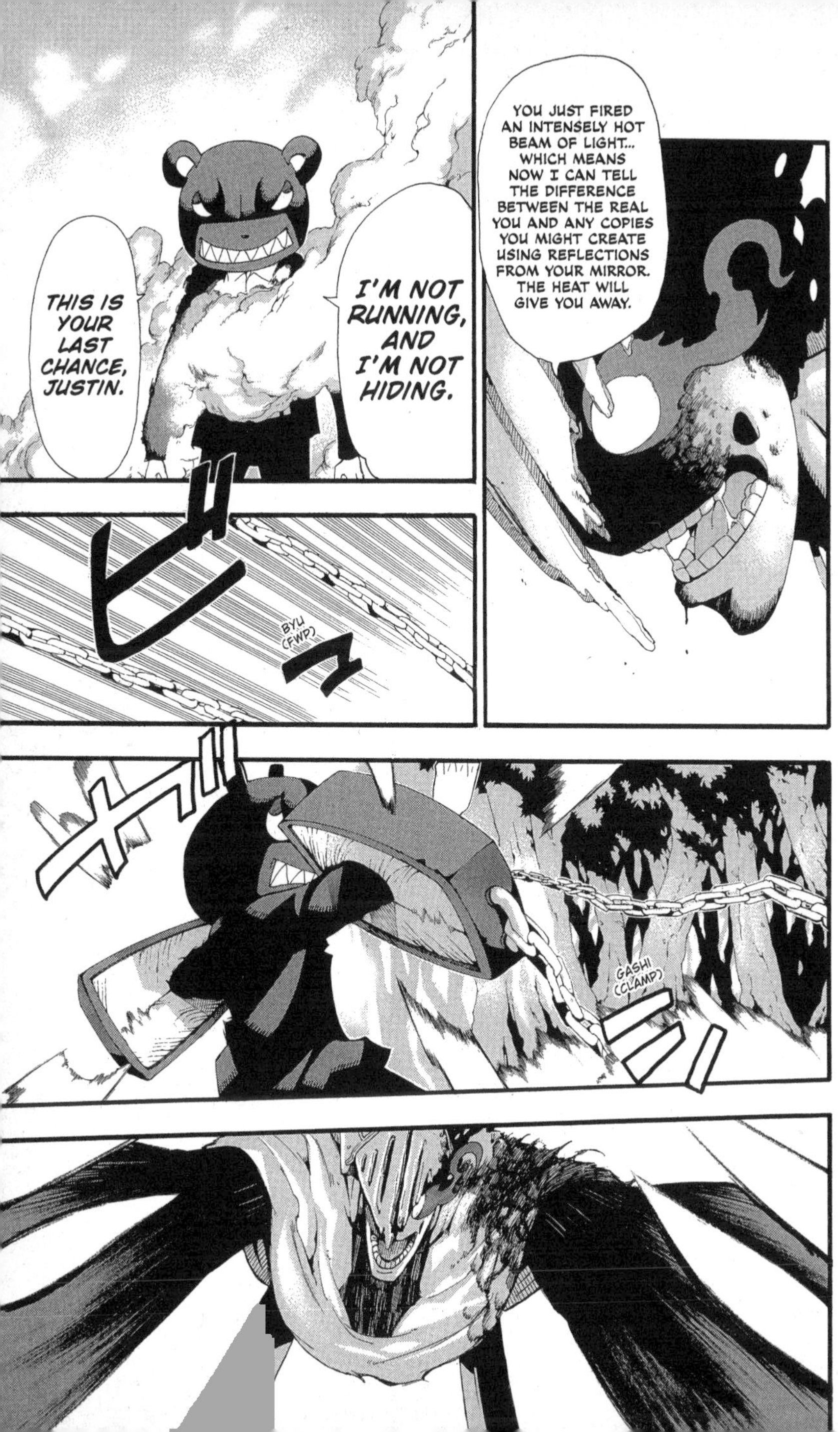

YOU JUST FIRED AN INTENSELY HOT BEAM OF LIGHT... WHICH MEANS NOW I CAN TELL THE DIFFERENCE BETWEEN THE REAL YOU AND ANY COPIES YOU MIGHT CREATE USING REFLECTIONS FROM YOUR MIRROR. THE HEAT WILL GIVE YOU AWAY.
I'M NOT RUNNING, AND I'M NOT HIDING.
THIS IS YOUR LAST CHANCE, JUSTIN.
BYU (FWP)
GASHI (CLAMP)

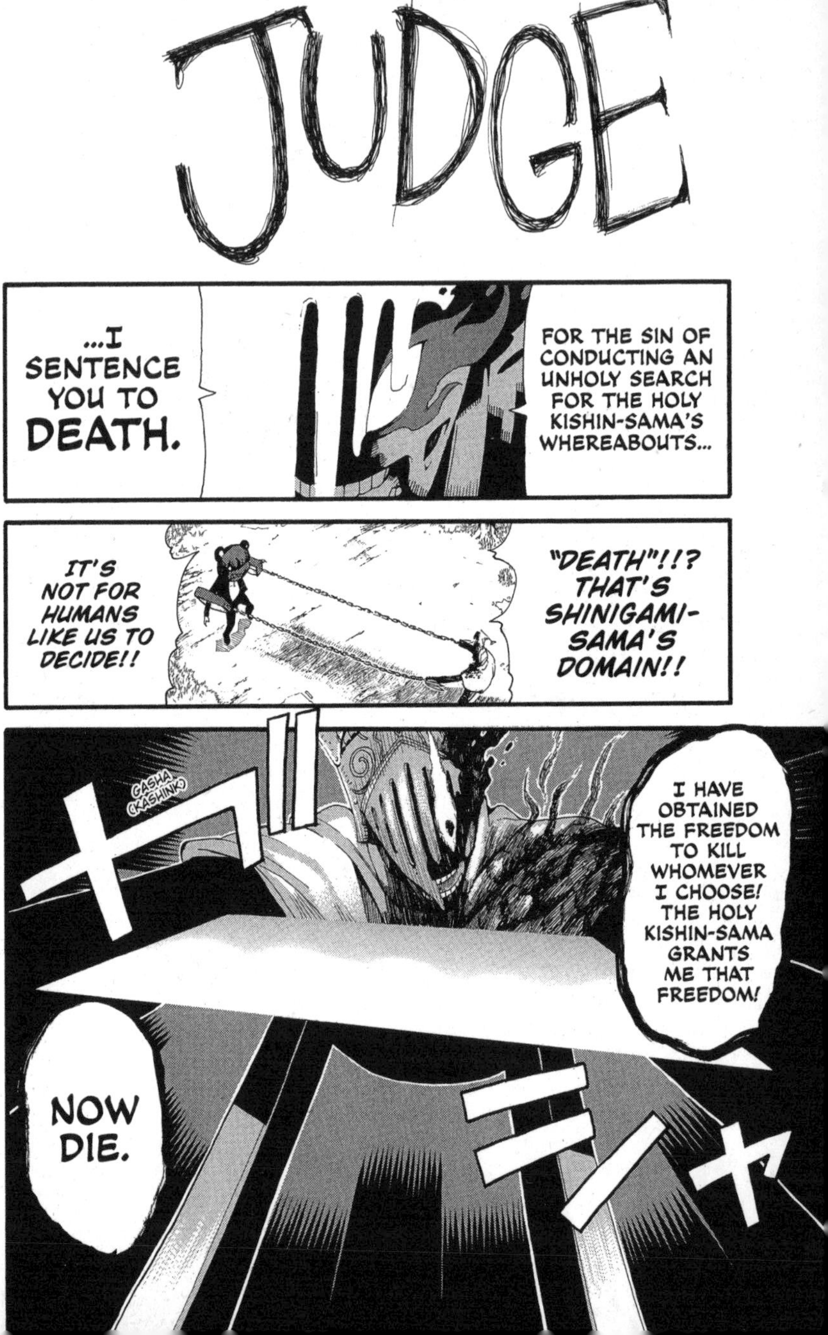
JUDGE
FOR THE SIN OF CONDUCTING AN UNHOLY SEARCH FOR THE HOLY KISHIN-SAMA'S WHEREABOUTS...
...I SENTENCE YOU TO DEATH.
"DEATH"!!? THAT'S SHINIGAMI-SAMA'S DOMAIN!!
IT'S NOT FOR HUMANS LIKE US TO DECIDE!!
I HAVE OBTAINED THE FREEDOM TO KILL WHOMEVER I CHOOSE! THE HOLY KISHIN-SAMA GRANTS ME THAT FREEDOM!
GASHA (KASHINK)
NOW DIE.

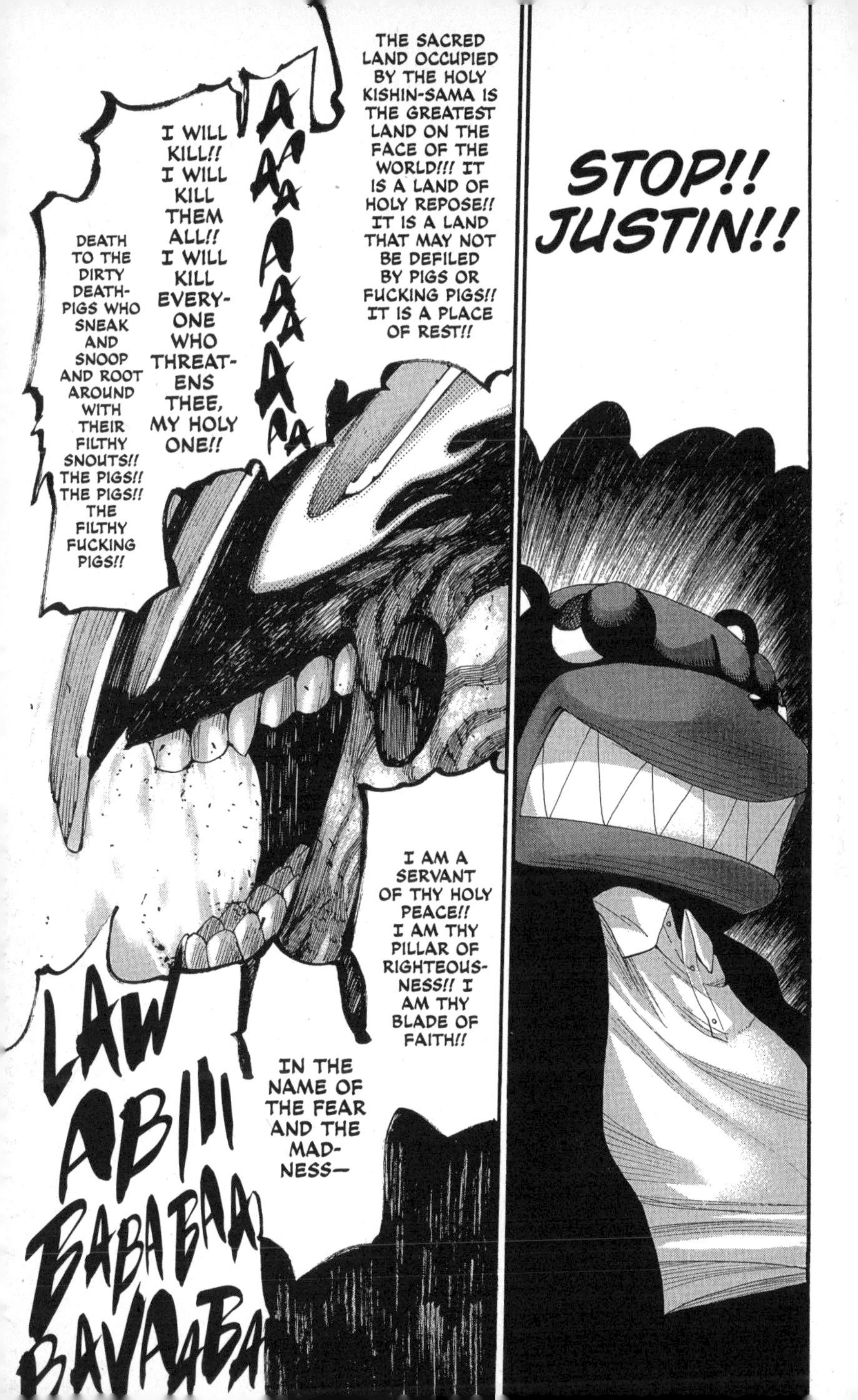
STOP!! JUSTIN!!
THE SACRED LAND OCCUPIED BY THE HOLY KISHIN-SAMA IS THE GREATEST LAND ON THE FACE OF THE WORLD!!! IT IS A LAND OF HOLY REPOSE!! IT IS A LAND THAT MAY NOT BE DEFILED BY PIGS OR FUCKING PIGS!! IT IS A PLACE OF REST!!
I WILL KILL!! I WILL KILL THEM ALL!! I WILL KILL EVERY-ONE WHO THREAT-ENS THEE, MY HOLY ONE!!
DEATH TO THE DIRTY DEATH-PIGS WHO SNEAK AND SNOOP AND ROOT AROUND WITH THEIR FILTHY SNOUTS!! THE PIGS!! THE PIGS!! THE FILTHY FUCKING PIGS!!
I AM A SERVANT OF THY HOLY PEACE!! I AM THY PILLAR OF RIGHTEOUS-NESS!! I AM THY BLADE OF FAITH!!
IN THE NAME OF THE FEAR AND THE MAD-NESS—
LAW ABIII BABABAA BAVAABA

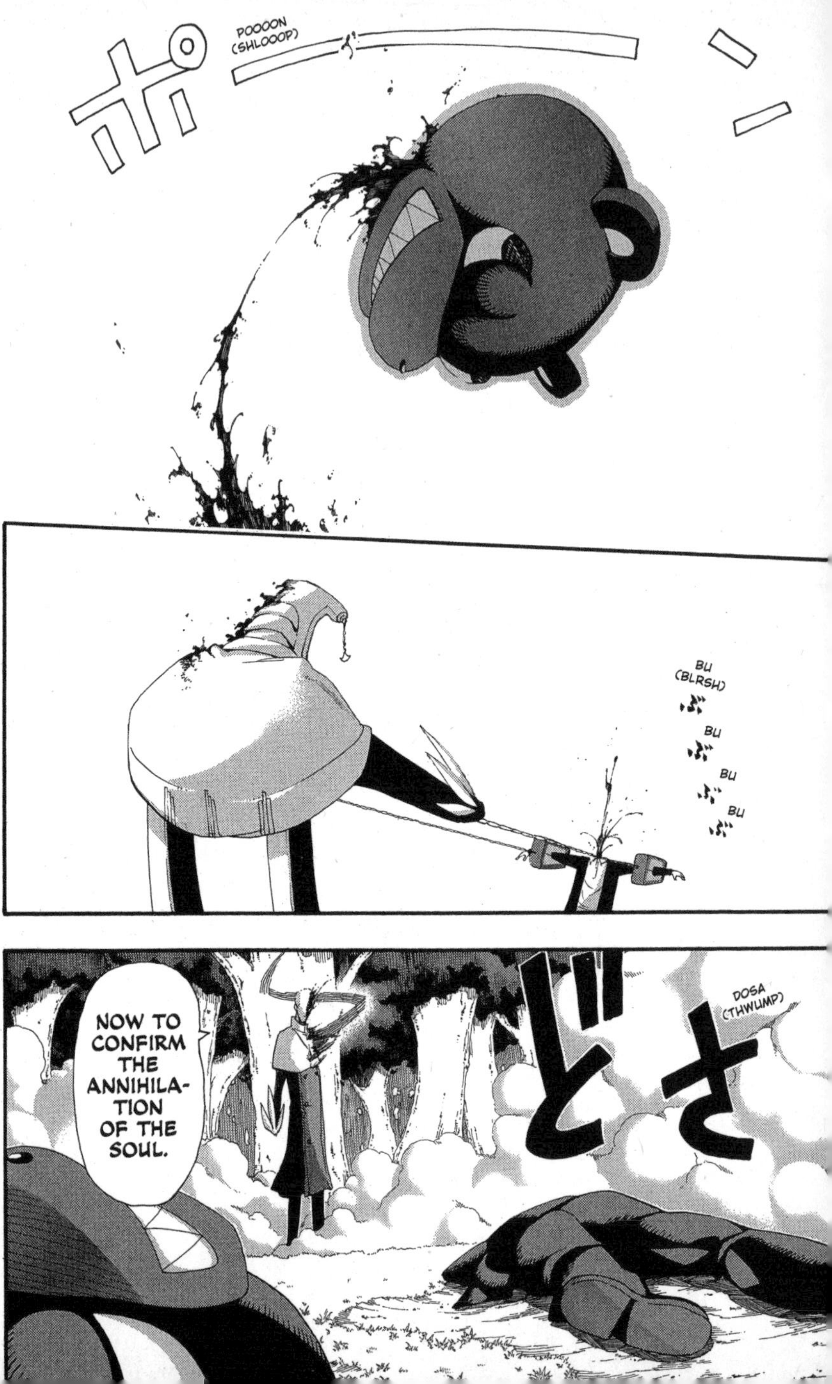
POOOON (SHLOOOP)
BU (BLRSH)
BU
BU
BU
DOSA (THWUMP)
NOW TO CONFIRM THE ANNIHILATION OF THE SOUL.

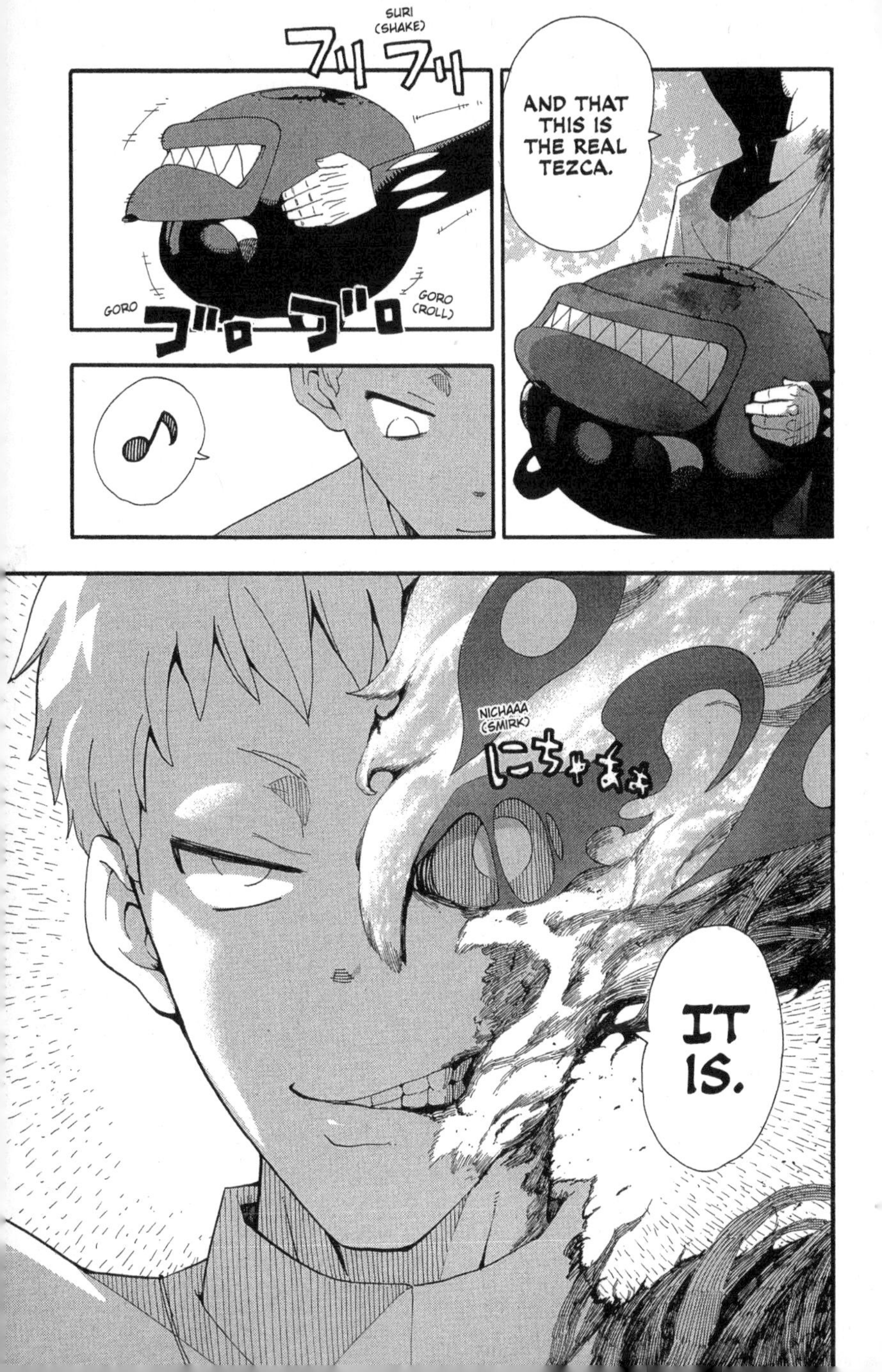
AND THAT THIS IS THE REAL TEZCA.
SURI (SHAKE)
GORO
GORO (ROLL)
NICHAAA (SMIRK)
IT IS.

SOUL EATER

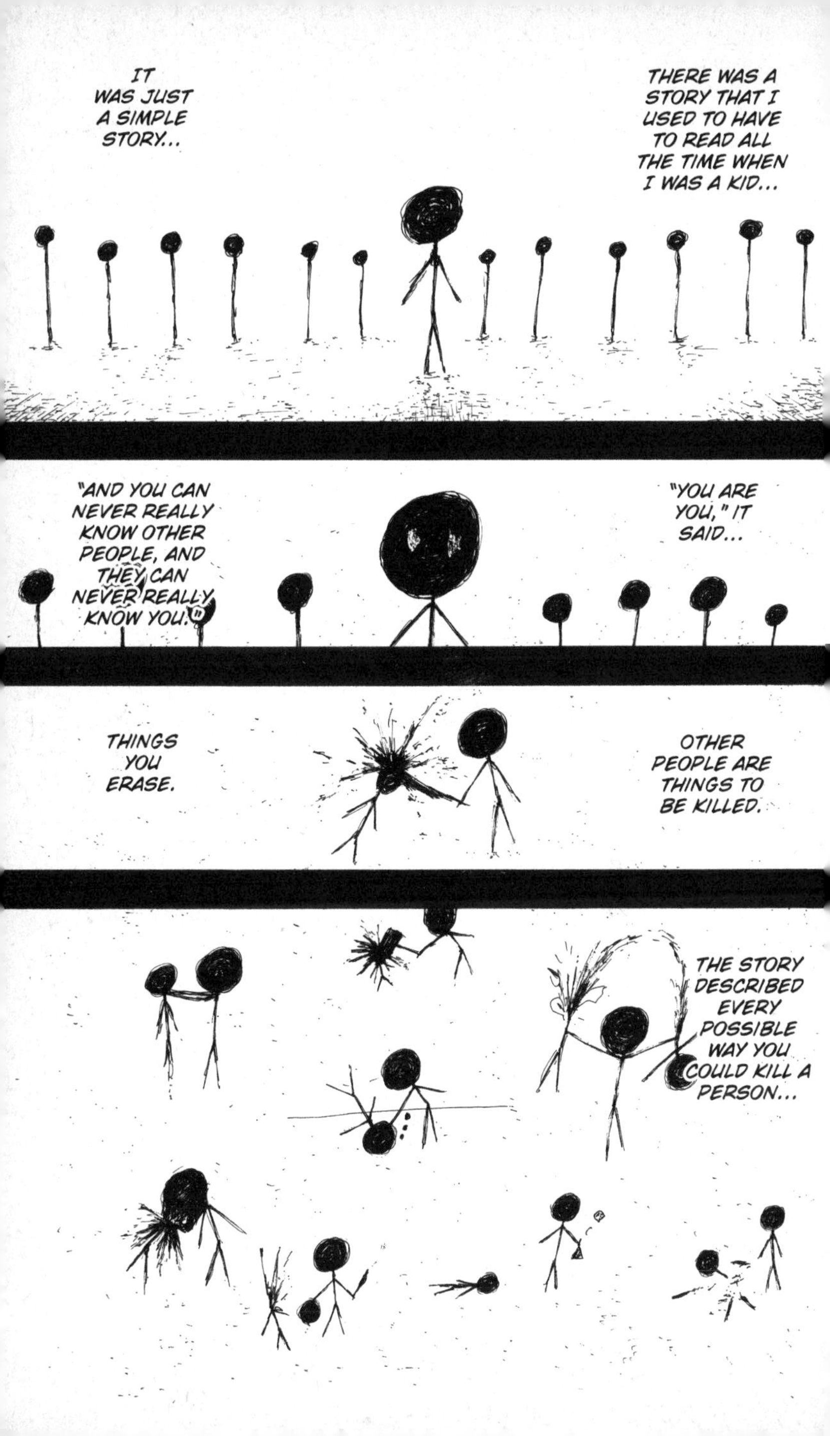
THERE WAS A STORY THAT I USED TO HAVE TO READ ALL THE TIME WHEN I WAS A KID...
IT WAS JUST A SIMPLE STORY...
"YOU ARE YOU," IT SAID...
"AND YOU CAN NEVER REALLY KNOW OTHER PEOPLE, AND THEY CAN NEVER REALLY KNOW YOU."
OTHER PEOPLE ARE THINGS TO BE KILLED.
THINGS YOU ERASE.
THE STORY DESCRIBED EVERY POSSIBLE WAY YOU COULD KILL A PERSON...

SOUL EATER

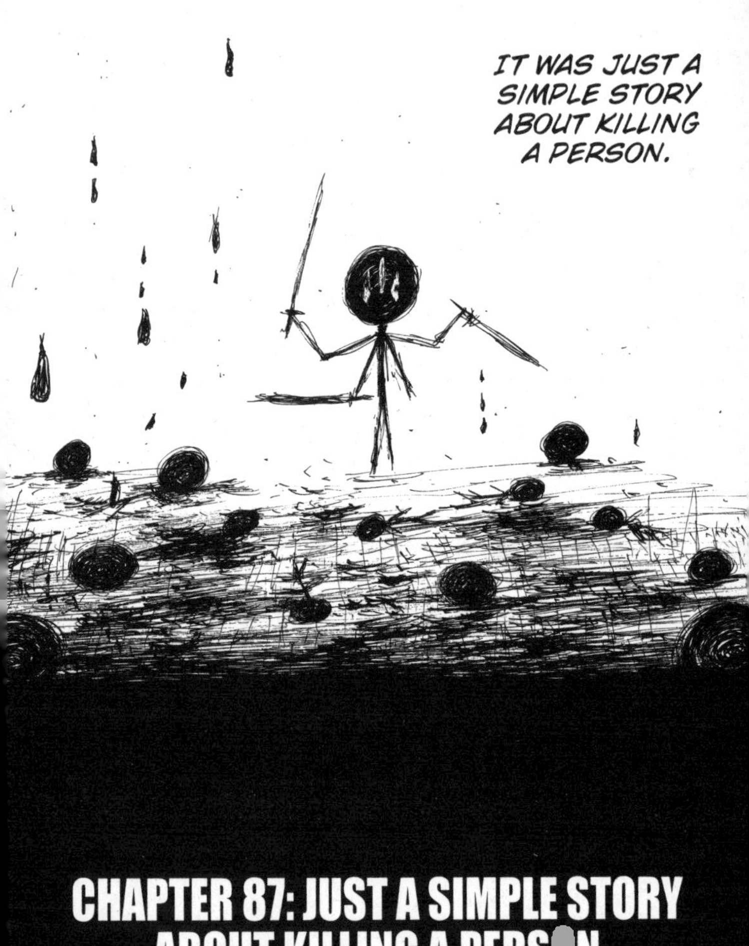
IT WAS JUST A SIMPLE STORY ABOUT KILLING A PERSON.

CHAPTER 87: JUST A SIMPLE STORY ABOUT KILLING A PERSON

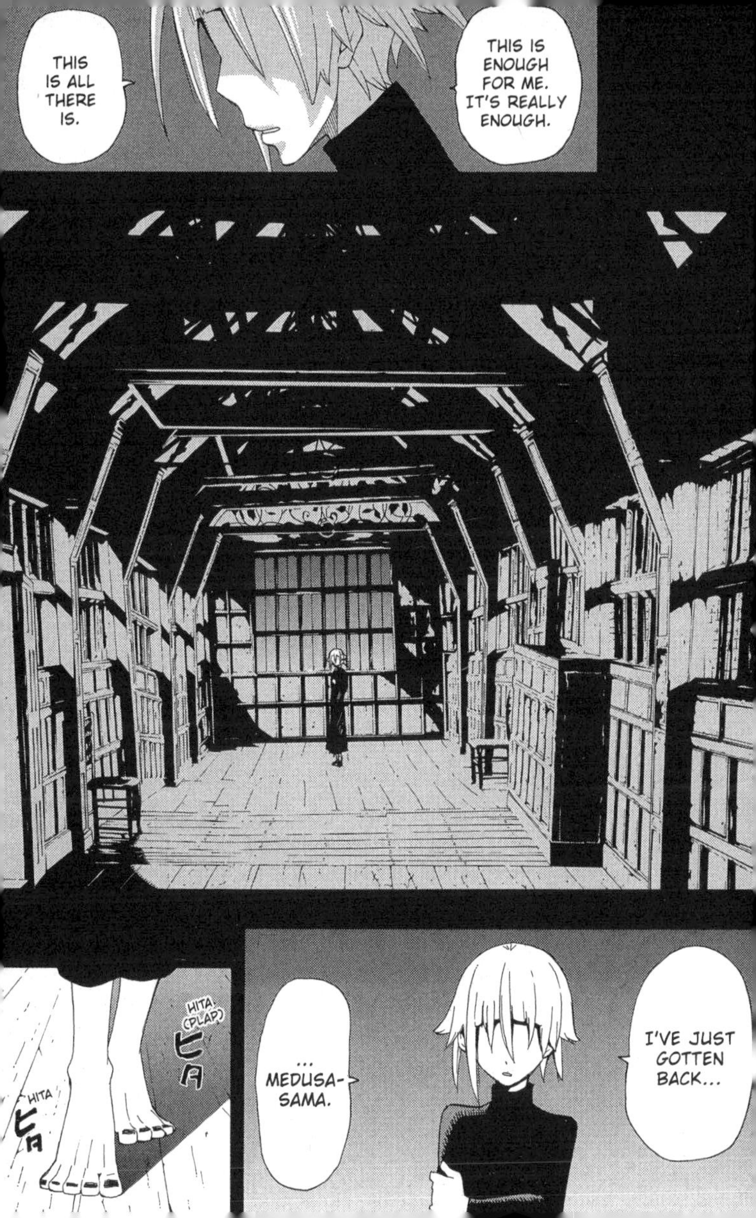
THIS IS ENOUGH FOR ME. IT'S REALLY ENOUGH.
THIS IS ALL THERE IS.
I'VE JUST GOTTEN BACK...
... MEDUSA-SAMA.
HITA (PLAP)
ヒタ
HITA
ヒタ

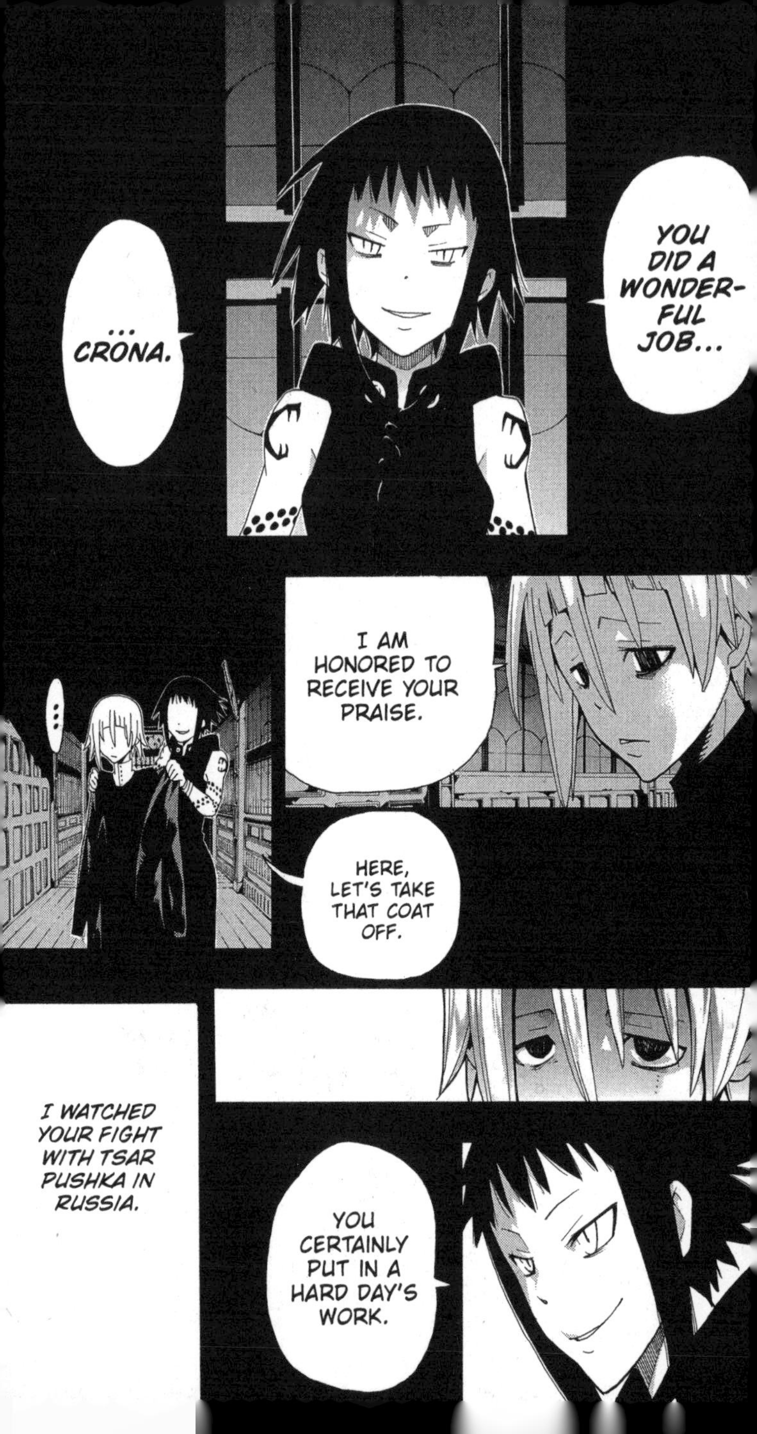
YOU DID A WONDER-FUL JOB...
... CRONA.
I AM HONORED TO RECEIVE YOUR PRAISE.
HERE, LET'S TAKE THAT COAT OFF.
...
YOU CERTAINLY PUT IN A HARD DAY'S WORK.
I WATCHED YOUR FIGHT WITH TSAR PUSHKA IN RUSSIA.

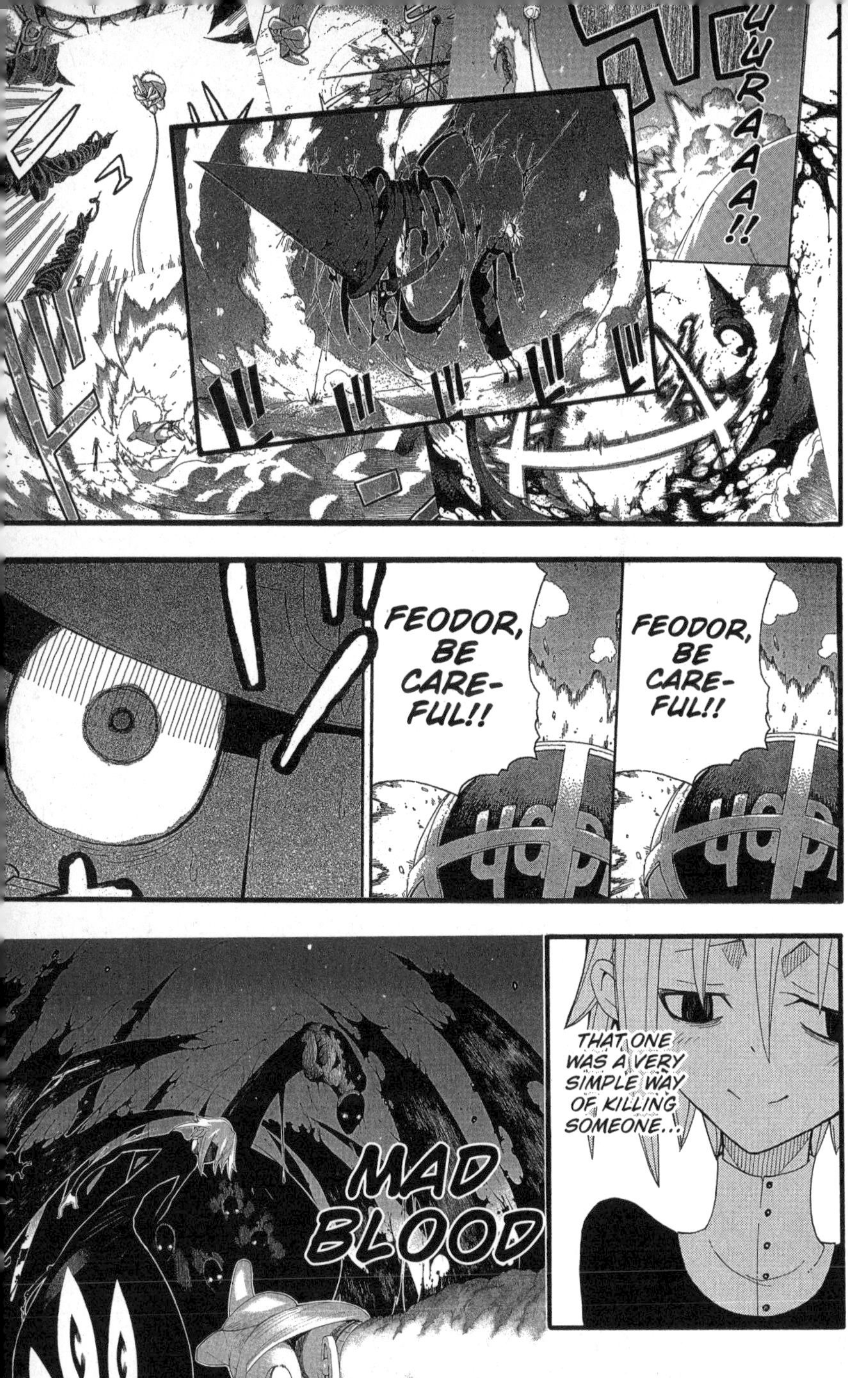
UURAAAA!!
FEODOR, BE CARE-FUL!!
FEODOR, BE CARE-FUL!!
THAT ONE WAS A VERY SIMPLE WAY OF KILLING SOMEONE...
MAD BLOOD

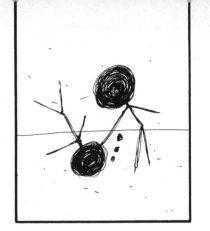

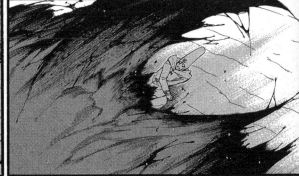

THINGS THAT GET SWALLOWED BY MADNESS...

...SWALLOW THE
MADNESS...

...AND MELT
INTO THE
MADNESS.

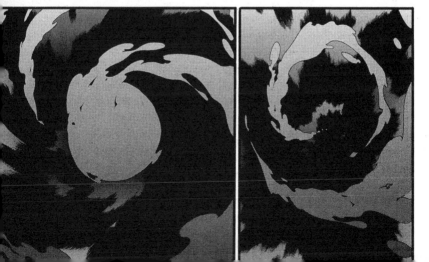

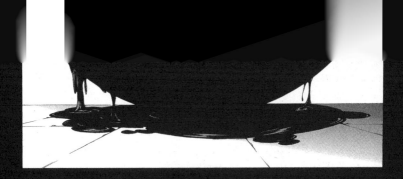

THEN THEY HARDEN IN THE MADNESS.

I WAS ESPECIALLY SURPRISED TO NOTE HOW THE BLACK SPHERES CREATED BY YOUR MAD BLOOD ATTACK EMITTED SUCH A HIGH CONCENTRATION OF MADNESS.

AND THEN, TO SEE IT TAKE OUT AN ENTIRE CITY IN UKRAINE WAS A SIGHT TO BEHOLD.

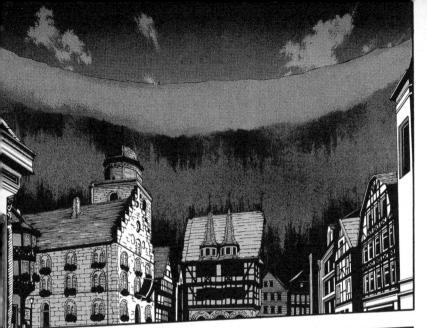

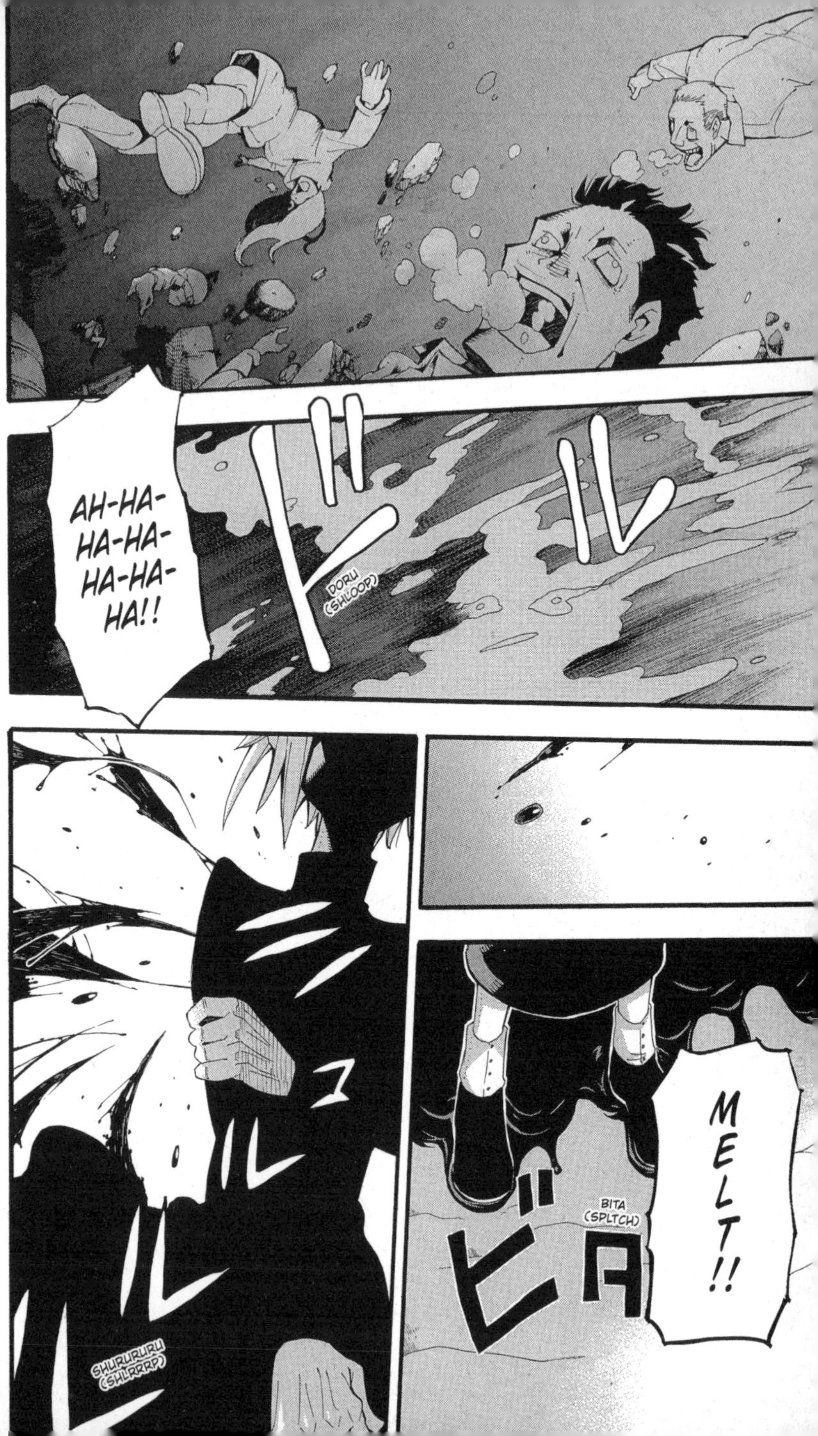
AH-HA-HA-HA-HA-HA-HA!!
DORU (SHLOOP)
SHURURURU (SHLRRRP)
MELT!!
BITA (SPLTCH)

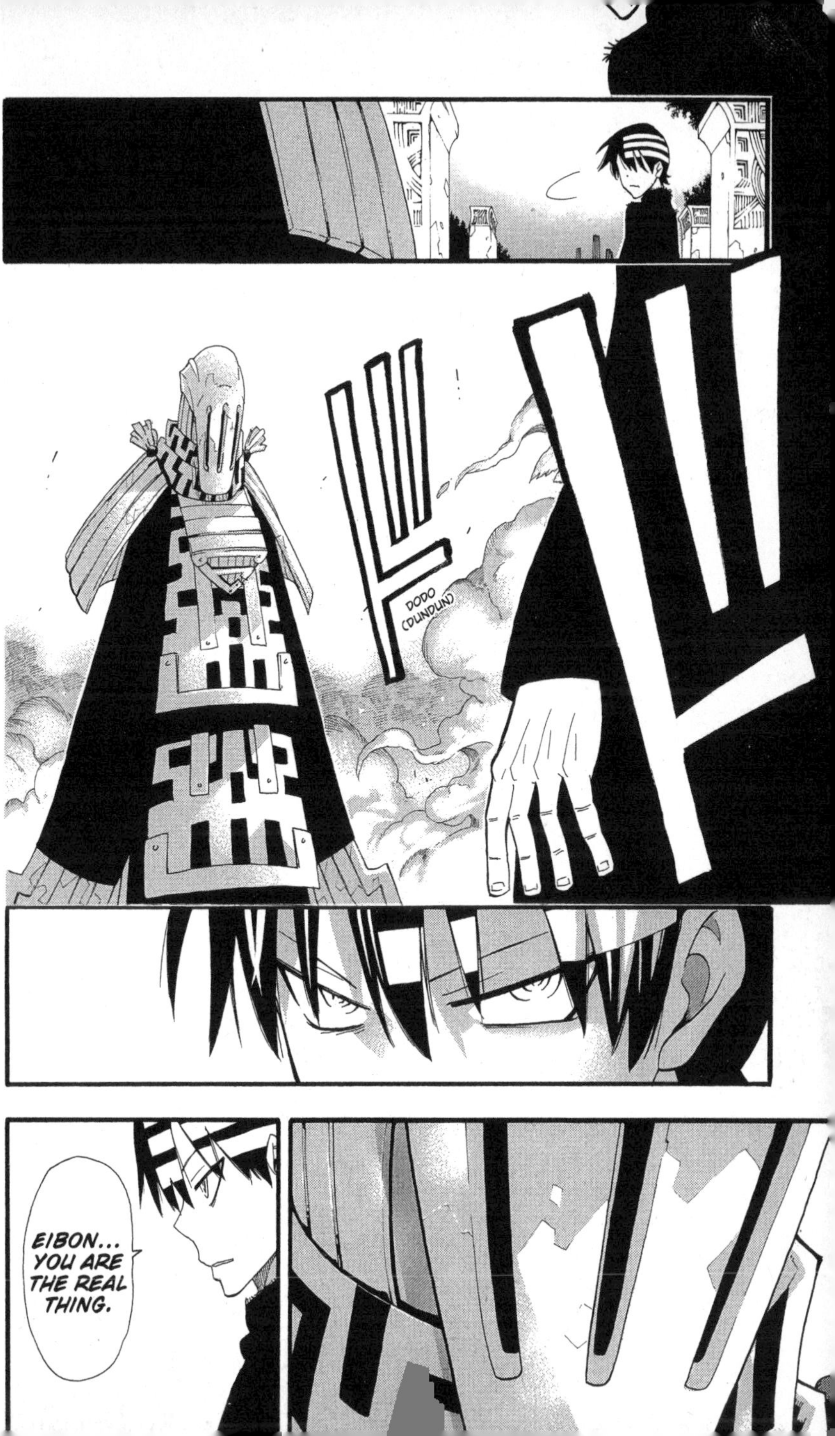
!
DODO (DUNDUN)
EIBON... YOU ARE THE REAL THING.

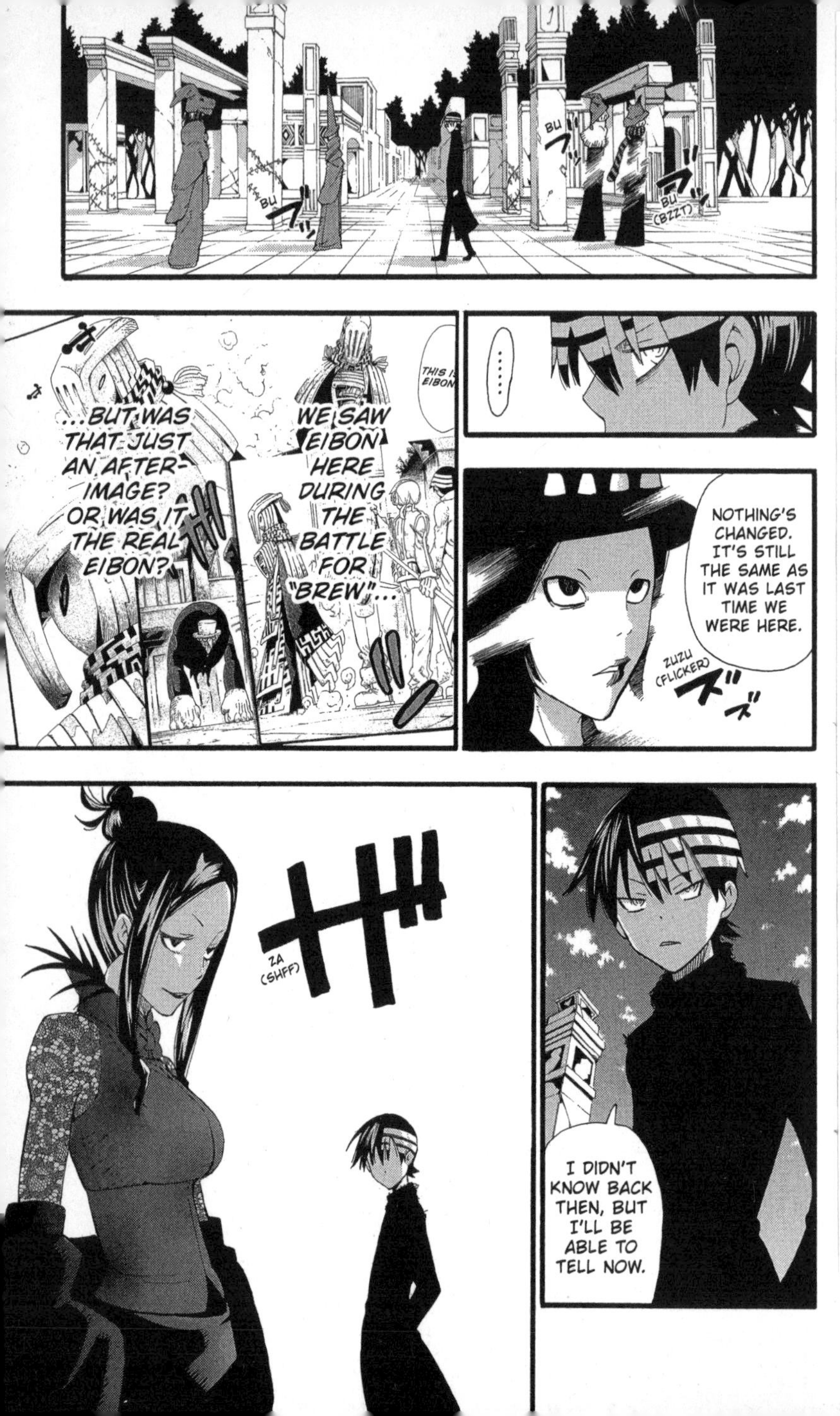
BU
(BZZT)
BU
BU
......
NOTHING'S CHANGED. IT'S STILL THE SAME AS IT WAS LAST TIME WE WERE HERE.
ZUZU
(FLICKER)
THIS I
EIBON
WE SAW EIBON HERE DURING THE BATTLE FOR "BREW"...
...BUT WAS THAT JUST AN AFTER-IMAGE? OR WAS IT THE REAL EIBON?
I DIDN'T KNOW BACK THEN, BUT I'LL BE ABLE TO TELL NOW.
ZA
(SHFF)

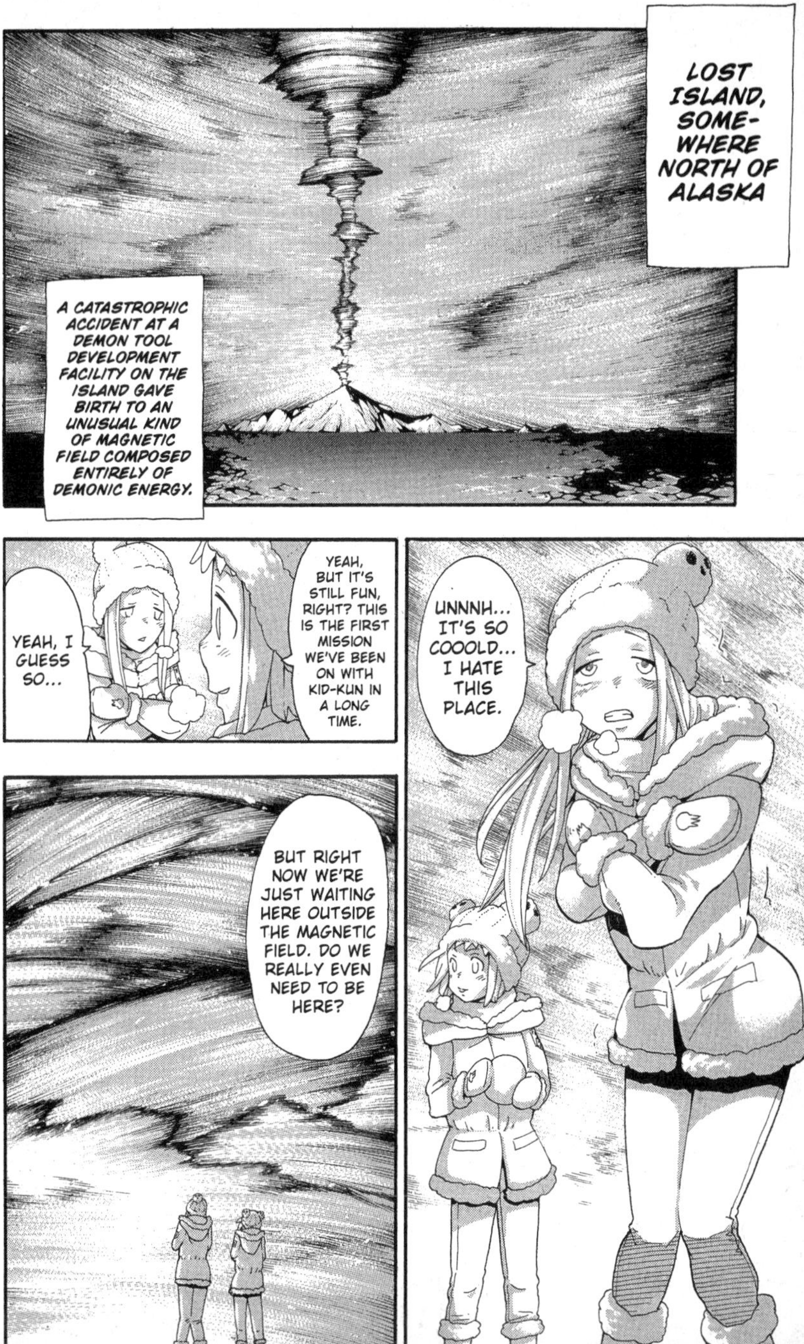
LOST ISLAND, SOMEWHERE NORTH OF ALASKA
A CATASTROPHIC ACCIDENT AT A DEMON TOOL DEVELOPMENT FACILITY ON THE ISLAND GAVE BIRTH TO AN UNUSUAL KIND OF MAGNETIC FIELD COMPOSED ENTIRELY OF DEMONIC ENERGY.
UNNNH... IT'S SO COOOLD... I HATE THIS PLACE.
YEAH, BUT IT'S STILL FUN, RIGHT? THIS IS THE FIRST MISSION WE'VE BEEN ON WITH KID-KUN IN A LONG TIME.
YEAH, I GUESS SO...
BUT RIGHT NOW WE'RE JUST WAITING HERE OUTSIDE THE MAGNETIC FIELD. DO WE REALLY EVEN NEED TO BE HERE?

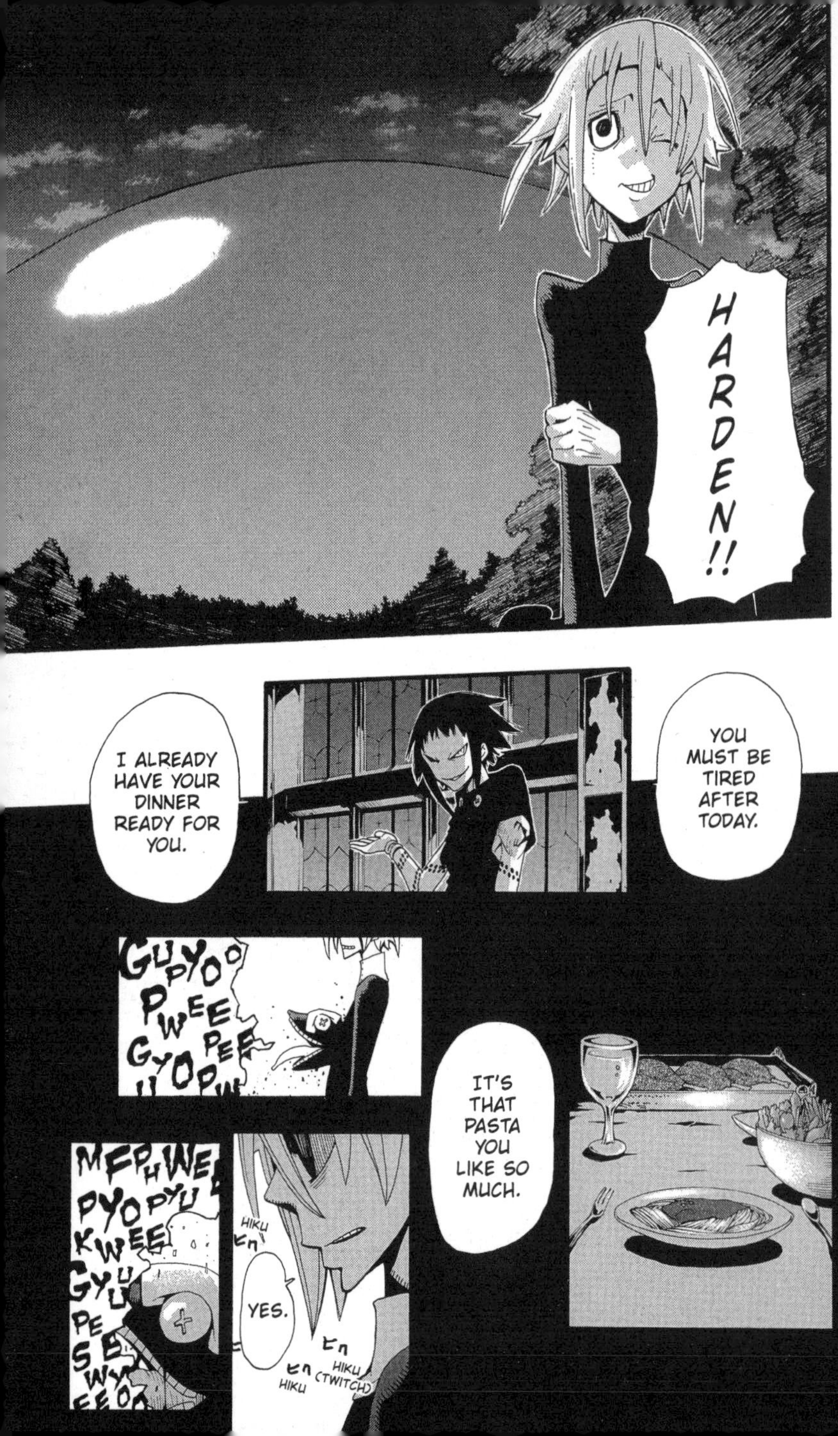
HARDEN!!
YOU MUST BE TIRED AFTER TODAY.
I ALREADY HAVE YOUR DINNER READY FOR YOU.
IT'S THAT PASTA YOU LIKE SO MUCH.
HIKU ヒク
YES.
ヒク HIKU (TWITCH)
ヒク HIKU

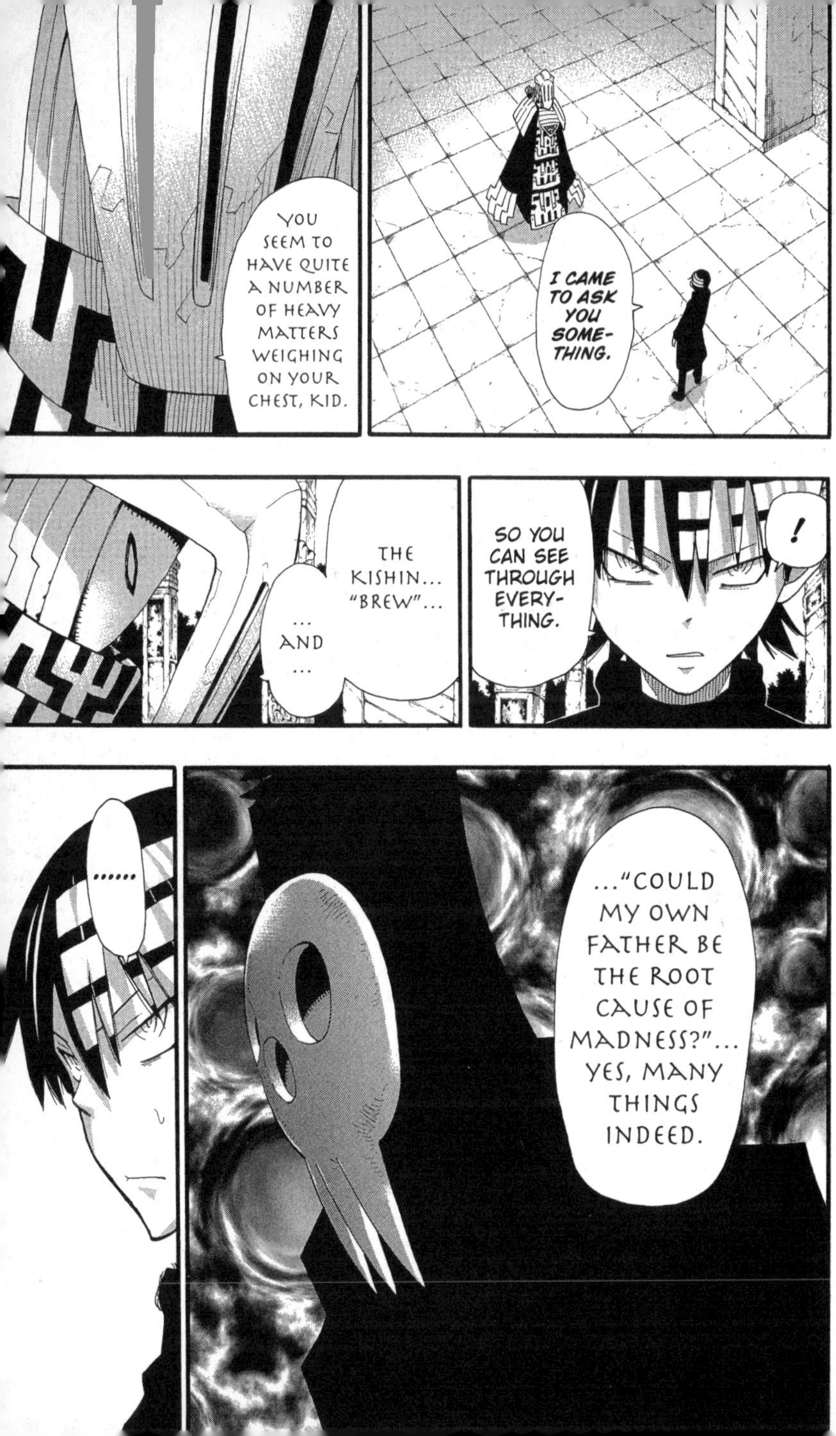
I CAME TO ASK YOU SOMETHING.
YOU SEEM TO HAVE QUITE A NUMBER OF HEAVY MATTERS WEIGHING ON YOUR CHEST, KID.
!
SO YOU CAN SEE THROUGH EVERYTHING.
THE KISHIN... "BREW"...
... AND ...
..."COULD MY OWN FATHER BE THE ROOT CAUSE OF MADNESS?"... YES, MANY THINGS INDEED.
......

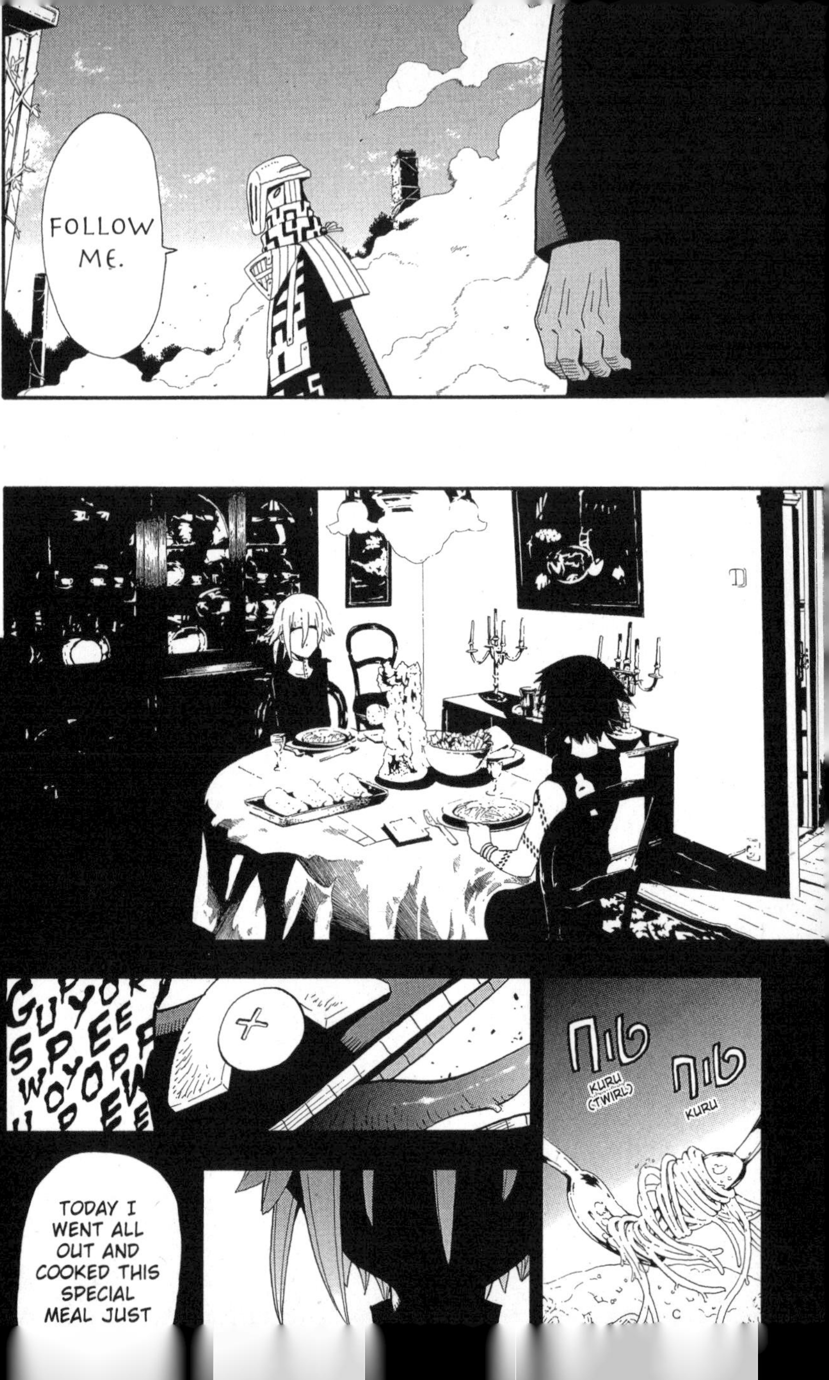
FOLLOW ME.
KURU (TWIRL)
KURU
TODAY I WENT ALL OUT AND COOKED THIS SPECIAL MEAL JUST

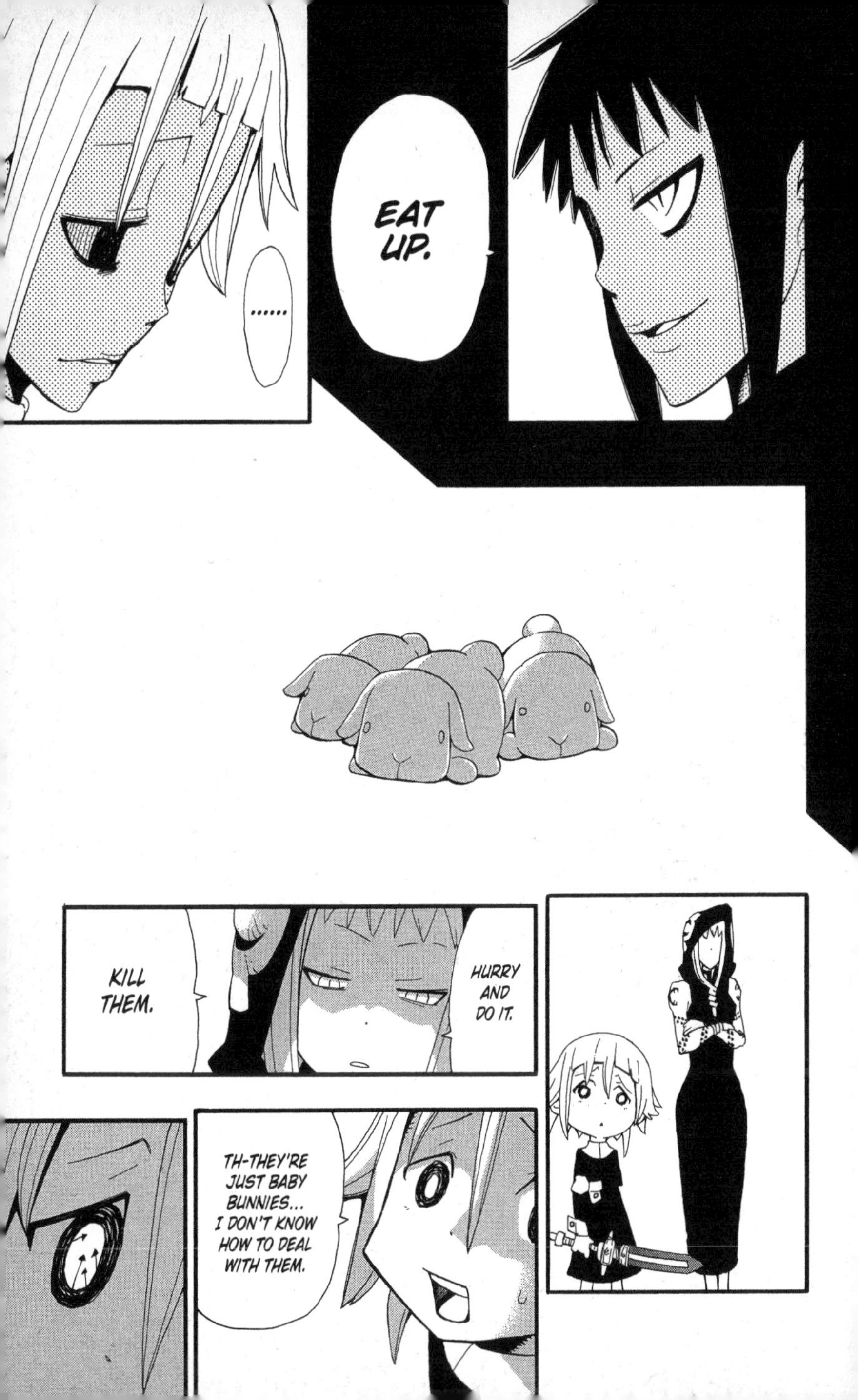
EAT UP.
......
HURRY AND DO IT.
KILL THEM.
TH-THEY'RE JUST BABY BUNNIES... I DON'T KNOW HOW TO DEAL WITH THEM.

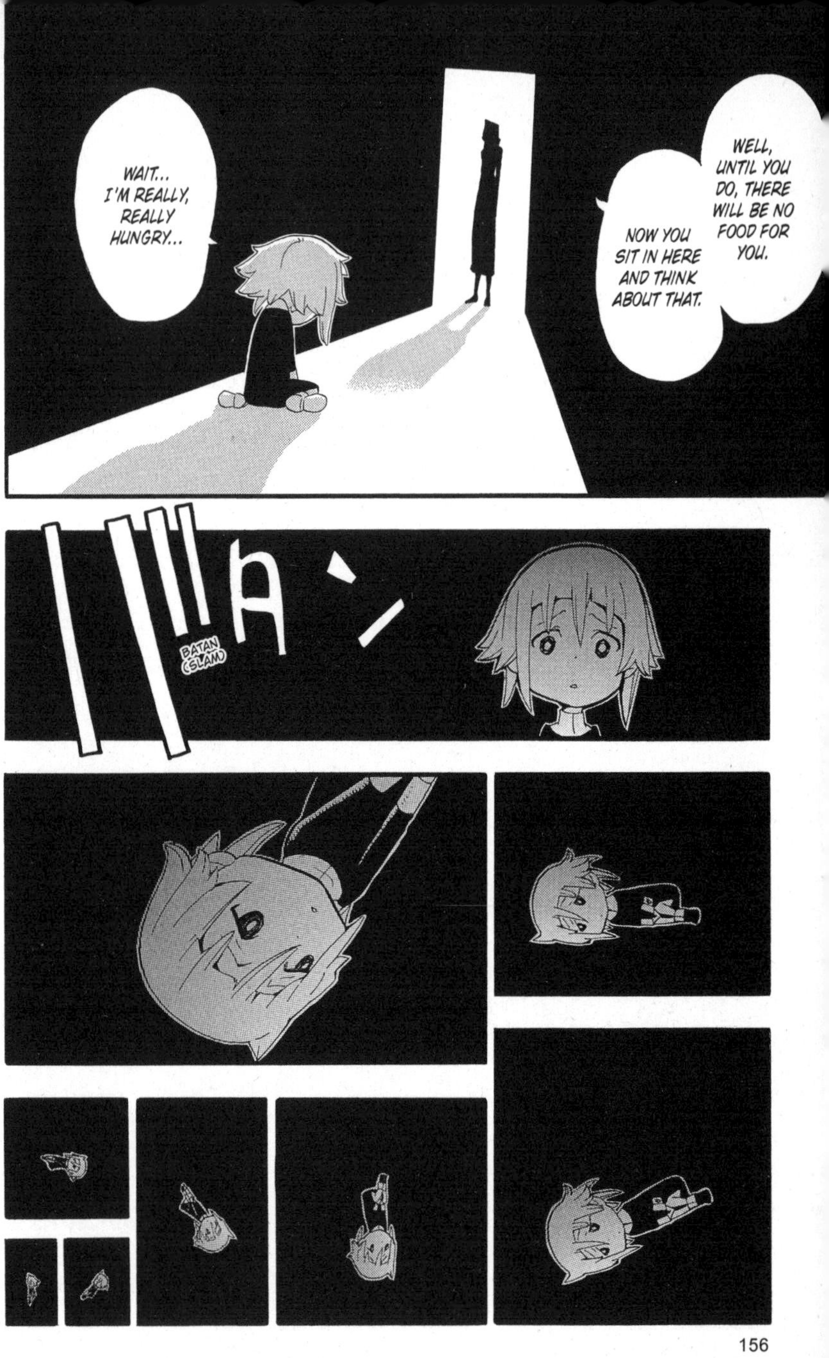
WELL, UNTIL YOU DO, THERE WILL BE NO FOOD FOR YOU.
NOW YOU SIT IN HERE AND THINK ABOUT THAT.
WAIT... I'M REALLY, REALLY HUNGRY...
BATAN (SLAM)

KACHI (CLICK)

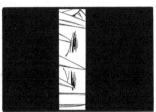

ALL RIGHT, IT'S BEEN FIVE DAYS. I'M GIVING YOU YOUR FIRST CHANCE TO EARN SOME FOOD.

KILL THE THREE LITTLE BUNNIES USING THREE DIFFERENT KILLING METHODS.

IF YOU DON'T DO IT NOW, THEN IT'S ANOTHER FIVE DAYS WITH NO FOOD.

IT'S JUST LIKE IN THAT PICTURE BOOK WE'RE ALWAYS STUDYING.

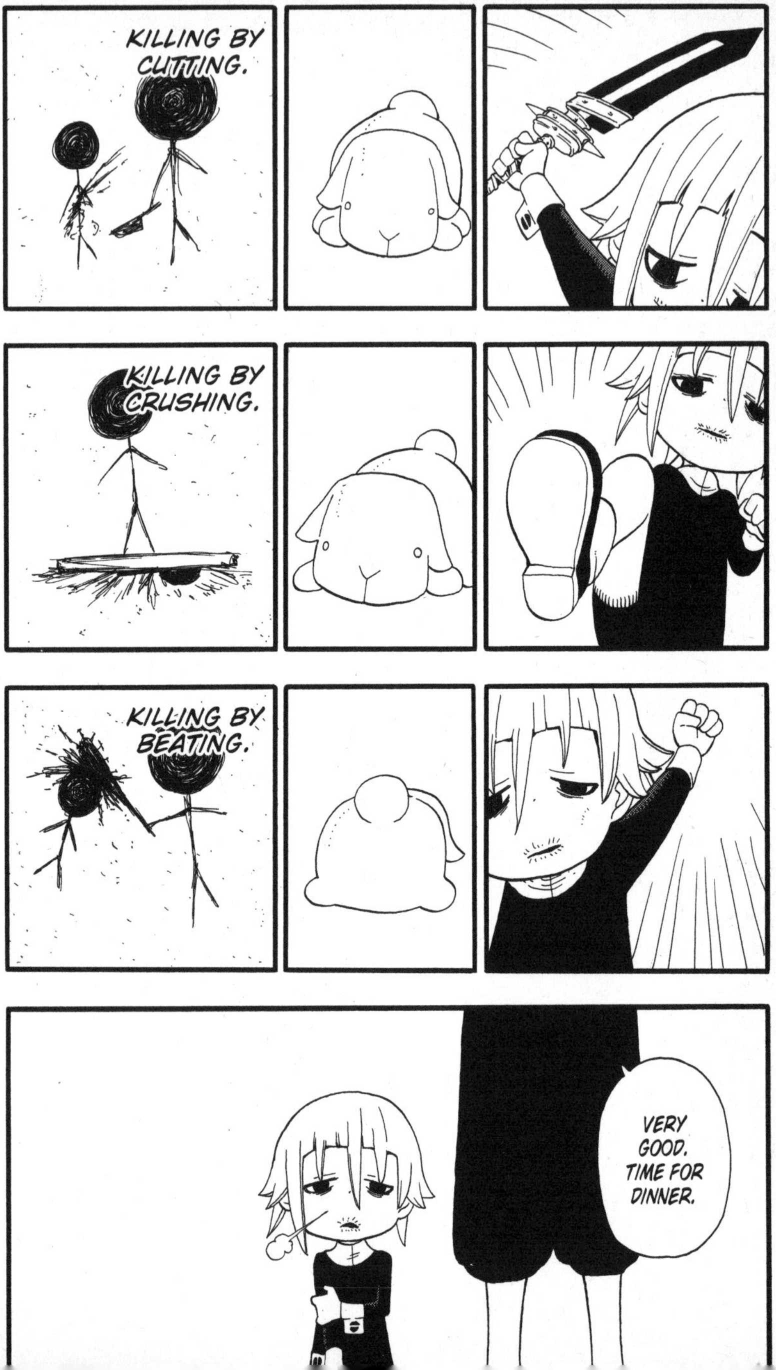
KILLING BY CUTTING.
KILLING BY CRUSHING.
KILLING BY BEATING.
VERY GOOD. TIME FOR DINNER.

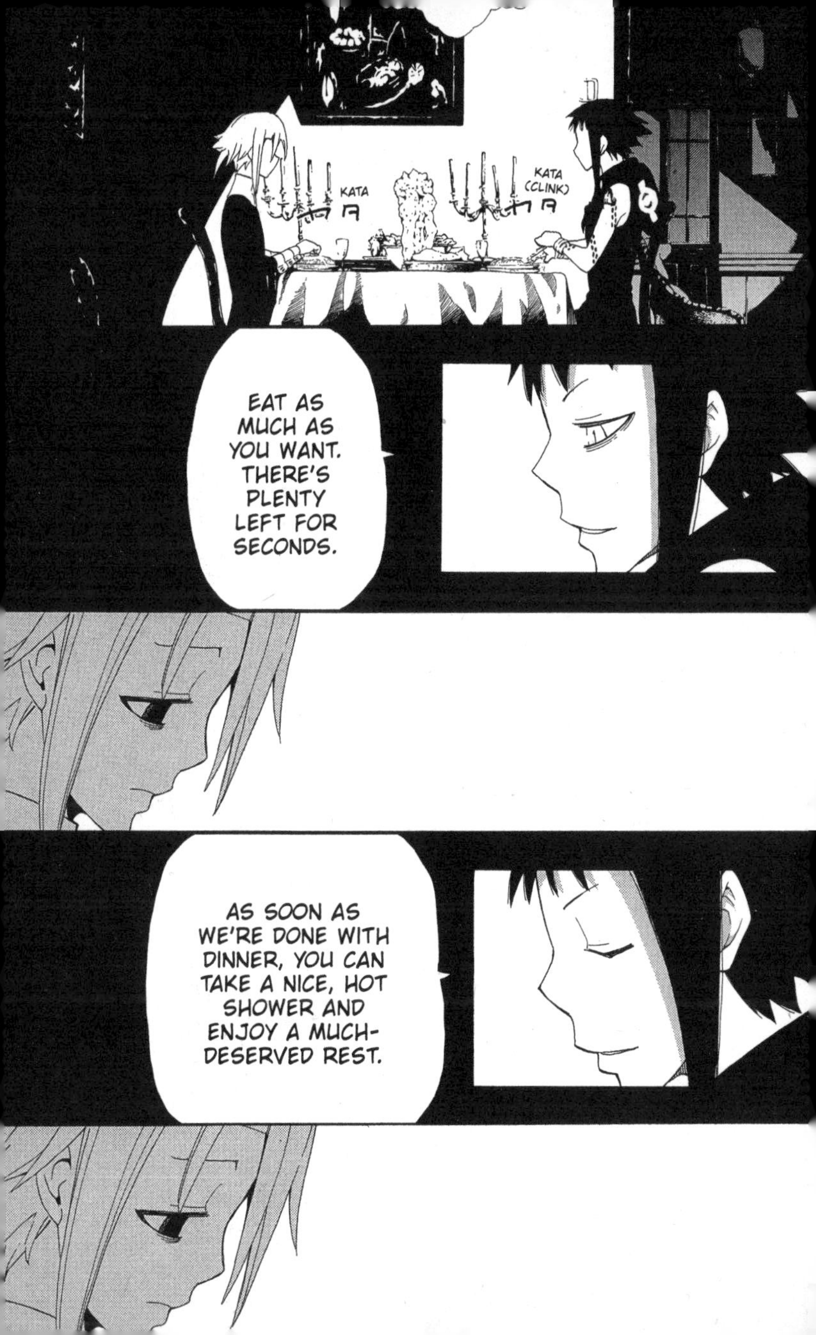
KATA (CLINK)
KATA
EAT AS MUCH AS YOU WANT. THERE'S PLENTY LEFT FOR SECONDS.
AS SOON AS WE'RE DONE WITH DINNER, YOU CAN TAKE A NICE, HOT SHOWER AND ENJOY A MUCH-DESERVED REST.

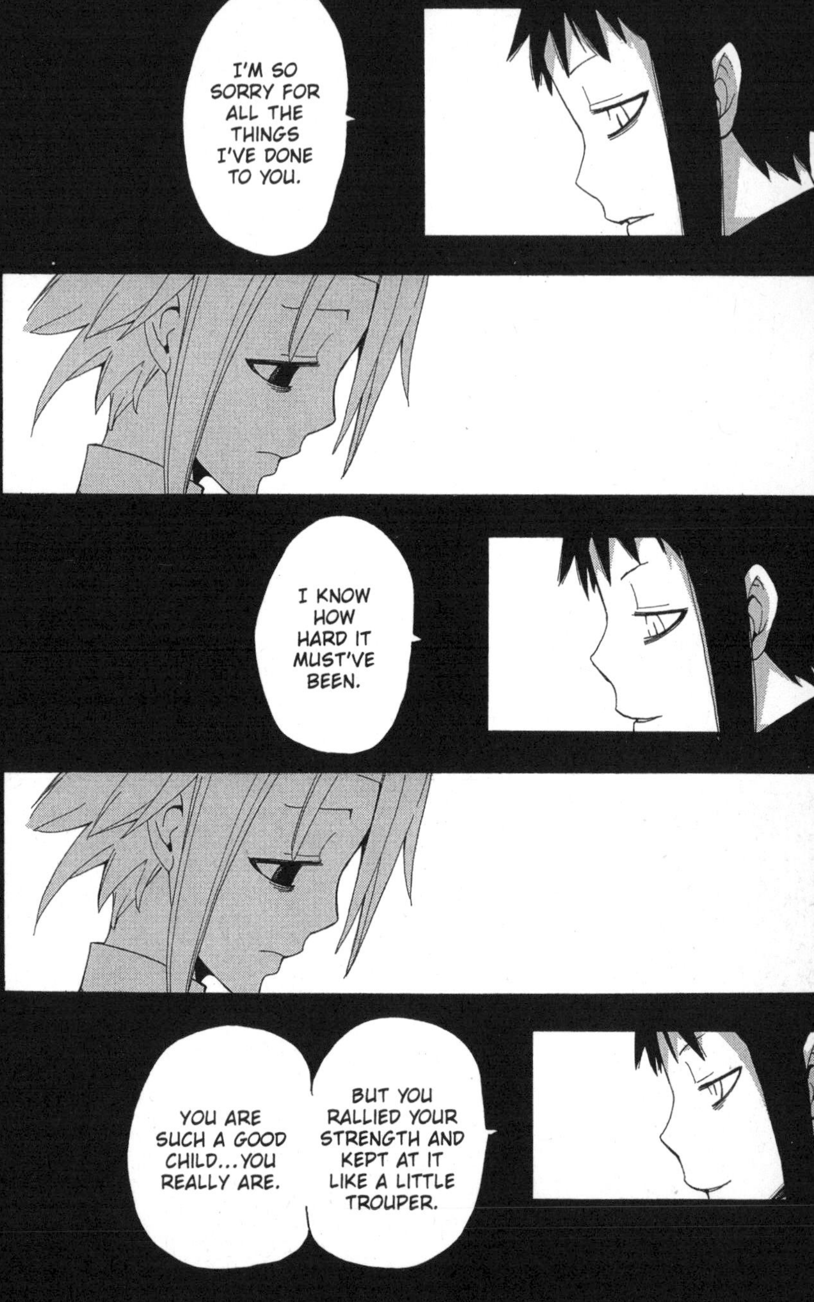
I'M SO SORRY FOR ALL THE THINGS I'VE DONE TO YOU.
I KNOW HOW HARD IT MUST'VE BEEN.
BUT YOU RALLIED YOUR STRENGTH AND KEPT AT IT LIKE A LITTLE TROUPER.
YOU ARE SUCH A GOOD CHILD...YOU REALLY ARE.

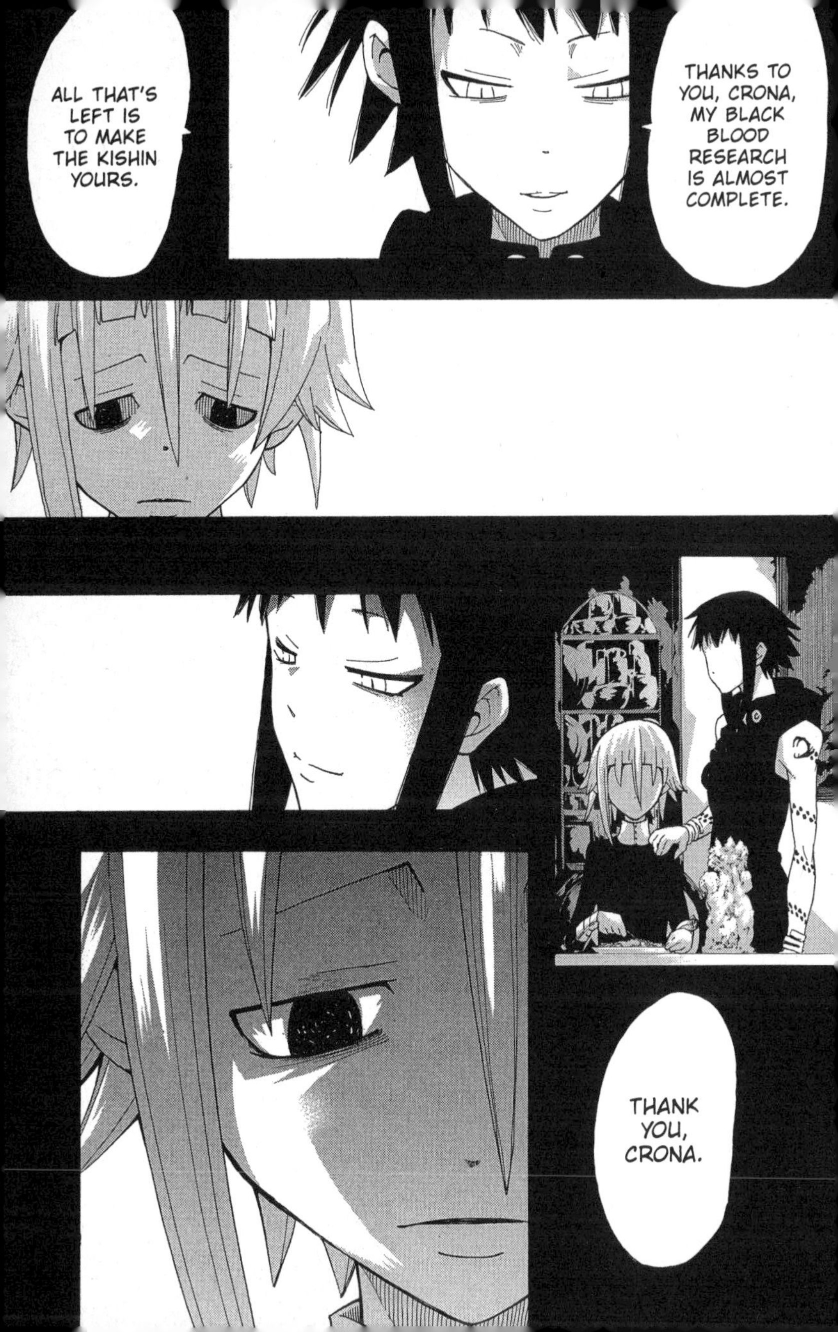
THANKS TO YOU, CRONA, MY BLACK BLOOD RESEARCH IS ALMOST COMPLETE.
ALL THAT'S LEFT IS TO MAKE THE KISHIN YOURS.
THANK YOU, CRONA.

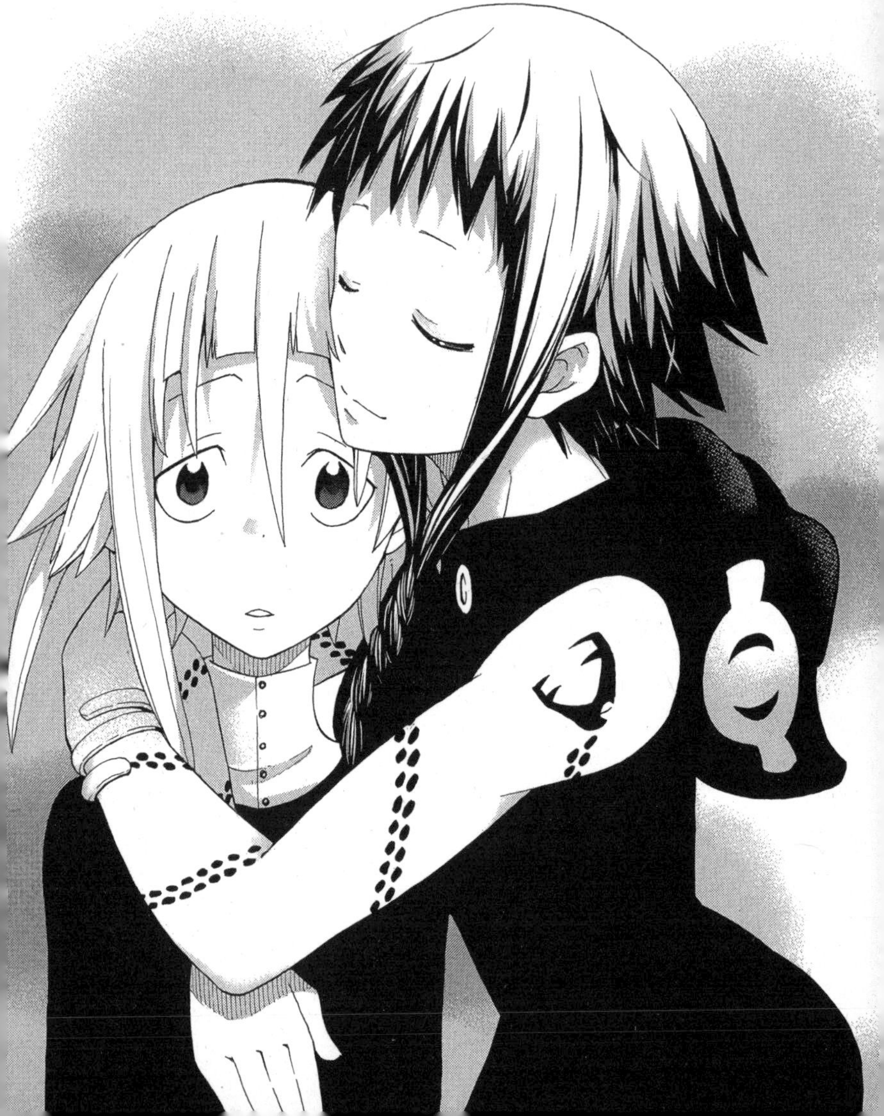

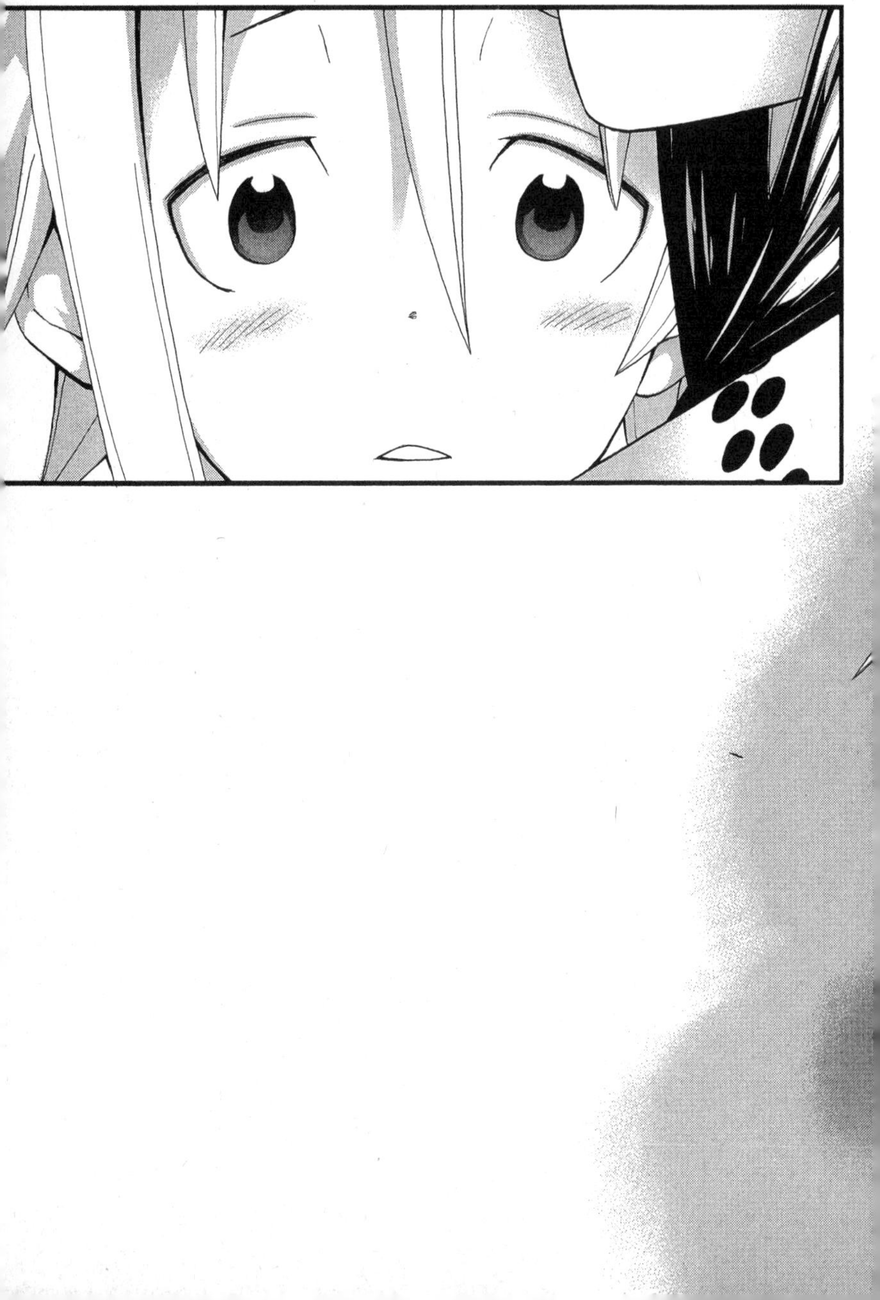

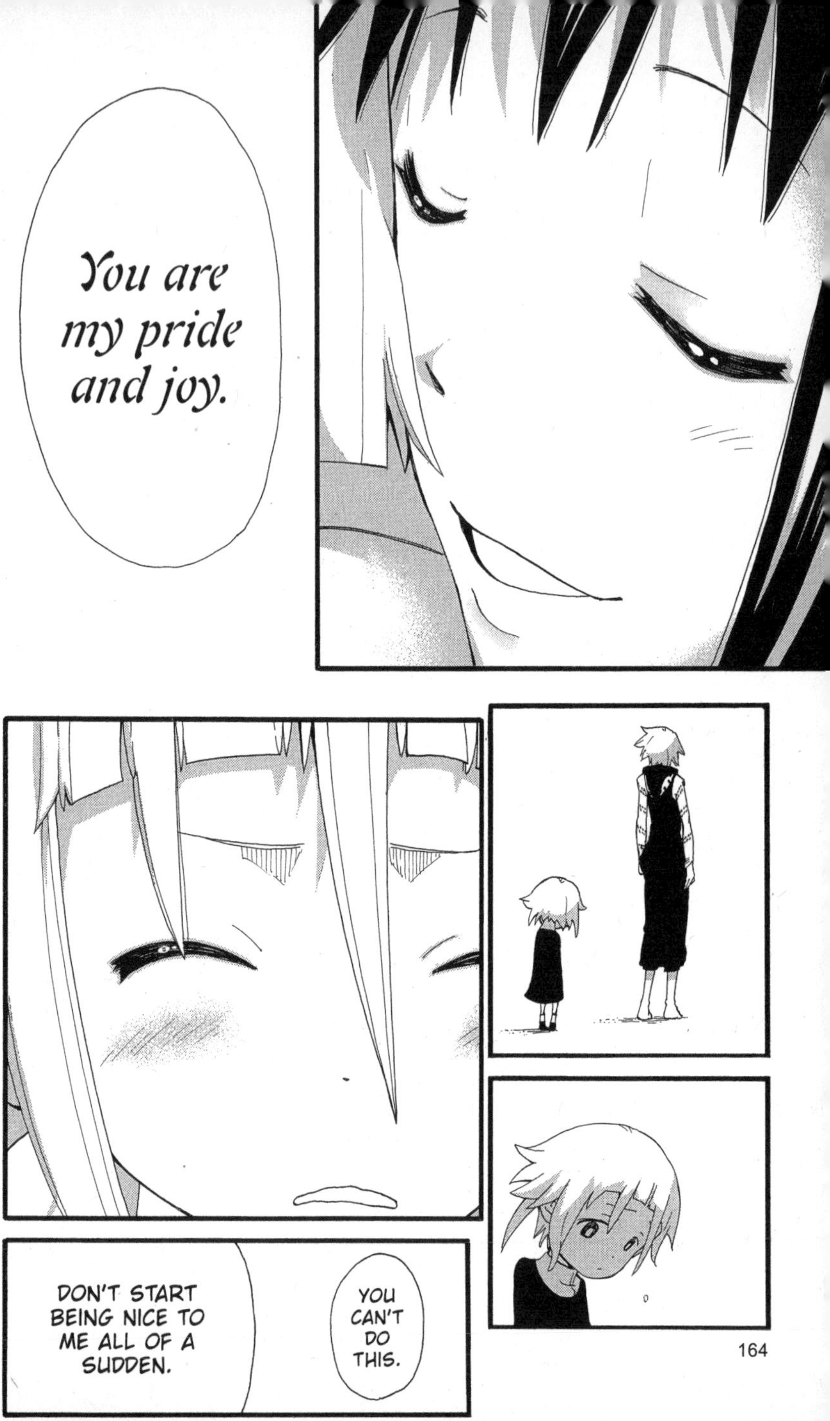
You are my pride and joy.
YOU CAN'T DO THIS.
DON'T START BEING NICE TO ME ALL OF A SUDDEN.

I... I JUST...
YOU'RE MEDUSA-SAMA. YOU'RE MY MOTHER...
IT'S BECAUSE YOU'RE MY MOTHER.
THAT'S WHY I ALWAYS DID WHAT YOU TOLD ME.

THAT'S HOW I COULD THROW EVERYTHING AWAY... LIKE YOU TOLD ME TO.

BUT THIS... WHEN YOU SUDDENLY ACT LIKE A NORMAL MOTHER, I JUST...

I don't know how to deal with it....

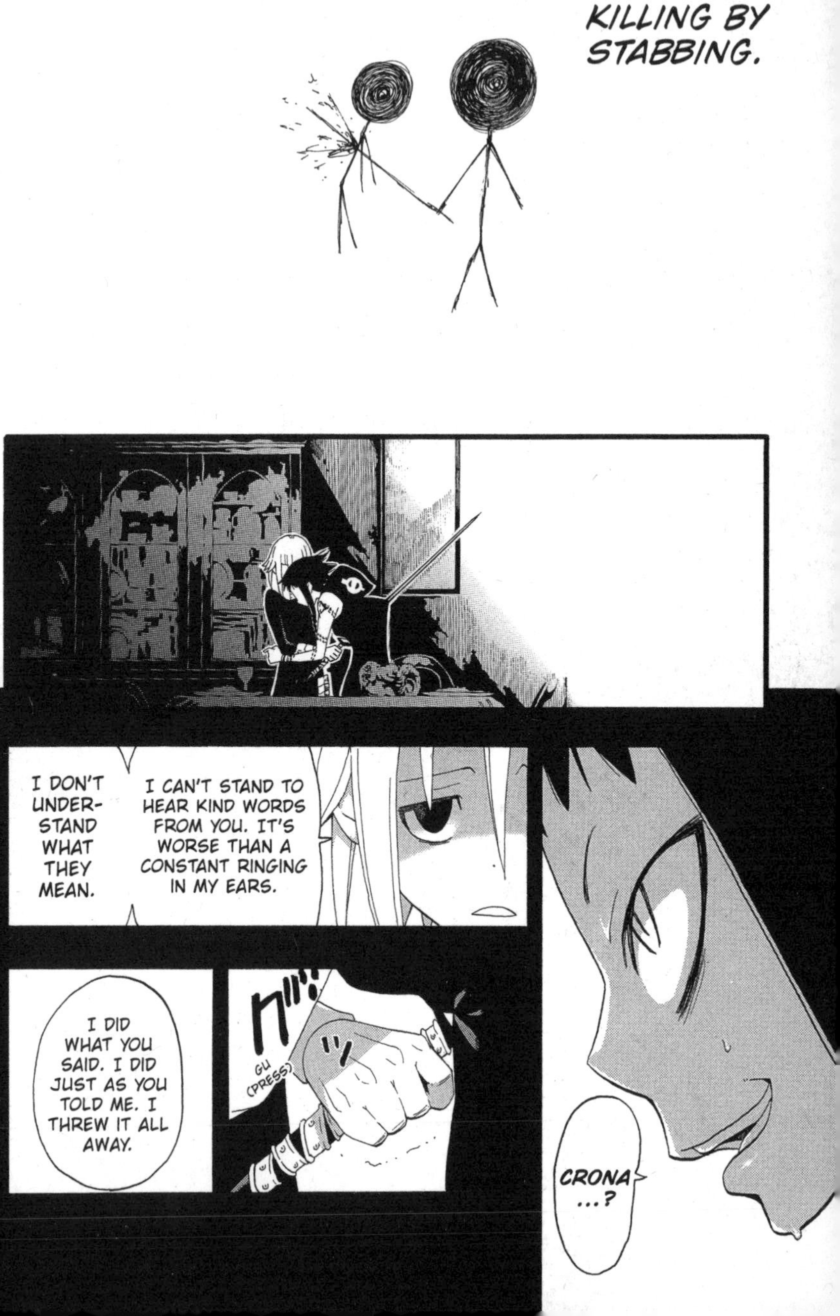
KILLING BY STABBING.
CRONA ...?
I CAN'T STAND TO HEAR KIND WORDS FROM YOU. IT'S WORSE THAN A CONSTANT RINGING IN MY EARS.
I DON'T UNDER-STAND WHAT THEY MEAN.
GU (PRESS)
I DID WHAT YOU SAID. I DID JUST AS YOU TOLD ME. I THREW IT ALL AWAY.

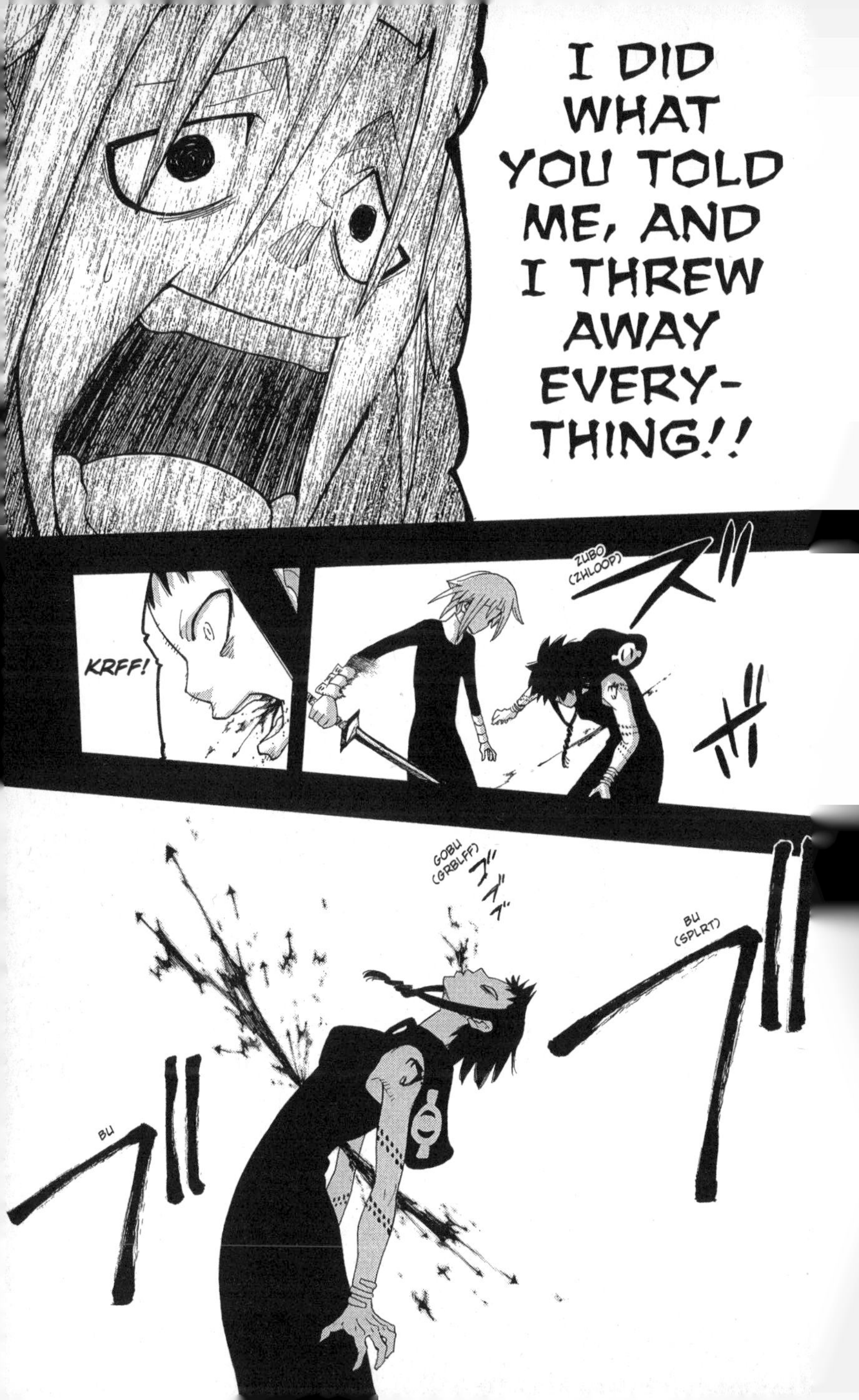
I DID WHAT YOU TOLD ME, AND I THREW AWAY EVERY-THING!!
ZUBO (ZHLOOP)
KRFF!
GOBU (GRBLFF)
BU (SPLRT)
BU

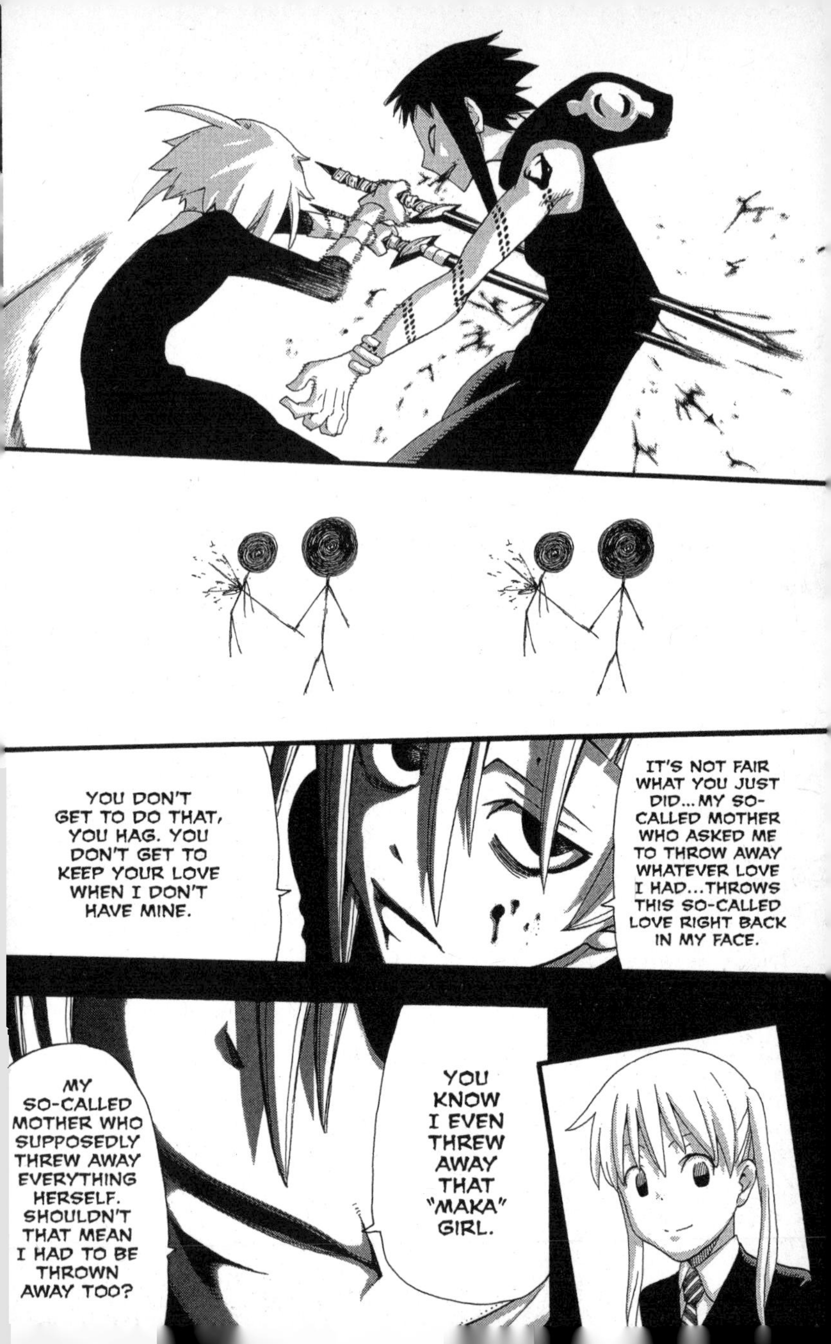
IT'S NOT FAIR WHAT YOU JUST DID... MY SO-CALLED MOTHER WHO ASKED ME TO THROW AWAY WHATEVER LOVE I HAD... THROWS THIS SO-CALLED LOVE RIGHT BACK IN MY FACE.
YOU DON'T GET TO DO THAT, YOU HAG. YOU DON'T GET TO KEEP YOUR LOVE WHEN I DON'T HAVE MINE.
YOU KNOW I EVEN THREW AWAY THAT "MAKA" GIRL.
MY SO-CALLED MOTHER WHO SUPPOSEDLY THREW AWAY EVERYTHING HERSELF. SHOULDN'T THAT MEAN I HAD TO BE THROWN AWAY TOO?

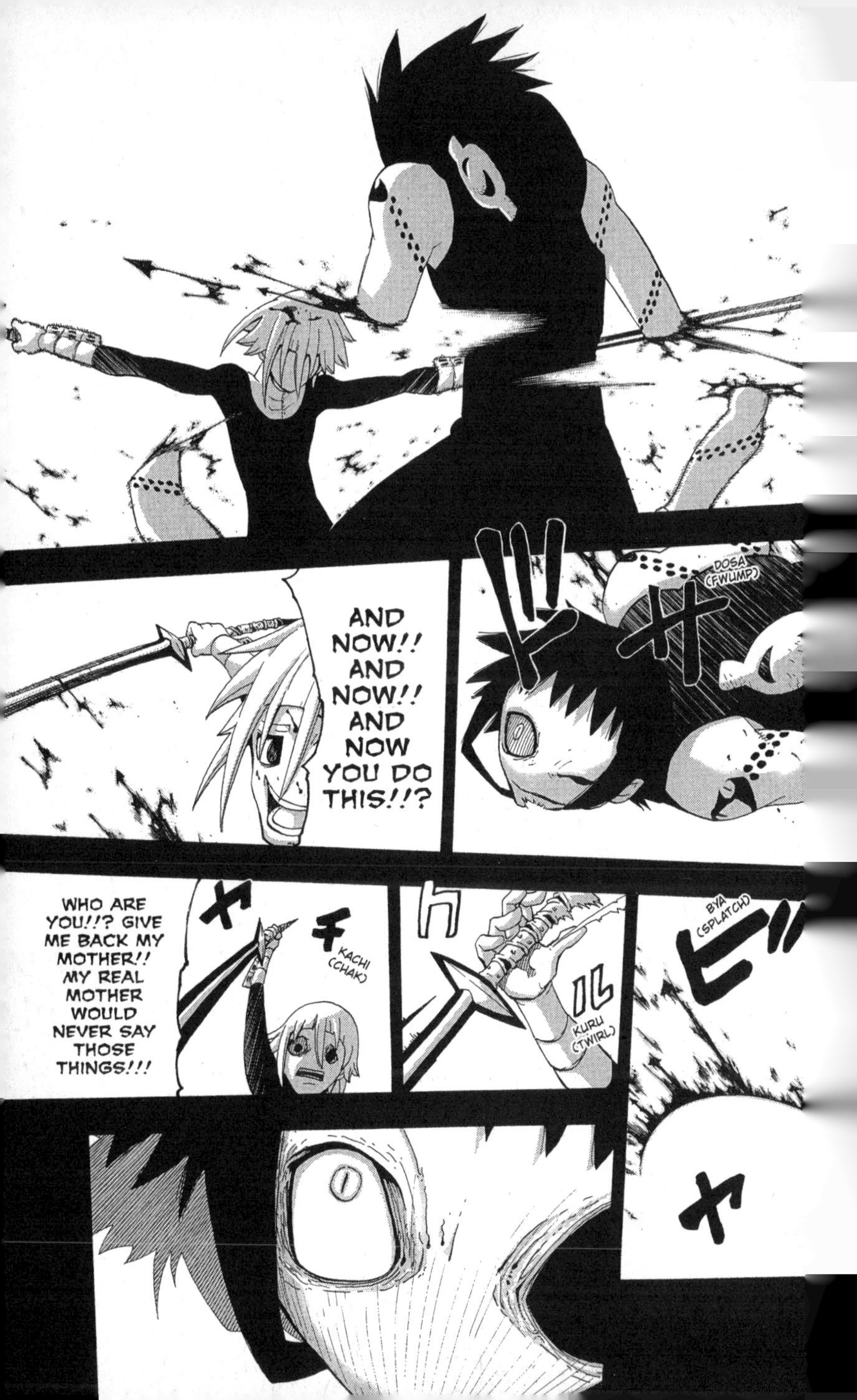
DOSA (FWUMP)
AND NOW!! AND NOW!! AND NOW YOU DO THIS!!?
BYA (SPLATCH)
KURU (TWIRL)
KACHI (CHAK)
WHO ARE YOU!!? GIVE ME BACK MY MOTHER!! MY REAL MOTHER WOULD NEVER SAY THOSE THINGS!!!

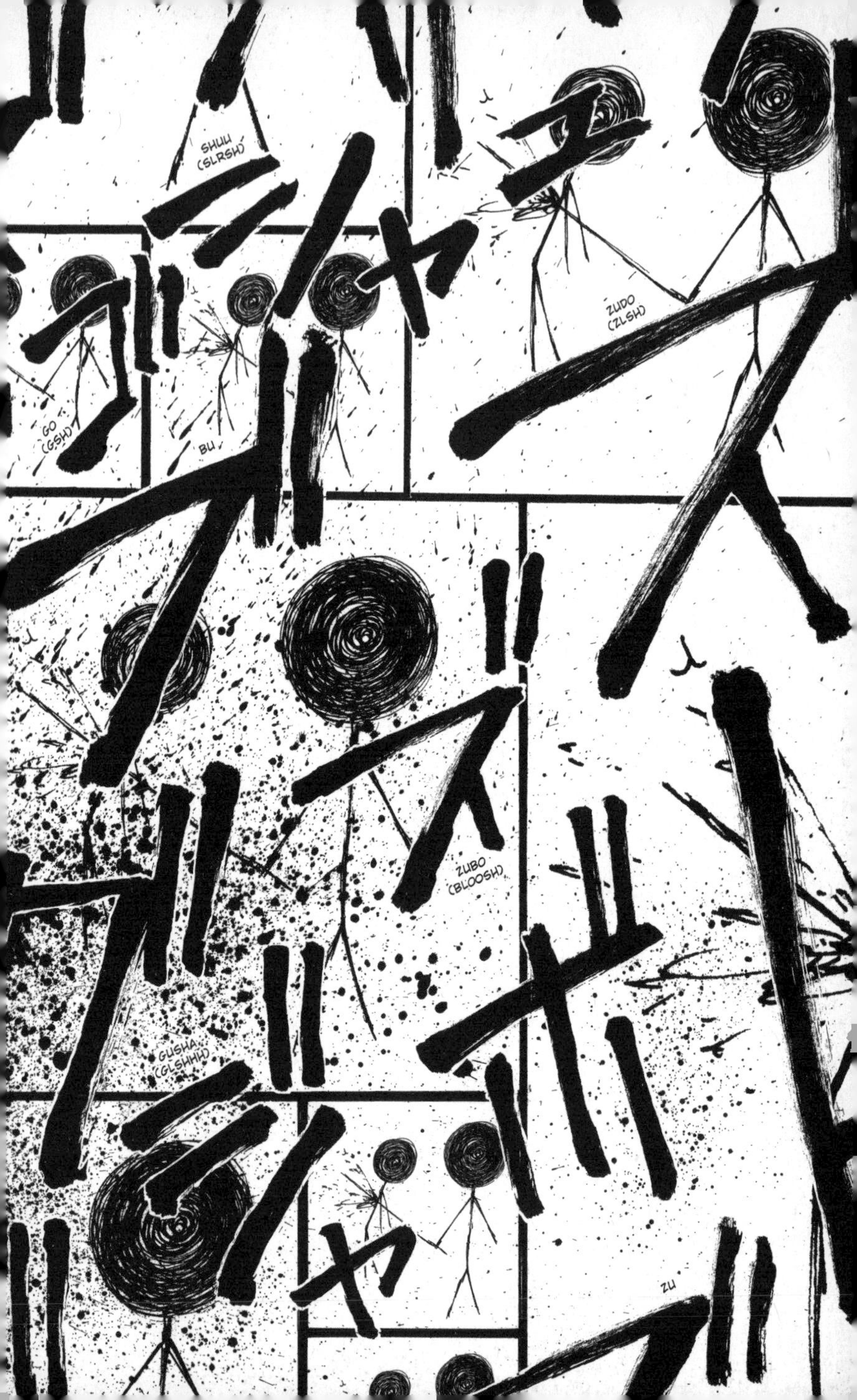
ZUDO
(ZLSH)
SHUU
(SLRSH)
BU
GO
(GSH)
ZU
ZUBO
(BLOOSH)
GUSHA
(GLSHHH)

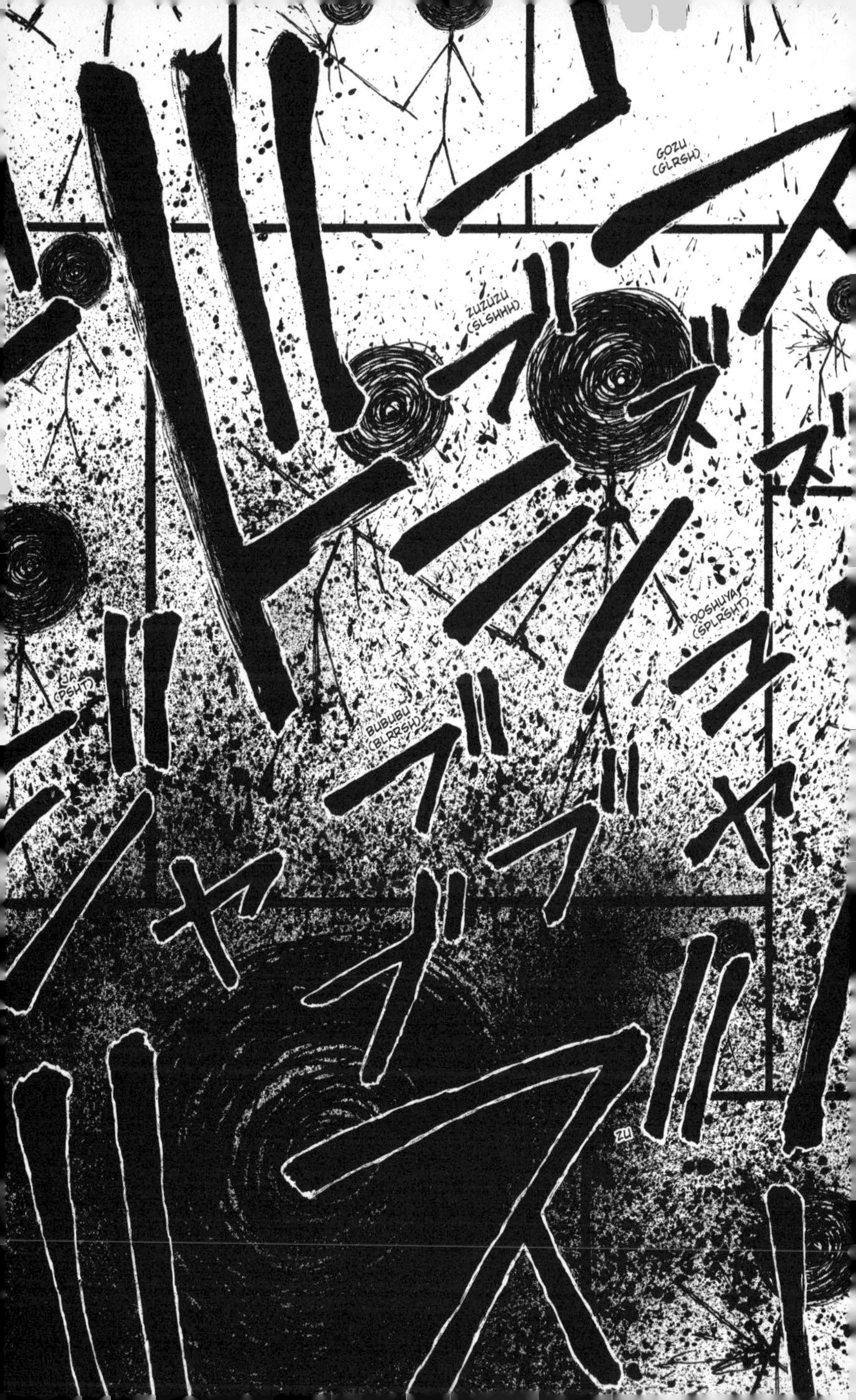
GOZU (GLRSH)
ZUZUZU (SLSHHH)
DOSHUYA (SPLRSHT)
BUBUBU (BLRRSH)
JA (PSHT)
ZU

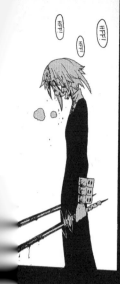

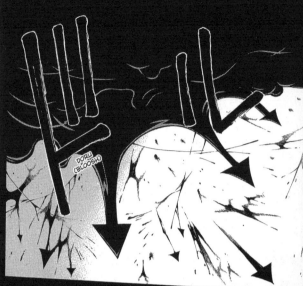

DORU (BLOOSH)
HFF!
HFF!
HFF!
SOMETHING DIED. I KILLED SOMETHING.
I THINK IT MIGHT'VE BEEN SOMETHING REALLY IMPORTANT, BUT I DON'T CARE...I DON'T KNOW ANYTHING ANYMORE.
IT'S COMPLETE!! YOU'VE CAST ASIDE YOUR FINAL SUPPORT, AND NOW THE BLACK BLOOD IS COMPLETE!!!
BACHI (CRRK)

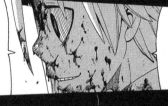

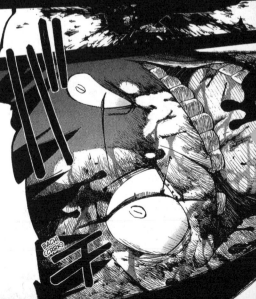

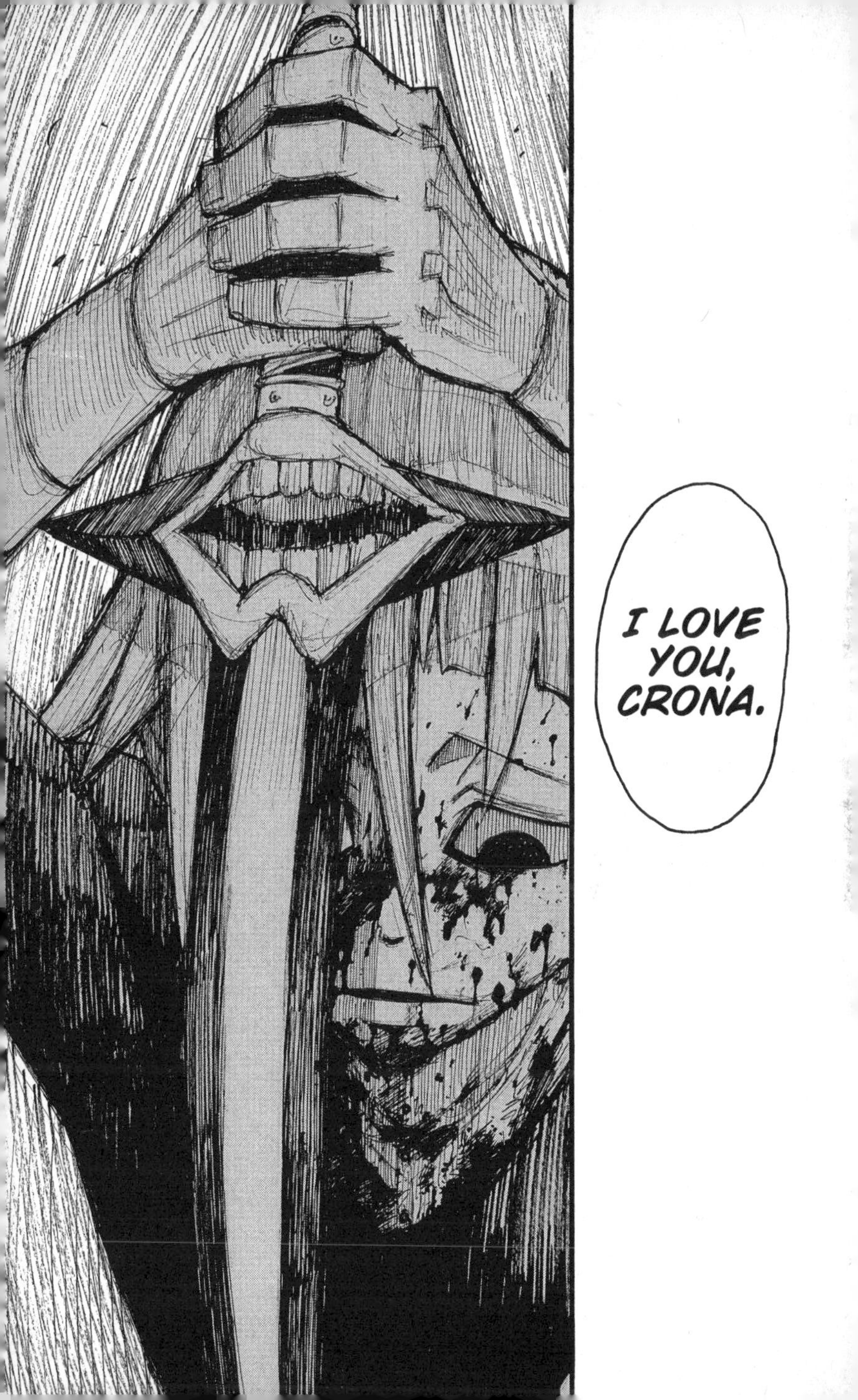
I LOVE YOU, CRONA.

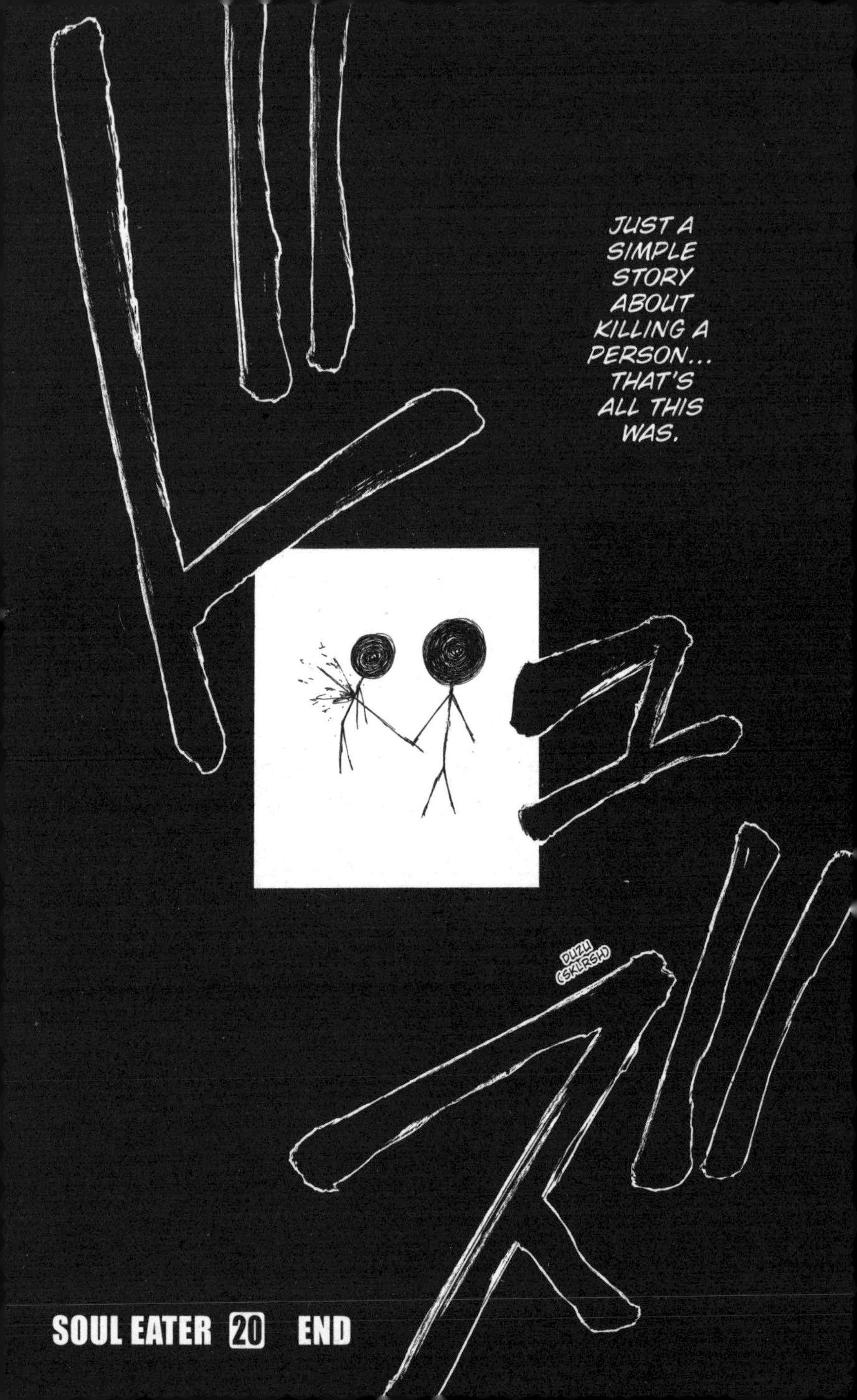
JUST A SIMPLE STORY ABOUT KILLING A PERSON... THAT'S ALL THIS WAS.
DUZU (SKLRSH)

SOUL EATER 20 END

SOUL EATER

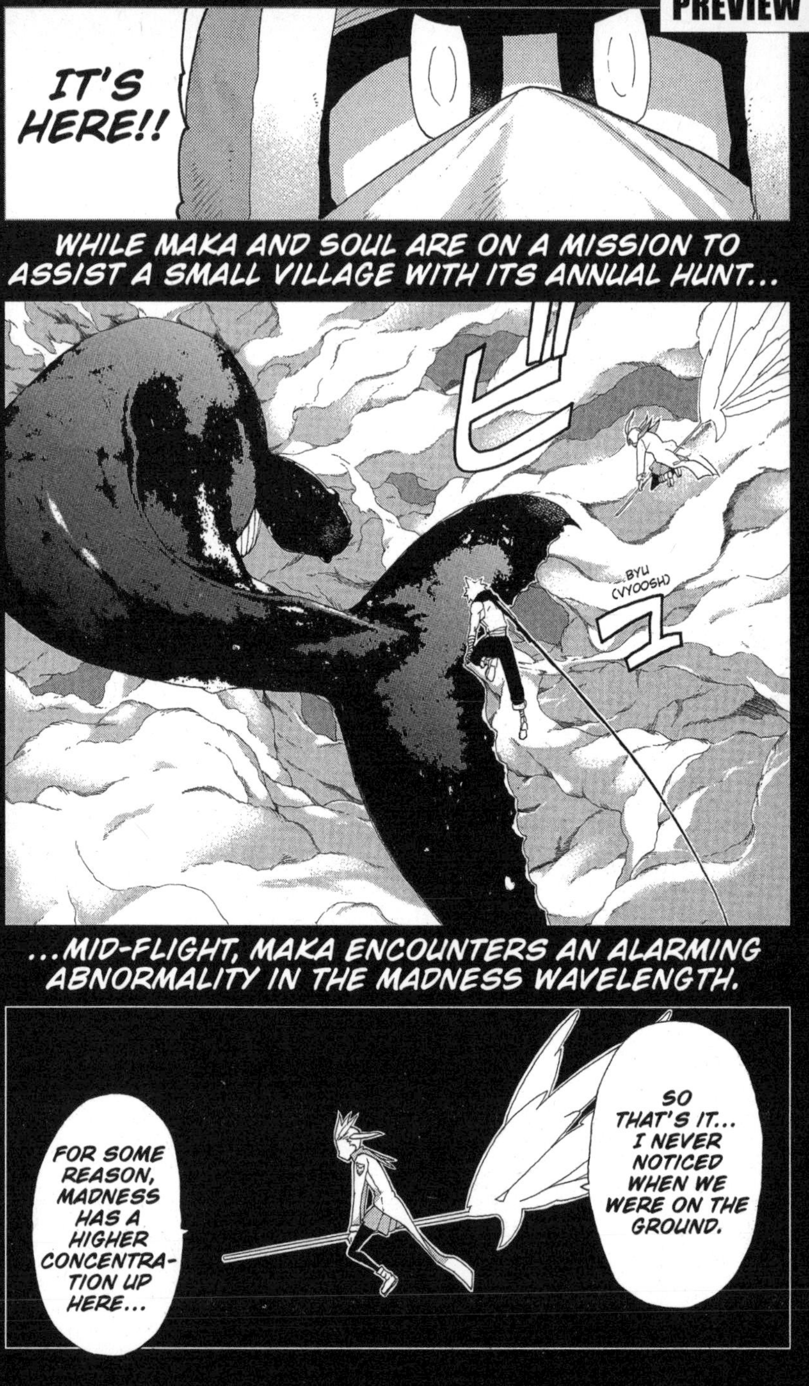
IT'S HERE!!
WHILE MAKA AND SOUL ARE ON A MISSION TO ASSIST A SMALL VILLAGE WITH ITS ANNUAL HUNT...
BYU (VYOOSH)
...MID-FLIGHT, MAKA ENCOUNTERS AN ALARMING ABNORMALITY IN THE MADNESS WAVELENGTH.
SO THAT'S IT... I NEVER NOTICED WHEN WE WERE ON THE GROUND.
FOR SOME REASON, MADNESS HAS A HIGHER CONCENTRATION UP HERE...

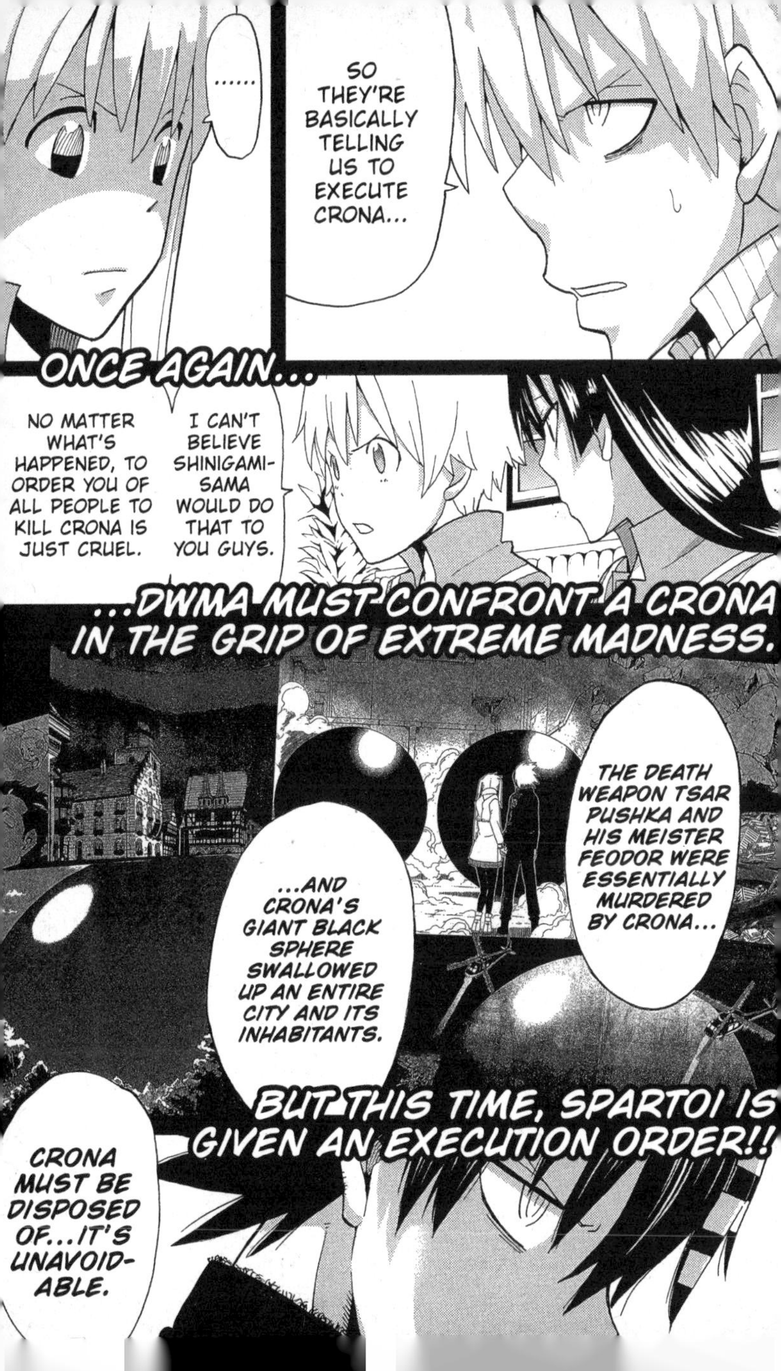
SO THEY'RE BASICALLY TELLING US TO EXECUTE CRONA...
......
ONCE AGAIN...
I CAN'T BELIEVE SHINIGAMI-SAMA WOULD DO THAT TO YOU GUYS.
NO MATTER WHAT'S HAPPENED, TO ORDER YOU OF ALL PEOPLE TO KILL CRONA IS JUST CRUEL.
...DWMA MUST CONFRONT A CRONA IN THE GRIP OF EXTREME MADNESS.
THE DEATH WEAPON TSAR PUSHKA AND HIS MEISTER FEODOR WERE ESSENTIALLY MURDERED BY CRONA...
...AND CRONA'S GIANT BLACK SPHERE SWALLOWED UP AN ENTIRE CITY AND ITS INHABITANTS.
BUT THIS TIME, SPARTOI IS GIVEN AN EXECUTION ORDER!!
CRONA MUST BE DISPOSED OF...IT'S UNAVOIDABLE.

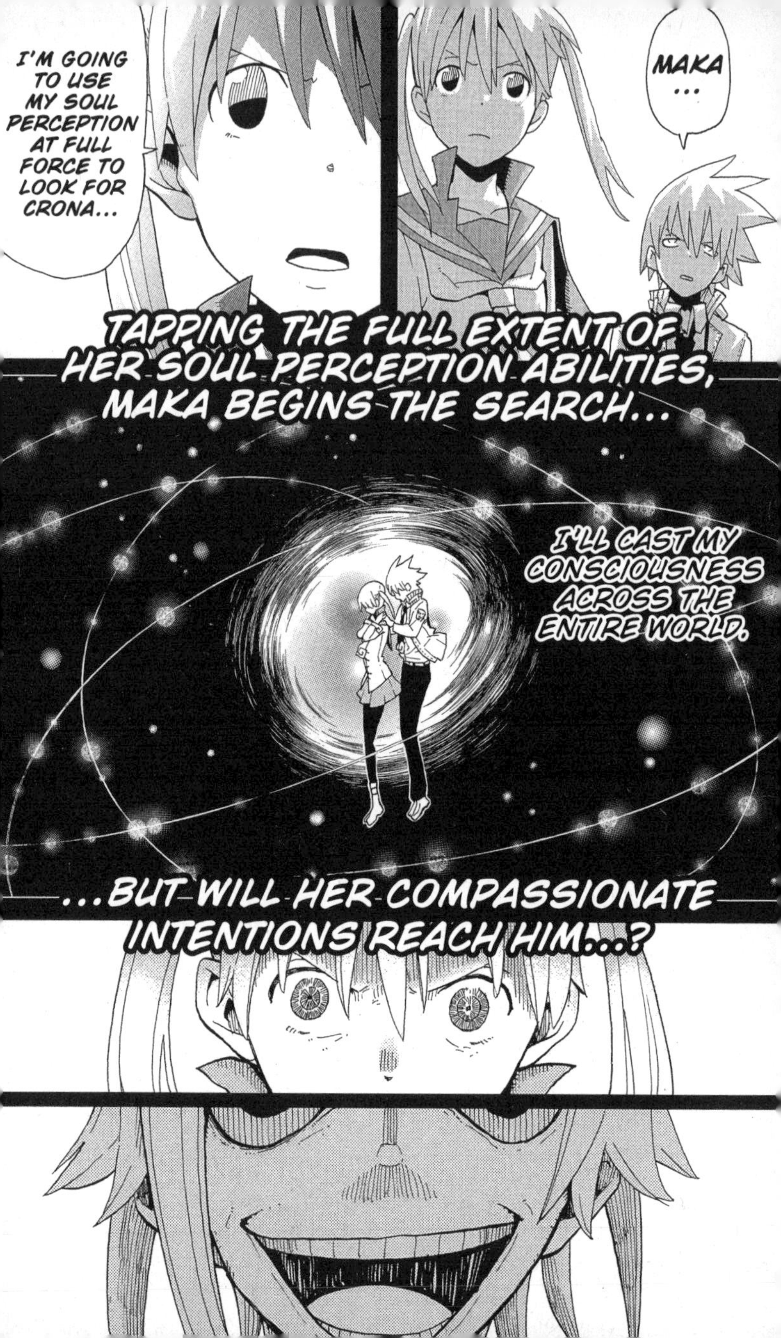
MAKA...
I'M GOING TO USE MY SOUL PERCEPTION AT FULL FORCE TO LOOK FOR CRONA...
TAPPING THE FULL EXTENT OF HER SOUL PERCEPTION ABILITIES, MAKA BEGINS THE SEARCH...
I'LL CAST MY CONSCIOUSNESS ACROSS THE ENTIRE WORLD.
...BUT WILL HER COMPASSIONATE INTENTIONS REACH HIM...?

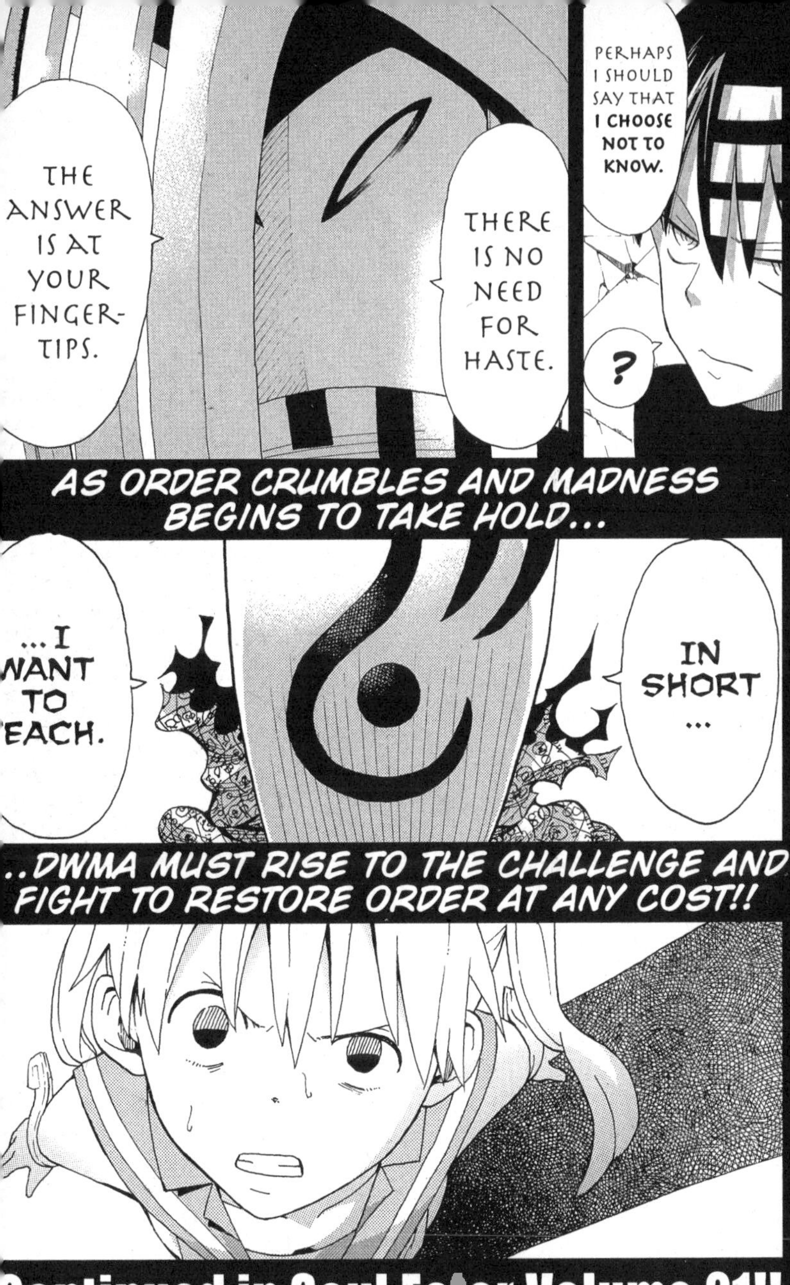
PERHAPS I SHOULD SAY THAT I CHOOSE NOT TO KNOW.
?
THERE IS NO NEED FOR HASTE.
THE ANSWER IS AT YOUR FINGER-TIPS.
AS ORDER CRUMBLES AND MADNESS BEGINS TO TAKE HOLD...
IN SHORT...
...I WANT TO TEACH.
..DWMA MUST RISE TO THE CHALLENGE AND FIGHT TO RESTORE ORDER AT ANY COST!!

Continued in Soul Eater Volume 21!!

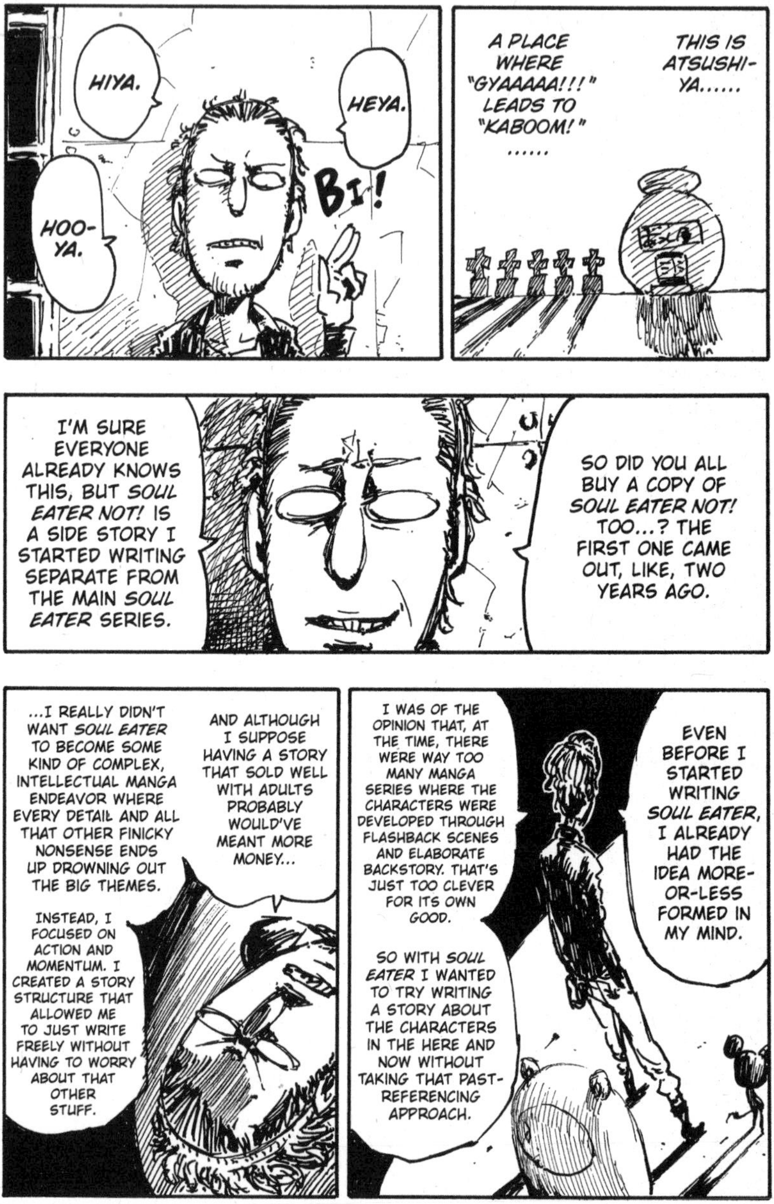

THIS IS ATSUSHI-YA......
A PLACE WHERE "GYAAAAA!!!" LEADS TO "KABOOM!" ......
HEYA.
HIYA.
BI!
HOO-YA.
SO DID YOU ALL BUY A COPY OF SOUL EATER NOT! TOO...? THE FIRST ONE CAME OUT, LIKE, TWO YEARS AGO.
I'M SURE EVERYONE ALREADY KNOWS THIS, BUT SOUL EATER NOT! IS A SIDE STORY I STARTED WRITING SEPARATE FROM THE MAIN SOUL EATER SERIES.
EVEN BEFORE I STARTED WRITING SOUL EATER, I ALREADY HAD THE IDEA MORE-OR-LESS FORMED IN MY MIND.
I WAS OF THE OPINION THAT, AT THE TIME, THERE WERE WAY TOO MANY MANGA SERIES WHERE THE CHARACTERS WERE DEVELOPED THROUGH FLASHBACK SCENES AND ELABORATE BACKSTORY. THAT'S JUST TOO CLEVER FOR ITS OWN GOOD.
SO WITH SOUL EATER I WANTED TO TRY WRITING A STORY ABOUT THE CHARACTERS IN THE HERE AND NOW WITHOUT TAKING THAT PAST-REFERENCING APPROACH.
...I REALLY DIDN'T WANT SOUL EATER TO BECOME SOME KIND OF COMPLEX, INTELLECTUAL MANGA ENDEAVOR WHERE EVERY DETAIL AND ALL THAT OTHER FINICKY NONSENSE ENDS UP DROWNING OUT THE BIG THEMES.
AND ALTHOUGH I SUPPOSE HAVING A STORY THAT SOLD WELL WITH ADULTS PROBABLY WOULD'VE MEANT MORE MONEY...
INSTEAD, I FOCUSED ON ACTION AND MOMENTUM. I CREATED A STORY STRUCTURE THAT ALLOWED ME TO JUST WRITE FREELY WITHOUT HAVING TO WORRY ABOUT THAT OTHER STUFF.

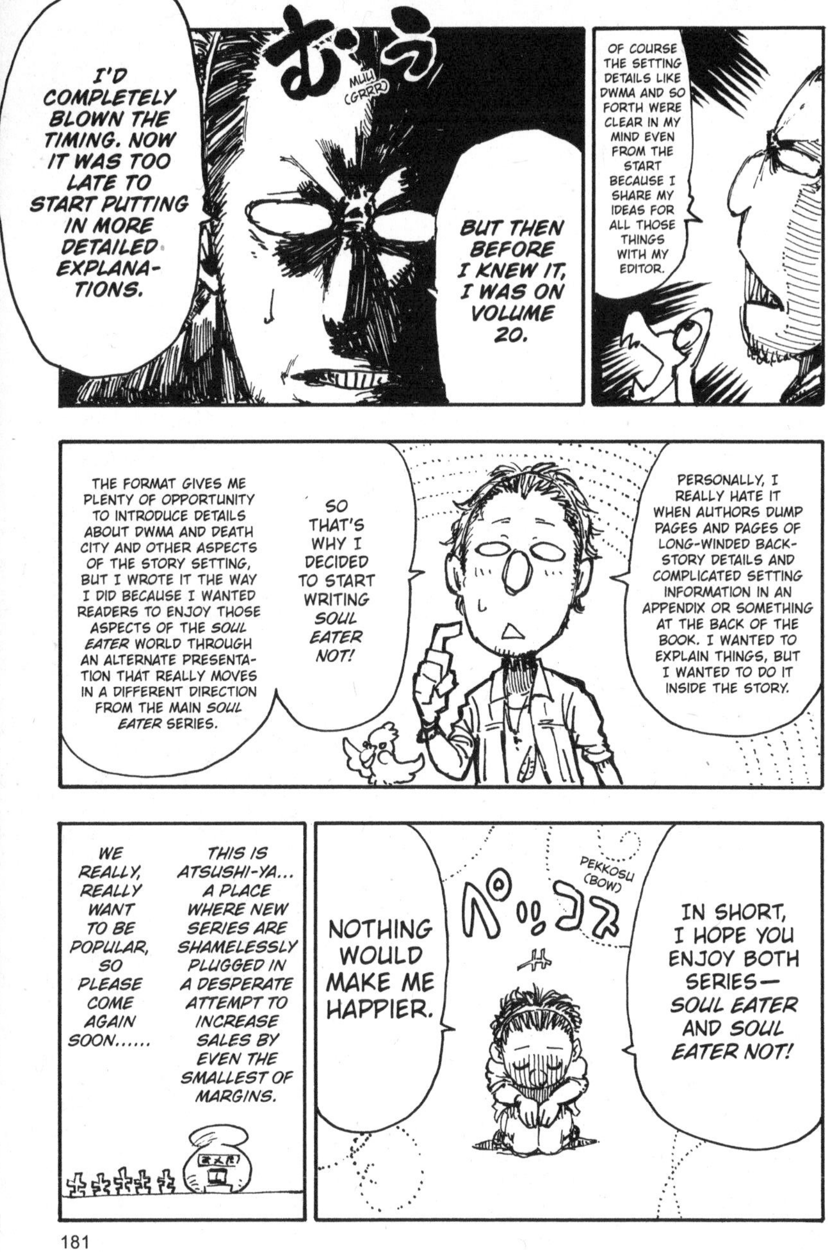
OF COURSE THE SETTING DETAILS LIKE DWMA AND SO FORTH WERE CLEAR IN MY MIND EVEN FROM THE START BECAUSE I SHARE MY IDEAS FOR ALL THOSE THINGS WITH MY EDITOR.
MULI (GRRR)
BUT THEN BEFORE I KNEW IT, I WAS ON VOLUME 20.
I'D COMPLETELY BLOWN THE TIMING. NOW IT WAS TOO LATE TO START PUTTING IN MORE DETAILED EXPLANATIONS.
PERSONALLY, I REALLY HATE IT WHEN AUTHORS DUMP PAGES AND PAGES OF LONG-WINDED BACK-STORY DETAILS AND COMPLICATED SETTING INFORMATION IN AN APPENDIX OR SOMETHING AT THE BACK OF THE BOOK. I WANTED TO EXPLAIN THINGS, BUT I WANTED TO DO IT INSIDE THE STORY.
SO THAT'S WHY I DECIDED TO START WRITING SOUL EATER NOT!
THE FORMAT GIVES ME PLENTY OF OPPORTUNITY TO INTRODUCE DETAILS ABOUT DWMA AND DEATH CITY AND OTHER ASPECTS OF THE STORY SETTING, BUT I WROTE IT THE WAY I DID BECAUSE I WANTED READERS TO ENJOY THOSE ASPECTS OF THE SOUL EATER WORLD THROUGH AN ALTERNATE PRESENTATION THAT REALLY MOVES IN A DIFFERENT DIRECTION FROM THE MAIN SOUL EATER SERIES.
IN SHORT, I HOPE YOU ENJOY BOTH SERIES—SOUL EATER AND SOUL EATER NOT!
PEKKOSU (BOW)
NOTHING WOULD MAKE ME HAPPIER.
THIS IS ATSUSHI-YA... A PLACE WHERE NEW SERIES ARE SHAMELESSLY PLUGGED IN A DESPERATE ATTEMPT TO INCREASE SALES BY EVEN THE SMALLEST OF MARGINS.
WE REALLY, REALLY WANT TO BE POPULAR, SO PLEASE COME AGAIN SOON......

Translation Notes

Common Honorifics

no honorific: Indicates familiarity or closeness; if used without permission or reason, addressing someone in this manner would constitute an insult.

-san: The Japanese equivalent of Mr./Mrs./Miss. If a situation calls for politeness, this is the fail-safe honorific.

-sama: Conveys great respect; may also indicate that the social status of the speaker is lower than that of the addressee.

-kun: Used most often when referring to boys, this indicates affection or familiarity. Occasionally used by older men among their peers, but it may also be used by anyone referring to a person of lower standing.

-chan: An affectionate honorific indicating familiarity used mostly in reference to girls; also used in reference to cute persons or animals of either gender.

-senpai: A suffix used to address upperclassmen or more experienced coworkers.

-sensei: A respectful term for teachers, artists, or high-level professionals.

Page 29
Feodor's name is a reference to Tsar Feodor I of Russia, son of Ivan the Terrible. His reign was a short and ineffectual one, and by most accounts he was feeble-minded and physically weak, dying heirless and without significant legacy beyond his commissioning of the famous Tsar Cannon (see below).

Page 30
Tsar Pushka's name is a direct reference to the Tsar Cannon (*tsar' pushka*), a magnificent cast-bronze cannon on display at the Kremlin in Moscow. It is a purely ceremonial cannon but impressively decorated and expertly cast in a massive caliber. Its size and ornamentation make it a popular tourist attraction in modern Russia. It was commissioned by Tsar Feodor I of Russia (see above) for reasons that are now lost to history.

Page 33
The writing seen on **Tsar Pushka's jacket** is пушка (*pushka* in Cyrillic), which means "cannon."

Page 35
The writing seen on **Tsar Pushka's helmet** is царь (*tsar'* in Cyrillic), which means "emperor."

Page 43
The battle cry **"ura"** is an actual Russian battle cry and is deliberately written in Cyrillic in the original (ура).

Page 90
When Soul is chided for his **limp attitude**, the ogre actually uses the Japanese phrase *chinkasu mitee na kibun*, which literally means "an attitude like penis smegma" but is being used in the figurative sense of "useless and lacking spunk."

Page 96
The **threat level indicators** used here are based on earthquake threat level codes used in Japan. The levels go from "S" ("severe," the highest threat; greater than 26% probability of occurrence) down through A, B, C, and D (the lowest threat; less than 0.1% probability of occurrence).

Page 121
Most of the **Death Times newspaper** shown on this page seems to be gibberish lettering, but the legible headline reads: "KATOLABOR BAKUHATUENZYOU," a nod to the Atsushi-ya bonus section at the end of every *Soul Eater* volume. *Katolabor* refers to the Catlabor robot (itself a parody of Patlabor). *Bakuhatuenzyou* is a Japan-style transliteration of what would normally be written *bakuhatsu enjo* ("explosion and fire") under the usual Japanese-to-English romanization rules. So the headline reads: "Catlabor explodes and goes up in flames!"

SOUL EATER

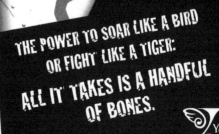

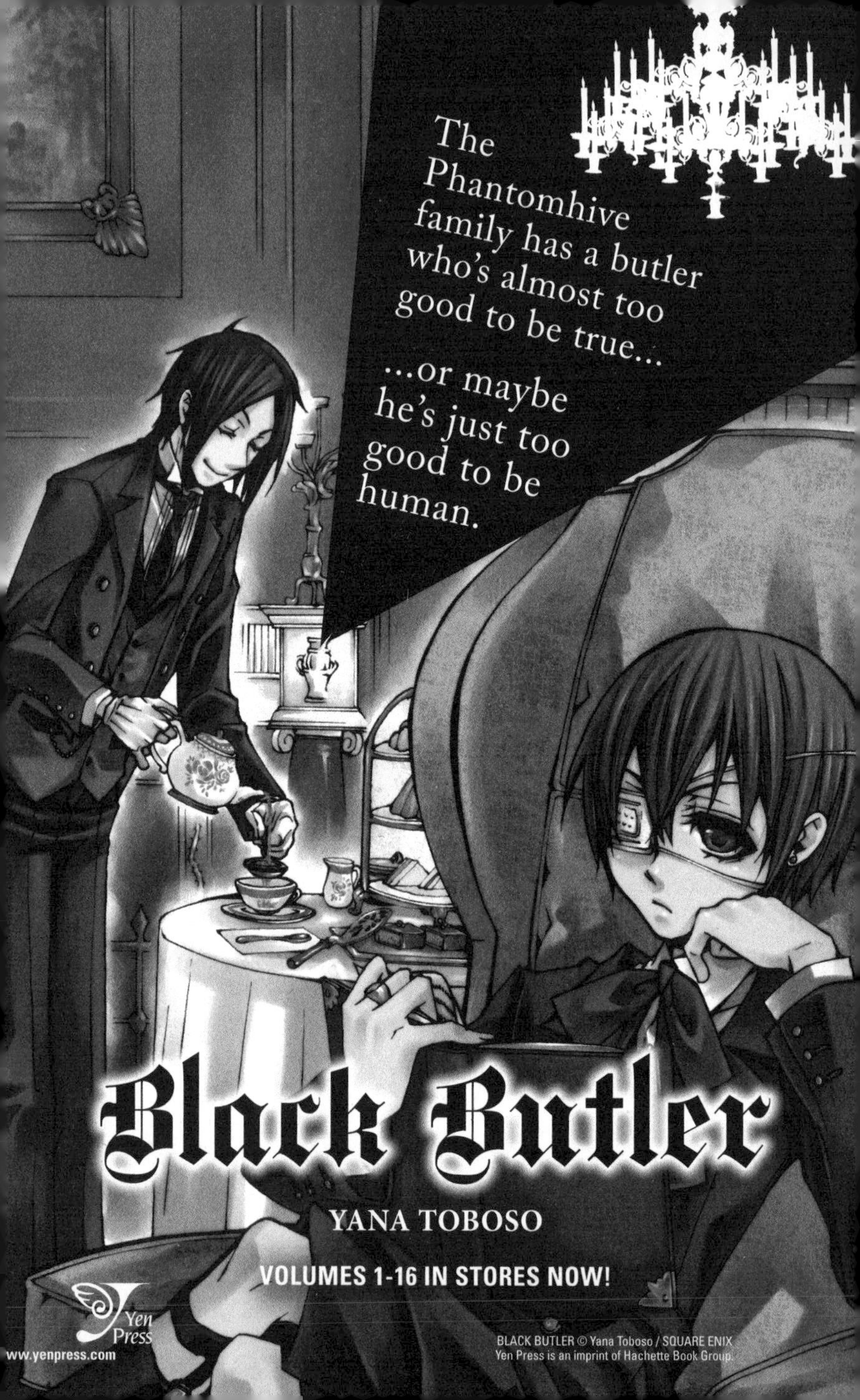
The Phantomhive family has a butler who's almost too good to be true...
...or maybe he's just too good to be human.
Black Butler
YANA TOBOSO
VOLUMES 1-16 IN STORES NOW!
Yen Press
www.yenpress.com
BLACK BUTLER © Yana Toboso / SQUARE ENIX
Yen Press is an imprint of Hachette Book Group.

**THE POWER
TO RULE THE
HIDDEN WORLD
OF SHINOBI...**

**THE POWER
COVETED BY
EVERY NINJA
CLAN...**

**...LIES WITHIN
THE MOST
APATHETIC,
DISINTERESTED
VESSEL
IMAGINABLE.**

Nabari No Ou
Yuhki Kamatani

COMPLETE SERIES 1-14
NOW AVAILABLE

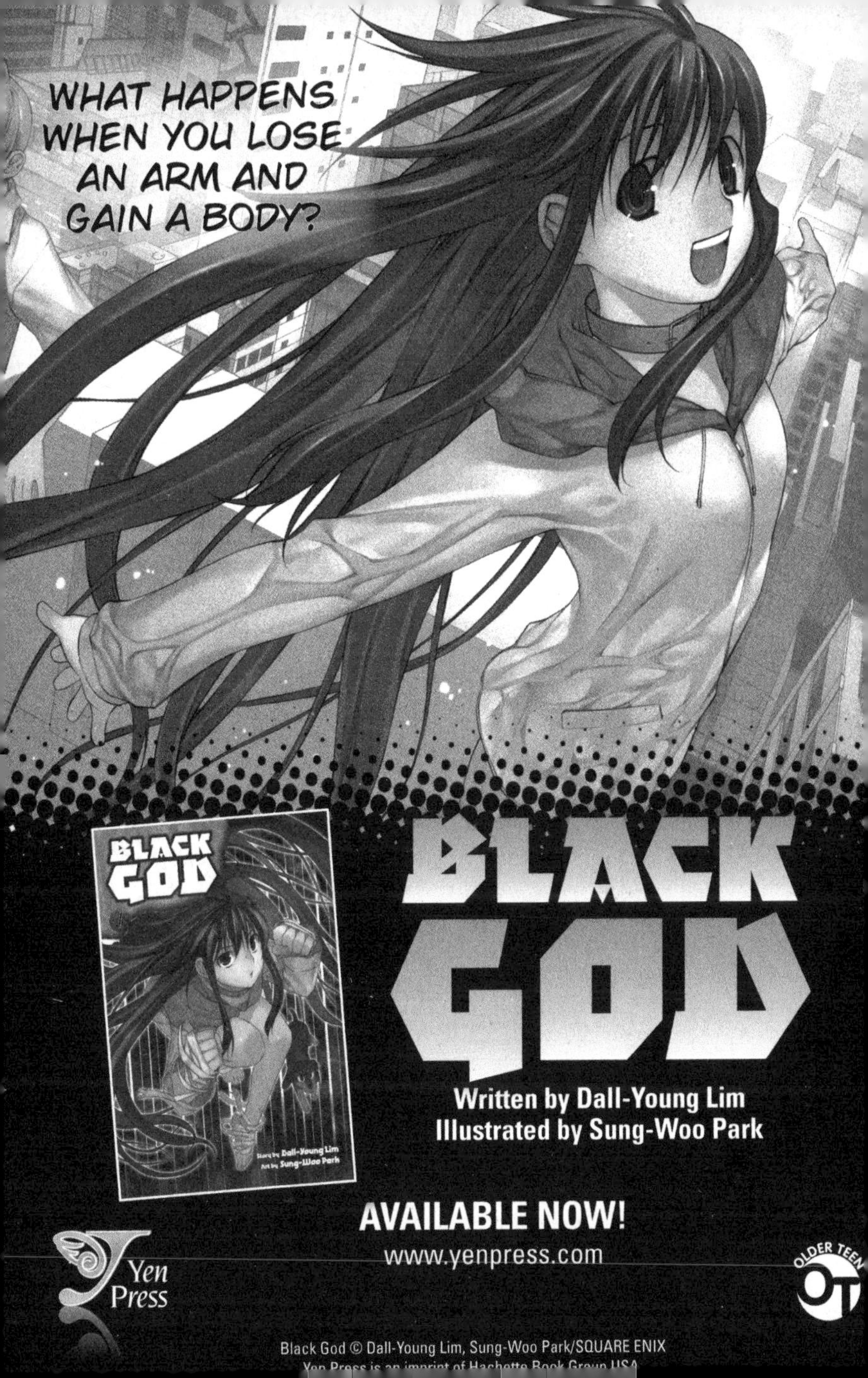
WHAT HAPPENS WHEN YOU LOSE AN ARM AND GAIN A BODY?
BLACK GOD
Story by Dall-Young Lim
Art by Sung-Woo Park
BLACK GOD
Written by Dall-Young Lim
Illustrated by Sung-Woo Park
AVAILABLE NOW!
www.yenpress.com
Yen Press
OLDER TEEN
OT
Black God © Dall-Young Lim, Sung-Woo Park/SQUARE ENIX

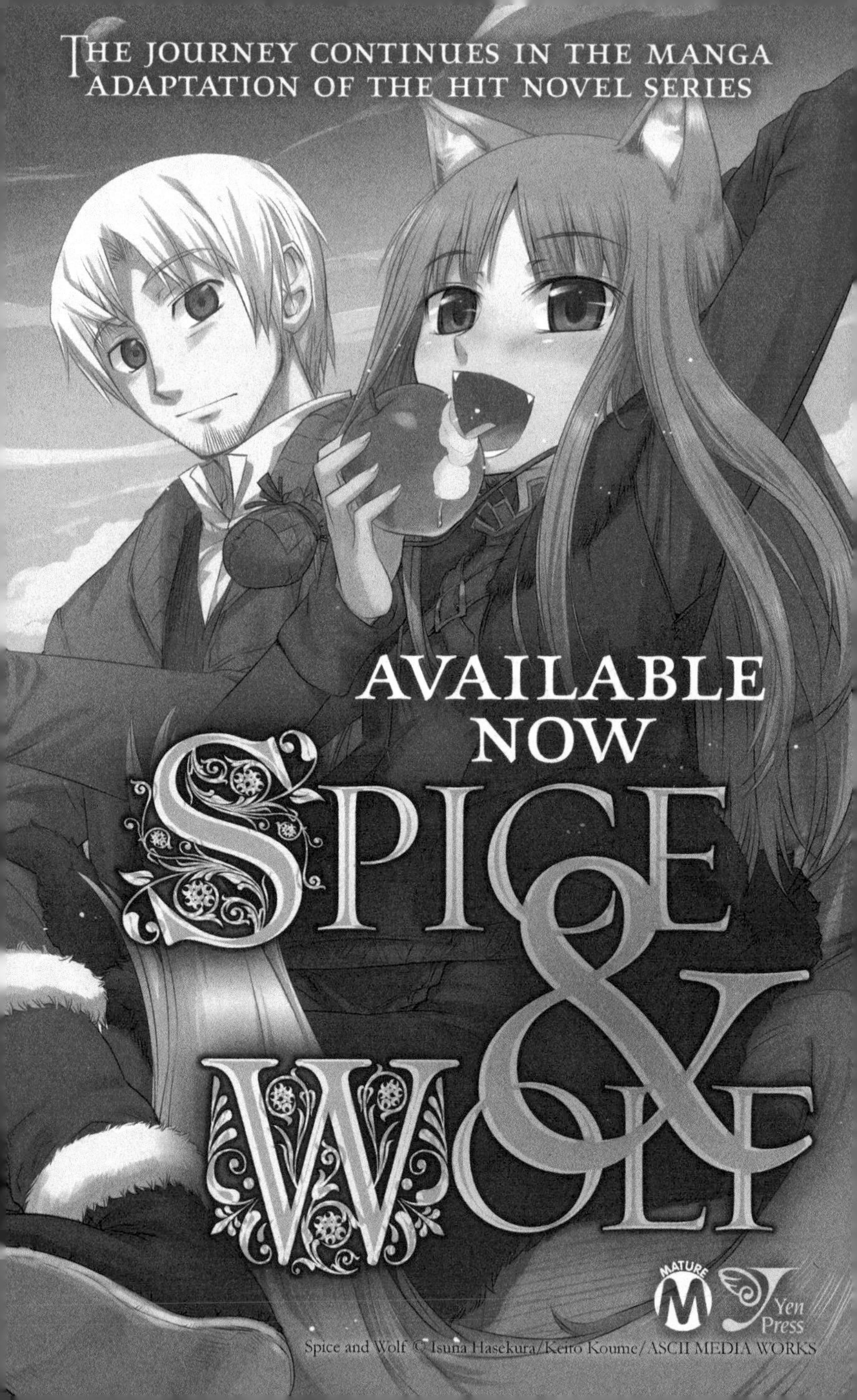
THE JOURNEY CONTINUES IN THE MANGA ADAPTATION OF THE HIT NOVEL SERIES
AVAILABLE NOW
SPICE & WOLF
MATURE
M
Yen Press
Spice and Wolf © Isuna Hasekura/Keito Koume/ASCII MEDIA WORKS

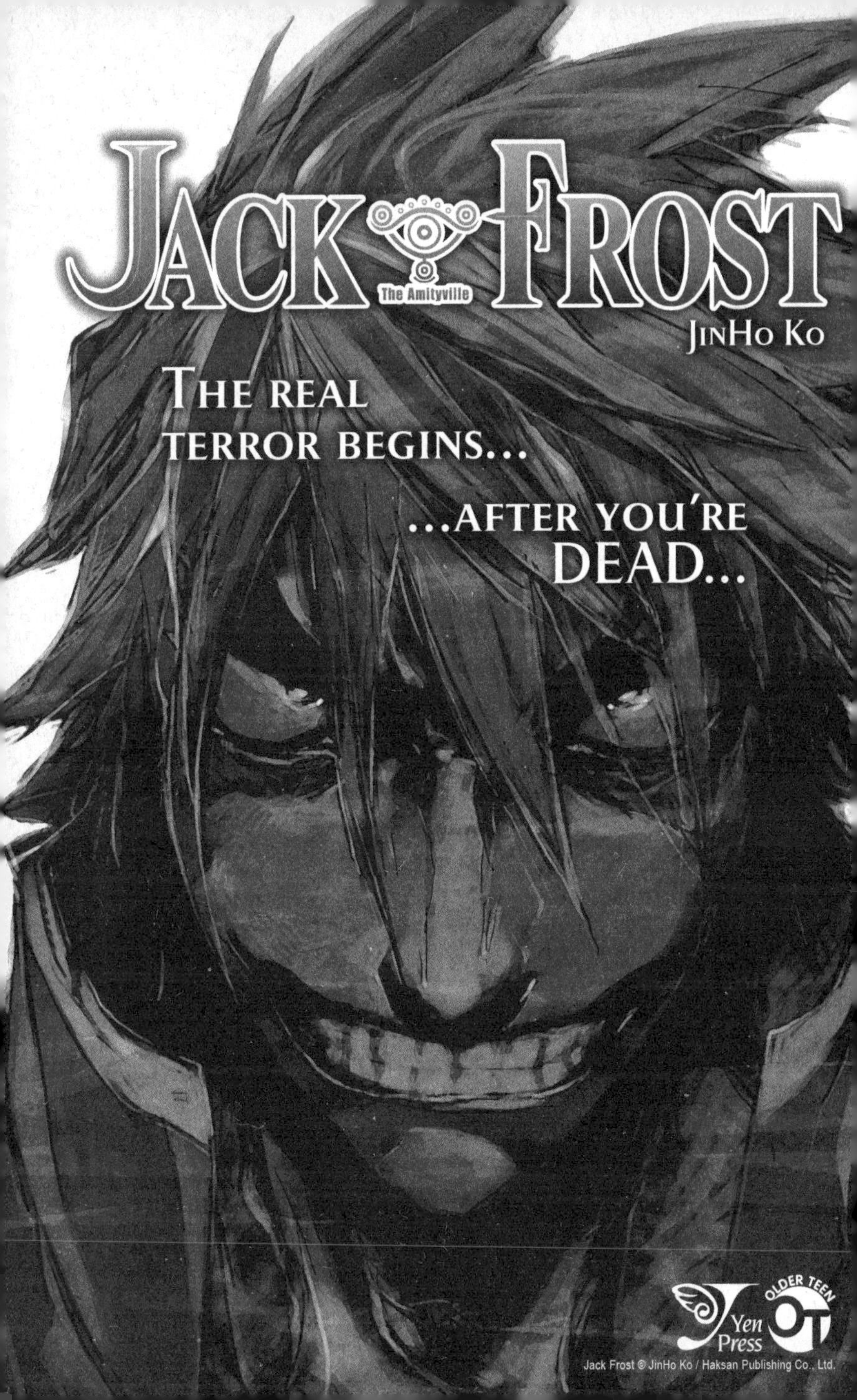
JACK FROST
The Amityville
JINHO KO
THE REAL
TERROR BEGINS...
...AFTER YOU'RE
DEAD...
OLDER TEEN
OT
Yen
Press
Jack Frost © JinHo Ko / Haksan Publishing Co., Ltd.

SOUL EATER ⑳

ATSUSHI OHKUBO

Translation: Jack Wiedrick

Lettering: Abigail Blackman

SOUL EATER Vol. 20 © 2011 Atsushi Ohkubo / SQUARE ENIX. First published in Japan in 2011 by SQUARE ENIX CO., LTD. English translation rights arranged with SQUARE ENIX CO., LTD. and Hachette Book Group through Tuttle-Mori Agency, Inc.

Translation © 2014 by SQUARE ENIX CO., LTD.

Yen Press
Hachette Book Group
237 Park Avenue, New York, NY 10017

HachetteBookGroup.com
YenPress.com

Yen Press is an imprint of Hachette Book Group, Inc. The Yen Press name and logo are trademarks of Hachette Book Group, Inc.

First Yen Press Edition: May 2014

ISBN: 978-0-316-40695-6

10 9 8 7 6 5 4 3 2

BVG

Printed in the United States of America